Integrated
Peacebuilding

Integrated Peacebuilding

*Innovative Approaches
to
Transforming Conflict*

EDITED BY **CRAIG ZELIZER**
GEORGETOWN UNIVERSITY

**WESTVIEW
PRESS**
A Member of the Perseus Books Group

Westview Press was founded in 1975 in Boulder, Colorado, by notable publisher
and intellectual Fred Praeger. Westview Press continues to publish scholarly
titles and high-quality undergraduate- and graduate-level textbooks in core
social science disciplines. With books developed, written, and edited with the
needs of serious nonfiction readers, professors, and students in mind, Westview
Press honors its long history of publishing books that matter.

Find us on the World Wide Web at www.westviewpress.com.
Every effort has been made to secure required permissions for all text, images,
maps, and other art reprinted in this volume.

Westview Press books are available at special discounts for bulk purchases in the
United States by corporations, institutions, and other organizations. For more
information, please contact the Special Markets Department at the Perseus
Books Group, 2300 Chestnut Street, Suite 200, Philadelphia, PA 19103, or
call (800) 810-4145, ext. 5000, or e-mail special.markets@perseusbooks.com.

Designed by Linda Mark
Text set in 10 pt Adobe Caslon Pro by the Perseus Books Group

A CIP catalog record for the print version of this book is available from the
Library of Congress

PB ISBN: 978-0-8133-4509-3 (alk. paper)
EBOOK ISBN: 978-0-8133-4510-9 (ebook)
10 9 8 7 6 5 4 3 2 1

This book is dedicated to the thousands of peacebuilders in the world. In particular, to the members of the Parents Circle–Families Forum, a joint Palestinian and Israeli organization, who demonstrate how people can transcend the worst tragedy of losing a family member, and build a constituency for peace through creative and ongoing work despite the many diplomatic setbacks. If everyone in the world could take a bit of courage and inspiration from the work of this amazing group, we would have much to celebrate and be much closer to building sustainable peace.[1]

In addition, the book is dedicated to the key peacebuilders in my life, Dr. Catalina Rojas–Zelizer and our son, Jacob Manuel Rojas–Zelizer, who inspire me every day to make the world a little better.

CONTENTS

LIST OF TABLES AND FIGURES

TABLES

FIGURES

PREFACE

I HAVE HAD THE PLEASURE of working in the peacebuilding field for over twenty years. During this time, the sector has grown from a small group of scholars, practitioners, and organizations on the margins of international affairs to a concept that is now beginning to influence official policy and practice in the halls of Washington, Paris, Addis Ababa, Geneva, and elsewhere.

I fell into this field in the early 1990s through working as a Fulbright Junior Scholar in Hungary. Although Hungary remained peaceful, unlike its neighbors in the former Yugoslavia, there were high levels of discrimination particularly between the Roma population and the Hungarian majority. To address these social tensions, a colleague and I founded a nonprofit organization, the TEAM Foundation, which was dedicated to improving relations among youth in the country. The more deeply I have become involved with the peacebuilding community since then, the more I am inspired by the rapid growth of the field in all sectors, and the innovative organizations, academic programs, and projects that are helping to foster sustainable peace around the globe. The idea that someone could have "peacebuilding" in their job title or job description seemed unfathomable twenty years ago, but now an increasing number of such positions are appearing across the globe, from multilateral institutions in Western capitals to grassroots organizations in conflict zones.

As will be explored in this book, a global infrastructure for peacebuilding is emerging, and with institutions and networks working on peacebuilding research, policy and practice in most regions. Local and international leaders are beginning to seek innovative ways of addressing conflict and fostering peace, and they are looking to the field for answers.

Despite the rapid growth in peacebuilding, it is important to emphasize that the world still tends to place a strong emphasis in terms of resources and policy on security-based approaches. Global military spending surpasses resources for international development by a ratio of more than 10 to 1, and for specific peacebuilding support the gap is even greater. The peacebuilding field is likely to continue to grow and hopefully increase its impact, but there is still a fundamental need to adjust global priorities to truly achieve sustainable peace in many of the world's most challenging contexts.

For many years, development, humanitarian relief, and peacebuilding largely operated as separate fields. Development and humanitarian relief sought to address immediate suffering resulting from humanitarian crises and work on advancing the long-term economic, health, social, and cultural aspects of society. Peacebuilders worked to build relations and institutions that could help to mitigate the outbreak of violent conflict, and to aid societies in moving toward a stable peace when severe violence did occur.

Over the past fifteen years it has become abundantly clear that development work cannot advance without addressing the underlying dynamics of violence, while peacebuilding is not effective without addressing the basic needs of people through economic opportunity, basic health services, and a functioning legal system. Much like the old saying "No justice, no peace," it could also be said, "No peace, no development" and vice versa.[2]

This book has been many years in the making: countless hours spent in the field interacting with colleagues; researching, writing, and working for and consulting with leading organizations; mentoring thousands of young professionals through my teaching at Georgetown University and other institutions; and through the creation of the Peace and Collaborative Development Network, a premier professional resource that has attracted over 30,000 individual and organizational members from around the world and serves as a central resource for peacebuilding and development.[3]

In my work with peacebuilding and development organizations, I have found it inspiring that many are trying to find the best approach to link peacebuilding to a related sector or particular programming effort. Through the pioneering work of organizations such as International Alert and CDA Collaborative Learning Project, and scholars such as Mary Anderson and Thania Paffenholz, we have improved knowledge of how to more effectively link development and peacebuilding. There is still a need, however, for much greater exploration of the opportunities, and ethical and practical challenges that go with integrating peacebuilding across a broad range of sectors.

Questions abound: Will the integration of peacebuilding lead, in some cases, to contradicting goals that can hurt programming and beneficiaries? Are there some sectors in which integrating peacebuilding is more effective? Does integrating peacebuilding into other sectors run the risk of diluting the peace aspect, and furthermore, how do organizations and professionals already strained for resources have the time to also consider how to integrate a peacebuilding perspective into sectoral-based programming?

Through my work with students and professionals over the past twenty years, every week via e-mail, on the phone, and in person, I am often asked how one develops a successful career in peacebuilding. My advice is usually that to pursue a successful career in peacebuilding, having advanced training through a graduate degree (or other experience) is critical but not enough. I strongly encourage aspiring professionals to pursue a degree in the field, but to also root their peacebuilding training in a particular sectoral and/or geographic area. I frequently repeat to many panicked students that a degree in peacebuilding does not often lead directly to a job in the field. However, I try to provide a strong note of encouragement that the key is to explore how to integrate peacebuilding across relevant sectors. Peacebuilding skills and knowledge are needed in many sectors, and individuals can pursue a successful career and make a difference in the world.

The hope is that individuals and organizations will be inspired through reading the text, and develop a better understanding of the theory and practice that makes integrated peacebuilding so important for some of the world's most challenging environments. Integrated peacebuilding does not offer a panacea that will magically resolve conflicts but can make important contributions.

I am never for want of inspiration when I think about the countless peacebuilders around the world, who, often at great risk to their personal safety, have dedicated themselves to ending conflict and rebuilding after periods of great violence. I hope the reader will see that building peace is not only possible, but inevitable with the collaboration of courageous actors at all levels—from the media professionals producing reports that challenge a dominant conflict narrative, to health professionals working across conflict divides, to legal experts fighting for transparency and access to justice in fragile states, to you.

Notes

1. For more on the PCCF, see www.theparentscircle.org.

2. See the World Bank's 2011 *World Development Report, Conflict, Security, and Development* for an excellent overview of the relationship of development, conflict and peace, http://wdr2011.worldbank.org/fulltext.

3. See http://internationalpeaceandconflict.org.

ACKNOWLEDGMENTS

THERE ARE MANY PEOPLE who deserve a thank-you for helping seeing this project through to fruition. First, thanks go to Mr. Anthony Wahl, executive editor of Westview Press, for inviting me to undertake this project and helping guide the project through all stages. I would also like to thank all the chapter authors for sharing your expertise and wisdom, respecting the time lines, and producing excellent work. Special gratitude goes to Aaron Chassy and Tom Bamat from Catholic Relief Services for helping to think through the concept of integrated peacebuilding and generously sharing their experiences.

I would like to express particular gratitude to my team of research assistants over the past two years, who have been students in the Conflict Resolution Program at Georgetown University. Each of you has provided invaluable background research and editing assistance, and served as a sounding board, and your contributions were invaluable to the completion of the project. In particular special thanks go to Samuel Feigenbaum, editor extraordinaire, and Stone Conroy, for his ability to balance so many tasks at once. In addition, thanks go to Sigma Chang, Valerie Oliphant, Deborah Drew, and Joshua Peacock.

Finally, special thanks go to my family, Dr. Catalina Rojas-Zelizer and our son, Jacob, for serving as a source of inspiration and constant support throughout the project.

CONTRIBUTORS

Paul Charlton: Works in the humanitarian relief and development fields, with a particular interest in Pakistan. Domestically he frequently provides training on conflict management and negotiation skills to health-care professionals. He holds a master of arts degree in conflict resolution from Georgetown University and is currently completing a medical degree from the Geisel School of Medicine at Dartmouth College in Hanover, New Hampshire.

Rhea Vance-Cheng: Holds a master of arts degree in conflict resolution from Georgetown University, where she focused on South Asian conflicts and art and peacebuilding. She received her bachelor of arts degree in theater from Mary Baldwin College. Currently she is associate director of civic and global engagement at the Spencer Center, located at Mary Baldwin College.

Sam Feigenbaum: Current student at Georgetown's master in conflict resolution program, where he works as a research assistant and freelance editor. His academic interests include security sector reform in East Asia, and counterterrorism in the Middle East.

Rachel Goldberg: Current student at Georgetown's master in conflict resolution program, where she focuses on the Israeli-Palestinian conflict. She has traveled to the region several times to study Hebrew and Arabic and to learn about the conflict. She received her bachelor of arts degree from the University of Delaware, where she studied psychology and political science and conducted research on the psychology of genocide architects.

Qamar-ul Huda: Scholar of Islam and senior program officer in the Religion and Peacemaking Center at the US Institute of Peace. His areas of interest are Islamic intellectual history, ethics, comparative religion, the language of violence, conflict resolution, and nonviolence in contemporary Islam. He earned his doctorate from the University of California, Los Angeles, in Islamic intellectual history, earned his bachelor of arts degree from Colgate University, and studied in Islamic seminaries overseas.

Mike Jobbins: Africa program manager for the Search for Common Ground, where he supports the management, design, and development of conflict resolution programming in fifteen countries across Africa. He worked in field programs in the Democratic Republic of the Congo and Burundi, where he supported the startup and management of projects on sexual and gender-based violence prevention, refugee reintegration, security sector reform, and postwar governance. He holds a master of arts degree from Georgetown University in conflict resolution and a bachelor of arts degree in government from Harvard University.

Shawn MacDonald: Director of programs and research at Verité, a civil society organization active globally in promoting sustainable business practices and corporate accountability for human rights, labor rights, and environmental protection. He has a degree in history from Harvard University and earned his doctorate in conflict analysis and resolution from George Mason University.

Katherine Marshall: Senior Fellow at Georgetown University's Berkley Center for Religion, Peace, and World Affairs, and visiting professor in the School of Foreign Service. She also serves as executive director of the World Faiths Development Dialogue, an NGO that works to bridge the worlds of development and religion. Her focus is on social justice, and she works to find more effective ways to address global poverty and inequity, through teaching, policy work, and research.

Valerie Oliphant: Current student at Georgetown's master in conflict resolution program. Her academic interests include women's involvement in peace processes and nonviolence movements, evaluation in peacebuilding, and resource conflicts. Valerie holds a bachelor of arts degree in international studies, with a focus on development in Africa, from the University of Arizona.

J. P. Singh: Professor of global affairs and cultural studies at George Mason University. He specializes in global economic policy and development, specifically exploring issues of information technologies, service industries, global governance and diplomacy, and cultural identity. He holds a PhD in political economy and public policy from the University of Southern California.

Evelyn Thornton: CEO of the Institute for Inclusive Security, which advances the participation of all those affected by violent conflict, especially women, in peace and security discussions. She has a master's degree in conflict resolution from Georgetown University and a bachelor's degree in international studies from Virginia Tech.

Tobie Whitman: Senior adviser, policy and research, at the Institute for Inclusive Security, where she leads its research program. She has written extensively on women and peacebuilding, including reports focused on women's contributions in Afghanistan, Cambodia, Chad, Liberia, North Ireland, Rwanda, and Uganda. She holds a PhD in international relations from Cambridge University and a bachelor of arts degree in social studies from Harvard University.

Andria Wisler: Executive Director of the Center for Social Justice Teaching, Research, and Service at Georgetown University. Her research focused on the transformation of post-Yugoslav higher education, based on substantial fieldwork and language training in southeastern Europe. She holds a master of arts degree in international educational development from Teachers College and a PhD in comparative and international education from Columbia University.

Craig Zelizer: Associate director of the Conflict Resolution Program, Georgetown University. Zelizer has over two decades of experience in conflict resolution practice and research. He has worked in over fifteen countries and conducted a wide variety of trainings, research, and applied projects for diverse clientele including USAID, the US Department of State, Rotary International, Partners for Democratic Change, and the US Institute of Peace. His research areas include examining the relationship between trauma and conflict, the impact of peacebuilding work, and the role of arts and peacebuilding, and exploring the professionalization of the field. He is also the founder of the Peace and Collaborative Development Network, a leading online portal focused on careers and networking. He holds a PhD in conflict analysis and resolution from George Mason University.

SECTION ONE

Integrated Peacebuilding and the Peacebuilding Business

chapter one

INTRODUCTION TO INTEGRATED PEACEBUILDING

Craig Zelizer and Valerie Oliphant

The more we sweat in peace the less we bleed in war.
—VIJAYA LAKSHMI PANDIT

OVERVIEW

THE THREAT OF VIOLENCE and ongoing conflict is ever present in today's globalized world. Despite recent research that suggests the possibility of a decline in global violence (Goldstein, 2011; Institute for Economics and Peace, 2012), there are currently more than fifteen major armed conflicts in the world, causing mass displacement, suffering, destruction of infrastructure, ruin of economies, and erosion of community solidarity (SIPRI, 2010). The long-term psychological and economic impact of violent conflict is enormous. Paul Collier (2007), a noted development economist, estimates that the average civil war in Africa has an economic impact in excess of US $64 billion. The Institute for Economics and Peace (2012) calculates that violence costs the global economy US $9 trillion per year. Even with international aid and economic support, many of today's conflicts have persisted for decades, as in the fifty-year conflict in Colombia that has displaced more than 3 million people. Other conflicts are more recent, including those in the Democratic Republic of the Congo and the surrounding region of East Africa, where millions have perished or suffered displacement over the past decade due to direct violence and the effects of war (IRC, 2007).

The field of peacebuilding has rapidly developed in scope and impact amid continued violence. What was initially carried out by a select group of scholars, citizen diplomats, and nongovernmental organizations is now being integrated into official discourse, policies, and practice. Bilateral aid agencies, the United Nations, the World Bank, government agencies, and thousands of nongovernmental and community-based organizations now focus part or all of their efforts on preventing and resolving conflicts. Networks such as the Global Partnership for the Prevention of Armed Conflict, the Alliance for Peacebuilding, and more specialized regional initiatives, such as the West African Network for Peacebuilding, are creating a global infrastructure for the field.

As will be explored in more detail in this chapter, there is no consensus on the precise definition of peacebuilding. The term originally referred to a distinct set of activities that took place at the end of a conflict in order to foster a more stable peace largely through reconciliation efforts and, to some degree, rebuilding (or creating) functioning institutions that society would see as legitimate. As the scope of the peacebuilding field grew, the term included a much broader set of processes that could take place at *any* stage of a conflict. Peacebuilding was originally seen as a distinct field. Over time, however, peacebuilding also began to be integrated into numerous sectors, ranging from humanitarian relief to international development. This book focuses on integrating peacebuilding across diverse sectors and explores the challenges and opportunities given the developments over the past decade. The reduction of conflict and promotion of peace requires the active involvement of many sectors to create economic opportunity, improve health systems, develop a more transparent media to hold leaders accountable, and reduce global violence (Diamond and McDonald, 1996).

For many years, most humanitarian practitioners working in international development did not explicitly address conflict issues beyond providing relief and security for beneficiaries and staff (Anderson, 1999; Paffenholz and Reychler, 2007; Rogers, Chassy and Bamat, 2010). This was primarily due to the desire to maintain neutrality, focus on saving lives, and improve overall development. Peter Uvin (2002), a noted peacebuilding and development scholar, explains:

> The development enterprise spent the first three decades of its charmed life in total agnosticism towards matters of conflict and insecurity. When violent conflict occurred, it was treated as an unfortunate occurrence, forcing development workers out and humanitarians in—an order to be reversed when the conflict was over and conditions were safe for normal development work to resume. (p. 2)

Much development work over the past fifteen years has occurred in societies that experienced a period of conflict. In 2010, more than one-third of overseas development aid went to fragile or conflict-affected states (OECD, 2011), yet to date, not one of these countries has achieved a single Millennium Development Goal (OECD Achieving, n.d.).[1] According to the Quadrennial Diplomacy and Development report of the US State Department (2010), "Close to 60 percent of State and USAID's foreign assistance goes to 50 countries that are in the midst of, recovering from, or trying to prevent conflict or state failure" (p. 122). Recognizing that development without peace is unsustainable, and peacebuilding without development often is ineffective, many organizations and professionals in agriculture, health, humanitarian relief, and related sectors are starting to integrate peacebuilding concepts and tools into their approach.

Evidence that peacebuilding can make a substantial contribution to fostering sustainable peace and positive growth in conflict-affected societies is building (Tongeren, Brenk, Hellema, and Verhoeven, 2005; Zelizer and Rubinstein, 2009). The field has begun to show its global potential, from helping to engage women in peacebuilding in Liberia, to creating peace media that fosters trust and understanding in the conflicts in the Caucasus, to reducing conflict in Colombia through the private sector. This is not to say that building peace is an easy task. At the policy level, an estimated 50 percent of all peace agreements fail within the first five years, and in many regions tensions and violence persist despite significant efforts to create positive change (Institute for Inclusive Security, 2011).

Along with the rapid increase in peacebuilding and conflict-related programming, there has also been exponential growth in academic programs focusing on peace and conflict issues (Fitzduff and Jean, 2011; Peace and Justice, 2007).[2] These range from school-based lessons that empower youth to rigorous academic training at the university and postgraduate levels. Thousands of courses are offered on conflict- and peace-related topics in a broad range of the social science and humanities disciplines, including programs dedicated to peacebuilding. Of particular relevance to this text are academic programs that offer a bourgeoning number of courses on the links between peacebuilding and sectoral areas, including in development, business, and gender.

Despite the plethora of courses available, many students and younger professionals who enter the peacebuilding field are not receiving adequate training in integrated approaches. While there is significant potential to impact regions affected by conflict through stand-alone programming, institutions in the field increasingly seek individuals with in-depth understanding of integrated programming (Carstarphen et al., 2010; Zelizer and Johnston, 2005). As Carstarphen et al. (2010) explain,

> Organizations working in more traditional sectors—such as humanitarian assistance, governance, and public health—increasingly find themselves addressing conflict directly, or at a minimum bringing a conflict-sensitive lens to their work. Those working to prevent, manage, or resolve conflict find that they also need to address the root causes of conflicts, such as poverty and lack of political participation through civil society, which have traditionally been the domain of development organizations. (p. 2)

Much like the courses in academic institutions, numerous peacebuilding texts exist, but they do not sufficiently address the importance of integrated approaches. While several highlight the need to conduct peacebuilding work across sectors (Paffenholz and Reychler 2000, 2007; Tongeren et al. 2005), there is still a need to explicitly map both the challenges and opportunities involved in integrated approaches. The challenges explored in this book include the danger of trying to do too much, setting unachievable goals, overburdening staff, distorting the potential nature of work to fit donor or funding priorities, and making efforts sustainable.

The goal of this text is to provide readers with a critical understanding of the growth and the future development of integrated peacebuilding in both theory and practice. The chapters focus on examples from international settings and provide a variety of frameworks for integrated peacebuilding. Furthermore, the text will highlight innovative organizations and possible career paths to inspire and prepare the next generation of peacebuilders.

The bulk of the book is composed of chapters written by expert scholars and practitioners in the field who are associated with Georgetown University, one of the world's premier institutions for the study of peacebuilding and conflict. The authors include leading faculty experts in their respective sectors, alumni who became seasoned practitioners through pursuits within their specialties, and current students of the master of arts in conflict resolution program.

The book is divided into two main parts. The first section provides a brief overview of peacebuilding, integrated approaches, the peacebuilding business, and the infrastructure of the field. The second part of the book is composed of ten chapters that explore integrated approaches within a specific sector, including international development, humanitarian relief, gender, religion, the private sector, the environment, security, media, health, and the rule of law. A concluding chapter highlights next steps for integrated peacebuilding and lessons learned to date.

This introductory chapter reviews relevant terminology, provides a more detailed explanation of peacebuilding and integrated approaches, reviews how important analysis is in conducting intervention, explores lessons from attempts to mainstream other fields (including gender, the environment, and HIV prevention), and offers a brief synopsis of each of the sectoral-focused chapters.

TERMINOLOGY AND KEY CONCEPTS

The peacebuilding field emerged in the early 1990s at the end of the Cold War, when the world saw a rash of new intrastate conflicts, often involving competing identity groups. Many of the conflicts that erupted, from Bosnia-Herzegovina, to Rwanda, to separatist movements in the Caucasus, required new tools and frameworks to help respond to the ensuing shift from largely interstate (between two or more states) to intrastate (civil) conflicts.[3]

Dr. Johan Galtung, one of the founders of the peace studies field, played a key role in developing the concept of peacebuilding. In 1975 Galtung outlined three broad approaches to conflict interventions that correspond with the stages of conflict: peacekeeping, peacemaking, and peacebuilding. His concepts have since been expanded, adding a fourth stage of conflict prevention. All of these are defined below:

Peacekeeping: Preventing conflict and violence from spreading through the intervention of a third party, such as the military or police. Peacekeeping largely focuses on the immediate crisis and violence, although it can be an integral part of a long-term process. The goal of peacekeeping is to stop the violence or help enforce a calm environment to enable peacebuilding processes to take place. The premier example of peacekeeping is the Blue Helmet Peacekeepers of the UN, but such efforts can also take place through policing or observers who report on cease-fire violations.

Peacemaking: An approach focused on resolving a specific conflict. Peacemaking takes place when parties gather and resolve specific issues through negotiations and/or other means, such as dialogue. These activities can include formal peace negotiations at the national level, as well as efforts to bring together parties at the community level. A trusted third party, such as a mediator or convener, can help to facilitate the process.

Peacebuilding: Focuses on transforming relationships and structures in society to decrease the likelihood of future conflicts. For many years, peacebuilding was seen as a process that occurred after conflict and violence ended. However, as described below, peacebuilding has become much broader and can take place in any stage of conflict. Examples include dialogue processes, reconciliation efforts, and creating or rebuilding institutions.

Conflict prevention: Seeks to stop or prevent conflict before it reaches a violent or highly escalated stage. This can take place at the latent or manifest stage of conflict. In general, conflict prevention activities can include mapping of the emergence of conflicts through new technology, media, and analysis, creating institutions and forums to bring together groups to constructively resolve issues, and rapid-response mechanisms to deal with violence before it spreads.[4]

One of the challenges in the peacebuilding field has been the lack of consensus over terminology (see Woodrow and Chigas, 2009). A recent study, the *Peacebuilding Mapping Project*, conducted by the Kroc Institute at the University of San Diego and the Alliance for Peacebuilding (2012), found that half of the alliance's members did not have a clear definition of the term. There is also considerable debate as to whether peacebuilding should be viewed as a discrete subsector of the conflict resolution field or as a broader approach that encompasses any effort to prevent, manage, or transform violence.

Conflict resolution emerged as a specific discipline starting in the 1950s. For many years it was used as a catchall term to refer to a rather general field of research and practice. However, over the past two decades, "peacebuilding" has begun to replace "conflict resolution" as a much broader term. This is particularly true for practitioners and policy makers who often associate conflict resolution with a narrower set of specific tools (negotiation, mediation, facilitation, conflict analysis, communication skills, and their theoretical underpinnings) in contrast to peacebuilding, which is seen as a broader approach to foster the longer-term relationship and structural changes needed to move toward peace. It is important to be aware that many other terms also are used in the policy, practitioner, and academic communities, such as "conflict mitigation," "conflict management," "crisis prevention," "stabilization," "conflict transformation," and "postwar recovery" (Carstarphen et al., 2010; Fitzduff and Jean, 2011; Zelizer and Johnston, 2005). The terms that institutions and individuals use, however, depend to a large degree on their training and institutional approaches. For example, military-based institutions tend to use the term "stabilization," whereas a nongovernmental organization might use "peacebuilding," and an academic institution might use "peace studies" or "conflict resolution." Several of the leading networks of practice-oriented organizations in the field, including the Alliance for Peacebuilding, the European Peacebuilding Liaison Office, and the West African Network for Peacebuilding, all use peacebuilding as the central concept to frame their work. The debate over terminology is unlikely to be settled anytime in the near future. For the purposes of this book, "peacebuilding" refers to the larger field of policy and practice (as defined below), and "conflict resolution" focuses on a specific subset of applied tools and theories that largely center on efforts to end outright violence.

Peacebuilding as a concept did not begin to have large-scale impact until 1992, when UN Secretary-General Boutros Boutros-Ghali published "An Agenda for Peace," in which he sought to encourage the UN and other international organizations to shift their focus from peacekeeping to conflict prevention and peacebuilding. Boutros-Ghali (United Nations, 1992) defined peacebuilding as "action to identify and support structures which will tend to strengthen and solidify peace in order to avoid a relapse into conflict," and "which can prevent the recurrence of violence among nations and peoples." Since 1992, the definition and scope of peacebuilding have expanded. The Organisation for Economic Co-operation and Development (2008, as cited in Development Assistance Committee, 2005), defines peacebuilding as "a broad range of measures implemented in the context of emerging, current or post-conflict situations and which are explicitly guided and motivated by a primary commitment to the prevention of violent conflict and the promotion of a lasting and sustainable peace" (p. 15).

The focus of this book is on integrated peacebuilding, which is defined as a set of processes and tools used by civil society and governmental actors to transform the relationships, culture, and institutions of society to prevent, end, and transform conflicts.[5] An integrated approach requires that organizations apply peacebuilding tools across their internal operations and external programs to ensure that, at a minimum, no harm is done, and ideally to achieve positive results in extremely difficult conflict environments.[6] The term is adopted in part from a publication by Catholic Relief Services examining how the organization's peacebuilding activities could be more effectively linked across its programming sectors, such as development, education, and microfinance (Rogers, Chassy, and Bamat, 2010).

The term "integrated peacebuilding" is also beginning to be used within the United Nations with the hope that UN agencies (such as the UN Development Programme, UN Women, and the UN Department of Peacekeeping Operations) will adopt a more coherent and coordinated approach while operating in conflict scenarios. In support of such efforts, the UN established its Peacebuilding Commission, Peacebuilding Fund, and Peacebuilding Support Office to link with external donor agencies.

Components of Peacebuilding

In the aforementioned Peacebuilding Mapping Project (Kroc/Alliance for Peacebuilding, 2012), peacebuilding is defined as having three separate components: peacebuilding as a profession, as a sector, and as a lens and set of tools.

First, peacebuilding is a profession. An increasing number of individuals are working for governments, multilateral organizations, and nonprofits with job titles such as peacebuilding specialist, peacebuilding program officer, and conflict prevention officer. The central focus of these positions is to use peacebuilding and conflict analysis tools (such as dialogue, mediation, facilitation, analysis, and cooperative planning in policy development) to make a direct impact on internal organizational and programming operations. An institution such as International Alert, for example, can employ a peacebuilding program officer to help private-sector companies integrate peacebuilding tools into their operations to reduce their negative impact and maximize their positive contributions in conflict regions.

Second, peacebuilding is a sector. As will be described in the second chapter, thousands of organizations around the world are dedicating all or part of their work to transforming conflict and building peace (Fitzduff and Jean, 2011). While the sector is much smaller than its development and humanitarian counterparts, it is growing rapidly. Many professional and academic networks now have emerging standards of practice, journals, and funders.

Third, peacebuilding as a lens and set of tools is a way of conducting programming across sectors. Conflict analysis tools are essential in exploring the root sources of a conflict, understanding key actors, looking at the potential negative or positive impacts of an intervention on a conflict context, examining the internal and external operations of an organization, and integrating peacebuilding tools where possible. A program designed to increase economic opportunities for women that integrated peacebuilding into its approach, for example, would also internally examine staffing, contracting, and its effect on relations between the identity groups to ensure that first, no harm is done to the community and second, that staff are trained in peacebuilding approaches, involvement is encouraged across the community, and relationships are mended.

While peacebuilding is increasingly becoming an area of focus for many organizations, institutions are struggling to find the best way to operationalize it. As Rogers, Chassy, and Bamat (2010) explain, "Efforts by international organizations to integrate or mainstream peacebuilding across the diverse spectrum of humanitarian and development work has tended to be opportunistic and ad hoc" (p. 1). Additionally, there is the challenge of establishing what exactly constitutes good integrated peacebuilding practice (Rogers, Chassy, and Bamat, 2010). It is important to emphasize that while the procedures and mechanisms of integrating peacebuilding vary according to the institutional context, each organization needs to invest resources, training, and ongoing learning to ensure that conflict issues not only are integrated across the organization, but also that they are not limited to a simple technical approach or single effort (Lange, 2004; Paffenholz and Reychler, 2007; Woodrow and Chigas, 2009). However, not all organizations agree with integrating peacebuilding, and some prefer to keep neutrality as the central component of their work by avoiding explicit engagement in conflict-related work that could pose a security risk to their operations and staff.

CONFLICT ANALYSIS

An organization that considers initiating peacebuilding or development work in a region affected by ongoing conflict and violence must take into account a number of factors before intervening. Conducting a rigorous analysis prior to starting programming can help an organization ensure that its work at a minimum will do no harm and, ideally, have a positive impact within the context of the conflict (Anderson, 1999; Bush, 1998; Paffenholz and Reychler, 2007). Analytical frameworks and tools provide the critical step linking theory to practice in integrating peacebuilding across sectors. A failure to conduct an adequate analysis at any level can subsequently lead to poorly planned programming attempts that can exacerbate conflict (Anderson, 1999; Conflict Sensitivity Consortium, 2004; Woodrow and Chigas, 2009). As Church and Rogers (2006), two leading experts in peacebuilding evaluation, suggest, "Designing peacebuilding programs and projects without a complete conflict analysis is irresponsible and potentially dangerous" (p. 12).

Saferworld and Conciliation Resources explain in their recent report, *From Conflict Analysis to Peacebuilding Impact* (2012), that "Conflict analysis is a means to understand better the complex dynamics of a conflict, set of conflicts or a situation of instability" (p. 5). Many variations of conflict analysis processes depend on the donor, the organization conducting the process, the audience, and the desired end product (Saferworld and Conciliation Resources, 2012).

Regular analysis is carried out in most sectors of development, to better understand the economic, social, political, and cultural conditions in a context and to conduct more effective programming. One of the challenges in the field is that many organizations have their own models of analysis based on a particular theoretical or sectoral approach (Hoffman, 2004; OECD, 2008). In 2004, the Conflict Sensitivity consortium identified fifteen different conflict analysis tool kits used by major donors and organizations. The frameworks differ based on methodology (desk- and/or field-based research) and focus (structural issues, identity groups, data, etc.).[7]

In general, most tools seek to answer the basic questions involved in developing a deeper understanding of an issue, including the who, what, why, when, and how of conflict (Susskind and Thomas-Warner, 1999). This data is then analyzed and incorporated to produce informed programmatic decisions (Conflict Sensitivity Consortium, 2004; Paffenholz and Reychler, 2007). Conflict analysis processes are not a magic way to identify all sources of conflict, but offer guidelines for helping to collect data that can lead to a stronger understanding of the potential means for intervention. The success of an analysis also depends on how the findings are used to develop and implement recommendations for policies or programming (Saferworld and Conciliation Resources, 2012).

There are many permutations of how an analysis may be performed depending upon the focus, levels, and goals of the analysis, as well as whether the organization seeks to work in, on, or around conflict (Department for International Development, 2006). In general, data is collected via desk- and library-based research while consulting with experts and informants. For more rigorous processes, technical experts and scholars will travel to a conflict and conduct a field-based assessment. These can last anywhere from a few days to several weeks, depending on the complexity of the conflict and capabilities of the organization.

In general, a conflict analysis will:

- Identify key parties and their underlying motivations and relationships (*who* is involved)

- Review the history and wider context of the conflict (*what* is the background/when events have occurred)
- Examine the dynamics of the conflict (*how* the conflict is being handled/escalated)
- Identify the root sources of the conflict (*why* the conflict is happening)
- Coordinate with other actors (local and international) already engaged in peacebuilding work to help strengthen local capacity and not needlessly duplicate efforts (Woodrow and Chigas, 2009; Diamond, 2002)

Key Stakeholders (Who)

One of the first steps in understanding potential avenues of intervention is to map the parties and stakeholders involved. There are numerous ways to analyze the key players in a conflict. The simplest method is to analyze groups as primary (those who are directly and significantly involved in the conflict), secondary (those who influence the conflict in some way), and tertiary (those who may play a role in trying to resolve or address the conflict context, but usually do not have a direct stake in the context). It is important not only to explore which groups generate the conflict, but also to examine which groups and institutions are actively working to build peace (Woodrow and Chigas, 2009).

Another issue to explore is that there are often power imbalances between groups. This can be caused by differences in economic, military, cultural, or political capital. A dominant party will often resist engaging with groups perceived as weaker or lacking a sufficient means of leverage.

Context and Background (What and When)

Developing an understanding of the historical context and the timing of events is another important aspect of conflict analysis. Conflicts have both recent and historical roots that are subject to differing interpretations by the stakeholders in conflict. For example, Israelis celebrate May 14, 1948, as the day Jews finally obtained a country, a safe haven after the horrific genocide in World War II. For many Palestinians, however, the same event is known as Naqba (catastrophe), a day that led to the mass displacement of Palestinians.

Dynamics of Conflict (How)

A third area that is critical to conflict assessment is exploring the stages of conflict, from latent to outright violence (Fisher and Keashely, 1991). As a conflict escalates, communication and interaction tend to become more inflamed, and trust decreases as violence becomes likely.

The challenge with models of conflict escalation is that most view conflict as a linear process that proceeds up a path of escalation until a tipping point, when there is a move toward de-escalation. In reality, conflicts are often long-term processes that ebb and flow with periods of heightened violence that may temporarily subside due to a change in leadership, cease-fire, or intervention. The staged model, however, is relevant for integrated efforts, as it is critical to understand the conflict trends before initiating programming.

Root Sources of a Conflict (Why)

Most conflict analysis models incorporate assumptions regarding the underlying sources of conflict, and the ability to identify these possible root causes is a skill required for conducting a conflict analysis. For example, the US government's *Interagency Conflict Assessment Framework* focuses on the role of identity groups in conflict-affected societies and how the institutions can either address the grievances of identity groups or fail to meet their demands.[8] Other frameworks may focus more on structural or resource issues. The World Bank's conflict tools, for example, have tended to focus more on socioeconomic issues (Conflict Sensitivity Consortium, 2004).

It is important to note that in both theory and practice, a conflict often cannot and should not be narrowed down to a single source. Issues of identity, structure, and resources are frequently intertwined, which makes deep-rooted, protracted social conflict difficult to resolve (Azar, Jureidini, and McLaurin, 1978). A conflict may start off largely as a resource-based issue, but expand to involve different identity groups vying for their various causes and interests. These complications can cause a dangerously increased level of polarization and conflict.

Conflict Analysis Tools

Integrated peacebuilding uses a number of key analytical tools, such as "do no harm" and "conflict sensitivity," which are first steps to begin to link programming in conflict regions to implicit peacebuilding (OECD, 2008; Paffenholz and Reychler, 2007; Rogers, Chassy, and Bamat, 2010; Saferworld; 2012). These are part of a larger group of tools, including Peace and Conflict Impact Assessment, Conflict Assessment, and Analysis Frameworks (Paffenholz and Reychler, 2007).

"Do no harm" comes from the pioneering research by Mary Anderson on development work in conflict regions, in which she demonstrated that introducing any human or financial resource into a conflict-affected environment has the potential to exacerbate the situation (as well as have a positive impact) if careful examination of the context is not undertaken. As Anderson (1999) explains,

> When international assistance is given in the context of violent conflict it becomes part of that context and also of the conflict. Although aid agencies often seek to be neutral or nonpartisan toward the winners and losers of a war, the impact of their aid is not neutral regarding whether conflict worsens or abates. When given in conflict settings aid can reinforce, exacerbate, and prolong the conflict; it can also help to reduce tensions and strengthen people's capacities to disengage from fighting and find peaceful options for solving problems. (p. 1)

For example, food aid in a war environment could be leveraged by various actors in the conflict setting to increase their influence or financial gains through taxing the humanitarian aid, setting up roadblocks, or limiting access to valuable aid-related resources (Anderson, 1999). "Do no harm" has become widely adopted by development, humanitarian, and peacebuilding organizations over the past decade. There are some critiques of "do no harm," as some contend it does not provide enough concrete guidance for mitigating the potential negative impact of programming (Rogers, Chassy, and Bamat, 2010).

In addition, Kenneth Bush advanced the concept of integrated approaches based on his Peace and Conflict Impact Assessments (PCIA), which he developed in the late 1990s to help development and humanitarian organizations work more effectively in conflict zones. Similar to Anderson, Bush (1998) raised the key concern that "*any* development project set in a conflict-prone region will *inevitably* have an impact on the peace and conflict environment—positive or negative, direct or indirect, intentional or unintentional" (p. 8). As such, PCIA is largely an analytical tool using a series of questions regarding programming goals, the context, and desired impact, that helps organizations examine a project's relationship to conflict and make adjustments where needed.

The Conflict Sensitivity Consortium (2004), a group led by International Alert in partnership with leading development organizations, conducted in-depth research on linking development and conflict work. The result was an improved set of conflict analysis frameworks and tools to help organizations thoroughly examine their operations and projects in order to minimize their negative impact on a conflict context, to maximize their positive impact, and to understand how changes in the conflict context could affect operations and programs. As Lange (2004) explains, conflict sensitivity is "the importance of seeing and treating conflict sensitivity as a cross-cutting lens that applies to every activity in, on or around a conflict-affected area, including peacebuilding programs" (p. 12).

Analysis tools are some of the preliminary steps in linking action to peacebuilding goals. An integrated peacebuilding approach requires that implicit or explicit linkages to peacebuilding be built into programming and policy. This goes beyond analysis to ensure that programs (in both internal and external operations) incorporate participatory processes, conflict resolution, and peacebuilding tools where possible, help to foster change in relationships and the larger conflict dynamic, and integrate into sectoral-based programming where appropriate.

Linking to Integrated Peacebuilding

Without such models to guide the analytic process of understanding the causes and possible interventions, there is a danger in making faulty assumptions, carrying out programming in the wrong areas, and failing to build cumulative knowledge in the field. Scholars can explain the same conflict from different theoretical viewpoints depending on the research and underlying assumptions about what causes conflict. In reality, any conflict analysis needs to explore multiple theoretical approaches to answer why the conflict is happening and how change is possible.

Recently, theories of change have developed as a key tool to better link analysis to programming. These theories help to connect an analysis to potential programming based on a more accurate understanding of the conflict context and the organization's particular strengths in sectoral or cross-sectoral programming. Using theories of change to articulate the rationale for programing choices can also be critical in determining the impact or results of a particular intervention (Search, 2006; Woodrow and Chigas, 2009; Vogel, 2012).

The next step after a conflict assessment is to begin exploring potential interventions rooted in possible theories of change based on the primary sources of the conflict. As a recent report from USAID (2010) explains, "A conflict assessment sets the stage for a theory of change. Once an assessment describes the conflict, a theory of change suggests how an intervention in that context will change the conflict" (p. 4). The basic concept is to articulate the theoretical and potentially casual assumptions of conflict intervention work. As Dr. Susan Allen Nan reports (USAID, 2010), "In general, a theory of change states what expected (changed) result will follow from a particular set of actions" (p. 1). For example, if a conflict assessment has identified poor governance (structures) and exclusion of minority groups (identity and structures) as factors driving conflict, programming to help address the conflict could take place at multiple levels and across sectors. An intervention could be designed to strengthen government bureaucracy through building institutions, reducing corruption, or increasing civic identity among the population.

Deciding on a theory or approach to change should be rooted in the analysis and key sources of conflict. In its conflict and peacebuilding programming, USAID (2010) has identified seven broad families of theories of change, each of which has a number of subtheories. These include the following:[9]

1. *Inside-out peacebuilding*—Largely focusing on promoting change in individuals that will then lead to change in society.
2. *Attitudes toward peace*—Influencing attitudes to make peace more attractive. Activities might include advocacy, peace education, and related efforts.
3. *Healthy relationships*—Promoting interaction and building bridges between groups.
4. *Peace processes*—Designing activities to encourage conditions for negotiation.
5. *Functioning institutions*—Working on improving judicial, security, economic, and other institutions to be more transparent, accountable, and effective.
6. *Reform the elite*—Targeting the elites to influence their behavior and actions.
7. *Come to terms with the past*—Working on transitional justice and trauma healing.

Once a theory of change is developed, programming options will be created and implemented, and ongoing monitoring and evaluation should occur to see what effects (expected and unexpected) the intervention has on the conflict context and parties involved (see Church and Rogers, 2006).

While the concept is evidently of increasing importance, not all agree with the significance of a theory of change. Critiques of the approach include that theories of change are often too simplistic and assume casual linkages that are not grounded in rigorous theoretical models; that they do not allow for flexibility in programming in conflict areas; and that they are driven by donor interests and that organizations may twist their theory of change to fit the type of work that is carried out (Woodrow and Chigas, 2009).

A Framework for Integrating Peacebuilding

As highlighted earlier, in the past, organizations working in conflict-affected environments tended not to factor conflict issues into their programming, apart from addressing security concerns. The underlying assumption was that achieving measurable development successes would eventually advance peace. The explicit link as to how this was to be accomplished was lacking. While development projects may help reduce conflict, they can also exacerbate tensions or fuel violence, particularly in resource-poor environments or where there is an active conflict (Anderson, 1999; Woodrow and Chigas, 2009). Organizations that work in conflict environments without factoring their work into the equation can be seen as "working around conflict" (Goodhand, 2001).

An important first step in moving beyond the traditional "working around conflict" approach: to use analytical tools to ensure that, at both the macro and micro levels, the intervention efforts themselves do not exacerbate an already tense situation. According to Goodhand (2001), this can be seen as "working in conflict," where organizations begin to reflexively integrate conflict considerations into their internal and external operations as the situation evolves.

While this is essential, it is important where possible to explicitly integrate peacebuilding *goals* into an organization's internal and external operations. An organization can help advance the capacity of its staff through training, coaching, and ensuring that conflict issues are factored into the decision-making process to the highest degree possible. Externally, explicit ways to reduce conflict and build peace should be integrated into all aspects of the program's life cycle, including program assessment, design, implementation, and monitoring and evaluation.

The following figure demonstrates the different approaches.

FIGURE 1.1. Approaches to Integrated Peacebuilding*

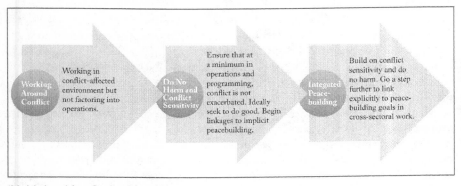

*Model adopted from Goodhand (2001).

The Multi-Track Diplomacy model established by Ambassador John McDonald and Dr. Louise Diamond (1996) provides a useful starting point. Their pioneering work demonstrates that building peace requires the involvement of multiple sectors, organized into the following tracks: 1. government, 2) NGO/professional, 3) business, 4) private citizen, 5) research, training, and education, 6) activism, 7) religion, 8) funding, and 9) communications and the media (Diamond and McDonald, 1996). In the peacebuilding community, it takes many levels of engagement to build peace. The model, however, does not provide adequate space for integrating peacebuilding *across* sectors or vice versa, and the skills needed to effectively conduct this work require further development.

Given the inalienable relationship between aid and conflict, where conflict can undermine development and aid may exacerbate conflict (Anderson, 1999; Bush, 1998, 2003; Goodhand, 2001), organizations must be careful in their attempts to integrate a peacebuilding approach into their operations without a sufficient understanding of the process. In practice, peacebuilding needs to be a both/and approach, where both dedicated funding and technical programming are conducted specifically around peace and conflict issues. Furthermore, many peacebuilding organizations have broadened their sphere of programming and now work across sectors that might have traditionally been under the purview of development organizations. A solid understanding of integrated approaches is invaluable to achieving shared goals of fostering peace and improving development as peacebuilding continues to merge into various sectors.

Lessons from Mainstreaming or Other Integrated Approaches

Mainstreaming cross-sectoral issues began in recognition that international development and relief efforts often overlooked critical issues in their programming. The mainstreaming movement, which strives to integrate sectoral issues into traditional development work, began with a push to include women and gender concerns in international development. For many years, aid was conducted in a gender-blind fashion. As the feminist movement developed, there was a correspondingly strong push to empower women to be active in economic development and related sectors. With the advent of gender mainstreaming, the international development field also began to have dedicated programming for other key areas, including environment, youth, and health/HIV (Paffenholz and Reychler, 2007).

Mainstreaming as a concept seeks to ensure that additional cross-sectoral concerns are factored into all stages of development and programming, as well as into an organization's internal practices (Lange, 2004; Tiessen, 2007). For example, in addition to a project's having the tangible goal of increasing economic opportunity by expanding agricultural production, there are the added criteria that such programs do not contribute to gender inequality or youth marginalization, or exacerbate conflict.

Mainstreaming efforts ideally should be conducted in both an organization's internal operations and in external programming (Paffenholz and Reychler, 2007). Internal mainstreaming for a development organization could involve building staff capacity on conflict issues, educating contracting and administration staff, improving analytical and evaluation tools, hiring more specialized staff, and providing mentoring and networking opportunities (Anderlini, 2007; Lange, 2004; Tiessen, 2007).

Mainstreaming in external programs occurs through integrating relevant cross-sectoral area, such as gender, peacebuilding, the environment, health, or HIV, into programming. This is accomplished by examining the impact of a project on a particular issue, and then training partners and beneficiaries, to create specific, context-oriented programming decisions that fulfill the "do no harm" mandate (Anderson, 1999; Bush, 1998, 2003; Conflict Sensitivity, 2004; Lange, 2004). A project designed to build infrastructure in a developing country, for example, can also incorporate environmental factors throughout the programming life cycle, by conducting an environmental impact statement, looking at sourcing of materials, transportation, construction, and potential long-term implications. The same project could also integrate HIV concerns by providing health services to workers in local communities and conducting educational campaigns about HIV prevention (Elsey, Tolhorst, and Theobold, 2005). From an implicit peacebuilding perspective, an infrastructure project could engage the local population in the process of deciding where the project will take place, ensure diversity in contracting and staffing of locals, and prevent programming from reinforcing conflict divisions. More explicit linkages to peacebuilding would examine how infrastructure projects could be used to address and transform underlying sources of conflict, as well as positively influence relationships, structures, and policies to reduce conflict and foster peace.

To look at the practical steps involved in integrating cross-sectoral issues, an example of integrating gender concerns into a development project in Pakistan will be discussed:

Assessment—A desk- or field-based assessment of conditions on the ground is conducted prior to starting many development projects. Integrating gender into the assessment might include the following: ensuring that the assessment looks at what factors encourage or discourage men/women from participating, ensuring that the assessment team has both men and women on the team where appropriate, that data collected is disaggregated according to gender, and that the team is sensitive to gender norms in society (for example, in more rural areas it might be appropriate to have women speak with women to encourage an open dialogue). In addition, mapping existing efforts in development and gender, as well as actors supporting and potentially opposed to such efforts, is critical.

Project design/implementation—The design of the project may also include the goal of empowering women without alienating men. In terms of designing the effort, special attention may be devoted to addressing gender aspects of a program. For example, how will the project work with both men and women in the cultural context? What power relations might exist that would hamper or encourage programming? Partners may also be trained in gender sensitivity issues. Ideally, exploring how the project connects to other efforts on the ground and possibly to larger strategic efforts is essential.

Project operations—In addition to considering the external project, gender can be integrated into internal operations. For example, a gender sensitive approach might examine what percentage of staff are men or women, or what percentage of project leaders are women. Opportunities might be provided to explore contracting and sourcing of materials for the project and to address gender concerns in budgeting decisions. On a macro level, attempts, if appropriate, might be made to influence how local/national policy or cultural beliefs related to gender roles might be changed in relation to the project.

Monitoring and evaluation—In addition to monitoring and evaluating for basic project activities, such as outputs (number of people trained or schools constructed), a gender-sensitive approach would also ensure that factors related to gender are part of the ongoing data gathering. For instance, a project might look at unexpected challenges, best practices, how participants in a project view gender relations, and so on. If collecting data through surveys, interviews, and/or focus groups, the project should ensure that both men and women are included in the sample. In short, the goal is to go beyond the "regular" project monitoring to try to avoid doing harm, and ideally improve gender equality.

These four steps are examples of the typical project life cycle, from start to finish. As can be seen, there are significant opportunities for integrating sectors within and across all stages.

REVIEW OF CROSS-SECTORAL MAINSTREAMING EFFORTS
Gender

The integration of gender by many organizations in the late twentieth and beginning of the twenty-first century was one of the first attempts at integrating a cross-sectoral issue across development sectors. While there is still considerable resistance to integrating gender into development, as some may view it as a soft or unnecessary issue, many development organizations have devoted considerable time and effort to the task (Tiessen, 2007; United Nations, 2002). The need to include the unique perspectives and concerns of both men and women prompted the concept of "gender mainstreaming" within the international development field, and has since spread throughout multiple sectors.

A movement to promote women in development emerged in the 1970s that largely focused on creating stand-alone programming to help address the needs of women and empower them as a means to advance economic growth in developing countries (Beal, 1998; United Nations, 2005). Despite the positive gains on this front, in many cases women were not enjoying improved conditions: little had changed in terms of societal norms, gender-based violence had not decreased, and in some cases women's empowerment had created a backlash from the community causing the "empowered" women to be targeted for daring to challenge social norms.

Over time, practitioners and scholars recognized the need not only to create programming that addressed the unique needs of women, but also to work on integrating gender across other aid sectors (Tiessen, 2007). It wasn't enough to simply create a separate program to empower women; organizations needed to factor in the role of gender in development programming for *all* stages, including program planning, hiring, selecting partners, implementation and evaluation, and monitoring. For example, an organization working to help increase productivity in the agricultural sector in a particular country might fail to consider how gender dynamics and roles would affect a particular project if women had access to credit or the ability to own or access land. A gender-sensitive approach involves examining how gender roles and institutions impact a particular intervention and vice versa, with the ultimate goal of setting up strategies to change unfair policies and practices.

Through the recognition of how women and men may have different contexts or needs, measures for including both genders in projects have made their way into many donor requirements to receive funding. While gender mainstreaming has yet to develop a single, agreed-upon definition, it refers to the idea that matters of gender must be taken into account in mainstream institutional activities and not marginalized into specialized programs. The UN Economic and Social Council (as cited in United Nations, 2002) defines gender mainstreaming as:

> The process of assessing the implications for women and men of any planned action, including legislation, policies or programmes, in all areas and at all levels. It is a strategy for making women's as well as of men's concerns and experiences an integral dimension of the design, implementation, monitoring and evaluation of policies and programmes in all political, economic and societal spheres, so that women and men benefit equally and inequality is not perpetuated. The ultimate goal is to achieve gender equality. (p. v)

The second round of gender mainstreaming initiatives focusing on transforming societal norms has worked on expanding the definition to include men, and now looks at gender as a broader concept. The incorporation of male allies, especially in patriarchal societies, is integral to success in changing community norms. Achieving gender equality is not about merely the advancement of women, but also the advancement of men. In many cases, men need to be engaged as allies to help work for positive change in gender relations and equality. In addition, programs and policies need to be examined for how they will impact men, women, boys, and girls differently.

Gender mainstreaming in development work has inspired an integration of gender into peacebuilding, giving women worldwide a space where they can be included and heard. In peace negotiations around the world, the overwhelming majority of people at the table are men, even though women are equally affected by conflict (Miall, Ramsbotham, and Woodhouse, 2005). Similarly, while in some conflict zones women compose up to 30 percent of insurgent forces, the majority of armed forces around the world are composed of men (International Labor Organization, 2010). The impact of including both men and women in building more effective policies and institutions is a critical factor that will be explored in more detail in Chapter 5 on gender and peacebuilding.

The Environment

As the environmental movement developed in the 1960s and 1970s, the link between environmental concerns and development became apparent. It wasn't until the 1990s, following the example set by gender, that environmental issues began to be integrated fully into development projects (Clayton and Bass, 2009). The issue gained further attention and traction after the Kyoto Protocol was first initiated in Japan in 1997.

The Kyoto Protocol helped make a correlation between environmental degradation and poverty, and articulated that addressing such concerns has been associated both with the successful reduction of poverty and with sustainable development strategies. Many argued that integrating environmental concerns with successful development could strengthen both sectors, while others noted that environmental concerns seem to be at odds with the economics-driven development strategy.

There are several definitions for "environmental mainstreaming" that more or less encompass similar core concepts. According to the International Institute for Environment and Development, environmental mainstreaming is "the informed inclusion of relevant environmental concerns into the decisions of institutions that drive national, local and sectoral development policy, rules, plans, investment and action" (Clayton and Bass, 2009, p. 11). Environmental mainstreaming aims to mitigate tensions between development and the environment by integrating the goals of both, showing how environmental management can actually further development goals, as well as decrease the associated costs of environmental degradation. The exact formula will vary depending on the particular situation, and thus it is important to tailor each one to the specific context.

Lessons learned from various environmental mainstreaming processes have shown that leadership buy-in, involving key sectors, communication, local ownership, transparency, and accountability are all integral components of successful mainstreaming (Clayton and Bass, 2009). Most important, various sectors must learn to collaborate so that environmental concerns are addressed broadly and with great care. A common concern in all attempts at mainstreaming and integration is that new programming requirements will be met haphazardly as a way of satisfying a checklist for donor requirements.

Although challenges with environmental mainstreaming are similar to those of gender mainstreaming, there has also been the additional economic debate on the costs and benefits of including environmental concerns. It is often more expensive to incorporate environmentally friendly practices, and many organizations claim that they simply do not have the financial resources to incorporate environmental concerns into their development activities. Furthermore, some organizations argue that enforcing new environmental protocols on developing nations is unfair and may further stunt their development in comparison to their more developed counterparts, who were allowed to grow during the Industrial Revolution without such restrictions. The linkages of environment and peacebuilding will be discussed in more detail in Chapter 8.

Health/HIV

Mainstreaming health into the development sector has included many operations, but most significantly those focusing on HIV/AIDS. This is represented through HIV-sensitive organizational workplace practices and through integrating HIV/AIDS concerns into external activities. It is increasingly important that international development and public health incorporate this type of programming into their practices, since most national budgets for health have remained the same or decreased in many developing countries, causing them to turn to international development agencies for help (Elsey, Tholhurst, and Theobald, 2005). Some scholars have estimated that

HIV/AIDS has contributed to a drop of 2–4 percent of GDP in some developing countries (Dixon, McDonald, and Roberts, 2002). People with HIV/AIDS may be doubly discriminated against in societies in which they are also marginalized. Furthermore, there is a strong catch-22 between health and poverty: those with diseases are more likely to be impoverished due to their circumstances, and those in poverty have an increased risk of contracting diseases from malnutrition, lack of access to education, poor health care, and dangerous living and work situations.

The call for increased attention to HIV and health mainstreaming began in the early 2000s, when the issue saw a large boost in the European Union and its use of health impact assessment tools to monitor the impact of health mainstreaming (Geyer and Lightfoot, 2010). Similar to other mainstreaming activities, a definition for health/HIV mainstreaming has yet to be agreed upon. The HIV/AIDS Mainstreaming Working Group developed this working definition in 2002: "Mainstreaming HIV/AIDS can be defined as the process of analyzing how HIV and AIDS impacts on all sectors now and in the future, both internally and externally, to determine how each sector should respond based on its comparative advantage," including implementing policies and procedures for ensuring that both staff and communities' vulnerability to infection is not increased and that staff and community members with HIV/AIDS are not discriminated against (cited in Elsey et al., 2005, p. 991).

A major challenge for HIV/health mainstreaming, as mentioned earlier, is the tendency for organizations to take a reductionist approach and simply add a prevention or treatment component into existing project structures without fully integrating HIV solutions into their programming. This is noticeable in Uganda, where the government has admirably taken on a multisectoral approach to HIV/AIDS. When evaluating their cross-sectoral impact, researchers in Uganda unfortunately found that attempts at mainstreaming HIV/AIDS into agricultural programming involved giving workers condoms and conducting a brief sexual education class instead of adapting agricultural work to address the needs of the HIV/AIDS-affected population, such as teaching households less labor-intensive farming techniques (Elsey et al., 2005). There is also a need for better indicators, so that organizations may monitor and evaluate the effects of mainstreaming. Health issues are now expanding to include disability mainstreaming. Health and peacebuilding practices and policy are discussed in Chapter 11.

Mainstreaming of Mainstreaming?

As highlighted above, with the onset of mainstreaming in development work, there are now a host of areas and issues that most development organizations consider essential. In addition to gender, there is an increasing emphasis on environment, health (HIV prevention), youth, and conflict.

One of the challenges in integrated approaches is how to define the boundaries of a particular project. For example, is it possible or realistic for a single development or peacebuilding project that attempts to engage youth leaders in a dialogue to also integrate environment, gender, health, HIV, and an expanding list of cross-sectoral areas into the project? Will this run the risk of diluting a project to such an extent that it no longer has a central focus? Will trying to integrate everything create competition between sectors, forcing organizations to choose between mainstreaming one or two aspects of the conflict in light of institutional capacity, feasibility, and financial and time constraints?

In support of integrated approaches, there is the central idea that for development efforts to succeed, there must be broad participation by the entire population and not just by groups of particular interest. Moreover, any project that does not at least minimally mainstream gender or other major concerns runs the risk of reinforcing and supporting unfair patterns of exclusion and discrimination on half of the population, which ultimately reduces the chances of sustainable development and growth. An additional challenge is that much of development work takes place at the project level, while the challenges that exist in society are often at the macro level. Thus, while much of development and peacebuilding work may make some contributions to improvements in the conflict context, it is a challenging feat to impact the overall level (Smith, 2004; Paffenholz and Rechyler, 2007; Woodrow and Chigas, 2009). There are also issues of poor coordination among multiple donors and competition among organizations that make having a larger impact across multiple programs more challenging (Smith, 2004). Furthermore, there may be tensions between the goals of international organizations and funders, who may want to push a certain agenda or goal, and local organizations or institutions, who may wish to pursue a different approach.

Purists might argue that integrating additional concerns into development programming undermines efforts to create long-term impacts and sustainability. For instance, would requiring a road construction project in Afghanistan to be gender sensitive in internal and external operations open a host of challenges, conflicts, or dangers to the implementing organization and local partners? An argument could also be made that development projects need technical experts in their particular sector, and that an attempt to do all this extra work would only dilute the impact of "hard" development work.

Another challenge is that many organizations and their individual staff are overburdened with heavy workloads. Trying to find time for integrating other concerns into development work can be exceedingly challenging for the following reasons:

1. *Lack of time*—For professionals working in the field, trying to find additional time to integrate cross-sectoral concerns into one's work can be exceptionally difficult.
2. *Lack of resources*—While there is debate about the level of resources needed (financial and human capacity) to integrate peacebuilding across sectors, it is clear that some additional resources may be needed. Many organizations do not have adequate resources set aside for such work, nor are donors always supportive of providing increased financing (Paffenholz and Reychler, 2007).
3. *Fad of the year*—The list of areas to be integrated continues to increase. Sometimes it is not clear if a particular area will sustain interest, or if it will be quickly replaced by a new one.
4. *How to integrate everything*—As indicated earlier, the list of important areas to be integrated is ever expanding. To date, there hasn't been a clear explanation of integrated approaches across sectors (Barbolet, Goldwyn,

Groewnewald, and Sherrif, 2005; Paffenholz and Reychler, 2007). Does integrating each respective area require a different set of assessment tools in the early stages of a project and different tools for programming and evaluation?

5. *Lack of clarity of terminology and tools*—For many of the approaches there is still considerable debate over appropriate definitions and methodology. Many organizations have developed their own methods, and while this can be useful for internal organizational control, it can raise challenges in building a coherent approach across the larger field.

6. *How to remain culturally sensitive*—Some say that a fear of perceived Westernization has led to being overly culturally sensitive, especially when it comes to integrating gender. How can one reconcile cultural differences that clash with the objectives of mainstreaming activities that may occur?

Despite the challenges raised in this chapter, integrated peacebuilding and other mainstreaming efforts are important in international aid and related sectors. Its inclusion in programming and organizational goals shows the effort and desire of the field to move toward sustainable development practices and more holistic, inclusive approaches. While this text cannot provide all of the answers to these challenges, it will attempt to clarify some of them. In particular, this text seeks to clarify terminology and tools that can be used in integrating peacebuilding approaches, identifying innovative practices and cases, and helping contribute to a more coherent approach across the larger field.

OVERVIEW OF THE TEXT

As stated earlier, this text is divided into two main parts. The first provides an overview of integrated peacebuilding, a discussion of the business of the field, and a discussion of key actors and their motivations.

Section two comprises the bulk of the work, and is composed of chapters that explore integrated peacebuilding in key sectors and disciplines, including international development, humanitarian relief, gender, religion, the private sector, the environment, media, security, and health.[10] The authors were asked to cover the following issues in each of their chapters:

- *Introduction to the sector*
  - ÷ What are the core conflict issues related to this sector?
  - ÷ How does the sector link with integrated peacebuilding?
- *Discussion of relevant theory*
  - ÷ What are the core theories that help explain conflict in this sector?
  - ÷ What are the main sources of conflict?
- *Discussion of processes/skills*
  - ÷ Which processes are being used to address conflicts in the sector?
  - ÷ What skills do practitioners need to be effective?

- *Impacting policy/systematic change*
  + What are the key policy debates in the sector related to integrated peace-building?
  + What are the key institutions working on peacebuilding in this sector?
  + What are some policy innovations that have been implemented to build peace?
  + What are indicators of success? Is change sustainable?
- *Challenges in the field*
  + What are some of the significant unresolved questions and ethical issues in this sector?
- *Complement the chapter with brief case studies and/or a profile of practitioners*

A brief overview of the chapters is provided below.

Section One

Chapter 2: The Business of Peacebuilding. This chapter explores the peacebuilding field as part of the larger international aid industry, reviews the different types of institutions involved in peacebuilding and their underlying motivations, and examines trends within the field.

Section Two

Chapter 3: International Development and Peacebuilding. This chapter, written by Andria Wisler, director of the Justice and Peace Studies Program at Georgetown, explores how for many years peacebuilding and international development operated as distinct areas of practice. More recently, scholars and practitioners have realized that with nearly two-thirds of development work taking place in conflict-affected countries, there is a strong relationship between the two. Effective and sustainable development cannot exist in countries with severe conflict, while peacebuilding practice and research need to also explore addressing the basic needs of communities. This chapter discusses the relationship between international development and peacebuilding.

Chapter 4: Humanitarian Assistance and Peacebuilding. In this chapter, Mike Jobbins, an alumnus of Georgetown University's Conflict Resolution Program and current Africa programs manager for Search for Common Ground, explores the theoretical and practical issues related to humanitarian relief and peacebuilding. Many challenges face the international community, including responding to natural disasters, handling massive population displacements, and providing rapid relief, that are key issues for integrated approaches.

Chapter 5: Gender and Peacebuilding. In recent years there have been extensive efforts to integrate gender into peacebuilding research and practice. Coauthors Evelyn Thornton, CEO of the Institute for Inclusive Security, and Tobie Whitman, senior adviser of policy and research at the institute, discuss recent efforts to ensure that gender is integrated into peacebuilding research and practice. Gender-sensitive programming looks at how programming affects men, women, boys, and girls in designing and implementing activities. Moreover, there is a strong push in the peacebuilding field to give women a central role in building peace at the grassroots and policy levels.

This chapter reviews the research supporting gender-sensitive peacebuilding programming, as well as the challenges in integrating this into practice.

Chapter 6: Peacebuilding and the Private Sector. This chapter is written by Shawn MacDonald, a frequent guest lecturer at Georgetown University and senior adviser at Verite. Traditionally, many practitioners and students of peacebuilding have failed to include the private sector as a significant actor in both generating conflicts and contributing to peace. With the globalization of the world's economy, the private sector has begun to play an increasingly important role in fostering competition and conflict over access to resources, as well as helping to fund and engage in innovative peacebuilding work. In addition, MacDonald explores the topic of for-profit businesses' directly contributing to peacebuilding as a core focus of their operations.

Chapter 7: Religion and Peacebuilding. This chapter is cowritten by Qamar-ul Huda, senior program officer at the US Institute of Peace, and Katherine Marshall of the Berkley Center at Georgetown University. In the twenty-first century, religion continues to be one of the primary identity markers around which groups coalesce. Many scholars and practitioners see religion as both a source of conflict and a potential means to bring groups together to work for peace. This chapter examines the role that religion plays in forming group identity and generating conflict, as well as innovative means by which religious leaders and members of their communities are using religion as a tool to engage in peacebuilding activities.

Chapter 8: Environmental Change and Peacebuilding. This chapter is written by Ashley Laura McArthur, an alumna of Georgetown University's Conflict Resolution Program and a senior analyst at the Cadmus Group. Over the course of the next few decades, many predict that one of the major sources of conflict in the world will be the increasing impact of environmental factors, such as overpopulation, arid climates, drought, and more. This chapter explores the current efforts to integrate peacebuilding and environmental issues, and the key challenges that are likely to emerge in the future.

Chapter 9: Security and Peacebuilding. This chapter is written by Rhea Vance-Cheng, an alumna of Georgetown University's Conflict Resolution Program, and Sam Feigenbaum and Rachel Goldberg, both current master's degree candidates of Georgetown University's Conflict Resolution Program. This chapter examines the need to balance a "3D" approach of defense, development, and diplomacy. Increasingly, peacebuilders and security actors are working together to help bring stability to fragile and weak states that are the site of many of the world's conflicts. The practical opportunities and ethical challenges of integrating hard and soft security approaches are explored in this chapter, as well as some innovative examples of collaboration.

Chapter 10: Media and Peacebuilding. This chapter is written by J. P. Singh, professor of global affairs and cultural studies at George Mason University. In the age of new media and globalization, the media is playing an increasingly important role in educating people around the world about conflict. Media can be a tool for inflaming violence, as seen in the hate-radio propaganda that helped to fuel the genocide in Rwanda, as well as an important process for fostering understanding among conflicted parties. This chapter examines the multiple roles of media related to conflict and focuses on how media can be used to both foster peace and generate conflict. Given the increasing impact of new media, the chapter also explores social media tools and processes in peacebuilding.

Chapter 11: Health and Peacebuilding. This chapter is written by Paul Charlton, an alumnus of Georgetown University's Conflict Resolution Program who is currently a second-year medical student at Dartmouth College. For many years there has been a strong relationship between health and conflict. During humanitarian crises, access to health services is often interrupted and disease and other epidemics may spread. Health workers have long sought to help ameliorate the suffering of populations affected by conflict. In more recent times, given the basic need of all humans for health and the negative impact of conflict on health, there has been increased interaction between medical and public health professionals and peacebuilding issues.

Chapter 12: The Rule of Law and Peacebuilding. This chapter is written by Brian Kritz, adjunct professor for Georgetown University's Conflict Resolution Program. It explores the need for and obstacles to developing a strong and transparent legal system in conflict-affected societies. Often in violent contexts, legal norms and institutions are decimated. One of the key steps in fostering a more stable postconflict period is to strengthen or develop a legal framework to address conflicts in society through peaceful means.

Chapter 13: Conclusion. In the last chapter, Craig Zelizer summarizes key lessons from the text and identifies future trends for integrated peacebuilding related to practice, research, and policy. A discussion of the critical issues of impact and sustainability of integrated approaches is also featured.

REFERENCES

Anderlini, S. 2007. *Women building peace*. Boulder, CO: Lynne Rienner.

Anderson, M. 1999. *Do no harm: How aid can support peace—or war*. Boulder, CO: Lynne Rienner.

Azar, E., P. Jureidini, and R. McLaurin. 1978. Protracted social conflict: Theory and practice in the Middle East. *Journal of Palestine Studies* 8:41–60.

Barbolet, A., R. Goldwyn, H. Groewnewald, and A. Sherrif. 2005. *The utility and dilemmas of conflict sensitivity*. Berghof Handbook for Conflict Transformation. Retrieved January 2, 2012, from www.berghof-handbook.net/dialogue-series/no.-4-new-trends-in -peace-and-conflict-impact-assessment-pcia.

Beal, J. 1998. Trickle-down or rising tide? Lessons on mainstreaming gender policy from Colombia and South Africa. *Social Policy & Administration* 32, no. 5: 513–534.

Bush, K. 1998. A measure of peace: Peace and Conflict Impact Assessment (PCIA) of development projects in conflict zones. Working Paper #1, Peacebuilding and Reconstruction Program Initiative and the Evaluation Unit, International Development Research Centre. Retrieved December 5, 2011, from http://web.idrc.ca/uploads/user-S /10533919790A_Measure_of_Peace.pdf.

———. 2003. *PCIA five years on. The Commodification of an Idea*. Berghof Handbook for Conflict Transformation. Retrieved April 2, 2011, from www.berghof-handbook.net /dialogue-series/no.-1-peace-and-conflict-impact-assessment.-critical-views-from -theory-and.

Carstarphen, N., C. Zelizer, R. Harris, and D. J. Smith. 2010. *Graduate education and professional practice in international peace and conflict.* Special report. Washington, DC: US Institute of Peace.

Church, C., and M. Rogers. 2006. Designing for results: Integrating monitoring and evaluation in conflict transformation programs. Search for Common Ground and United States Institute of Peace. Retrieved April 1, 2011, from www.sfcg.org/Documents/manualpart1.pdf.

Clayton, D. B., and S. Bass. 2009. *The challenges of environmental mainstreaming: Experience of integrating environment into development institutions and decisions.* London: International Institute for Environment and Development.

Collier, P. 2007. *The bottom billion: Why the poorest countries are failing and what can be done about it.* New York: Oxford University Press.

Conflict Sensitivity Consortium. 2004. Conflict-sensitive approaches to development, humanitarian assistance and peace building: Tools for Peace and Conflict Impact Assessment. Retrieved April 1, 2011, from www.conflictsensitivity.org/publications/conflict -sensitive-approaches-development-humanitarian-assistance-and-peacebuilding-res.

Department for International Development. 2006. Consultation questions for DFID conflict policy paper. Retrieved April 1, 2011, from www.dfid.gov.uk/consultations/conflict -consultation.pdf.

Diamond, L. 2002. Who else is working there. In J. P. Lederach and J. Janner, eds. *A handbook of international peacebuilding* (pp. 25–36). San Francisco: Jossey-Bass.

Diamond, L., and J. W. McDonald. 1996. *Multi-track diplomacy: A systems approach to peace,* 3rd ed. West Hartford, CT: Kumarian Press.

Dixon, S., S. McDonald, and J. Roberts. 2002. The impact of HIV and AIDS on Africa's economic development. *British Medical Journal* 324 (7331): 232–234.

Elsey, H., R. Tolhurst, and S. Theobold. 2005. Mainstreaming HIV/AIDS in development sectors: Have we learnt lessons from gender mainstreaming? *AIDS Care* 17, no. 8: 988–998.

Fitzduff, M., and I. Jean. 2011. Peace education: State of the field and lessons learned from USIP grantmaking. Peaceworks No. 74, United States Institute of Peace. Retrieved April 5, 2012, from www.usip.org/files/resources/PW74.pdf.

Fisher, R. J. 1993. The potential for peacebuilding: Forging a bridge from peacekeeping to peacebuilding. *Peace and Change* 18, no. 2: 247–266.

Fisher, R J., and L. Keashly. 1991. The potential complementarity of mediation and consultation within a contingency model of third party intervention. *Journal of Peace Research* 23, no. 1: 29–42.

Galtung, J. 1975. Three approaches to peace: Peacekeeping, peacemaking, and peacebuilding. In J. Galtung. *Peace, war and defence—Essays in peace research,* vol. 2 (pp. 282–304). Copenhagen: Christian Ejlers.

———. 1995. Peace and change graduate course. Institute for Conflict Analysis and Resolution, fall semester.

Geyer, R., and S. Lightfoot. 2010. Strengths and limits of new EU governance: The cases of mainstreaming and impact assessment in EU public health and sustainable development policy. *Journal of European Integration* 32, no. 4: 339–359.

Goldstein, J. 2011. *Winning the war on war: The decline of armed conflict worldwide.* New York: Dutton.

Goodhand, J. 2001. Aid, conflict and peacebuilding in Sri Lanka. Conflict and Security Development Group, King's College London. Retrieved October 5, 2011, from www.dfid.gov.uk/pubs/files/conflictassessmentsrilanka.pdf.

Hoffman, M. 2004. Peace and Conflict Impact Assessment methodology. Evolving art form or practical dead end? Berghof Handbook for Conflict Transformation. Retrieved April 1, 2011, from www.berghof-handbook.net/dialogue-series/no.-1-peace-and-conflict -impact-assessment.-critical-views-from-theory-and.

Institute for Economics and Peace. 2012. *Global Peace Index 2012, Fact Sheet*. Retrieved June 14, 2012, from www.visionofhumanity.org/globalpeaceindex/2012-gpi-findings.

Institute for Inclusive Security. 2011. Recommendations for elevating the role of women in mediation. Retrieved December 5, 2011, from www.huntalternatives.org/pages /8641_women_mediating_across_conflict_lines_inclusive_security_s_12th_annual _colloquium.cfm.

International Labor Organization. 2010. Socio-economic reintegration of ex-combatants. Geneva, Switzerland: Author. Retrieved September 1, 2012, from www.ilo.org/employment /Whatwedo/Instructionmaterials/WCMS_141276/lang--en/index.htm.

International Rescue Committee. 2007. Measuring mortality in the Democratic Republic of the Congo. Retrieved June 7, 2012, from www.rescue.org/special-reports/congo -forgotten-crisis.

Kroc Institute, University of San Diego, and the Alliance for Peacebuilding. 2012. *Presentation of the Peacebuilding Mapping Project* by Necla Tschirgi and Elena McCollim, Conference, Peàcebuilding 2.0: Managing Complexity and Working Across Silos, May 11, 2012, US Institute of Peace, Washington, DC.

Lange, M. 2004. *Building institutional capacity for conflict-sensitive practice: The case of international NGOs*. London: International Alert. Retrieved April 1, 2011, from www .conflictsensitivity.org/node/102.

Miall, H., O. Ramsbotham, and T. Woodhouse. 2005. *Contemporary conflict resolution* (2nd ed.). Cambridge: Polity.

Organisation for Economic Co-operation and Development (OECD). 2007. Principles for good international engagement in fragile states and situations. OECD publishing. Retrieved April 1, 2011, from www.oecd.org/dataoecd/61/45/38368714.pdf.

————. 2008. Guidance on evaluating conflict prevention and peacebuilding activities. OECD publishing. Retrieved April 5, 2011, from www.oecd.org/dataoecd/36/20 /39289596.pdf.

————. 2009. *Ensuring fragile states are not left behind. Summary report*. OECD publishing. Retrieved April 5, 2011, from www.oecd.org/dataoecd/50/30/42463929.pdf.

————. 2011. *International engagement in fragile states: Can't we do better?* OECD publishing. Retrieved April 5, 2012, from www.oecd.org/dataoecd/14/14/48697077.pdf.

————. n.d. Achieving the MDGs—Addressing conflict, fragility and armed violence. Retrieved April 5, 2012, from www.oecd.org/document/19/0,3746,en_21571361 _43407692_46008211_1_1_1_1,00.html.

Paffenholz, T., and L. Reychler. 2000. *Peacebuilding a field guide*. Boulder, CO: Lynne Rienner.

————. 2007. *Aid for peace: A guide to planning and evaluation for conflict zones*. Baden-Baden, Germany: Nomos.

Peace and Justice Studies Association. 2007. Global directory of peace and conflict resolution programs. Retrieved April 1, 2011, from www.peacejusticestudies.org/globaldirectory/index.php.

Rogers, M., A. Chassy, and T. Bamat. 2010. Integrating peacebuilding into humanitarian and development programming (Catholic Relief Services). Retrieved January 1, 2012, from www.crsprogramquality.org/publications/2010/10/5/integrating-peacebuilding-into-humanitarian-and-development.html.

Saferworld and Conciliation Resources. 2012. From conflict analysis to peacebuilding impact. Lessons from the People's Peacemaking Perspectives Project. Retrieved June 10, 2012, from www.c-r.org/resources/PPP-lessons.

Sandole, D. J. 1998. A comprehensive mapping of conflict and conflict resolution research: A three-pillar approach. *Peace and Conflict Studies* 5, no. 2: 1–30.

Smith, D. 2004. Towards a strategic framework for peacebuilding: Getting their act together. Overview report of the Joint Utstein Study of Peacebuilding. Royal Norwegian Ministry of Foreign Affairs. Retrieved December 5, 2011, from www.prio.no/Research-and-Publications/Project/?oid=92706.

Stockholm Peace Research Institute. 2010. SIPRI yearbook, 2010. Appendix 2A. Patterns of major armed conflicts, 2001–10. Retrieved January 2, 2012, from www.sipri.org/yearbook/2011/02/02A.

Susskind, L., and J. Thomas-Warner. 1999. Conducting a conflict assessment. In L. Susskind, S. McKearan, and J. Thomas-Warner, eds. *Consensus-building handbook: A comprehensive guide to reaching agreement* (pp. 99–136). Thousand Oaks, CA: Sage Publications.

Tiessen, R. 2007. *Everywhere/nowhere: Gender mainstreaming in development agencies.* Bloomfield, CT: Kumarian.

Tongeren, P., M. Brenk, M. Hellema, and J. Verhoeven, J., eds. 2005. *People building peace II: Successful stories of civil society.* Boulder, CO: Lynne Rienner.

United Nations. 1992. An agenda for peace: Preventive diplomacy, peacemaking and peace-keeping. Retrieved April 1, 2011, from www.un.org/Docs/SG/agpeace.html.

———. 2002. Gender mainstreaming: An overview. Office of the Special Adviser on Gender Issues and Advancement of Women. Retrieved January 3, 2012, from www.un.org/womenwatch/osagi/pdf/e65237.pdf.

———. 2005. From WID to GAD: Conceptual shifts in the women and development discourse, by S. Razavi and C. Miller. Research Institute for Social Development. Retrieved January 2, 2012, from www.eldis.org/assets/Docs/17140.html.

USAID. 2010. Theories of change and indicator development in conflict management and mitigation, by Dr. Susan Allen Nan. Retrieved April 1, 2011, from http://pdf.usaid.gov/pdf_docs/PNADS460.pdf.

US Department of State. 2010. Leading through civilian power: The first quadrennial diplomacy and development review. Retrieved April 1, 2012, from www.state.gov/s/dmr/qddr/index.htm.

Uvin, P. 2002. The development/peacebuilding nexus: A typology and history of changing paradigms. *Journal of Peacebuilding and Development* 1, no. 1: 5–24.

Vogel, I. 2012. Review of the use of "Theory of Change" in international development. Department for International Development. Retrieved October 30, 2012, from

www.dfid.gov.uk/What-we-do/Research-and-evidence/news/research-news/2012/Review
-of-the-use-of-Theory-of-Change-in-International-development.

Woodrow, P., and D. Chigas. 2009. A distinction with a difference: Conflict sensitivity
and peacebuilding. CDA Collaborative Learning Projects. Retrieved January 1, 2012, from
www.cdainc.com/cdawww/news_announcement.php#key763.

Zelizer, C., and L. Johnston. 2005. *Skills, networks and knowledge: Developing a career
in international peace and conflict resolution.* Fairfax, VA: Alliance for Conflict Transformation.

Zelizer, C., and R. Rubinstein. 2009. *Building peace: Practical reflections from the field.*
Bloomfield, CT: Kumarian.

NOTES

1. Similar to peacebuilding, there is no universal agreement on fragile and conflict-
affected countries. The Organisation for Economic Co-operation and Development (2007)
defines fragility as such: "States are fragile when state structures lack political will and/or
capacity to provide the basic functions needed for poverty reduction, development and to
safeguard the security and human rights of their populations" (p. 2).

2. For a useful history of the emergence of graduate programs in the field, see Polking-
horn, B., H. La Chance, and R. La Chance, R. "Understanding of Developmental Trends
in Graduate Conflict Resolution Programs in the United States," *Research in Social Movements, Conflicts and Change* 29 (2009): 233–265.

3. Interstate conflict was viewed as the norm for most of the Cold War and involves
conflicts between governments of two or more nations, while intrastate conflict entails
conflict within a state's boundaries that could involve a government versus rebel or insurgent groups.

4. Adapted from Fisher (1993); Diamond and McDonald (1996); Galtung (1995); and
Sandole (1998).

5. The inclusion of civil society and government actors is adopted from the definition
of peacebuilding provided by Chic Dambach, former CEO of the Alliance for Peacebuilding. See www.allianceforpeacebuilding.org/?page=aboutmission.

6. The term "do no harm" is adopted from the work of Mary Anderson (1999).

7. For more details, see www.conflictsensitivity.org.

8. The ICAF is an interagency framework developed collaboratively by eight US federal
agencies to help guide joint conflict-analysis processes. For more info, see www.state.gov
/documents/organization/187786.pdf.

9. See Appendix A of the *USAID* (2010).

10. There are many other sectors in which integrated peacebuilding is taking place, such
as democratization, agriculture, education, public policy, and arts. For this text, a number
of key areas were selected based on trends in the field and author expertise.

chapter two

THE BUSINESS
OF PEACEBUILDING

Craig Zelizer

Peacebuilding is a long-term investment by all relevant actors, and requires a shared vision and long-term strategy to address the root causes of conflict.

—REPORT OF THE UN WORKING GROUP ON LESSONS LEARNED
OF THE PEACEBUILDING COMMISSION (2010, P. 8)[1]

OVER THE PAST TWO DECADES peacebuilding has grown from a minor academic discipline to an independent field of practice, policy, and study made up of actors who develop, fund, implement, and evaluate programming. As the field has grown, there has also been an expansion of efforts to integrate peacebuilding into related sectors and institutions, including humanitarian and development organizations, the military, multilateral organizations, donors, and the private sector.

Although the integration of peacebuilding across a wide array of sectors is a promising endeavor toward positively impacting areas embroiled in protracted conflict, substantial challenges remain. First, there is the risk that attempts will be treated as superficial, as another box to check in an already crowded field of other mainstreaming sectoral priorities, from gender to the environment and health (Lange, 2004; Paffenholz and Reychler, 2007). Second, donor funding for peacebuilding projects is often short-term in nature due to shifting priorities and donor fatigue, but building peace requires longer-term fixes. Third, organizations may be at risk when addressing issues of social change and justice given the strong dependency on government funding.

This chapter explores the business of peacebuilding as a sector of the larger international aid industry in terms of funding, practice, goals, and key actors in both developed and developing countries. First, the chapter presents a general overview of
the development industry, a brief history, and key actors. This is particularly important
since many individuals and organizations in peacebuilding and related fields are motivated to a large degree by a desire to alleviate and prevent suffering but may lack
an understanding of the funding, human capital, and other resources required to go
about the business of integrated peacebuilding. Second, the chapter reviews many of
the relevant challenges that actors in the field face while pursuing the difficult goal
of effecting sustainable, peaceful, and positive change in fragile societies. Additionally,
given the increasing linkages between security, peacebuilding, and development, the
chapter will explore the securitization of the field.

PEACEBUILDING AND THE INTERNATIONAL AID INDUSTRY

Peacebuilding has developed into an independent field in terms of both theory and
practice. It is important, however, to note that this field exists within the much greater
constellation of the international aid industry. The funding sources, structures, and motivations of actors in peacebuilding are largely the same as in the field of international
assistance. Moreover, given the increase in integrated efforts, many peacebuilding programs are conducted by development and humanitarian organizations. International
assistance as an industry amounts to more than US $100 billion annually and includes
a diverse range of actors, from bilateral donors, such as the US Agency for International Development (USAID); multilateral organizations, including the United Nations (UN) and its affiliate agencies; international and local nonprofit organizations,
such as Mercy Corps; for-profit businesses, including DAI and Chemonics; grassroots
community-based organizations in developing societies; foundations, such as the Ford
and Rockefeller Brothers Foundations; and academic institutions conducting applied
practice, education, and research.

The goal of the international aid industry is to foster positive change in the economic, social, and political spheres of developing countries. Although many practitioners involved in the industry are motivated by altruistic desires to alleviate suffering,
violence, and predation, the business of aid is a multibillion-dollar industry that often
involves the consideration of political and economic factors.

Aid is no longer solely under the purview of donors and nonprofit organizations.
For-profit companies that work in development, individual consultants, universities,
and private-sector businesses all employ hundreds of thousands of people around the
world. Due in part to the size of the industry and the nature of the work that is done,
aid significantly impacts the economies of both recipient and donor countries.[2] While
organizations vary in their motivations for carrying out aid work, all (including nonprofits) must generate revenue to keep their staff and operations running in order to
meet their ultimate goals, which in turn range from altruistic crisis management to
advancing political, economic, and security interests.

International assistance programming can be divided between development programming and humanitarian relief/aid. Development supports longer-term assistance

to build or develop a country's economy and infrastructure, while humanitarian relief activities focus on short-term assistance in crisis settings. *Humanitarian aid* is defined as "aid and action designed to save lives, alleviate suffering and maintain and protect human dignity during and in the aftermath of emergencies" (Global Humanitarian Assistance, n.d., para. 1). Humanitarian aid is provided in response to natural disasters, such as the earthquake and flooding in Pakistan in recent years, as well as human-made disasters, such as the election-related violence in Kenya in 2007 that led to the displacement of several hundred thousand people.

International development tends to focus on long-term assistance to help build the capacity of societies through strengthening economic, social, cultural, and educational institutions and human capacity. Relief and development activities take place at the community, regional, and national levels, and can support a broad range of activities across sectors, including economic growth, infrastructure, social services, health, agriculture, and education (de Haan, 2009). Development assistance includes loans to help finance infrastructure, educational projects, programming grants to nonprofits, contracts for for-profits and universities to support work, and direct budget support to governments in developing countries for specific programming (Vidal and Pillay, 2004). As outlined in Chapter 1, in recent years the fields of development and humanitarian relief have begun to integrate peacebuilding into some of their programming and operations in conflict-affected areas.

For many years, humanitarian aid and international development functioned as separate sectors of practice, even while many organizations conducted work in both areas. It was only in the 1990s that a conceptual model called the Relief to Development Continuum was developed, outlining the following stages:

1. *Humanitarian relief*—Crisis response.
2. *Rehabilitation*—Initiate work on immediate infrastructure and economic needs.
3. *Development*—Long-term sectoral programming (economic, education, agriculture, health, etc.) aimed at fostering stability and growth within society. (Smillie, 1998)

Conflict-related concerns and activities can be integrated into any of these stages. It is important to note that although the continuum model provided an important conceptual step to better link relief and development, there have been many critiques of this approach. The first is that the model is seen as overly simplistic, suggesting a simple transition from one stage to another. Second, many organizations carry out work in both relief and development, and the model as it stands envisions an unrealistic division of organizational responsibility. Third, the model does not emphasize preventive efforts to stop crises and work to change the conditions that lead to the need for relief activities. Although the relief and development continuum model is still a useful concept, Smillie (1998) explains that

from the 1960s into the 1980s, the standard approach to relief and development was a linear one, with both seen as distinct and essentially sequential types of effort. The concept of a "continuum" in which the external response to an emergency moves from relief through reconstruction to development represented a useful conceptual innovation. However, the approach was still based on the notion that at each distinct stage there would be specialized institutions to take and then pass on responsibility for discrete and phased programming. In the early 1990s, the continuum concept gave way to more holistic thinking. As a result, relief and development are no longer viewed as self-contained and mutually exclusive. Linkages can and must be made if reconstruction and development are to be sustainable and recurring relief avoided. (p. xiii)

Revising Aid: A Critique of International Development

International development emerged in the post–World War II era, when developed countries sought to increase the capacities of states emerging from colonialism. Additionally, countries recovering from the devastation of World War II needed substantial assistance in caring for refugees and rebuilding their societies. Many of these newly independent states suffered from weak economies and a high dependency on the agricultural sector. Through technical assistance, grants, loans, and other forms of support, the developed countries provided aid to their poorer and under-resourced counterparts.

Initially, international development efforts primarily focused on promoting economic growth and modernizing societies (Harrison, 1981). The goal was to assist poorer countries in developing industrial sectors and transitioning into economies similar to those of their Western counterparts (Tomlinson, 1999). Formulas for development were, for the most part, based upon Western countries' own paths to modernity. As such, measures of successful development were calculated by how quickly countries converted to a "modern" economic system (Frank, 1966). For decades, success in these cases was measured by increases in gross domestic product (GDP) and per capita income. The objective was to largely transform rural-based, poor economies into active members of the global economic and political system.

Over time a strong critique emerged from academics, development practitioners, and policy makers that challenged the notion of an international development model that largely prioritized economic growth. This often meant imposing a particular type of Western economic and political structure, a one-size-fits-all model, on developing countries. As a condition for obtaining aid, host countries were often forced to cut back government spending, privatize key industries, and open up their economies to receive large-scale development and infrastructure projects. This can be seen in the controversial "structural adjustment programs" (SAPs) of the World Bank and the International Monetary Fund (IMF), which were popular for several decades starting in the 1970s. To receive aid, countries needed to comply with a list of demands and implement a series of SAPs, which focused on reducing deficits on external accounts and decreasing public spending, and aimed to achieve a balanced government budget (de Haan, 2009).

There are a number of other significant critiques of aid. While advocates of the aid industry may cite beneficence as their rationale for advancing poorer societies, critics indicate that the ultimate aim tends to coincide with the establishment of a global free-market economy, which pushes liberal democracy as the dominant political system. Although there is much talk about participation and accountability, critics argue that the goal is ultimately to integrate poorer countries into the dominant, unfair economic system that benefits the more powerful countries by increasing their access to natural resources and additional markets.

Another point of note is that the decisions regarding the provision of aid have frequently been guided by political and not needs-based considerations. During the Cold War, aid was often targeted to countries that were at risk of aligning too closely with the Soviet Union and socialism (Lundborg, 1998). At times, this meant that aid was provided to leaders who engaged in undemocratic practices and led corrupt governments. This trend continues today, as political and security considerations may trump other factors, such as need, in deciding where aid is given.

Another critique is that outside donors and international organizations working in developing societies strongly influence decisions regarding the types of programs and initiatives that can receive support. This means that programs may not be based on the local context or needs, which in turn raises a host of ethical issues about power, ownership, and sustainability (CDA Collaborative Learning Projects, 2011a; 2011b). It is important to note, however, that over the past few decades there has been a strong push for much more inclusive and locally led development. Furthermore, in almost all societies there are strong civil-society, volunteer, nonprofit, and community- and faith-based organizations that carry out locally designed and led development projects. In many cases these organizations may be working with funding or in partnership with international organizations. For example, under its new Forward Policy, USAID is seeking to increase support provided directly to local organizations in developing countries, as opposed to contracting via US-based companies and nonprofits.[3]

In addition to local concerns, there are some macro-level critiques of aid in general. Research shows that several countries, all of which have received aid for more than four decades, have fared much worse than countries that have received little or no aid (Easterly, 2006). Although these findings are disputed, there are success stories of countries that have prospered without substantial aid: Singapore, Taiwan, and South Korea (commonly dubbed the East Asian Tigers). According to William Easterly (2006), between 1950 and 2001, "countries with below-average aid had the same growth rate as countries with above-average foreign aid. Poor countries without aid had no trouble having positive growth" (p. 39). Furthermore, another study found that countries in which aid represented 8 percent or more of their gross domestic product (GDP) actually had a negative growth rate (p. 50).

Advocates for a more innovative, market-based approach to change, both from within and without the field, often cite the bureaucratic largesse of the aid industry. Easterly (2006) suggests that there is not enough support in international development for innovation to occur naturally from within the field. There is too much emphasis on macro-level plans, often taking place in headquarter settings located in the capitals of Western countries, rather than conduct operations based upon the reality and context-specific challenges on the ground. Instead, Easterly advocates for an innovative, grassroots approach that coordinates with agents of change on the ground in a flexible, creative manner. Easterly (2006) and other scholars (Polak,

2008) have also emphasized that the way to transform poorer communities around the world is to focus on economic empowerment and integrate a market-based approach to fostering change, instead of doling out aid that can lead to a dependency relationship. Of course these critiques portray an overly simplistic view of aid and bureaucracy, as on-the-ground events are often extremely complex and do not account for the many successes and the innovation taking place around the world.

Still, there are many defenders of international aid as a vital movement that makes a concrete difference and improves economic and living conditions for millions around the world. For example, in 2000 the Millennium Development Goals (MDGs) were created to target eight areas designed to reduce poverty, empower women, increase educational access for children, and improve health. Although it is unlikely the MDGs will be fully realized by the target date of 2015, there have been significant strides in areas such as the poverty rate in Africa, which has fallen from 52 percent in 1990 to 48 percent in 2008 (Overseas Development Institute, 2010, p. 11). Individuals such as Jeffrey Sachs, director of the Earth Institute at Columbia University, and singer Bono have long pushed for increased spending on aid as a means to promote improvements in the damaged sectors of conflict-ridden societies, while others critique the push for market-driven approaches to aid, as they fear this is not the way to provide support for the neediest of the world.

Due to the numerous critiques outlined above, the aid industry has attempted to change by incorporating other perspectives. For example, Amartya Sen helped to advance the notion of human development and the need to focus on the welfare of people, beyond focusing purely on economics as the goal. Human development theory is based on the idea that a nation's true wealth comes from the people and that "the basic objective of development is to create an enabling environment for people to live long, healthy and creative lives" (UNDP, n.d., para. 4). This stands in contrast to some of the traditional notions of development, which place a strong emphasis on growth in macroeconomic indicators, such as GDP, as a means of measuring progress.

To date, the majority of funding for the international aid industry has come from developed countries via their governments, foundations, private businesses, and individual donors. In recent years, however, emerging developing countries, such as India, China, Qatar, and Brazil, have become active in international development initiatives.

The debate about the nature of development also has strong connections to peacebuilding. As peacebuilding has begun to increase in prominence and attract further support and legitimacy from governments and international donors, some have warned there is a danger that the field will be used as a tool to keep power imbalances and systems of inequality in place instead of as a method to seek transformative change at the macro level (Bendana, 1996; Francis, 2010; Zimina and Fisher, 2008). Moreover, others suggest that peacebuilding may impose onto societies a Western notion of dealing with conflict, one that is rooted in a liberal democratic individualistic tradition and may not work across cultures (Francis, 2010). Critics maintain that the nature of funding in the field, which in most cases depends heavily on government and intergovernmental support, biases in favor of projects that might prioritize stability or economic growth over other goals.

ACTORS IN AID AND PEACEBUILDING

According to de Haan (2009), there are four key categories of actors in the aid industry: *bilateral aid agencies, multilateral aid organizations, NGOs,* and *philanthropic organizations/foundations.* There are also many informal community-based organizations, volunteer groups, and faith-based organizations, as well as increased activity by military and private-sector actors. Each of the actors will be reviewed below along with its connection to integrated peacebuilding, beginning with where the majority of funds for aid and conflict work originate.

Overseas Development Assistance

The main mechanism through which the governments of developed countries provide support to the developing world is through overseas development assistance (ODA). According to the Development Assistance Committee (DAC) of the Organisation for Economic Co-operation and Development (OECD), ODA is defined as "those flows to countries and territories on the DAC List of ODA Recipients and to multilateral development institutions," with the goal of helping to promote "the economic development and welfare of developing countries as its main objective" (OECD, 2008). Originally, the 1970 UN General Assembly passed Resolution 2626, which urged donor countries to set a target goal of providing 0.7 percent of their gross national income (GNI) to international assistance programs (Millennium Project, n.d.).[4]

Some forty years later, few countries have met this target. While total ODA from donor countries in 2010 was US $128.7 billion (OECD, Members, 2011), only a few countries have met or surpassed the 0.7 percent target. The average percentage across donor countries in 2010 was 0.32 percent, with Luxembourg being the most generous donor country in the world, providing 1.09 percent of GNI in ODA. The US (the largest donor in total monetary value) provided 0.21 percent of GNI in ODA (OECD, Net ODA, n.d.).

As stated earlier, there is also increasing support for humanitarian and development activities that originate in emerging economies, including Qatar, Saudi Arabia, Brazil, United Arab Emirates, Turkey, and China. This is likely to increase in the future. Non-DAC countries contributed 8 percent of all international aid in 2009 (OECD, Open Doors, n.d.).

The Development Assistance Committee categorizes development projects in a number of broad sectoral areas including: Social and Infrastructure Services, Health, Economic Infrastructure and Services, Productive Services, Government and Civil Society, Multisector, and specific areas such as Humanitarian Relief (OECD, 2011a).[5] Within each category are subthemes, including several specifically focused on peacebuilding or conflict issues. For example, "Government and Civil Society" is a category with conflict resolution and prevention, and peace and security (OECD/DAC, List, 2011) services falling within this area. Humanitarian aid is classified as a separate area and includes emergency response, reconstruction relief, rehabilitation, disaster prevention, and preparedness. It was only in 2004 that peace- and conflict-related issues became an official area for funded activities. Within the category of conflict prevention, the OECD/DAC (List, 2011) identifies six types of activities, including:

Security system management and reform—Having to do with the restructuring of military- and civilian-institution relations.

Civilian peacebuilding, conflict prevention, and resolution—Focused on civilian and civil-society activities to help prevent, transform, and resolve conflicts.

Participation in international peacekeeping operations—This does not include direct support for peacekeeping missions, only related activities that take place in such contexts including human rights programming, security sector reform, and election monitoring.

Reintegration and small-arms and light-weapons control—Preventing and controlling the spread of weapons to help reduce violence and prevent conflict.

Removal of land mines—Land mines are often placed in conflict zones and pose a critical danger to civilians, particularly those working in agriculture.

Child soldiers (prevention and demobilization)—This is a special area of emphasis given the large number of youth who are forced into or engaged in fighting in conflicts in the world. (pp. 9–10)

The programming areas listed above explicitly focus on conflict issues in terms of DAC-supported activities. Other areas are connected to conflict from an integrated perspective, such as components of humanitarian programming and rule of law. It is important to note that although the field is growing in terms of programming and support, the total amount of dedicated peace and conflict funding in relation to overall development remains small, with approximately US $3 billion provided in 2010 (OECD, 2011b).[6]

The funding figures for dedicated peace and conflict work from the DAC countries have increased by over 200 percent since the category was created in 2004. This is illustrated in Figure 2.1, which explores the level of funding for conflict, peace, and security issues:

FIGURE 2.1. Total DAC Spending on Conflict, Peace, and Security, 2004–2010[7]

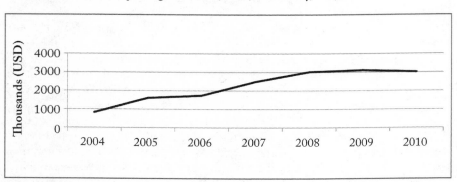

Source: OECD Stats Database, http://stats.oecd.org/Index.aspx?DatasetCode=ODA_SECTOR

In calculating international assistance, official ODA totals do not include funding provided by foundations, individual charitable contributions (largely from individuals and corporations via nongovernmental organizations), the private sector, the military, and remittances sent by migrants to their home countries. These are considerable funds, as foreign direct investment in developing countries far surpasses ODA, totaling over US $600 billion in 2011 (United Nations Conference on Trade and Development, 2011), while remittances to developing countries (money sent back by immigrants to their home country) in 2011 topped over US $350 billion (World Bank, 2011b). It is important to note other areas of funding, such as the military, foundations, and other sectors, are also providing support for peacebuilding-related activities.

Bilateral Aid Agencies

Bilateral aid agencies are the official institutions through which developed countries provide the bulk of their development assistance. There are currently twenty-four official bilateral aid agencies in the world, located in the wealthier countries of North America, Western Europe, East Asia, and the Pacific. The agencies regularly interact with one another, share information, and try to coordinate their aid work through the OECD/DAC. The oldest members of the DAC are Belgium, France, Germany, Italy, Japan, the Netherlands, the UK, and the US (OECD, n.d.). The newest to join the DAC is South Korea, which became a member in 2010.

This committee has taken a leading role in helping members to establish more effective programming in conflict-ridden and fragile environments by conducting research on best practices, policy guidelines, and convening key stakeholders. Conflict, security, fragile states, and peacebuilding have become relatively new focal areas for the DAC in the past decade. The groundbreaking Peace and Development Policy Statement in 1997 (OECD, 2001) explored the relationship between development and conflict:

> Work in war-torn or conflict-prone countries must be seen as an integral part of the co-operation challenge. Wars have set back development severely in many countries, including in some of the poorest; excessive military expenditures have too often taken priority over more productive public investments and responses to complex emergencies have come to represent a major claim on development co-operation budgets. More basically, helping strengthen the capacity of a society to manage conflict without violence must be seen as a foundation for sustainable development. (p. 79)

Some institutions, such as USAID, have created explicit subunits to help the agency work on conflict as a cross-cutting theme. For example, in 2003 USAID created the Conflict Management and Mitigation Unit to "work with USAID's missions and partners to integrate or 'mainstream' best practices in conflict management into more traditional development work."[8] The unit is relatively small, with a staff of about fifteen people and budget of US $6 million (Beller, Klein, and Fisher, 2010). They also award approximately US $20 million in grants related to conflict and peacebuilding each year. Other units at USAID explicitly work on peacebuilding or conflict, such as the

Office of Transitions Initiatives, which had a budget of US $55 million in 2010 and does rapid response and programming in insecure and conflict-affected environments.[9]

Other bilateral aid agencies that focus on conflict as part of their programming include the Swedish International Development Agency (SIDA), the Department for International Development in the UK, the Canadian International Development Agency, and the Swiss Development Agency. Calculating the total funds spent on conflict initiatives is challenging since many list conflict or peace as a subunit of broader areas, such as security. The agency of SIDA, in 2008, estimates that 20 percent of their funds went to efforts that had peace or security as a primary or secondary focus.[10] In the US, according to the Congressional Research Service (2011), total USAID and State Department funding for conflict mitigation and reconciliation totaled over US $700 million in 2010 (p. 5). The total US international-aid budget was US $39 billion in 2010 (Congressional Research Service, 2011), while total US defense spending in 2010 was over US $600 billion.

A further complication in methodological approaches to understanding funding levels occurs when conflict offices in bilateral agencies change their mandate or structure according to government policies. For example, the Department for International Development (DFID) set up a unit in 2004 called the Post-Conflict Reconstruction Unit to help integrate conflict sensitivity into their development programming, but the office was renamed the Stabilization Unit in 2007 to broaden the focus also to security issues and strengthening linkages with the Ministry of Defense and the Foreign Office.[11]

In terms of programming areas, bilateral donors engage in peacebuilding work across a variety of sectors. For example, USAID/CMM (Conflict Management and Mitigation) focuses on integrating peacebuilding issues across a diverse range of development sectors that include economic growth, natural resources, security sector reform, social development, and focused conflict programming.[12] DFID recently grouped together conflict and governance into two broad areas, with a number of specific areas of programming, including security and justice, conflict prevention, public financial management, women, and peace and security. In a recent review of programming, DFID determined that twenty-one of its twenty-eight priority countries "are fragile or conflict affected" and is seeking to increase its expenditure of resources in this area.[13]

Multilateral Organizations

A number of multilateral organizations work on development and peacebuilding issues. The UN has over thirty specialized agencies such as the UN Development Programme (UNDP), which is engaged in development and conflict work (de Haan, 2009). The blue helmets of the UN Department of Peacekeeping Operations currently number over 95,000 and are involved in more than sixteen missions worldwide (United Nations, 2011).

The World Bank and its associated international financial institutions (such as the International Monetary Fund and the International Bank for Reconstruction and Development) are often engaged in macro-level efforts that finance and support economic development, infrastructure, and related projects. Over the past two decades, the World Bank has taken an explicit look at their programming in conflict and fragile environments, and subsequently established a small Conflict Prevention and Reconstruction Unit in the late 1990s. The conflict work has since been integrated into new areas at the bank, including the Fragile and Conflict Affected Countries Group and the Social Cohesion and Violence Prevention cluster in the Social Development Department as well as the recently created Global Center on Conflict Security and Development.[14] In "The World Development Report: Conflict, Security, and Development" (2011a), the Bank made some of the strongest linkages between development and conflict to date. As Robert Zoellick, president of the World Bank, states in the report,

> A civil conflict costs the average developing country roughly 30 years of GDP growth, and countries in protracted crisis can fall over 20 percentage points behind in overcoming poverty. Finding effective ways to help societies escape new outbursts or repeated cycles of violence is critical for global security and global development. (p. xii)

One of the premier UN agencies working on peacebuilding is the UNDP. The organization has been engaged in conflict and peacebuilding work for many years, but the Bureau for Crisis Prevention and Response was created in 2001 to help improve and coordinate the agency's work on conflict issues. As with any larger institution, there are other divisions conducting peacebuilding work, such as UNESCO (education), UNDPKO (peacekeeping/security), UNWOMEN (gender and conflict/peace), UN Trust Funds, and the UN Peacebuilding Commission, which was formed in 2005.

Many regional multilateral organizations have also developed an explicit focus on conflict and peace issues, such as the Organization of American States, the African Union, and the Organization for Security and Cooperation in Europe, which has taken a pioneering role among regional organizations through its conflict prevention work in Europe, particularly the Balkans, the Caucasus, and the former Soviet Union.

Nongovernmental Organizations

Much of the activity taking place around the world is conducted by local, national, and international nongovernmental organizations (NGOs). According to de Haan (2009), approximately 15 percent of ODA flows through NGOs. In addition, many NGOs receive direct support from charitable contributions, foundations, and fee-for-service activities that fall outside of the official ODA tally.

NGOs range in size from community-based organizations at the grassroots level in local contexts, to World Vision, an international NGO that conducts development, peace and conflict work, and humanitarian relief in over one hundred countries with the help of over 30,000 staff.

Although many leading development and humanitarian organizations have been involved in peacebuilding work for a significant period, it is only in the past decade that a number have created units specifically designed to conduct peacebuilding work. For example, Catholic Relief Services (CRS), a global organization with over 4,500 staff, made peacebuilding a priority area in 2001 and has since hired additional personnel to work on developing this capacity. CRS (n.d.) explains that

> over time we learned that the way we do our emergency and development programming helps prevent or transform conflicts. If we ignore conflicts and their underlying causes then our work prolongs the conflict by providing new resources to the warring parties (like food and supplies), or our programs are destroyed in the chaos and violence. If we help our partners address the injustices in their society that cause conflict and facilitate respectful relationships between conflicting parties then our work together builds sustainable peace. (para. 1)

A significant number of additional development and relief organizations have incorporated similar issues into their work and have begun to integrate matters of conflict and programming into their core.

There are also a plethora of organizations that focus specifically on peacebuilding. Most of these organizations are smaller in both staff and budget than their development counterparts, yet still work with great dedication on an international scale; these include Search for Common Ground, which works in more than twenty-five countries with over 350 staff; Partners for Democratic Change, in eighteen countries; and International Alert, in twenty countries. Some regionally based organizations also have played a strong role in conflict activities. For example, ACCORD, an organization based in South Africa that was started in 1992 and played an important role in that country's transition, is a leading institution working across Africa.

A worldwide alliance of peacebuilding organizations, the Global Partnership for the Prevention of Armed Conflict, was created in 2003 and now has over 1,000 members.[15] There are also networks of organizations, both local and international, that focus on nearly every region of the world. Some of these include the Alliance for Peacebuilding, the European Peacebuilding Liaison Office (which coordinates thirty organizations in the European Union), and the West African Network for Peacebuilding.[16]

It is important to again emphasize that in overall size, the development and humanitarian industry far surpasses the size and budget of dedicated international peacebuilding work. For example, in the US, Interaction is the main network organization for international development and humanitarian organizations. Interaction has over 180 members whose combined total revenue is nearly US $19 billion, with a number of organizations having budgets in excess of US $500 million or $1 billion per year.[17] The Alliance for Peacebuilding comprises over seventy member organizations, most with budgets under US $10 million.

Foundations

In recent years, foundations have acted in an increasingly important role in the world of international development and peacebuilding. Foundations traditionally have provided support for development assistance related to research and programming. This has shifted in recent years to include their own programming and agenda related to international assistance programs (Haan, 2009). The Gates Foundation in particular, the world's largest foundation, has placed a strong emphasis on improving impact and evaluation in international development.

Numerous large foundations, including Ford, Hewlett, MacArthur, and the Ploughshares Fund, have supported the growth of the peacebuilding and conflict field in both scholarship and practice. The Hewlett Foundation was the largest private donor in peacebuilding and conflict resolution for twenty years, and helped support scholarship, practice, and networks with over $160 million, until they changed priorities in 2004 (Hewlett, 2004). In recognition of the need to better coordinate efforts, the top foundations in support of conflict and peace work in the US formed the Peace and Security Funders Group in 1999. Between 2008 and 2009, the member foundations provided over US $250 million in funding to support peace and security programs at universities, think tanks, and nonprofits in the US and abroad (Peace and Security Funders Group, 2010).[18]

Military

Military actors have not traditionally been seen as purveyors of aid or advocates of peacebuilding programs, nor have they been included in official development assistance programs. In recent years, however, Western militaries have become increasingly involved in development and conflict projects, largely due to the wars in Iraq and Afghanistan. The concept is not new, however, as the US and other militaries have engaged in humanitarian relief, assistance, and small-scale development in countries such as Somalia and Haiti starting in the 1990s. Peacekeepers have also been a fixture of international peace efforts for more than six decades.

While the military has been involved in building ties through training programs and other types of exchanges with nations in the development world, military actors have increasingly focused on fostering new types of operations called "stabilization operations." In 2008, the US military issued a new Stability Field Operations Directive, which elevates development and stability to the level of offensive and defensive operations.[19] These types of projects often take place in regions where there is a military intervention and a need to, among other factors, build goodwill among the population and reduce extremism. The military has invented a number of new programming initiatives that touch on conflict-related themes, such as the provincial reconstruction teams (PRTs) and human terrain teams (HTTs). These are units in which development specialists and/or anthropologists are embedded to help assist with civilian relations. As explained in a US Army handbook about the teams (Center for Army Lessons Learned, 2007), "The PRT is designed to help improve stability by building up the capacity of the host nation to govern; enhance economic viability; and deliver essential public services, such as security, law and order, justice, health care, and education" (p. 2). The role of the military will be addressed in more detail in Chapter 13.

Private-Sector Actors

Much of the development work funded through bilateral aid agencies is implemented by hundreds of for-profit international development contractors who conduct projects on behalf of donors. These contractors implement development projects in the field and obtain funds from agencies such as USAID and DFID. Many contractors are also active in implementation and research for conflict-related issues on behalf of USAID, DFID, the World Bank, and other donor agencies. One reason for the explosion of contractors in international aid and development work (including conflict) is the general push within the US and in some other countries, such as the UK, to outsource some government functions.[20]

In addition to private contractors, a growing number of businesses have been involved in international development, especially as donors push for increased public/private partnerships.[21] Over the past decade, the role of business has been both a force for peace and a source of conflict. Many international businesses (particularly extractive industries, such as oil, timber, gas, and minerals) also operate in conflict zones and have the potential to significantly impact, knowingly or otherwise, the regional conflict dynamics. Local businesses can also play a critical role in integrating peacebuilding into their operations to ensure that, at a minimum, they do not enflame the conflict and, ideally, that they build relationships and help foster a positive impact.

The emphasis on private-sector actors and conflict has increased over the past two decades, as companies have begun to play more important roles in certain positive transitions, such as in South Africa and Northern Ireland. There are also many examples of businesses that promote conflict-reducing activities in Colombia and Sri Lanka under the motto that "peace is better business" (Rettberg, 2004, p. 7). The role and motivations of private-sector actors will be explored further in Chapter 10.

Other Actors

The list above does not cover all the actors involved in international aid or peacebuilding activities, but rather represents the core groups that provide funds and implement projects. Other groups are also involved in aid and conflict-related activities, including faith-based groups and indigenous communities. These actors may fall into one of the categories described, such as a religious group that operates a faith-based nonprofit organization. There are also countless community-based organizations (CBOs) that may not have an official status, but carry out vital work nonetheless. Additional actor profiles will be discussed in subsequent chapters.

WHY IS AID PROVIDED?

In exploring the industry, it is essential to understand why donors provide funding for aid and peacebuilding work. The majority of organizations that work in integrated peacebuilding rely to a large degree on funding from bilateral and multilateral aid agencies. While it is difficult to obtain exact data, for a large number of for-profit organizations (particularly for-profit contractors), upward of 90 percent of their budgets comes from government sources. For nonprofits, some are entirely dependent on government funding mechanisms while others can maintain a balance of individual, foundation, and corporate donors.[22]

Within the peacebuilding field, there is tension between advocates who stress social justice as a core approach of the field and believe that the only way to truly end conflicts is to seek an end to power imbalances at all levels of society. Others stress the technical process of managing and reducing conflict, and ensure that ongoing conflicts do not escalate and spread. As a result, there may be a tension between efforts that seek to promote justice and change versus those that seek to maintain the status quo and stabilize power relations. Many organizations that depend on international and local funding mechanisms come to face this conundrum in a very real sense. As a longtime peacebuilding practitioner, Diana Francis (2010) elaborates:

> I suspect that, despite our theory about conflict and change, we are not only reluctant to compromise our impartiality, but also (properly) wary of action to confront structural violence and bring hidden conflict into the open—afraid that it could make things worse rather than better. (Maybe we are also aware that most major donors will be unwilling to support interventions that lift the lid off of conflict, rather than turning down the heat.) (p. 103)

Governments, foundations, and individuals who provide funding for international assistance and conflict work for a variety of reasons. According to the Congressional Research Service (2011), the three broad goals for official US foreign assistance support include:

- **National Security** has been the predominant theme of U.S. assistance programs. . . . Since the September 11, 2001, terrorist attacks in the United States, policymakers frequently have cast foreign assistance as a tool in the global war on terrorism, increasing aid to partner states in the terrorism war and funding the substantial reconstruction programs in Afghanistan and Iraq.
- **Commercial Interests**. Foreign assistance has long been defended as a way to either promote U.S. exports by creating new customers for U.S. products or by improving the global economic environment in which U.S. companies compete.
- **Humanitarian Concerns**. Humanitarian concerns drive both short-term assistance in response to crisis and disaster as well as long-term development assistance aimed at reducing poverty, hunger, and other forms of human suffering brought on by more systemic problems. Providing assistance for humanitarian reasons has generally been the least contested purpose of aid by the American public and policymakers alike. (pp. 2–3)

Other organizations have their own rationale for supporting foreign aid programs. At times the goals of donor nations in supporting security or advancing other strategic interests may not match the priorities of locals. Often the ideal standard of aid as an apolitical force for good represents a smaller fraction of a larger project designed to promote a particular agenda. For example, the top three countries that received US foreign assistance in 2010 were Afghanistan, Israel, and Pakistan (Congressional Research Service, 2011). Some question if these are the countries that are most in need, or if this is due to important political and security considerations.

KEY DEBATES IN THE FIELD

A number of key debates relevant to integrating peacebuilding are currently being discussed in the aid and peacebuilding fields. These include the increasing linkage of aid and security, participation and accountability, and projectification and donor fatigue.

Securitization of Aid and Conflict

Since 9/11, there has been a strong move toward the securitization of aid by some donors as outside assistance has become increasingly linked to larger security and military objectives. To some degree the discourse of aid has moved away from a sectoral focus on providing economic, educational, and health assistance across a broad spectrum of areas, to a centralized need to strengthen weak or fragile states. According to the World Bank (2011a) over 1.5 billion people today live in states that are experiencing conflict or fragility, "periods when states or institutions lack the capacity, accountability, or legitimacy to mediate relations between citizen groups and between citizens and the state, making them vulnerable to violence" (p. xvi).

While this has clear implications in undermining development, security, and safety for local citizens of fragile states, there is also a significant security motivation by some donors to help reduce the chances of terrorists or other nonstate armed actors from operating in weak or ungoverned spaces. While this may be a laudable goal, a number of practitioners and scholars in the aid industry are concerned that aid is being distributed to support a security-first agenda for donors concerned about terrorism. Development assistance in some areas is now even being linked to counterinsurgency programming. As stated in one recent guide linking development and insurgency (Moyar, 2011):

> The primary purpose of development aid in counterinsurgency should be to improve local security and governance, because development is less important than security and governance and is effective only where security and governance are present. Development aid should be used to co-opt local elites, not to obtain the gratitude of the entire population, and should be made contingent on reciprocal action by those elites. (p. 1)

This is not to say that all agencies are moving in this direction, and there are significant debates about the best and most ethical way to link development, conflict, and security, but it is clear that there are increasing linkages between development, security, and peacebuilding programming.

Given the limited amount of funding for international aid, this has serious implications for how aid is distributed within both countries and sectoral areas. As Oxfam International (2011) found in a recent report, "Whose Aid Is It Anyway? Politicizing Aid in Conflicts and Crises," "Since 2002 one-third of all development aid to the 48 states labeled 'fragile' by the OECD has gone to just three countries: Iraq, Afghanistan and Pakistan" (p. 72). The report goes on to explain that the use of aid

> for military or security objectives has been increasingly justified by development approaches that seek to integrate humanitarian action and poverty reduction with

efforts to stop violent conflict and political instability: combining activities ranging from counter-insurgency to conflict resolution, military training to community development and food aid to reconstructing agricultural markets. (p. 72)

There are also strong critiques that see the securitization of aid as another example of liberal elites or Western societies seeking to impose their view on developing countries. Duffield (2002, 2007) argues that the linking of security and aid is another in a long series of steps by liberal Western countries to impose a normative order onto states and societies perceived as "backward" or "dangerous." He sees this effort as a new form of colonialism under the guise of aid and security, stating that "within a developmental security frame-work, borderland states have lost most of their relevance except as 'facilitators' or things to be 'reformed' or 'reconstructed'" (Duffield 2002, p. 1066).

Another fundamental issue for bilateral aid agencies concerns the degree to which they provide assistance based on local needs versus larger economic, political, or security agendas. Calculations about which country receives aid and of the sector it enriches can be significantly influenced by political considerations within a donor country (Center for Global Development, 2006).

Given the reliance many organizations have on government funding, a number of critical questions result. For instance, what does it mean for a private company or non-profit organization to be engaged in peacebuilding activities in a country such as Afghanistan, which is dominated by a large-scale international military conflict? Is it possible and ethical to engage in conflict and peace work that is funded by the same actors directly or indirectly engaged in the conflict? Considering the significant bias toward military support, what does it mean for organizations to engage in peace work in regions where the same donors may also be supporting military or security goals? For example, in Colombia, over the past ten years the US has invested over US $5 billion in Plan Colombia to help stabilize the country. While some of the funds have gone for peacebuilding-related activities, approximately 80 percent has gone to more security-oriented programming (Isacson and Poe, 2009).

One of the challenges for organizations is that with the focus on security increasing over the past decade, the space for individuals and organizations to be engaged with actors in conflict-affected countries has been severely hampered. A basic rule of peacebuilding practice is that "we don't make peace by talking to our friends," and that fostering peace requires direct engagement with insurgent actors.[23] The US and other countries, including the UK, India, and Russia, however, have developed lists of terrorist groups with whom these countries refuse to negotiate. This has made it extremely difficult, if not illegal, for US-based third-party actors to engage with groups. The June 2010 *Holder v. Humanitarian Law Project* ruling by the US Supreme Court has made it largely illegal for US peace and humanitarian actors to interact with groups who may be seen as having terrorist affiliations, and severely limits space for peacebuilding in challenging environments. As Guinane and Sazwal (2010) explain, "Chief Justice Roberts argued that conflict mediators and peacebuilding trainers 'legitimize' terrorist groups by teaching nonviolent conflict resolution skills. This ignores the fact that conflicts cannot be effectively resolved unless all parties are part of negotiations. It also confuses the role of independent civil society groups with governments" (para. 6).

Participation and Accountability

One major focus in the aid community over the past two decades has been to recognize the need for participation from the local communities that often receive aid. There have been numerous terms for this, such as "participatory approaches at the grassroots level," or "country ownership" (Center for Global Development, 2006). The real challenges lay in building truly participatory processes given the power dynamics between donors and recipients. There is also the critical question as to what entity should hold the donors and aid/conflict organizations accountable. In reality most of the funding for aid comes from governments and, to a lesser degree, foundations, businesses, and individuals. For example, US or British overseas aid comes from their respective taxpayers. This can create a problem in that beneficiaries who are the target of programming may not be the ones who have the direct power to influence how the program is conducted. As Bertin Martens (as cited in Center for Global Development, 2006) explains,

> A unique and striking characteristic of foreign aid is that the people for whose benefit aid agencies work are not the same as those from whom the revenues are obtained; they actually live in different countries and different political constituencies. This [separation] blocks the normal performance feedback process: beneficiaries may be able to observe performance but cannot modulate payments (rewards to agents) as a function of performance. Although donors are typically interested in ensuring that their funds are well spent, it is extremely difficult for them to do so, since there is frequently no obvious mechanism for transmitting the beneficiaries' point of view to the sponsors. (p. 12)

Rigorous analysis and emphasizing local participation can help to address this issue in conflict and mainstreaming work. Still, a great deal remains to be done in terms of ultimate accountability. As CDA Collaborative Learning Projects (2011b) found in their research with beneficiaries of development and peacebuilding projects around the world, some of the key challenges to developing accountability include:

> The systems and structures of international assistance (the "business model") are too focused on the quick and efficient delivery of goods and services and not enough on relationships.
> External agendas, priorities, fads and trends determine the types of assistance people receive or can access, but are often disconnected to the realities on the ground.
> People in recipient societies want more ownership and to play a more active role in their own development, saying that they want to "discuss together, decide together, and work together." (p. 1)

Although there have been positive steps toward developing stronger partnerships and interactions with local organizations and constituencies over the past decade, significant challenges remain at both the micro and macro levels. As outlined in the CDA report, sometimes donors and implementing organizations do not have the time or capacity to perform rigorous consultation, as this is a time-consuming process.

Projectification

Building peace and reducing conflicts in highly polarized situations is a long-term process that requires sustained effort and activity. As highlighted earlier, there are often setbacks in peacebuilding processes when agreements fail, conflicts escalate, violence persists, or conflicts become further entrenched. Noted peace scholar and practitioner John Paul Lederach (1997) estimates that it can take a generation or more to truly build the chance for a sustainable peace.

One of the fundamental challenges in the international aid and conflict industry is that most donors support efforts on a short-term, project-focused basis. To give and receive funding, large societal problems need to be atomized into discrete project-focused interventions. Most funding from foundations, governments, and individuals is provided on a shorter-term basis than what may be required to sustain long-term change and is often provided in brief one- to three-year periods, and in rare cases five years. Thus, interventions designed to address systematic issues have to be projectified to fit into discrete segments that may not correspond with the actual needs of society.

A key part of projectification is donor fatigue, as the priorities or funding available to support projects changes over time. Whenever there is a large-scale international conflict situation, there will be a correspondingly huge increase in available funding and resources. Over time, however, these dwindle.

CONCLUSION

A diverse set of actors and motivations is involved in peacebuilding and aid work. As highlighted throughout the chapter, it is essential to see the business side of the field, along with the dynamic, altruistic work conducted by most individuals and organizations. Having a deeper understanding of the reasons funding is offered, the challenge of developing long-term partnerships and programming in many cases, combined with the long-term nature of conflict, is fundamental to address the issues that pose difficulties from within integrated peacebuilding programming.

QUESTIONS FOR FURTHER DISCUSSION

1. What is the relationship between funding and practice in peacebuilding and development?

2. What are some of the pros and cons of the increasing securitization of international assistance?

3. How do organizations working in peacebuilding fund and sustain themselves? And how does the push for funding possibly affect their programmatic choices?

4. How would you define and operationalize accountability in the international development industry? What can be done to improve this?

5. What are some emerging trends in the international development industry that might affect peacebuilding?

REFERENCES

Beller, S., G. Klein, and R. Fisher. 2010. *US government innovations in peacebuilding and conflict resolution: Implications for the IPCR Program.* Washington, DC: American University. Retrieved April 5, 2011, from www.american.edu/sis/ipcr/loader.cfm?csModule =security.

Bendana, A. 1996. Conflict resolution: Empowerment and disempowerment. *Peace and Change* 21, no. 1: 68–77.

Catholic Relief Services. n.d. Background of CRS Peacebuilding Program. Retrieved December 1, 2011, from http://crs.org/peacebuilding/general_background.cfm.

CDA Collaborative Learning Projects. 2011a. The Listening Project issue paper: Perceptions of aid in places affected by conflict. Retrieved April 1, 2012, from www.cdainc .com/cdawww/pdf/issue/conflict_sensitivity_ip_Pdf.pdf.

Center for Army Lessons Learned. 2007. PRT playbook: Tactics, techniques, and procedures. Retrieved April 5, 2011, from http://usacac.army.mil/cac2/call/docs/07–34 /toc.asp.

Center for Global Development. 2006. A primer on foreign aid. Working Paper 92, by Steven Radelet. Retrieved October 5, 2011, from www.cgdev.org/content/publications /detail/8846.

———. 2011b. Policy brief: The Listening Project and Good Humanitarian Donorship. Retrieved January 2, 2012, from www.cdainc.com/cdawww/project_profile.php?pid =LISTEN&pname=Listening%20Project.

Congressional Research Service. 2011. Foreign aid: An introduction to U.S. programs and policy. By C. Tarnoff and M. L. Lawson. Retrieved December 10, 2011, from http: //fpc.state.gov/documents/organization/157097.pdf.

de Haan, A. 2009. *How the aid industry works.* Sterling, VA: Kumarian.

Duffield, M. 2002. Social reconstruction and the radicalization of development: Aid as a relation of global liberal governance. *Development and Change* 33, no. 5: 1049–1071.

———. 2007. Development, territories, and people: Consolidating the external sovereign frontier. *Alternatives* 32: 225–246.

Easterly, W. 2006. *The white man's burden. Why the West's efforts to aid the rest have done so much ill and so little good.* New York: Penguin.

European Network on Debt and Development. 2011. How to spend it: Smart procurement for more effective aid, by B. Elmmers. Retrieved June 10, 2012, from http://eurodad .org/?p=4639.

Francis, D. 2010. *From pacification to peacebuilding: A call to global transformation.* New York: Palgrave MacMillan.

Frank, A. G. 1966. *The development of underdevelopment.* Boston: New England Free Press.

Global Humanitarian Assistance. n.d. Defining humanitarian aid. Retrieved December 12, 2011, from www.globalhumanitarianassistance.org/data-guides/defining-humanitarian -aid.

Guinane, K., and S. K. Sazawal. 2010. Supreme Court's Humanitarian Law Project Ruling fails the common sense test. Charity and Security Network. Retrieved October 11, 2011, from www.charityandsecurity.org/blog/Supreme_Court_Humanitarian_Law_Project _Ruling_Fails_Common_Sense_Test.

Harrison, P. 1981. *Third World tomorrow: A report from the battlefront in the war against poverty.* New York: Penguin.

Hewlett Foundation. 2004. The Hewlett Foundation's conflict resolution program: Twenty years of field-building, by D. Kovick. Retrieved April 1, 2011, from www.hewlett .org/programs/past-programs/conflict-resolution.

Isacson, A., and A. Poe. 2009. After Plan Colombia: Evaluating "Integrated Action," the next phase of U.S. assistance. Center for International Policy, Washington, DC. Retrieved January 2, 2012, from http://justf.org/content/after-plan-colombia.

Lange, M. 2004. *Building institutional capacity for conflict-sensitive practice: The case of international NGOs.* London: International Alert. Retrieved April 1, 2011, from www .international-alert.org/sites/default/files/publications/building-_institutional_cap.pdf.

Lederach, J. P. 1997. *Building peace: Sustainable reconciliation in divided societies.* Washington, DC: US Institute for Peace.

Lundborg, P. 1998. Foreign aid and international support as gift exchange. *Economics and Politics* 10, no. 2: 127–141.

Millennium Project. n.d.. The 0.7% target: An in-depth look. Retrieved November 2, 2011, from www.unmillenniumproject.org/press/07.htm.

Moyar, M. 2011. *Development in Afghanistan's counterinsurgency: A new guide.* Orbis. Retrieved on January 13, 2012, from http://smallwarsjournal.com/blog/development-in -afghanistans-counterinsurgency.

Organisation for Economic Co-operation and Development (OECD). n.d. DAC members and date of membership. Retrieved October 10, 2011, from www.oecd.org /document/38/0,3746,en_2649_34603_1893350_1_1_1_1,00.html.

———. n.d. *Development aid reaches an historic high in 2010.* Retrieved October 1, 2011, from www.oecd.org/document/35/0,3746,en_2649_34447_47515235_1_1_1_1,00.html.

———. n.d. Net ODA in 2010. Retrieved January 2, 2012, from http://webnet.oecd .org/oda2010.

———. n.d. Official development assistance—Definition and coverage. Retrieved October 1, 2011, from www.oecd.org/document/4/0,3746,en_2649_37413_46181892_1_1 _1_37413,00.html.

———. n.d. Open doors: Engaging beyond the DAC. Retrieved October 10, 2011, from www.oecd.org/document/29/0,3746,en_2649_33721_46886749_1_1_1_1,00.html.

———. 2001. DAC guidelines: Helping to prevent violent conflict. OECD publishing. Retrieved October 10, 2011, from www.oecd.org/dataoecd/15/54/1886146.pdf.

———. 2008. Is it ODA? Fact sheet. Retrieved January 2, 2012, from www.oecd .org/dataoecd/21/21/34086975.pdf.

———. 2010. DAC members' aid performance in 2010. In *Development co-operation report 2011: 50th anniversary edition.* OECD Publishing. Retrieved November 5, 2012, from www.oecd-ilibrary.org/development/development-co-operation-report-2011/dac -members-aid-performance-in-2010_dcr-2011–17-en;jsessionid=1duotlfyeosyn.epsilon.

———. 2011a. List of CRS purpose codes. Retrieved January 1, 2012, from www.oecd .org/document/21/0,3746,en_2649_34447_1914325_1_1_1_1,00.html.

———. 2011b. Statistics on resource flows to developing countries. Retrieved January 2, 2012, from www.oecd.org/document/9/0,3746,en_2649_34447_1893129_1_1_1_1,00 .html.

Overseas Development Institute. (2010). Millennium Development Goals Report Card: Measuring progress across countries. Retrieved December 5, 2011, from www.odi .org.uk/resources/details.asp?id=5027&title=millennium-development-goals-mdg-report -card-measuring-progress-across-countries.

Oxfam International. 2011. Whose aid is it anyway? Politicizing aid in conflicts and crises. Briefing paper 145. Retrieved October 4, 2011, from www.oxfam.org/en/policy /whose-aid-it-anyway.

Paffenholz, T., and L. Reychler. 2007. *Aid for peace: A guide to planning and evaluation for conflict zones*. Baden-Baden, Germany: Nomos.

Peace and Security Funders Group. 2010. Peace and security grantmaking by US foundations, 2008–2009. Retrieved April 1, 2011, from www.peaceandsecurity.org/415/32532 .html.

Polak, P. 2008. *Out of poverty: What works when traditional approaches fail*. San Francisco: Berrett-Koehler.

Rettberg, A. 2004. Business-led peacebuilding in Colombia: Fad or future of a country in crisis? Working Paper #56, Crisis States Program Development Research Centre, London School of Economics, London. Retrieved November 1, 2011, from http://eprints .lse.ac.uk/28201.

Smillie, I. 1998. Relief and development: The struggle for synergy. Occasional Report #33, Watson Institute for International Studies, Brown University, Providence, RI. Retrieved November 5, 2011, from www.watsoninstitute.org/pub/OP33.pdf.

Tomlinson, J. 1999. Globalized culture: The triumph of the West. In T. Skelton and T. Allen, eds. *Culture and global change* (pp. 23–31). New York: Routledge.

United Nations. 2011. Peacekeeping fact sheet. Retrieved December 15, 2011, from www.un.org/en/peacekeeping/resources/statistics/factsheet.shtml.

United Nations Conference on Trade and Development. World Investment Report Overview 2012. New York: Author. Retrieved November 10, 2012, from www.unctad -docs.org/UNCTAD-WIR2012-Overview-en.pdf.

United Nations Development Programme (UNDP). n.d. About human development. Retrieved June 1, 2011, from http://hdr.undp.org/en/humandev.

Vidal, C., and R. Pillay. 2004. Official development assistance as direct budget support: An issues paper for UNDP. Retrieved November 1, 2011, from www.unssc.org/web1 /programmes/rcs/cca_undaf_training_material/teamrcs/file2.asp?ID=1815.

World Bank. 2011a. World development report: Conflict, security, and development. Washington, DC. Retrieved December 14, 2011, from http://go.worldbank.org /QLKJWJB8X0.

World Bank. 2011b. Migration and Development Brief. Outlook for Remittance Flows 2012–2014. Washington, DC. Retrieved January 2, 2012, from http://go.worldbank.org /R88ONI2MQ0.

Zimina, L., and S. Fisher. 2008. An open letter to peacebuilders. Retrieved June 10, 2012, from www.internationalpeaceandconflict.org/forum/topic/show?id=780588%3ATopic%3A53963.

Notes

1. For more detail, see www.un.org/en/peacebuilding/doc_lessonslearned.shtml.

2. A recent report from the European Network for Debt and Development (2011) explains that over 50 percent of international aid is still tied (meaning only institutions from the donor country are eligible). Although there has been a push to change this among OECD countries, it is still prevalent. As explained in the report, "Many donors considered tied aid as a win-win approach—it allowed them to deliver development aid while at the same time promoting business opportunities for their own firms in developing countries" (p. 13).

3. For more info, see http://forward.usaid.gov.

4. Originally the ODA goal was a target % of Gross National Product. However, beginning in 1993, the term Gross National Income began to be used. See the OECD for details: http://www.oecd.org/dac/aidstatistics/theo70dagnitarget-ahistory.htm.

5. For a full list of OECD programming areas and codes, see www.oecd.org/dac/aidstatistics/purposecodessectorclassification.htm#bottom.

6. Data from OECD Stats Extract, http://stats.oecd.org/Index.aspx?lang=en&DataSetCode=TABLE5 for sector I.5.b: Conflict, Peace & Security.

7. Ibid.

8. USAID/CMM mission statement: www.usaid.gov/our_work/cross-cutting_programs/conflict.

9. OTI, www.usaid.gov/our_work/cross-cutting_programs/transition_initiatives/faq.html.

10. SIDA, www.sida.se/English/About-us/our-fields-of-work/Human-security1/Human-security.

11. See www.stabilisationunit.gov.uk/about-us.html.

12. See the CMM website, www.usaid.gov/our_work/cross-cutting_programs/conflict.

13. See www.dfid.gov.uk/What-we-do/Key-Issues/Governance-and-conflict.

14. See http://go.worldbank.org/ZVG4I1OHY0 and http://go.worldbank.org/AXLFGVT540.

15. See www.gppac.net.

16. For more information, see http://allianceforpeacebuilding.org, http://eplo.org and http://wanep.org.

17. Personal correspondence with Go Funai, former staff member at Interaction, October 10, 2010.

18. The group provides funding for a broad array of programs related to peace and security. The three areas receiving the greatest support in 2008 and 2009 are controlling and eliminating weaponry, preventing and resolving conflict, and promoting international peace and security.

19. For more information, see the US Army's Stability Operations Manual, http://usacac.army.mil/cac2/repository/FM307/FM3–07.pdf.

20. For more on privatization and contracting, see A. Stanger, *One Nation Under Contract: The Outsourcing of American Power and the Future of Foreign Policy* (New Haven, CT: Yale University Press, 2009).

21. A public/private partnership is when the government and private sectors collaborate through joint funding or other initiatives to support development-related activities.

22. These are estimates based on the author's personal interactions and research in the field. More detailed research is needed in this area.

23. This quote is generally attributed to Moshe Dayan, an Israeli military leader: www.arikpeace.org/Eng/Index.asp?CategoryID=357&ArticleID=1065.

SECTION TWO

Sectoral Approaches to
Integrated Peacebuilding

chapter three

INTERNATIONAL DEVELOPMENT AND PEACEBUILDING

Andria Wisler

Fragile states are the toughest development challenge of our era. Too often, the development community has treated states affected by fragility and conflict simply as harder cases of development. Yet these situations require looking beyond the analytics of development—to a different framework of building security, legitimacy, governance, and economy. This is not security as usual, or development as usual. Nor is it about what we have come to think of as peacebuilding or peace-keeping. This is about Securing Development—bringing security and development together first to smooth the transition from conflict to peace and then to embed stability so that development can take hold over a decade and beyond. Only by securing development can we put down roots deep enough to break the cycle of fragility and violence.

—ROBERT ZOELLICK (2008, PARA. 12)

PEACEBUILDING AND INTERNATIONAL development historically have functioned as discrete sectors of practice. The schism was made apparent in a variety of venues, including academic literature, public discourse on political affairs, and media reports broadcast from conflict zones. More recently, scholars and practitioners have recognized that there exists an undeniable correlation between the two sectors that necessitates collaboration. Nearly two-thirds of development programming now operates within conflict-affected countries. Actors within both fields agree that social, economic, and political development is unsustainable in societies with violent conflict, and recognize that addressing the basic needs of these communities is both a moral and a practical imperative. This chapter discusses the relationship between international development and peacebuilding, the challenges of integrating peacebuilding into development, and how stakeholders responsible for peacebuilding interventions are becoming more accountable to the survival and sustenance needs of the communities they serve.

INTRODUCTION TO THE SECTORS

In the summer of 1944, over 700 delegates from forty-five countries convened in Bretton Woods, New Hampshire, for the United Nations (UN) Monetary and Financial Conference. Their goal was to consider the economic- and development-based causes of World War II, and to plot a course for ending the conflict and securing the peace. As the war dragged on, delegates signed the Bretton Woods Agreements that fashioned a system of rules, institutions, and procedures to regulate the international monetary system. These agreements eventually manifested into the International Monetary Fund (IMF) and the International Bank for Reconstruction and Development (IBRD), which was the precursor to the World Bank. The IBRD's (1989) first stated purpose was

> to assist in the reconstruction and development of territories of members by facilitating the investment of capital for productive purposes, including the restoration of economies destroyed or disrupted by war, the reconversion of productive facilities to peacetime needs and the encouragement of the development of productive facilities and resources in less developed countries. (para. 1)

Despite the initial understanding that international development was closely tied with processes to end violent conflict, the two sectors diverged as Cold War rivalries and subsequent UN Security Council vetoes began to regulate intervention in conflict-affected countries. Peace and security was sought by nation-states through the protection of their sovereignty and economic development. Driven by modernization theory, this development was addressed by international financial institutions, the UN, and donor agencies.[1]

Nearly half a century after the historic Bretton Woods meeting, additional players in the prevention, response, and transformation of violent conflict began to act to prevent intrastate civil flare-ups from erupting into cross-border wars. In 1992, former UN Secretary-General Boutros Boutros-Ghali sketched his vision for how UN interventions could expand in conflict-affected countries that were once made inaccessible due to Cold War politics in his "Agenda for Peace." His follow-up report in 1994, "Agenda for Development," showcased development's potential for reducing tensions caused by underlying socioeconomic, cultural, and humanitarian inequalities. Practitioners at this time recognized the "importance of moving beyond the artificial separation between 'conflict' as belonging to the field of security issues and 'development' as the domain of economics" (Smoljan, 2003, p. 240).

While Boutros-Ghali's architecture for building peace and fortifying development made a convincing *theoretical* claim for practical, ethical, and political implementation, the first two decades of the post-1989 era quickly underscored the *practical* difficulties of linking development and conflict. According to the 2011 *World Development Report,* some 1.5 billion people live in countries affected by repeating cycles of social, political, and criminal violence (World Bank, 2011). Seven of the ten lowest-ranking countries on the 2011 Human Development Index (HDI) published by the UN Development Programme (UNDP) are in or emerging from conflict. According to the *UN Millennium Development Goals Report,* Goal 2, "to achieve universal primary education by 2015," is in serious jeopardy given that 42 percent (28 million) of children of primary-school age live in poor countries affected by conflict (United Nations, 2011, p. 17). On a global scale, the economic tax that violence levies on development programs is staggering: the Global Peace Index estimates that $9 trillion in income—a brick of the development foundation—is lost to violence *annually* (Institute for Economics and Peace, 2012).

Although the relationship between conflict and development has been demonstrated quantitatively, human and organizational roadblocks frustrate collaboration and result in circumspect communication between theorists and practitioners. The relationship between conflict and development continues to be "contested in terms of worldview, assumptions about human nature and society, and intended outcomes for peace and security that underpin various policies and approaches" (O'Gorman, 2011, p. 11).

In her recent book, *Conflict and Development: Development Matters,* Eleanor O'Gorman (2011) contributes to breaking down these obstructions by outlining three arguments to persuasively delineate the relationship between conflict and development. First, as noted earlier, violent conflict has proven to be a consequential hindrance to achieving the Millennium Development Goals (MDGs); not one conflict-affected country has yet to achieve a single MDG (World Bank, 2011). Second, O'Gorman notes how Mary Anderson (1999), in her book *Do No Harm,* asked, "How can humanitarian or development assistance be given in conflict situations in ways that rather than feeding into and exacerbating the conflict help local people to disengage and establish alternative systems for dealing with the problems that underlie the conflict?" (p. 2). Anderson recognized the impact of development in three ways: as a possible force for and driver of peace, which interacted with conflict; as having the potential for inflicting harm and engineering good; and as not neutral in any context. Anderson's "do no harm" principle highlights the responsibility of development, aid, and humanitarian actors to not cause, enable, or inflame violent conflict through their policies and programs. This idea garnered both resistance and support from a spectrum of actors who found themselves rethinking development as exclusively a postwar occurrence with limited time frames. Third, O'Gorman (2011) underscores how development is contestably "well-placed" to respond to a number of the root causes of violent conflict, such as poverty, social injustice, and ethnic tensions, through structural interventions with the state and economy.

In contrast to the arguments put forth by O'Gorman,[2] who favors strengthening the link between peacebuilding and international development, a counterargument maintains that the two sectors are—in agenda and discourse, although not in practice—embroiled with each other, to the point of resemblance. Pushpa Iyer (2011) asserts that the liberal peacebuilding model, as forwarded by Boutros-Ghali and supported by the UN and other international donor agencies, parallels the neoliberal economic development models championed by the aforementioned international financial institutions.[3] This conformity creates an environment in which donors dictate the ingredients of a formulaic peace, a vision currently dominated by traditional economic development initiatives that can ignore many other locally driven visions for peace. Iyer contends that "peacebuilding," as defined and developed in the field of conflict resolution, is a much broader concept than "development," and as such requires a longer-term engagement than development donors and workers traditionally commit. The donors' current development-driven solutions for peace in conflict-affected countries overstress economics, and in turn understate the "oppression, discrimination, and rights abuses that societies in conflict experience" through the inequitable distribution of wealth and ensuing competition for resources (p. 17).

O'Gorman (2011) and Iyer (2011) both reveal some of the tensions and the opportunities arising from cross-sector work between development and peacebuilding. Given the current status of underdevelopment in conflict-affected countries and communities, it is imperative to get beyond the chicken-and-egg debate: whether peace is a prerequisite for development or whether development is a necessary condition for peace. The authors support the argument for an "inclusivist" (Smoljan, 2003) approach to integrating development and peacebuilding, a timely change given parallel shifts in both sectors regarding the movement in peacebuilding from national to *human* security and the trend from strictly economic growth to *human development* in international development. These advancements provide a fertile ground for cooperation, as human security moves beyond freedom from physical fear to include economic, food, health, personal, and additional elements ordinarily under the purview of development. Similarly, human development considers the satisfaction of basic human needs along with the eradication of poverty, disease, and injustice. Continued and deeper cross-sector interoperability would ensure an understanding and praxis of peacebuilding, with sustainable development as means, or process, and not simply as product (Barbanti, 2004).

RELEVANT THEORY

Theories from the fields of peacebuilding, conflict resolution, and development studies help inform and explain the relative discrepancies between two sectors. While occasionally at odds, the respective theories uncover some of the areas that have challenged the sectors in their individual missions and in their attempts at coordination.

Two major ideas from peacebuilding and conflict resolution have illuminated the potential conflicts for development practitioners and donors in societies on the brink of, in, or emerging from violent conflict. The first is the changing nature of the dominant form of conflict in the past few decades—a shift from interstate to intrastate—with an emphasis on revitalized nationalism, civil war, ethnic hostilities, and the transnational systems of conflict finance (Kaldor, 1999). Since Mary Kaldor first published the seminal text *New and Old Wars,* the field of peacebuilding has reacted to her understanding of the blurry distinctions of the "old war," being between the armies of two or more states, and the "new war," which emerged at the end of the Cold War and includes the state or group use of political violence, organized crime, and large-scale violations of human rights. In the past decade, this changing global context, as described by Kaldor, has been further shocked by terrorist activity, particularly emanating from failed, fragile, or broken states where extremist groups use the fractured communities as grounds for recruiting and training.

Kaldor's (1999) contribution caters directly to the second idea that has the practice of peacebuilding in impoverished, conflict-affected contexts. A challenge is that much of development theory and some practice still focuses on a realist, state-building development model, despite the nonexistence of the state in many areas, or the "sovereignty gap" (Zoellick, 2008). One of the challenges in a state-building-focused development model is that it displaces attention from the larger historical dynamics of the conflict context (Goodhand, 2003). In contrast to the emphasis on state-focused models, many peacebuilding workers have begun to professionalize their work with players and institutions beyond sovereign heads of state, bearing in mind that modern conflicts involve a range of actors, including cross-border rebel groups, transnational terrorist cells, civil-society organizations funded by the diaspora, and de facto military camps. Furthermore, peacebuilding actors, more habituated to a contextual long-term vision, in both the past and the future, often strive to understand how periods of colonialism, global legacies of economic disenfranchisement, and previous armed conflicts leave consequential residue that even the most well-intentioned development models have difficulty controlling for (Cerretti, 2009).

In turning to development studies, Olympio Barbanti (2004) opines that "because development aid does not deal directly with violence, conflict and conflict resolution have not been topics of major concern to development workers or theorists" (para. 4). While this gap of cross-sectoral understanding has been alleviated somewhat with the work of theorists, practitioners, and groups cited in this chapter, Josh Cerretti (2009) notes that dominant strains of development discourses continue to trivialize the realities of many societies that they target in relation to conflict. For those influenced by modernist or neoliberal economic thought, development theory and practice maintained a one-size-fits-all direct transferability of prescriptions well into the new millennium, through which industrialized countries imposed moral views and policies benefiting themselves (Escobar, 1995).

Specifically, Cerretti (2009) names the aforementioned neoliberal economic policies of the major international financial institutions (IFIs), which traditionally support less public involvement in the economy through reductions in government spending and barriers to international trade. At times they insist on conditions for development aid, which can lead to the marginalization of key segments of the society, particularly women. Further, as a model that encourages competition, its policies can exacerbate inequalities when cooperation and solidarity are most compelling for a highly stressed conflict environment. The neoliberal discourse popularizes personal utility and self-interested behavior despite such messages often being culturally inappropriate and irrelevant in a conflict-sensitive context. In some cases, development organizations and programs have refueled conflicts and even concealed corruption and human rights abuses.

Cerretti (2009) continues his critique of development to include the gender and development (GAD) model, forwarded as an alternative to male-dominated discourses. Although GAD responded to the exclusion of women and a lack of a gendered analysis of other economic development models, Cerretti claims it may unintentionally entrench a false binary between men and women, which may be exacerbated during times of conflict: men-as-violent and women-as-victims or male-as-protector and female-as-protected. Such binaries—if reinforced by postconflict development and peacebuilding models—may become reified in discourse and through routine action. Cerretti asserts that GAD can do more to address masculinities in conflict-sensitive development contexts, in order to encourage gender equity and prevent a resurrection of gender-based direct violence or an institution of structural violence.

The field of development studies has embraced a number of critical frameworks, including those of the dependency theorists of Latin America (e.g., Frank, 1966) and the world-systems models of Immanuel Wallerstein (2004). The 1990s ushered in a series of UN conferences to discuss development in multi-sectoral ways. A transdisciplinary view of development has garnered access to experts, practitioners, and donors through the contributions of Nobel laureates of the 1990s and the MDGs. These efforts underscore the need to consider the means—not only the ends—of achieving better and more equitable living conditions for the most impoverished of communities, most of which fall within conflict contexts. In tandem, theories from both conflict resolution and development studies expose a history and propensity for "a vicious cycle in which development leads to conflict, and the lack of conflict resolution practices interferes with further development" (Barbanti, 2004, para. 7). This chapter will now turn to the processes proposed by these theories through the cross-sectoral work of peacebuilding and international development.

INTEGRATING PEACEBUILDING PROCESSES AND SKILLS FOR INTERNATIONAL DEVELOPMENT

A brief survey of the literature, including practitioners' field notes, organizational evaluation reports, articles in academic journals, and more, reveals a set of similarly varied processes being used to address conflicts from various levels. These processes include the fieldwork, funding, evaluation, and research of development in conflict-sensitive contexts. The processes attempt to take values and insights from peacebuilding and integrate them into development practice, hopefully with value-added outcomes. Oshita, Okwunwa, and Bakut (2007) write that this does not change what development practitioners do, "but it has everything to do with how we do them [development practices]. It is about adding value to a good process such that it results both in the achievement of the planned development targets and contributing to building lasting peace" (p. 255). This section attends to: first, the design and use of conflict analysis as a tool for development (O'Gorman, 2011); second, the *Principles for Good International Engagement in Fragile States and Situations* (OECD, 2007); and third, the importance of context as well as a regional vision for sustainable development and peace, particularly in light of sovereignty gaps and cross-border smuggling. Needless to say, the inventory here is incomplete and is meant to offer the reader a glimpse of the scope of possible integrated measures.

Conflict Analysis

O'Gorman (2011) succinctly describes the necessity of effective conflict analysis for conflict and development contexts:

> The task is one of tracking dynamism and not allowing the conflict to be taken as a single snapshot at a given moment, but rather to be sequenced as a film that moves: conflict analysis should edit and capture the back story, the key event, the actors and their complex interactions over time. (p. 44)

O'Gorman notes that conflict analysis and assessment tools became normalized for development practitioners in the 1990s as conflict-sensitive programming was broached and actors' roles became more reflexive. She offers Mitchell's "basic conflict structure," defining the conflict situation, behaviors, and attitudes as well as other tools that highlight elements such as parties, goals, issues, interests, values, strategies, dynamics, relationships, and interventions. A "levels of analysis" approach that is built through tiers or systems of the conflict considers regional players, effects, and dynamics (Ramsbotham, Woodhouse, and Miall, 2011, p. 117), whereas a "conflict cycle" or "stages of conflict" model allows for users to identify stages or triggers tied to temporal signposts (O'Gorman, 2011).

While the methods for conflict analysis and assessment are diverse, they operate at both *strategic* and *project* levels to inform development actors about relevant sites for action to promote peace, reduce the resurgence of violence, and de-escalate conflict. Routinely couched under the term Peace and Conflict Impact Assessment (PCIA), these tools have been integrated into several major bilateral development institutions (DFID, SIDA, GTZ/BMZ, UNDP, USAID), as well as small development NGOs. For example, in the case of community-based development in a recently violent area, USAID (2007) suggests a micro-level "rigorous, participatory and grounded assessment, rather than a desk-based conflict analysis" (p. 23). With new information, the hope is that development actors can engage confidently in conflict dynamics and context with some measure of preemption, and not limit their abilities to a reactionary toolkit.[4]

These advancements are not without their challenges. For example, looking through the lens of conflict requires reenvisioning traditional conceptualizations of success in development terms. Peacebuilding typically mandates involvement beyond what a development agency is accustomed to, namely with the matter of impartiality. Questions abound on who owns the process and outcome of the analysis; as O'Gorman (2011) writes, "Analysis is not a research paper but a live information source" (p. 61). She cites authors who argue that as an act of social justice, the process must be owned by the conflict-affected communities and not external practitioners, much akin to their development counterparts who purport participatory development as a framework. O'Gorman alerts the demotion of conflict sensitivity as a "tool" rather than a paradigmatic and cultural shift in perspective by those individuals and organizations working in conflict zones. In turn, this leads to an overbearing focus on a checklist's deconstruction of the conflict, which steals time and energy from the creative processes generating a construction of peace.

Principles for Good International Engagement in Fragile States and Situations

The *Principles of Good International Engagement in Fragile States and Situations* were formally endorsed by ministers and heads of agencies at the Development Assistance Committee's (DAC) High Level Forum in April 2007 to help maximize the positive impact of international engagement, minimize unintentional harm, and support existing dialogue and coordination processes. In partnership with the *Paris Declaration on Aid Effectiveness,* the Principles highlight the need to assist national reformers: "the most fragile states will need to be driven by their own leadership and people . . . to build effective, legitimate, and resilient state institutions, capable of engaging productively with their people to promote sustained development" (OECD, 2007, Preamble). While the term "fragile state" does not preclude a state in conflict, it does denote a state that exhibits persistent social tensions, violence, or the legacy of war, and is thus a necessary addition to peacebuilding processes for international development settings.

The Principles (OECD, 2007) are broken down into three segments: the basics (numbers 1–2); the role of state-building and peacebuilding (numbers 3–6); and the practicalities (numbers 7–10). In short, they underscore the need to:

1. take context as the starting point;
2. do no harm;
3. focus on state-building;
4. prioritize prevention;
5. recognize the links between political, security and development objectives;
6. promote non-discrimination as a basis for inclusive and stable societies;
7. align with local priorities in different ways in different contexts;
8. agree on practical coordination mechanisms between international actors;
9. act fast . . . but stay engaged long enough to give success a chance; and
10. avoid pockets of exclusion, i.e. "aid orphans."[5]

The Principles were field-tested in nine countries prior to their formal endorsement, and later reports in 2009 and 2011 document their effectiveness through a variety of methods and fragile contexts. The findings suggest the execution of Principle 10 to be the weakest, citing frequent disparities in the provision of aid between countries, provinces, and social groups within a state—all triggers of development-induced conflict (OECD, 2010). Principle 6 was deemed the strongest in implementation on the ground in the tested sites, as international actors have increased their surveillance of inclusive policies, particularly in the area of gender (OECD, 2010).

Keeping the Individual Context and Region in Perspective

Development is easily critiqued for its reliance on one-size-fits-all transferability, a feature that quickly fractures in a conflict context. Nigerian researchers lament the "dearth of accurate data for planning [that] has forced development programmers to rely on concepts, frameworks and applications that hardly apply to the peculiar references of development, conflict and security in Africa" (Oshita et al., 2007, p. 256). The local context assumes prominent prioritization in conflict-affected countries where development programming is used as an intervention for both conflict preventative and ameliorative purposes. Goodhand (2003) underscores the obligation for peace and development workers to know the history of the country and its people in order to understand who holds power, how power is brokered, and the relationship between these actors and both formal and informal institutions. The inclusion of the state as a co-actor in programming addresses the government's need to garner legitimacy and develop capacities by delivering basic, visible services. On another note, it is advantageous for practitioners of any kind on the ground in a conflict setting to know their locality to be more effective and to help ensure their own security and safety. Conflict creates risk not only for local peoples, but for external teams as well; effective evacuation plans can be established only with intimate local knowledge. Facilitating this local knowledge is a key constituent of any process.

In addition to attending to the specific history and current needs of a given country, tracking conflicts to, and across, borders is imperative. Few if any conflicts are contained within a country's borders; violence, narcotics, arms, piracy, people, disease, and extremism are some of a conflict's features that flow across territorial boundaries into neighbors' domains, welcome or not. Typically, economic relations worsen as investment, transit, and trade become increasingly difficult to maintain as a result of the displaced goods and people. Sesay (2004) found that a country's being in even a minor conflict significantly reduces neighboring countries' GDP per capita, life expectancy, and domestic and foreign investment, and significantly increases the illiteracy rate of nearby countries. Collier and Hoeffler (2004) estimate that a civil war reduces the growth rate in surrounding countries by an average of 0.9 percent per year (p. 6). Fragility is contagious, and conflict-affected states can easily set off a chain reaction within an unprepared region.

Related Conflict Skills

As we move from processes to skills, it is easy to expand the inventory commenced above. With an overall view to integrating conflict-sensitive approaches into development programming, both fields of peacebuilding and international development offer much to the discussion. An interdisciplinary discourse helps actors progress beyond what they know as "business as usual" and deal with issues such as the political implications of aid in conflict-prone environments and changing notions of peacebuilding dependent upon the context (Iyer, 2011).

"Business as usual" for both peacebuilding and development workers also refers to with whom they are accustomed to working in the field. Zoellick (2008) reminds his audience that external actors, including soldiers, diplomats, and aid workers, among others, need to be able to work together. For example, development and aid convoys often need to communicate with peacebuilding workers and military or peacekeeping presences to get basic humanitarian supplies to their destinations. Such collaboration is not without its risks and ethical concerns regarding armed humanitarians and the securitization of development (MacGinty and Williams, 2011). Moreover, in contexts in or emerging from violent conflict and fragility, actors must be willing to identify and build credibility with the people and institutions beyond the sovereign, which is likely to be weak with its responsibilities under control by nongovernmental establishments. In the pursuit of breaking down normalized habits of working, development practitioners need to further familiarize themselves with the indisputable certainty that human development and peacebuilding require a much longer time commitment than do conventional notions of economic development implementation driven by modernization theories.

Although the subject is the focus of an increasing number of volumes (see, for example, Zarkov, 2008), it is important to at least mention the practitioner's skill of using a deeply gendered understanding of violent conflict, its resolution, and how development can both negatively and positively impinge upon women's lives and roles. Policy makers and workers who represent aid agencies, development donors, and peacebuilding programs continue to make worrying assumptions that lead to repeated mistakes in assistance and protection. The ordeals women face in conflict, including sexual violence and increased familial economic responsibilities, must be met with an understanding of women's resiliency and agency in safeguarding survival. A gender analysis must move beyond the checking of a box on an economic results-based management list and look toward the transformation of roles, institutions, masculinities, and everyday lives in conflict-ridden contexts.

Individuals and organizations implementing and executing development activities in conflict contexts often lack the appropriate tools and capacities for evaluation and thus pay scant regard to this necessary step in successful program management. Reasons for this inattention are related to the perceived urgency to prioritize new and more action in the context of scarce financial and human resources, notwithstanding violence or conflict; the lack of skills and time to indulge in a thorough evaluative strategy; and the absence of institutional incentives and support. Evaluation is currently demand-driven externally by donors who emphasize accounting and does not result from the internal insistence for learning from experience and past programming. It thus is often considered an added burden to overtasked field workers who are unaware of the incentives and added value of successful assessment techniques or are faced with forcing evaluation frameworks, techniques, and norms that are standardized for development programs in nonsensitive contexts. Together these conditions create an unfavorable environment in which evaluation becomes undervalued, deprioritized, and mythologized for its laboriousness and drudgery (Del Felice and Wisler, forthcoming).

The skills and processes detailed in this section have much to offer international development practitioners in their conflict-affected work, not to mention for their own safety in difficult contexts. In many instances, development actors are already on the ground as violence as a symptom of burgeoning conflict spreads, forewarning the potential of a tinderbox setting. Thus, the conflict-sensitization of the development field has the added value of increasing those capable of seeing predictors or indicators of civil violence before it spirals into chaos or full-fledged war.

CREATING SYSTEMIC CHANGE AND IMPACTING POLICY

*There is, however, a fairly obvious consensus that the politicization
of ethnic and religious identities in the contest for material objectives
has unleashed turbulent and catastrophic impact for development*

programmes. Whether the root cause (or causes) is to be attributed to ethno-linguistic fragmentation of these countries or "high level of poverty, failed political institutions and economic dependence on natural resources," there is a considerable case in the literature for a multi-sectoral policy response that seeks to establish the priorities for structural risk-reduction and a governance regime that "mitigates existing differences and supports peaceful ways of solving disputes."
—CELESTINE OYOM BASSEY (2007)

Goodhand (2003) synthesizes some of the larger policy debates that revolve around the cross-sectoral relationship between peacebuilding and international development with the assertion that "mainstream conflict and policy analysis tends to place emphasis on internal problems and external solutions" (p. 640). Zoellick (2008) provides evidence to Goodhand's claim with the observation that the responsibility for services delivering basic human needs to a country's constituents is often transferred away from ministries and local authorities to outside actors. Although external assistance can act as a necessary stopgap in the face of complete government shutdown or disintegration, Zoellick stresses that it is not only the services that matter but also who performs them. Coming from the government, services to ensure people's material well-being can also symbolize the deliverance of distributive justice, the legitimacy of government, and the assurance of basic human rights to all people (Evans, 1998). Thus, there is an increasing consensus on building government capacity, securing government budget support, and training in good governance.

A second major point of contention concerning these policy debates is, according to Goodhand (2003), the continued inattention to the dynamics between "greed" and "grievance" at the metalevel of international public policy. This inattention fails to create global financial regulation or effective tracking mechanisms on investment in sensitive commodities, such as arms, oil, gems, and timber or alternative debt repayment plans for countries in conflict. Moreover, these two conflict phenomena do not necessarily exist at odds even while global policy players appear to suggest they do, where their perception of conflict and development is often restricted to the unit of the singular nation-state. Regionalized conflict systems are more accurately the norm in today's arena. Donor policy and development planning frameworks are often constrained by country-level analysis despite the aforementioned reality that a fragile state can quickly spread throughout a fragile region, and that people, weapons, disease, drugs, and violence are quick to permeate sovereign borders (Zoellick, 2008). Donor organizations and countries could model sound global policies exhibiting the mutually reinforcing relationship of good governance and poverty alleviation for conflict-affected countries by shifting priority to protection, such as compensatory transfers and safety nets, and away from a traditional focus on economic production (Goodhand, 2003).

Individual organizations that reacted to the integration of peacebuilding and international development practices have proven to be more attentive to incurring positive changes to policy and practice. For example, USAID (2007) notes that "community cohesion—the interpersonal relationships and the formal and informal networks and associations that help to build mutual trust, common purpose and a sense of community"—is sacrificed greatly in violent conflict, yet is an integral ingredient of success for a society's economic development (p. 8). Thus, USAID conceives of rebuilding relationships and reconciliation as fundamental goals of community-based development (CBD) in conflict-affected contexts and envisions long-term projects in which communities develop their own initiatives and create spaces for people to act in nonviolent ways. USAID notes, however, that CBD can also instigate conflict if myths arise regarding the unequal distribution of program resources or benefits, or the domination of one group in decision-making. Development programmers responsive to conflict resolution processes must ensure transparency and monitor benefits carefully to allay complaints about corruption or discrimination. Conflict assessment and analysis, as well as dialogue with knowledgeable local partners, are tools for programmers as they work to create a safe, neutral environment.

Through the Department for International Development (DFID), the United Kingdom recently clarified its policies for development programming in unstable contexts shouldering violent conflict (DFID, 2011). Characterizing war as "development in reverse," this strategy paper reminds readers that an "'average' civil war costs a developing country the equivalent of 30 years of GDP growth. It can take 14 years for a country to return to its pre-war growth path and 20 years to reach its pre-war trade levels" (p. 7). In addition to these figures, Collier (2008) recognizes a "conflict trap," the time in which countries recently emerging from a major conflict are likely to relapse back into civil war; each civil war, he estimates, costs the country and its region $64 billion. Recognizing how its prosperity and well-being are interconnected with peaceful development around the world, the UK government prioritizes three mutually supporting policy pillars to its development initiatives in conflict-affected areas: early warning, rapid crisis prevention and response, and investment in upstream prevention. Given this prioritization, the report underlines the basic premise for the various institutions to work as "one government" in tandem with multilateral organizations and international partners on an integrated approach utilizing skills and capacities, including: strong intelligence and assessment, diplomacy, development work, defense engagement, work to promote trade and open markets, and the creation of a stabilization unit. A new early warning system and watch list of fragile countries will trigger systematic reviews of UK activity in fragile countries, and an early action facility within the government's conflict pool will enable swift response to warnings and opportunities, including quick assessments. Overall, the policy paper accredits the UK government with its strong fiscal and human capital supporting development in low-performing countries but notes the impending ruination of such advancements given conflict's pervasive effects on a country's infrastructure, social networks, and economic systems.

The sustainability of change and definitive measures of success regarding the marriage of best practices of international development and conflict resolution in contexts affected by violence have yet to be fully understood or documented and are issues for the international community at large. As O'Gorman (2011) writes, "Rarely is accountability understood or measured from below. Rarely do we ask those we claim to help how they experience international aid and what they think needs to be done to improve it" (p. 18). What is commonly understood, however, is that "it is far more cost-effective to invest in conflict prevention and de-escalation than to pay the costs of responding to violent conflict" (DFID, 2011, p. 4).[6] Stability is an attribute to successful development initiatives. Characterized by legitimate political systems, stable environments showcase a respect for human rights and rule of law, the meeting of basic human needs, security, and other economic and social opportunities for all constituents. As they continuously evolve, their changes withstand violent upheaval despite system shocks or conflict.

PROFILE OF A PRACTITIONER

Dr. Robin-Edward Poulton is a specialist in terrorism, disarmament, conflict transformation, and peacebuilding. He is the founding managing director of EPES-Mandala,[7] a global consultancy group of trainers, researchers, and conflict workers at the nexus of international development, conflict transformation, and peacebuilding. A British citizen raised in West Africa, Dr. Poulton is the author of several publications in French and English on international development and conflict resolution processes in relation to disarmament. He is a graduate of the University of St. Andrews in Scotland and Oxford University, attended Fourah Bay College in Freetown, Sierra Leone, and wrote his PhD dissertation on Afghanistan at the Ecole des Hautes Etudes in Paris. He has lectured at the University of Richmond in Virginia, Virginia Commonwealth University, and European Peace University in Austria, among other universities.

With over twenty-five years of field experience with the UNDP, the EU, USAID, and various NGOs, Dr. Poulton has long understood the inescapable connections between sustainable economic and political development and durable peace in conflict-ridden regions of the world. He is pragmatic about the role of external development in countries emerging from conflict and is incredibly mindful of the endogenous capacity for resolution and peacemaking that exists, waiting to be mobilized, in war-torn communities. Dr. Poulton has used local conflict resolution processes, such as the palaver tree in West Africa, or traditional societal values, such as valor in Afghanistan, to implement sustainable and complementary development and disarmament processes.

When Dr. Poulton served as a senior research fellow at the United Nations Institute for Disarmament Research, he initiated and supported groundbreaking micro-disarmament work on weapon collection, destruction, and security sector reform in West Africa, Central Asia, and Cambodia. This included the Weapons for Development program in Mali and Cambodia, which exchanged weapons for community development assistance; instead of providing cash

(continues)

PROFILE OF A PRACTITIONER *(continued)*

payments to individuals who handed in their weapons, the program provided development assistance to communities for projects such as improved water systems and schools. This innovation reduced the number of weapons circulating in an unstable, postwar country as well as bringing communities together as agents of change for their security and development.

PROFILE OF AN INTERNATIONAL AGENCY: MERCY CORPS

Mercy Corps (2012) is an international development agency that embodies core peacebuilding principles. The organization, headquartered in Portland, Oregon, operates with the motto "Be the Change" and intervenes in transitional communities impacted by disaster, conflict, or economic collapse. Founded in 1979, Mercy Corps uses ground-level, community-led, and market-driven development programs. In 2010 Mercy Corps employed 3,700 personnel worldwide with a budget of approximately $300 million (Griffin and Moorhead, 2012, p. 29) and operated in twenty-three out of forty failed states (Foreign Policy Group, 2010). The organization works across many sectors and started conducting peacebuilding activities in the late 1990s and to date has implemented "over 100 peacebuilding programs in over 30 countries and regions" (Mercy Corps, 2009, p. 1).

As part of an initiative to strengthen their peacebuilding work in 2004, Mercy Corps merged with the Conflict Management Group, founded by Harvard law professor Roger Fisher (coauthor of the foundational text *Getting to Yes*), to better inform its peacebuilding work. Through this partnership staff are taught conflict-management and peacebuilding techniques with the goal that these skills and knowledge will be passed on from the programmer to youth, women, and local leaders in the conflict region. Their peacebuilding work is based on three core approaches, including promoting dialogue and rebuilding relationships, addressing the underlying causes of conflict, and working on impact and advocacy (Mercy Corps, 2009). In particular their work to address the sources of conflict is strongly related to integrated peacebuilding. As stated in their peacebuilding vision (Mercy Corps, 2009),

> The second key component of our peacebuilding work is to help local communities develop and implement programs that address the underlying causes of violence they identify through dialogue. Most of the issues that fuel violence are at the heart of development assistance, whether this is poverty and unequal access to economic development, competition over

natural resources, political discrimination or youth alienation and unemployment. The vast majority of our peacebuilding programs therefore, have a strong development component. However, they differ from traditional development programs in that the ultimate goal of the assistance is to promote *both* development and conflict management objectives. Our work falls into several key areas: economic growth, natural resource management, youth engagement, and local governance. (p. 2)

For example, in a project in Guatemala to address land disputes between indigenous groups and large landowners, Mercy Corps helped provide direct mediation services to help poorer groups gain access to land. However, the organization realized this wasn't sufficient and that they also needed to provide small-scale farmers with access to funding and technical assistance to be able to improve their economic status (Mercy Corps, 2010).

Mercy Corps's peacebuilding work also has a strong emphasis on economic empowerment and opportunity. As the organization (Mercy Corps, 2011) explains, "Mercy Corps' integrated economic development and peacebuilding programs go beyond conflict sensitivity to actively build peace through market development and economic activity" (p. 1).

In Guatemala and elsewhere, Mercy Corps has integrated peacebuilding practices discussed in this chapter: long-term time commitment to regional peacebuilding; operational transparency; integration of ground-level stakeholder perspectives and interests; holistic understanding of local and wider impacts of the conflict and peacebuilding, as well as immediate and long-term consequences; conflict-sensitivity training for their employees; and most important, expanding beyond traditional development processes.

Moving Forward with Challenges in the Field

Conflict is complex, unpredictable, often long-term, and rarely the result of one root cause. Thus, a cross-sectoral approach is preferable when ascertaining the hoped-for outcome of reducing violence and constructing peace. In a conflict-sensitive context, the international development field requires flexibility of practitioners and programming so that unmet expectations do not forestall success or inspire delusion. This flexibility entails the allowance of the community to maintain ownership of development activities that seek tangible results in meeting basic human needs, communication with a wide variety of actors while attempting political neutrality, and a longer-term vision in balance with simple, quantifiable goals.

Challenges abound for development practitioners working in stable environments, let alone those marred by violence, and for conflict workers regardless of the triggers, players, or prevalence of bloodshed in their environments. When we consider underdeveloped contexts engaged in or emerging from violent conflict, very difficult ethical, pragmatic, and economic challenges must be raised. How do we all work together? How do we measure success? Theoretical quandaries resurface: Are the differences between old and new wars overstated? Is development, particularly if managed by neoliberal-leaning international financial institutions, a new form of colonialism in weakened states?

The peacebuilding and development sectors are at a crucial juncture to respond to these questions and participate in larger, ongoing conversations about the role of international aid in war-affected situations: Does aid fuel conflict and generate more harm than good? As MacGinty and Williams (2011) express, "One important question that all who now study the conflict-development nexus are now asking is whether they can provide any kind of solution to the evident suffering of developing countries' populations, or whether they are indeed part of the problem" (p. 153). Often called the "Nightingale risk," it is the reality that humanitarian help given to people in conflict contexts—in the form of development or conflict interventions—might also aid the war effort. The actors discussed in this chapter must weigh in on current veins of this discussion that examine the extent to which development and peace can and should be separated from, for example, security and counterinsurgency strategies, if not remain mutually exclusive. While their assessment sounds overwhelming, MacGinty and Williams (2011) also identify this as an "exciting time in our evolution of the relationship between conflict and development," one they compare to circumstances faced by seventeenth- and eighteenth-century cartographers in their quest to map new terrains. Development and peacebuilding actors must keep those who are intended to be the main beneficiaries—fellow human beings—the focal point of their work, from their anxieties to their actions.

QUESTIONS FOR FURTHER DISCUSSION

1. What events and institutions have acted as impediments for conflict-sensitive international development?

2. What practices of development have been most successful in promoting peacebuilding? What conflict-resolution and peacebuilding skills and capacities are most amenable to development practices?

3. What are the ethical dilemmas that development organizations and peacebuilding interveners must consider in their interactions with all local actors, including those labeled terrorists or rebel groups?

4. Peacebuilding and conflict work typically mandates involvement beyond what a development agency is used to—impartiality." Who owns the conflict analysis process?

5. How does integrating peacebuilding into development change the peacebuilding processes?

6. What could strengthen OECD's Principle 10 of Good International Engagement?

7. What forms of "interdisciplinary discourse" might be most helpful for a development or peacebuilding practitioner? How could such interdisciplinary communication be encouraged or institutionalized?

REFERENCES

Anderson, M. B. 1999. *Do no harm: How aid can support peace—or war*. Boulder, CO: Lynne Rienner.

Barbanti, O. 2004, August. Development and conflict theory. Beyond Intractability website. G. and Heidi Burgess, eds. Conflict Research Consortium, University of Colorado, Boulder. Retrieved October 15, 2011, from www.beyondintractability.org/bi-essay /development-conflict-theory.

Bassey, C. 2007. Introduction: The nexus of conflict and development crisis in Africa. In C. Bassey and O. Oshita, eds. *Conflict resolution, identity crisis, and development in Africa* (pp. xv–xxxiii). Lagos, Nigeria: Malthouse Press Ltd.

Boutros-Ghali, B. 1992, 31 January. An agenda for peace: Preventive diplomacy, peace-making and peace-keeping, United Nations Secretary-General's Report A/47/277-S/24111. New York: United Nations. Retrieved October 15, 2011, from www.un.org/Docs/SG /agpeace.html.

————. 1994, May 6. An agenda for development, United Nations Secretary-General's Report A/48/935. New York: United Nations. Retrieved January 5, 2011, from www.un .org/Docs/SG/agdev.html.

Cerretti, J. 2009. Hurdles to development: Assessing development models in conflict settings. *Peace & Conflict Review* 4, no. 1. Retrieved January 5, 2011, from www.review .upeace.org/index.cfm?opcion=0&ejemplar=18&entrada=88.

Chalmers, M. 2007. Spending to save? The cost-effectiveness of conflict prevention. *Defence and Peace Economics* 18, no. 1: 1–23.

Collier, P. 2008. *The bottom billion: Why the world's poorest countries are failing and what can be done about it*. New York: Oxford University Press.

Collier, P., and A. Hoeffler. 2004. The challenge of reducing the global incidence of civil war. Centre for the Study of African Economies, Department of Economics, Oxford University, Copenhagen Challenge Paper. Retrieved November 5, 2012, from www.uib.es /depart/deaweb/smed/pdf/collier.pdf.

Del Felice, C., and A. Wisler. Forthcoming. *Peace education evaluation: Exploring prospects, learning from experiences*. Ashgate, NC: Information Age.

Department for International Development (DFID). 2011. *Building stability overseas strategy*. London: DFID. Retrieved January 5, 2011, from www.dfid.gov.uk/Documents /publications1/Building-stability-overseas-strategy.pdf.

Escobar, A. 1995. *Encountering development: The making and unmaking of the Third World*. Princeton, NJ: Princeton University Press.

Foreign Policy Group LLC and the Fund for Peace. 2010. The failed states index 2010. *Foreign Policy*. Retrieved October 15, 2011, from www.foreignpolicy.com/articles/2010/06 /21/2010_failed_states_index_interactive_map_and_rankings.

Francis, D. F. 2006. Linking peace, security, and developmental regionalism: Regional economic and security integration in Africa. *Journal of Peacebuilding & Development* 2, no. 3: 7–20.

Frank, A. G. 1966. The development of underdevelopment. *Monthly Review* 18, no. 4: 17–31.

Gagnon, V. P. Jr. 2002. Bosnia & Herzegovina. In S. E. Mendelson and J. K. Glenn, eds. *The power and limits of NGOs* (pp. 206–226). New York: Columbia University Press.

Goodhand, J. 2003. Enduring disorder and persistent poverty: A review of the linkages between war and chronic poverty. *World Development* 31, no. 3: 629–646.

Griffin, R. W., and Moorhead, G. 2012. *Organizational behavior: Managing people and organizations.* Mason, OH: South-Western.

Institute for Economics and Peace. 2012. Global Peace Index 2012, fact sheet. Retrieved June 14, 2012, from www.visionofhumanity.org/globalpeaceindex/2012-gpi-findings.

Iyer, P. 2011. Development versus peacebuilding: Overcoming jargon in post-war Sierra Leone. *Africa Peace and Conflict Journal* 4, no. 1: 15–33.

Kaldor, M. 1999. *New and old wars: Organized violence in a global era* (1st ed.). Palo Alto, CA: Stanford University Press.

MacGinty, R., and A. Williams. 2011. *Conflict and development.* London: Routledge.

Mercy Corps. 2009. Conflict Management Group Sector Overview. Retrieved April 5, 2012, from www.mercycorps.org/sectors/conflictmanagement.

———. 2010. Seventeen years of restarting broken lives. Web log comment. Retrieved October 15, 2011, from www.mercycorps.org/countries/bosniaandherzegovina/20627.

———. 2011. *Peacebuilding through economic development approach 2011* by J. Vaughn, S. Morris, and D. Johnson. Portland, Oregon.

———. 2012. About us. Retrieved October 15, 2011, from www.mercycorps.org/aboutus.

O'Gorman, E. 2011. *Conflict and development: Development matters.* New York: Zed Books.

Organisation for Economic Co-operation and Development (OECD). 2007. *Principles for good international engagement in fragile states and situations.* Retrieved November 1, 2012, from www.oecd.org/dataoecd/61/45/38368714.pdf.

———. 2009. Aid orphans: Whose responsibility? Development Brief, Issue no. 1.

———. 2010. *Monitoring the principles for good international engagement in fragile states and situations: Fragile states monitoring survey: Global report.* Paris: OECD. Retrieved November 1, 2012, from www.oecd.org/dacfragilestates/44651689.pdf.

Oshita, O., V. Okwunwa, and B. Bakut. 2007. Conclusion. In C. Bassey and O. Oshita, eds. *Conflict resolution, identity crisis, and development in Africa* (pp. 253–268). Lagos, Nigeria: Malthouse Press Ltd.

Ramsbotham, O., T. Woodhouse, and H. Miall. 2011. *Contemporary conflict resolution.* London: Polity.

Read, R. 2010, September 19. Mercy Corps' Neal Keny-Guyer: In failing nations, it's all about community. *Oregonian.* Retrieved October 15, 2011, from www.oregonlive.com/opinion/index.ssf/2010/09/mercy_corps_neal_keny-guyer_in.html.

Rostow, W. W. 1960. *The stages of economic growth: A noncommunist manifesto.* Cambridge: Cambridge University Press.

Sesay, F. L. 2004. Conflict in neighbouring (developing) countries: Direct and indirect effects on economic growth. TIGER Working Paper Series, no. 68. Department of Applied Economics, Ludwig Maximilian University, Munich, Germany.

Smoljan, J. 2003. The relationship between peace building and development. *Conflict, Security & Development* 3, no. 2: 233–250.

United Nations. 2011. *The Millennium Development Goals Report 2011*. New York: Author.

United States Agency for International Development (USAID). 2007. *Community-based development in conflict-affected areas, Office of Conflict Management and Mitigation*. Washington, DC: Author. Retrieved January 5, 2012, from www.usaid.gov/our_work/cross-cutting_programs/conflict/publications/docs/CMM_CBD_Guide_May_2007.pdf.

Wallerstein, I. 2004. *World-systems theory: An introduction*. Durham, NC: Duke University Press.

World Bank. 2011. *World development report: Conflict, security, and development*. Washington, DC: Author.

Zarkov, D. 2008. *Gender, violent conflict, and development*. New Delhi: Zubaan Books.

Zoellick, R. B. 2008, September 12. Fragile states: Securing development. International Institute for Strategic Studies, Global Strategic Review. Retrieved January 5, 2012, from www.iiss.org/conferences/global-strategic-review/global-strategic-review-2008/keynote-address.

ACKNOWLEDGMENTS

Thank you to Monica Scheer for her contribution to the Questions for Further Discussion and case study of Mercy Corps.

NOTES

1. Proponents of modernization theory, such as Rostow (1960), argued for "the adoption of 'modern' forms of administrative and political organization in imitation of western states and businesses, the transfer of western knowledge and skills through education programs, and a 'green revolution' of increased agricultural productivity through the use of western farming methods" (MacGinty and Williams, 2011, p. 10).

2. For similar critiques, see Francis (2006) and Smoljan (2003).

3. The neoliberal economic model champions paring back the state; freeing the market from regulation; privatizing state assets; and lifting exchange controls and industrial licenses to provoke increased exposure of the market to the developing state. MacGinty and Williams (2011) write about the hegemony arising from the intellectual dominance of this mode of thought: "Cloaked in a populist mantle of the empowerment of entrepreneurs and the cutting of public sector waste, neo-liberal truisms became the new orthodoxy" (p. 12).

4. For further information, see www.conflictsensitivity.org.

5. Aid orphans are the countries that compose the geographical gaps of donor giving. Donors decide separately which countries and programs to assist, and to what extent, based on their particular values, priorities, missions, and historical relationships. An asymmetry ensues in which actual aid allocation is driven by factors other than need and merit; certain areas become forgotten and thus more deeply entrenched in poverty (OECD/DAC, 2009).

6. Chalmers's (2007) main conclusion is that undertaking targeted programs of conflict prevention can be highly cost-effective for the international community. In all twelve of the conflict prevention (CP) packages he examined in a study, the anticipated cost savings from avoiding conflict were calculated to exceed the costs of the packages.

7. See www.epesmandala.com.

chapter four

HUMANITARIAN ASSISTANCE AND PEACEBUILDING

Mike Jobbins

Humanitarian assistance does not in and of itself create either war or peace, and the ultimate responsibility for ensuring peace and stability falls to national governments and the international community. However, poorly planned and/or executed aid programmes in conflict zones may fail to reduce suffering or may at worst inadvertently exacerbate it. (p. 5)

—MARIA LANGE AND MICHAEL QUINN (2003)

THIS CHAPTER EXPLORES THE INTEGRATION of humanitarian assistance and peacebuilding in conflict and immediate postconflict settings. During and after violent crises, humanitarian, development, and peacebuilding programs feature many of the same actors, sometimes operate in the same geographic areas, and often share an underlying sense of purpose in improving the human condition. These programs, however, often differ in their core assumptions and operating principles. This chapter begins with a brief overview of international humanitarian action and recent trends in the field. It then considers the integration of peacebuilding into humanitarian programming in both theory and practice, before outlining some remaining challenges.

PEACEBUILDING AND HUMANITARIAN ASSISTANCE

Crises and emergencies, large and small, affect millions of people each year. In poor and developing countries, when natural disasters or violent political crises strike, these often result in a humanitarian crisis, that is, an emergency whose effects are so profound that the country is unable (or unwilling) to meet the needs of the affected population. In such situations, international organizations, such as the United Nations, and governments often take on the significant responsibility to provide assistance, generally citing formal or customary principles of humanitarianism.[1] Unlike other forms of development assistance, which target long-term growth and structural change, humanitarian aid focuses on saving lives and responding to the immediate aftermath of an emergency.

Organizations tend to use different criteria to characterize humanitarian responses. Perhaps the most coherent common statement of the humanitarian mission is outlined in a 2003 joint document developed by sixteen donor countries and other stakeholders, known as the "Principles and Good Practice of Humanitarian Donorship" (Good Humanitarian Donorship, 2003). These begin with three objectives:

Objectives and definition of humanitarian action
1. The objectives of humanitarian action are to save lives, alleviate suffering and maintain human dignity during and in the aftermath of man-made crises and natural disasters, as well as to prevent and strengthen preparedness for the occurrence of such situations.

2. Humanitarian action should be guided by the humanitarian principles of humanity, meaning the centrality of saving human lives and alleviating suffering wherever it is found; impartiality, meaning the implementation of actions solely on the basis of need, without discrimination between or within affected populations; neutrality, meaning that humanitarian action must not favor any side in an armed conflict or other dispute where such action is carried out; and independence, meaning the autonomy of humanitarian objectives from the political, economic, military or other objectives that any actor may hold with regard to areas where humanitarian action is being implemented.

3. Humanitarian action includes the protection of civilians and those no longer taking part in hostilities, and the provision of food, water and sanitation, shelter, health services and other items of assistance, undertaken for the benefit of affected people and to facilitate the return to normal lives and livelihoods. (lines 9–17)

These objectives, while straightforward and well intentioned, raise two main complications in practice, particularly in conflict or postconflict settings. First, the basic principles of humanitarian assistance focus on providing short-term palliative care, aimed at saving lives and preventing suffering in an emergency—but not necessarily in addressing the root causes of a crisis. For example, humanitarian aid is rarely designed to address long-standing social inequalities, or the sometimes desperate situation in which populations found themselves before an emergency. As organizations face complex emergencies where cyclical violence leads to a protracted crisis, it is difficult to separate the ongoing suffering from the social conflicts that fuel militancy. As a result of decades-long crises in the Democratic Republic of Congo (DRC), Afghanistan, and Sudan, the international community is beginning to reconsider the role of humanitarian assistance beyond short-term palliatives.

Second, although it is recognized that assistance should be neutral, impartial to local politics, and distributed on objective criteria "solely on the basis of need," humanitarian assistance—like any other program—the choice of criteria in allocating resources, and the selection of beneficiaries are part of an inherently political process. Most of the decisions taken by international humanitarian agencies in an emergency situation and supported by external donors are the same kinds of decisions that would ordinarily be undertaken by government, such as reconstructing schools. As a result, the mechanisms through which citizens provide input into the process, how decisions are then made, and for what overall objectives are particularly important and potentially controversial.

The intersection of international assistance and local politics has made the humanitarian enterprise much more complicated, particularly in violent and divided societies. As a result, the integration of a wide array of tools from the field of conflict resolution and peacebuilding into humanitarian and emergency settings has gathered considerable interest. This has occurred in three ways:

- First, a number of organizations develop and implement traditional peacebuilding programs alongside, and in coordination with, humanitarian actors during an emergency. This includes programs by major humanitarian and development organizations, such as Mercy Corps, Catholic Relief Services, or the Norwegian Refugee Council, which also have peacebuilding sections; larger international peacebuilding groups, such as Search for Common Ground or International Alert, which manage programs "on the ground" in emergency settings; and national nongovernmental organizations (NGOs), often in coordination with the UN Development Programme (UNDP), another UN agency, or a larger NGO. While these programs often have similar donors and might coordinate closely with humanitarian actors, they typically have separate goals, personnel, and resources.
- A second strand focuses specifically on humanitarian negotiations. Agencies such as the International Committee of the Red Cross/Red Crescent and the UN Office of the Coordinator of Humanitarian Affairs negotiate with governments and other parties to a conflict, to ensure the humanitarian space to operate. While these programs often use negotiation, mediation, and other conflict resolution techniques, they do not seek to address the overall conflict dynamic.
- The third strand seeks to integrate peacebuilding tools directly into relief programs, to address some aspect of how the humanitarian program relates to the conflict dynamic. This is generally referred to as conflict-sensitive response. This trend has led a number of other major NGOs and UN agencies, such as CARE, Save the Children, the International Rescue Committee (IRC), World Vision, and UNICEF, to hire conflict advisers and to integrate peacebuilding into their program response.

The remainder of this chapter looks at the major changes in the humanitarian sector that have facilitated the integration of peacebuilding, before discussing the theoretical and practical considerations, particularly in developing conflict-sensitive humanitarian programming, as well as the major challenges.

THE MODERN HUMANITARIAN AGENDA

Humanitarian programming is a growing field of practice. The main humanitarian research network, the Active Learning Network for Accountability and Performance in Humanitarian Action (ALNAP), in its 2012 "State of the Humanitarian System" report, estimated that there were 274,000 humanitarian professionals worldwide in 2010, of whom nearly half worked for the UN or Red Cross/Red Crescent. The remainder were based at major international or national NGOs (Harvey et al., 2012).[2] Although estimates and definitions vary widely, there is clear consensus that humanitarian funding increased dramatically over the past decade. Even after accounting for spikes driven by major emergencies, such as the 2005 Indian Ocean tsunami or the Iraq war, there has been a consistent upward trend in humanitarian funding.

The increase in funding and personnel has coincided with the professionalization of the sector. Increased resources have led organizations and donors to focus energies on ensuring responsible and transparent stewardship of donated funds to maximize their effectiveness. The push for improved effectiveness has contributed to the development of norms, standards, and a community of practice. This broader community—the "humanitarian system"—now includes a bewildering array of actors, including international NGOs, UN agencies, and the Red Cross/Red Crescent federations that deliver aid, as well as university departments and think tanks, private-sector consult-

FIGURE 4.1. Humanitarian Aid Spending, 2000–2011[3]

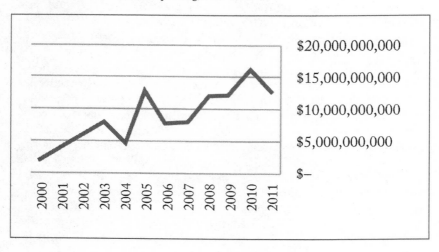

ants and vendors, donor organizations, professional journals and associations, and, increasingly, national and local organizations based in developing countries.

At the same time, professionalization has also been driven by practical challenges humanitarian responders face, particularly following the humanitarian response during violent conflicts in the mid-1990s. High-profile interventions in the Balkans and Somalia, and the nonintervention in Rwanda, brought new attention to the role of the international community as a whole in responding to major emergencies. Protracted wars alongside aid operations in Sudan and Afghanistan, and the Goma refugee crisis in the Democratic Republic of the Congo and Rwanda raised troubling questions about the role of humanitarian actors within the conflict space.

Without the overarching political logic of the Cold War, international bodies, NGOs, governments, and private donors considered a host of new questions: What role should nonmilitary, nondiplomatic assistance play (directly and indirectly) in shaping the political outcomes of a conflict? What criteria should determine whether assistance is provided, and to whom? How should assistance programs be organized when a state's capacity has been so weakened as to prevent it from playing that role? How should aid providers identify priorities?

The Professional Humanitarian System

These questions led to three major initiatives that advanced the development of norms in humanitarian response, and particularly in the context of armed conflict or complex emergencies.

In 1993 the organization Collaborative for Development Action Inc. (CDA), based in Cambridge, Massachusetts, launched the Local Capacities for Peace Project.[4] The CDA worked with local and international NGOs to develop a series of case studies, workshops, and training modules to capture experiences of international assistance in conflict settings. Later known as the Do No Harm Project, named after its core principle, the project drew attention to the unintended consequences of humanitarian assistance, particularly during complex political emergencies. The Do No Harm Project drew attention to the danger of political manipulation of assistance, the sometimes adverse economic effects of aid programming, and inadvertent reshaping of the social landscape. "Do no harm" and risk analysis have become foundational principles of humanitarian action and still provide a basis for most organizations in the responsible design of humanitarian response activities. Mary Anderson's seminal book *Do No Harm: How Aid Can Support Peace—Or War,* captured many of the lessons of the project, spawned a literature of handbooks and training curricula, and influenced many aid actors' policies. The Do No Harm Project (2004) proposed its own analytical framework to apply these lessons to humanitarian and development assistance programming, and increased humanitarian agencies' interest in integrating conflict assessments into their program design.

The second major initiative came in 1997, when a group of NGOs and the Red Cross and Red Crescent movement came together to develop a common set of quality standards. Officially known as the Sphere Humanitarian Charter and Minimum Standards in Disaster Response, or Sphere Standards, the result is a periodically updated set of guidelines for acceptable humanitarian action.[5] In the context of conflict, this handbook defines humanitarian response as actions centered on alleviating suffering of the beneficiaries, placing the immediate well-being of beneficiaries above all other considerations (such as political concerns, visibility, and long-term sustainability). The Sphere Standards reinforced the accountability of humanitarian actors to the people they serve, and built upon the idea that assistance should be delivered based on objective criteria and needs. The standards—with specific guidelines relevant to most major aspects of humanitarian response—have become the yardstick against which aid agencies and their donors assess whether programs meet the minimum requirements of good practice.

Finally, in 2005 and 2006 the UN agencies involved in emergency response underwent a series of changes in the way they coordinate during crises. The Interagency Standing Committee (IASC) was created in 1992 to coordinate humanitarian response between UN agencies and other key relief and development actors at the global level. The reforms resulted in the introduction of the "cluster system" as the main strategy for coordination in emergencies. This system, now widely used in emergencies, divides humanitarian actions into eleven key thematic areas, or "clusters."[6] Within each cluster, a specialized UN agency or major international organization is charged with convening regular meetings, at the global, national, regional, and field levels, to analyze needs, share data, and plan a coherent response. Within this system, two clusters explicitly address themes related to conflict issues. The UNHCR-led Protection Cluster is charged with protecting vulnerable populations—including their rights to not be physically harmed—as well as issues of discrimination and marginalization. The UNDP-led Early Recovery Cluster has a wide mandate that "encompasses the restoration of basic services . . . governance, security and the rule of law, environment and social dimensions, including the reintegration of displaced populations. It stabilizes human security and addresses underlying risks that contributed to the crisis" (Cluster, n.d., para. 1). Direct peacebuilding programs fall within both of these mandates: as prevention of violence, human rights abuses, and discrimination in the context of "protection," or in addressing governance, security, or underlying social issues in the context of "early recovery." In practice, the location of peacebuilding activities within the cluster system usually depends upon the type of program or issue being addressed, as well as the individuals and organizations involved in the response.

Changing Aims and Objectives

In the context of increasing professionalization, the aims of humanitarian programs have continued to emerge. As outlined in the principles of good humanitarian donorship quoted earlier, the first two aims—reducing suffering, and doing so with neutrality and impartiality—fit within classic notions of relief work. The third aim, however, includes several objectives beyond material aid provision, notably "protection of civilians" and "facilitating the return to normal lives and livelihoods." These objectives cover types of activities not typically associated with emergency assistance, such as promoting human rights (the general interpretation of "protection") and seeking an exit to the crisis or conflict. Two main trends have led to greater emphasis on programs that have aims other than immediate lifesaving assistance.

Humanitarian Assistance, Development, and Relief-to-Development

First, there is increasing emphasis on the "relief-to-development" transition, ensuring that actions undertaken in poor countries to address the immediate effects of a disaster also enhance long-term well-being and sustainability. Although humanitarian organizations and development organizations share the same overall goal of reducing human suffering, and in many cases include many of the same actors, institutions, and funding streams, the logic of interventions is distinct. Humanitarian assistance programs are usually launched quickly following an emergency and operate with relatively short time horizons; programs are typically designed and budgeted in twelve-month increments. Development programs operate with longer time horizons (often three or five years) and aim for sustainable change. While development programs may be closely coordinated with host governments, humanitarian programs might value neutrality and independence. Humanitarian programs might use international experts and professional staff to deliver assistance quickly, while development programs might aim to build local capacities to leave behind sustainable change.

In some cases, these two imperatives run in opposite directions. For example, an emergency feeding program designed to save lives during a famine might undermine local food prices and deprive local farmers of capital that might otherwise be invested in improving their yields. In other cases, there is a logical complement. Poverty exacerbates social tensions and vulnerability to natural disasters. A humanitarian agency might provide assistance and care to people displaced by flooding, while a development agency might craft a plan to build dikes in the long term or reduce poverty to enable the affected people to move to another area.

This tension is not a new one. In 1994 London's Overseas Development Institute's Relief and Rehabilitation Network's newsletter (Humanitarian Practice Network, 1994) ran an article in its second issue titled "The Upsurge of Interest in the 'Relief-Development Continuum': What Does It Mean?" In the article, the network saw the driving factors primarily as a response to the increasing cost of humanitarian emergencies (and thus increasing donor interest in prevention mechanisms), as well as competition for scarce donor resources and confusion over the missions of different actors. Early references go back to the late 1980s. In the fifteen years following the network's article, the focus has shifted slightly. Actors recognize that in complex emergencies, there is not so much of a progression between the two forms of assistance and needs as is implied by the "continuum" metaphor, and that in many cases, both relief and development needs occur simultaneously. Some now refer to a "contiguum" situation, in which organizations describe the transition as something to be encouraged, rather than taken for granted as a linear progression (Koddenbrock and Büttner, 2009).

Protracted or repeated crises, stemming from natural or man-made disasters, have led humanitarian aid organizations to question how their assistance can be best used to respond simultaneously to the symptoms as well as the causes of the problem. Thus, food assistance can include food distribution as well as seeds and irrigation. Emergency medicine shipments are often accompanied by training and equipment for local clinics.

While this is fairly straightforward in the context of natural disasters, identifying and treating the causes of human-made or political emergencies through humanitarian programming require a diverse skill set, a distinctive form of engagement with political actors, and different forms of analysis from what humanitarian organizations cultivate. The professionalization of the humanitarian sector has led to increased specialization and subject matter expertise in areas such as public health, agronomy, nutrition, emergency education, and international or human rights law. The transition from relief to development, however, also requires strong process management expertise, ensuring that projects are socially and politically sustainable. In deeply divided societies, this has led to increased efforts to integrate peacebuilding expertise.

Stabilization Programming

In chronically unstable places like the DRC, Sudan, Iraq, and Afghanistan, a succession of humanitarian crises is linked directly to the ongoing political emergency at the national level. In these countries, both national governments and international actors draw linkages between international assistance and political outcomes. Broadly referred to as stabilization programs, these programs generally start from the assumption that some combination of underdevelopment, a lack of opportunities for young people, perceived inequalities, weak local governments, and unaddressed local frustrations drive continued violence and crisis. The analysis and prioritization of the causes of the crisis and the response strategies vary widely. Stabilization programs, however, tend to prioritize the immediate drivers of conflict and instability, rather than the underlying long-term causes.

Humanitarian actors have become increasingly involved in stabilization programs—particularly those dealing with refugees and internally displaced people (IDPs). Large numbers of displaced people can be a driving factor in the continuation of conflicts, and the assistance and eventual return of displaced people are often explicit demands by parties in a peace process.[7]

In many protracted conflicts, it is difficult to separate the reintegration of displaced people back to their homes in safety and dignity from the need to ensure a more stable environment in those areas.[8] This is particularly true in protracted crises characterized by cyclical displacement where civilians return to their homes at the end of one crisis, only to be uprooted again by violence, as in civil wars in Guatemala, Bosnia and Herzegovina, and the DRC. Just as organizations that help people return home after a flood might recognize a responsibility to ensure that homes are rebuilt in a way that prevents disasters in the long term, many organizations helping to return refugees or IDPs after a political crisis recognize an obligation to help ensure their safety. This raises a host of challenges, discussed in a later section of this chapter.

Stabilization programs often include among their goals the restoration of state authority to a given area. As a result, the lines between political, military, and humanitarian aims can blur and contradict principles of independence or neutrality. This uncomfortable commingling makes many humanitarian actors uneasy. Close identification with military actors risks limiting the effectiveness of humanitarian actors and the ability to access populations in areas outside of government control. Close association with military or political actors can also endanger the security of humanitarian personnel. In Afghanistan, Iraq, Kenya, Somalia, and Nigeria, humanitarian organizations have been targeted by armed groups that saw their actions as proxies for political interests. For many relief agencies, participating in stabilization operations challenges the humanitarian principle of neutrality. As the humanitarian system has become the dominant framework for assistance to war-affected populations in the post–Cold War era, there has been a further blurring of the line between military "hearts and minds" operations and humanitarian relief. Stabilization programs, often implemented in the context of ongoing armed conflict and in coordination with local governments, are particularly likely to be perceived as overtly political.

INTEGRATING PEACEBUILDING INTO HUMANITARIAN RESPONSE

Most international organizations and donor agencies have recognized the need to integrate conflict analysis and programming into their interventions of political emergencies. In the humanitarian realm, the "do no harm" principle is well known, reflected in the Sphere Standards, and is among the foundational principles of modern humanitarian response. Alongside the "do no harm" tool kit developed by CDA, many agencies have adopted their own guidelines, tool kits, and methodologies for addressing conflict through their work (Conflict Sensitivity Consortium, 2010). These methodologies and approaches are most commonly referred to as "conflict sensitivity."

Conflict sensitivity recognizes the political nature of assistance, and shows "politically informed neutrality" (active awareness of attempts to manipulate aid), integrates conflict prevention to avoid latent tensions, does no harm, and engages with development and peacebuilding actors. Conflict sensitivity means not only considering the potential adverse effects of assistance in a given conflict or crisis environment, but also how humanitarians understand the systemic political impact of their presence.

Conflict Sensitivity and Peacebuilding

The most common definition of conflict-sensitive programming is this one, put forward by the Conflict Sensitivity Consortium,[9] a network of major, primarily UK-based, humanitarian and development NGOs involved in encouraging conflict-sensitive approaches to emergencies and piloting conflict sensitive programming in Kenya, Sierra Leone, and Sri Lanka:

> Conflict sensitivity can be defined as the capacity of an organization to (1) understand the (conflict) context in which it operates, (2) Understand the interaction between its intervention and the (conflict) context; and (3) Act upon the understanding of this interaction in order to avoid negative impacts and maximize positive impacts on the (conflict) context and the intervention. (Lange and Quinn, 2003, p. 6)

Valeria Izzi and Christof Kurz (2009), writing for Search for Common Ground, one of the largest peacebuilding organizations, put out a slightly different formulation:

> The notion of conflict sensitivity is the idea that no intervention can be neutral in a conflict setting: there is necessarily an impact—positive or negative—on conflict dynamics. The definition of conflict sensitivity revolves therefore around two pillars:

(1) the imperative to "do no harm" and (2) the effort to actively contribute to peace-building. (p. 3)

Each definition recognizes the political nature of humanitarian assistance and the potential for humanitarian assistance to contribute to either positive or negative outcomes, beyond its intended scope. Both definitions presume that humanitarian assistance is inevitably political, whether the humanitarian intervention "necessarily" has an impact on conflict dynamics or "interacts with the conflict context." The notion that aid should take efforts to "maximize positive impacts" or to "contribute to peace-building" suggests that assistance should aspire to some positive social function of aid beyond its sector, a far more ambitious and difficult task.

Many organizations fear that linking material assistance with a maximalist "peace writ large" (of impacting peace at the macro level) definition of peacebuilding might dilute the focus of humanitarian actions,[10] put their entire missions in jeopardy by expanding beyond their core functions and mission, or support unrealistic expectations that material aid in and of itself will solve thorny political problems. Furthermore, there is a clear difference in ambition and timing, while the notion of "peace writ large" envisions an end state where all forms of conflict can be dealt with constructively. This is an aspiration well beyond what is achievable within the relatively limited time frame of humanitarian programming.

In practice, the conflict advisers, analytical frameworks, and tools used within conflict-sensitive approaches draw largely from the field of peacebuilding, but the distinction lies in the aims of conflict-sensitive humanitarian programs that work *in* a conflict context, from those of peacebuilding actors who work *on* conflict issues (Goodhand, 2001). Dianne Chigas and Peter Woodrow (2009), in response to concerns that these lines were blurring, argue that "peacebuilding" should refer to stand-alone responses to particular social and political problems, with "conflict sensitivity" used to refer to an approach or method of doing a program aimed at achieving other overall goals, and thus cannot—and should not—target the same results. This distinction is relatively straightforward in classic humanitarian programming whose only aim is to provide lifesaving relief. The distinction is more subtle in situations where humanitarian programs do envision some longer-term outcomes, such as in the relief-to-development programs or the stabilization programs described above, and where programs are designed with the aim to ensure that crises do not recur.

Chigas and Woodrow (2009) also raise the important observation that there is a common myth across the humanitarian and development sectors that by its very nature, assistance contributes to "peace writ large." There is little evidence to support this claim, and there is a danger that conflict-sensitive emergency assistance will come to replace other forms of peacebuilding programs, particularly because these programs have quicker and more tangible results. Host-country governments that see these programs as boosting the government's popularity find them attractive and are less likely to seek more serious reconfigurations in state–society relations.

Just as conflict exists at an interpersonal, community, and society level in war-affected areas, conflict sensitivity can exist at many levels. While most would readily agree that humanitarian aid should be conflict sensitive with regard to its direct beneficiaries, such as improving their lives and not putting them at risk of violence, opinions differ over the degree to which a humanitarian project, such as building a school or shelter, should contribute to social change. While a survey by the Conflict Sensitivity Consortium (Zicherman et al., 2011) found that 84 percent of humanitarian practitioners felt that increased conflict sensitivity should be a "top priority," few could cite specific examples of conflict resolution or peacebuilding activities within their agency's programs (p. 6).

Underlying Theories and Concepts
Prioritization of Human Needs

Appropriate to a sector that focuses on distributing and allocating scarce resources in an environment, underlying theories of conflict tend to be principally materialistic. Much of humanitarian program design focuses on prioritizing needs, inevitably focusing on the most urgent and basic. Prioritization tools, such as Maslow's hierarchy of needs and similar models clearly distinguishing between urgencies and second-order priorities, have a large influence on program design, either explicitly or implicitly. Maslow (1954) distinguishes between basic first-order priorities, such as biological/physiological (such as food or water) and safety (security), and second-order ones, including belonging (friendship, family), esteem, and finally self-actualization.

Humanitarian assistance focuses primarily on the bottom level of the pyramid—responding immediately to physiological needs. While the undeniable focus of assistance is on saving lives and alleviating physical suffering, the so-called hard elements of relief work, there has been increasing recognition that there is also a need to consider higher-level aspects.

Most individuals and agencies recognize a moral obligation to treat beneficiaries with respect, and to ensure that basic assistance is delivered in a way that recognizes the range of needs and interests of beneficiaries. Many groups have adopted codes of conduct and best practices that consider the psychological and emotional well-being of aid recipients. This is reflected in a number of guidelines and best practices that expand upon the basic notions of reducing suffering through neutral and impartial aid. For example, UNICEF (2003) has added several humanitarian principles focused on higher-level needs:

The humanitarian imperative. Human suffering must be addressed wherever it is found, with particular attention to the most vulnerable in the population.

Neutrality. Humanitarian agencies must not take sides in the hostilities or in controversies based on political, racial, religious or ideological identity.

Impartiality. Aid is delivered to all those who are suffering; the guiding principle is only their need and the corresponding right. Human rights are the basis and the framework for an assessment of needs.

Do no/less harm. Although aid can become part of the dynamics of the conflict and may even prolong it, humanitarian organizations must strive to "do no harm" or to minimize the harm they may be inadvertently doing.

Accountability. There are four stakeholders in the provision of aid assistance: the beneficiary community; the national/local authority; the donor and the aid agency. Within this relationship, international aid agencies shall hold themselves accountable to both the beneficiary communities and the donors.

Participation of affected populations. Humanitarian action tends to look at short-term needs and forget the responsibilities of the aid community to give sustainable aid in a way that realizes the right of affected populations to participate in decisions that affect their lives.

Respect for culture and custom. Understanding local customs and traditions is, of course, important, not only in carrying out your work, but also in understanding local values. (pp. 1–3)

Horizontal Inequalities and Intergroup Tensions

Many analyses of conflict-sensitive humanitarian response focus on the ways in which distributing goods and assistance might interact (or be perceived to interact) with existing divisions in society (Anderson, 1999). Particular attention focuses on how aid can inadvertently favor different segments of the population or social groups—particularly groups already in conflict. The underlying logic is that by providing assistance in a way that appears uneven among groups, resentment may give way to new kinds of inequalities that potentially exacerbate conflict.

The theory of "horizontal inequalities," advocated in the field of development and conflict by Frances Stewart and the Centre for Research on Inequality, Human Security and Ethnicity at Oxford University, argues that the most significant drivers of conflict are inequalities among groups, rather than those among individuals. According to the theory, individuals not only are concerned about their own relative status within a larger society, but also actively monitor the status of their social group and respond to perceived slights irrespective of their personal situation. While this observation is fairly straightforward and commonsensical, it is fundamental in the context of humanitarian work, in which needs are analyzed objectively, looking primarily at individuals and households without accounting for group belonging.

Human Rights, Protection, and Peacebuilding

Activities falling under the scope of "protection" typically include monitoring and reporting abuses, conducting advocacy to rectify past abuses, and raising awareness of general rights principles, all of which encourage accountability, and perhaps deterrence, within a justice framework. While these address many of the same issues as peacebuilding programs, there are some fundamental differences in how peacebuilding practitioners and the human rights community address the problems. The focus on legal rights under domestic or international law and judicial accountability represent a targeted end state, where every citizen is protected within the formal system. But this focus does not always address issues of historic grievances or identity between groups, or the sorts of informal problem-solving between individuals and communities that take hold in contexts where the institutional capacity (courts, governments) is unlikely to extend formal protections.

TABLE 4.1. Concepts in Protection and Peacebuilding

PROTECTION	PEACEBUILDING
Aims at an end state of guaranteed rights	Aims at a process of achieving long-term interests
Focuses on individual victims, including vulnerable people	Often focuses on social groups, including perpetrators of abuses
Grounded in universal rights inherent to all individuals	Focused on specific interests (land, resources, identity) and interest groups (ethnic, social)

CONFLICT SENSITIVITY IN PRACTICE

There are a number of common ways that that aid can cause conflict or miss opportunities to create peace. The Conflict Sensitivity Consortium survey (Zicherman et al., 2011, p. 5), referenced above, found that 85 percent of humanitarian workers had seen or worked on a project that they felt had inadvertently caused conflict or made a conflict worse. The results often are documented long after a project is completed, and sometimes appear clear in retrospect. Consider this example from interviews with a woman in South Kivu in the DRC.

> The natural spring here is the only upgraded water source in the entire area. It was fixed up by an aid agency. All the other villages prefer to come here, to draw their drinking water from our village. Some families send their children, and there are so many that the small ones do not have the force to push in line. Other people come from afar and don't know the agreed-upon norms on how the spring should be maintained. Every day there is a long line, and every day there are conflicts over water. Even me, I was a victim of verbal disputes and beatings by another lady. We women, we live this conflict each day. If only the humanitarian organizations could come to save us, by improving the springs in the other villages, so that we could have some peace![11]

This section considers some of the common causes of conflict within humanitarian programs and provides response strategies.

Conflict Linked to Identifying Beneficiaries

Perhaps the most common forms of humanitarian-linked conflict relate to the identification of beneficiaries and aid recipients. The humanitarian principle of impartiality means that agencies deliver aid based on objective needs and human rights, and is the main humanitarian principle guaranteeing that aid does not favor one group in society over another. As a result, agencies typically design programs to be as objective as possible, often in accordance with international standards. However, the objective criteria often do not align with communities' own expectations, and these criteria often seem opaque or illegitimate to beneficiaries. To cite several examples:

- When spraying houses with insecticide to kill mosquitoes and prevent malaria, it is sometimes mathematically optimal to spray only a percentage of the households in a given community. Because the spray will kill mosquitoes that enter, each house sprayed lowers risk of malaria for its neighbors. Thus, by spraying 80 percent of households, an agency can cover ten villages with the number of resources technically needed for eight. However, such a strategy is unfeasible, given the likelihood of causing or exacerbating perceptions of inequality for the remaining 20 percent.

- One recent program aimed at building schools to facilitate the return of refugees was designed based on the understanding that for school rehabilitation to have maximum educational benefits, it is necessary to rehabilitate the classrooms that accompany the students over their educational career. There is little educational value in rehabilitating one classroom in a school, when students will move back to a dilapidated classroom the next year. This raised communication challenges. Staff had a budget to rehabilitate a limited number of classrooms, and perpetually struggled to explain why they were building four or five new classrooms all at one school, rather than distributing the rehabilitated classrooms among all the schools in the region. It inevitably caused rumors of corruption and nepotism about why one school and not another was chosen for rehabilitation.

- Different communities may have different coping mechanisms in times of emergency, which can impact the provision of humanitarian aid. For example, during the 2011 elections crisis in Côte d'Ivoire, large numbers of Christians and Muslims were displaced by fighting in Abidjan. Christian churches organized relief efforts for their flock, establishing safe refuge and camps within church compounds. Muslim community associations organized networks of host families to provide food and shelter to displaced people. Because it is easier to identify and provide assistance to displaced people centralized in camps, rather than dispersed through households, agencies worked to ensure that assistance reached the neediest from across the spectrum and was not perceived as favoring one group over another.

Furthermore, it risks creating conflicts and resentment between beneficiaries and nonbeneficiaries of aid, exacerbating tensions. To address these issues, a number of conflict resolution tools or processes can be used to mainstream and reduce potential conflict:

- **Communication and transparency** in explaining how the program is designed and how beneficiaries are being identified. Humanitarian groups might meet with key stakeholder groups, publish project summaries, or even give interviews to local media, to explain how they are going about the selection process, in order to prevent rumors and misunderstandings, both before the project begins and throughout its implementation. However, one challenge and obstacle that many aid workers face is the fear of raising unrealistic expectations that the subsequent program might not live up to.

- **Community participation in identifying beneficiaries** through consultations with local leaders or civic groups, by holding public meetings, or by drawing upon existing community groups and structures to identify needy groups and deliver assistance. However, one challenge is that if the process is not carefully designed, and if there has not been a proper analysis, it might reinforce existing inequalities and grievances, particularly where there are existing power imbalances within the community. This also raises complications in cases where community priorities do not align with either the capacity or the funding available to humanitarian organizations, or—as in the case of the schools listed above—it does not align with international best practices.
- **Community participation in the design of the program.** In many cases—such as the classroom rehabilitation example above—community preferences for how aid is delivered directly contradict the design of assistance programs. There are also several challenges to community participation, including limits on what agencies can deliver, the need to balance agencies' expertise with the community's knowledge, and the risk of reinforcing power imbalances. In areas where there are significant displacements, one key challenge may be that the community physically present when the program is being designed may not anticipate—or focus on—the needs that will be required as the crisis ends and people return.
- **Conflict mapping and analysis focused on identifying main social cleavages** are critical within the affected society. While acceptance of the value of conflict analysis is nearly universal, there are a number of challenges when applied in practice. Conflict analysis often requires specific expertise, tools, and processes, some of which might be resource-intensive or time-intensive. Within these limits, capturing the knowledge of nonspecialist staff and partners is crucial, and many initiatives focus on ways to integrate conflict analysis into other assessment tools. Integrating several conflict-developed indicators into existing assessment tools can be an excellent way to collect large amounts of information at relatively low cost, as well as to correlate individuals' and households' perception vis-à-vis the conflict with other indicators (demographic, health needs, food security) that are the subject of the investigation. On the other hand, the data is inevitably less rich; in some cases, information relevant to conflict (for example, respondents' ethnic background) might be politically sensitive to integrate into a routine needs assessment. Other questions may appear jarring if not framed properly within the context of a larger study. Furthermore, regardless of the data-collection strategy, conflict analysis requires human resources to analyze the conflict-specific data.

Conflict Linked to How Programs Are Managed

The second broad form of conflict that often arises in humanitarian operations is linked to the way in which humanitarian programs are managed. Programs are typically implemented under pressure, in difficult environments, and sometimes with incomplete information. In this context, a number of challenges arise within the scope of operational decision-making:

- One key challenge is the recruitment of staff and contractors. In many societies around the world, there are deep social inequalities in terms of access to education and the resources needed to access desirable technical jobs requiring advanced degrees, including in the humanitarian sector. As a result, the recruitment for national staff humanitarian programs can be a source of conflict that can shift perceptions of agencies' activities in a given community, or subtly alter the way assistance is delivered and the way the agency understands the needs. Because crises necessitating large-scale responses typically affect already vulnerable communities, skilled national employees are recruited from elsewhere, and so the delivery of assistance can be altered by conscious or unconscious regional, ethnic, urban/rural, or religious stereotypes.

- Diversion of aid and the infiltration of assistance programs by combatant groups has been a concern in some areas, since it contradicts the humanitarian mission and risks drawing agencies into the broader conflict. Among many examples, Human Rights Watch (2002) observed that the Sudan People's Liberation Army (SPLA) had infiltrated refugee camps, as far as Kampala, quoting a local organization that "SPLA influence is very strong in the camps. There are informers in the camps, and there is a problem with forced recruitment. Uganda turns a deaf ear to refugees with this problem. . . . The SPLA stays in the camps with their guns and uses the camps for rest and recover[y] and to plan" (p. 140).

- There is a risk of creating unwieldy social systems. For example, take the following story, recounted by a national NGO in Niamey, Niger: "There was a village not far away. An NGO went there to improve the drinking water. When they left, they created a water committee to maintain and continue the work. Then, another NGO came, to provide veterinary support to the livestock. To make it sustainable, they created a livestock committee. The livestock needed water, and where there had never been any problems before, now there is a big conflict between the livestock committee, and the water committee. It all could have been avoided if they had sat [and] worked with the single development committee."[12]

A number of strategies have emerged to manage these kinds of conflict, although the solutions tend to be very context-specific:

- **Reflecting local diversity in recruitment.** One of the most common strategies suggested by those working in conflict is to ensure a diverse representation of all groups in society—including marginalized groups and all perceived parties to a conflict. While "positive discrimination" policies and other forms of recruitment that explicitly take account of applicants' social identity raise challenges in many organizations, recruitment policies are particularly problematic in humanitarian organizations because of the mandate to impartiality in humanitarian action and because of the extremely high stakes involved in humanitarian programming. Furthermore, where staff represent different identities involved in a conflict, moving beyond tokenism can be a challenge and requires team-building efforts to ensure that individuals work as a mixed unit, while also recognizing that in the most divided cases, "working with the other side" can expose staff to security concerns.

- **Strong ethical code, guidelines, and enforcement.** The risk of ethical lapses by humanitarian staff is well recognized. These include kickbacks and exploitation (including sexual) of beneficiary populations, diversion of funds, corruption, and diverting business through family members. In some cases, there are examples of aid personnel engaging directly in illegal business transactions fueling conflicts (Plaut, 2011). This preoccupation has led organizations to adopt stronger codes of conduct, ethics training modules, and internal control processes, including complaint lines, ombudsmen, and in some cases internal investigators.

- **Engaging with existing capacities.** One tenet of good humanitarian practice focuses on working through existing local structures, including local authorities, civil society groups, and coordination mechanisms, as discussed above. In practical terms, one element of this engagement is ensuring that the collaboration strengthens the capacity of these institutions in the long term. This includes both building the skills of local partners and helping partners identify clear goals for their organization, and ensuring the project fits within their own goals, rather than vice versa. In addition, humanitarian programs often bring substantial resources and activities that can inundate the capacity of local partners, co-opting them for the project effort, but undermining the organization's long-term stability once the particular funding ends. One key challenge is managing precedents. For example, many UN agencies and international organizations tend to pay per diems for participants in workshops and trainings. The merits of this practice are much debated, but it has become the norm in many places. However, there is a danger that paying per diem for community members to participate in activities that they would have otherwise done might create unrealistic expectations and lead to activities' evaporating once international resources dry up.

Opportunities to Help Address Causes of Conflict

Humanitarian assistance programs reshape the social and physical landscape, changing the futures of individuals and communities. This is particularly the case in programs focused on the return and reintegration of displaced people. Infrastructure, including roads, schools, and water pumps built during the emergency phase, last long afterward.

Education provided in displacement camps lasts with children long after they leave the camp. The moments of crisis are likely the most dramatic in the life of individuals and communities, with long-lasting effects on individual psyches and social relationships. Aiding people in these moments holds the potential to address long-standing grievances and root causes of conflict, or to create fractious social relations in the future, at the level of the household, community, or society.

Peacebuilding actors often refer to the concept of "growing the pie"—increasing the total value—as a way to transform seemingly zero-sum competition among parties to a conflict. The massive investments that humanitarian programming brings to communities can result in this added value, but they also can raise many of the questions of the limits of this kind of work. For example:

- Developing shared infrastructure between communities is one key element. For example, a French NGO was reconstructing a clinic in a town that had been decimated by an armed militia during interethnic fighting in northwestern DRC. During the consultation process, the NGO discovered that the community wanted the clinic to be reconstructed because members of the local ethnic group had been unable to go to clinics in neighboring communities since the violence. The NGO suspected that once the new clinic was rehabilitated, the local community would reciprocally exclude their neighbors. Recognizing the larger challenge of segregation in the sector in which the humanitarian community would be investing heavily, the humanitarian community engaged traditional chiefs, local government, and the health staff to help ensure access to the hospitals.

- As part of its mission to ensure that refugees return to a safe environment, the office of the UN High Commissioner for Refugees (UNHCR) often works to help restore functioning local governments, which in turn help restore functioning local authorities and support dispute resolution processes. Other UN agencies work closely with national counterpart institutions (the World Health Organization and national Ministries of Health; UNICEF works with the Ministry of Education; etc.). This gives these agencies significant influence with national and local governments. As international bodies bound to principles of international law, including the Universal Declaration of Human Rights, these agencies are often in the position of advocacy and advancing human rights principles, such as nondiscrimination, gender inclusivity, and others within state institutions that might address root causes of conflict.

- Some programs deliberately alter the geography and social makeup of communities. For example, from 2002 to 2008, agencies faced the challenge of reintegrating more than 450,000 refugees in Burundi, the second–most densely populated country in Africa. In an agricultural economy, with a high incidence of land conflict, reintegration was a zero-sum game. To break out of this, the government, UNHCR, other UN agencies, as well as a number of NGOs worked together to try to devise Pareto-efficient strategies to break the dynamic whereby every refugee resettled necessarily comes at the expense of someone already using the land.[13] The strategy included giving cash grants to inject resources into poor communities, and developing "peace villages" to host returning landless IDPs and refugees in ethnically mixed communities with support from the donor community. The peace villages were designed to break down stigmas between surrounding communities and the returning refugees—many of whom had been outside the country for decades—and encourage the intermingling of Hutus and Tutsis, residents and returnees. Although the long-term outcomes of the project are not yet clear and have been plagued with challenges in implementation, this effort represents an innovative response to a difficult situation (Telyukov and Paterson, 2008).

To leverage the potential positive effects of humanitarian interventions on the conflict dynamics, there are several key strategies:

- **Adding resources for Pareto-optimal solutions.** As the examples above from the DRC and Burundi lay out, the resource investment by humanitarian actors can hold out the opportunity to "grow the pie," as in Burundi by adding resources in an absolute sense, or by using planned investments as leverage to encourage cooperation, as in the DRC. However, these kinds of programs are among the most complicated and challenging, and are a form of social engineering that strict humanitarian agencies rarely have the capacity, time, or resources to engage in.
- **Spreading human rights principles.** NGOs and UN agencies often make support and collaboration with government agencies contingent on respect for human rights issues. Direct advocacy to governments and other actors can shift their practices, while the simple presence of humanitarian actors committed to human rights principles can reinforce the visibility of these notions among government and among the general public. However, while the respect for human rights may, in many ways, address social inequalities and injustices that might drive conflict, the concepts are not the same. In politically sensitive areas, rights-based advocacy can inflame rather than resolve conflict, by accentuating horizontal inequalities and perceptions of injustice between communities.
- **Modeling gender and inclusive decision-making.** Another potential positive effect of humanitarian programming on conflict lies in modeling participatory decision-making processes. This is particularly true with regard to the inclusion of women and marginalized groups in decision-making. By actively including traditionally marginalized groups and emphasizing diversity in their own staffing, in community partner structures, and in decision-making processes, humanitarian agencies can empower these groups, and design programs and infrastructure that are more responsive to their needs. In cases where social exclusion is a driver of conflict, this may address some conflict causes. However, this process of encouraging inclusivity can also cause a backlash. If it is not handled sensitively, it may be perceived as an affront to cultural

norms or a threat to established social systems, aggravating stigma for participants or shifting public attitudes about the overall program or agency.

UNICEF PEAR Plus Program (adapted from Izzi and Kurz, 2009)

In the Democratic Republic of Congo, UNICEF manages a number of multi-sectoral relief and relief-to-development programs to IDPs. This includes the Program for Expanded Assistance to Returns (PEAR). The program fits within the UN's overall stabilization strategy and is designed to assist the return of formerly displaced people to key areas in the fragile East, and to give them basic assistance to help them resume normal activities. A follow-up program, PEAR Plus, is designed to provide integrated support to these communities with longer-term infrastructure, including schools, health clinics, water, and sanitation, and to support the protection of human rights. The program was designed to invest heavily in a relatively small group of communities, to jump-start normal life.

About twelve months into the project, UNICEF was interested in the program's effect on conflict in the areas in which it was investing, and asked Search for Common Ground to conduct a study of the degree to which the program was "conflict sensitive." The research found that field-level staff of UNICEF and its partners were recognizing potential harm from their interventions, and were working to ensure that the project avoided pitfalls. However, at the same time, the project did not systematically focus on conflict sensitivity, and relied largely on improvisation and common sense of its staff. The study laid out three scenarios for UNICEF: Because the risk of harm from the program was relatively low and was being managed, UNICEF could (a) choose not to invest limited resources in further conflict sensitivity without fundamentally violating core principles. If UNICEF wanted to go further, it could (b) adopt a minimalist approach, focused on incorporating conflict sensitivity tools into existing processes without adding any new aims, working *in* conflict but not addressing the issues, or (c) adopt a maximalist approach, and integrate activities specifically designed to achieve peacebuilding outcomes, alongside the humanitarian aims, and accept to work *on* conflict.

Because of the "stabilization" mandate of the program, and the desire to see the cycles of violence, displacement, and reintegration in these same communities, UNICEF adopted a maximalist approach, which includes both conflict monitoring and training for program staff, increased transparency around the program's activities as well as specific peacebuilding activities, such as community dialogues using participatory theater, conflict resolution training for local authorities, festivals, and "solidarity events," and training for local radio stations in conflict-sensitive journalism. Since its inception in 2009, the program has worked to address dozens of conflicts, both preexisting conflicts over land, returning displaced persons, and gender violence, as well as conflicts linked to humanitarian assistance between beneficiaries and nonbeneficiaries, particularly in the field of education.

Case Studies from Refugee Reintegration Programs

For the reasons described at the outset of this chapter, the return of displaced people is among the most challenging and conflict-prone areas of humanitarian programs. In situations where the international community—often UNHCR or another UN agency—takes on responsibility for the safety of large numbers of vulnerable people, there is a particular obligation to consider the conflicts they face when they return. Nearly all comprehensive evaluations of reintegration programming, including recently concluded protracted crises in Angola, South Sudan, East Timor, and Kyrgyzstan-Uzbekistan, have cited the need for increased attention and capacity to address conflicts:

- **Between returnees and non-displaced persons** resulting from the perceived advantages accorded to returnees or other social differences and distinctions. While some people flee across borders and become refugees, others stay, or become internally displaced. As difficult as the experience of the refugees was, those who lived through the war at home often faced similar abuses, with less international assistance. As a result, there is sometimes a sense of resentment among the communities based on the assistance that refugees receive. On the other hand, refugees who have lived in camps for a decade or more have in some cases lost touch with their home culture, or language. An evaluation of the refugee return program in Angola found that there was a "strong sense of alienation expressed by many returnees in relation to Angolan society and the state. Some said that they were resented by other members of the population. . . . Social relations between the returnees and resident populations were also constrained by the fact that a large proportion of the former refugees spoke little or no Portuguese. As a result, they were dismissively referred to by other Angolans as 'Zambianos' and 'Zairenses'" (Crisp, Riera and Freitas, 2008, p. 24).

- **Over land, assistance, natural resources, other issues in the return process.** Refugees who have been out of the country for years typically return home and face new conflicts. During their absence, new families have moved into their houses. Someone else is cultivating their fields. The head of the family passed away, and a family member inside the country inherited the entire estate, leaving nothing for the refugees. Water infrastructure has been destroyed, and the population has grown. Agricultural feeder roads have fallen into disuse, making farming less viable in some areas. These kinds of conflicts are predictable and inherent to almost any refugee crisis, but require in-depth local knowledge and conflict resolution skills, which are distinct from the skill sets of typical aid workers. An evaluation in Sudan wrote that "to play a meaningful role on reintegration, there is a need for UNHCR to strengthen its staffing profile . . . which in reintegration operations may require specialist expertise on issues such as land and property rights and conflict resolution" (Duffield, Diagne, and Tennant, 2008, p. 46). An evaluation in central Asia observed that, given the likelihood of future conflict in the region, it was logical to begin planning for how to resolve these conflicts in advance: "[UNCHR's Central Asia Strategy] should give particular attention to . . . a strengthened programme of local capacity building with governmental and non-governmental institutions that have the potential to contribute to conflict resolution" (Crisp, Bowman, and Prokopchuk, 2011, p. 3). Strong state institutions capable of preventing or resolving conflict are critical to preventing new displacements, and ensuring the longer-term safety of returnees.

- **Ensuring the reintegration process does not leave the seeds for longer-term conflict.** Humanitarian crises reshape communities, and the postemergency period is critical in shaping where people live and how people rebuild. The way that refugee return operations are conducted can set the tone for future conflict. One example of this is in East Timor, where Daniel Fitzpatrick, a former UN official writing in UNHCR's "New Issues on Refugee Research," reported complaints from Timorese leaders that UNHCR was "dumping" the displaced in the capital of Dili during the hectic postemergency period. The first displaced people to return secured land through legal and illegal means, creating a new elite. Later returnees and migrants from rural areas found their houses occupied and rental prices unaffordable. Land issues later exploded again in Timor-Leste, contributing to a second round of violence and house-burning several years later (Fitzpatrick, 2002).

CHALLENGES IN THE FIELD

Integrating peacebuilding through conflict sensitivity and other tools in an emergency context raises a number of serious challenges.

At the theoretical level, there are fundamental unresolved differences in logic, skill sets, and operating norms. Peacebuilding practitioners typically focus on engaging multiple parties to a conflict, and historically have drawn a distinction between themselves and rights-based advocates. However, the underlying justification for humanitarian action depends on notions of basic and universal human rights. Within the cluster system, peacebuilding actions often fall under the broad mandate of "protection," which aims to prevent and seek redress for human rights abuses, including both physical violence and discrimination. In this realm, protection actions are generally guided by international and national law and rights principles, which are in most cases nonnegotiable and thus in some ways antithetical to the process of conflict resolution. While many conflict-sensitive approaches seek to ensure that assistance is not perceived as disproportionately favoring one social group, the humanitarian principle of impartiality implies that aid should be given to the neediest, without regard to their identity.

Unresolved practical questions relate primarily to the fact that in any crisis or post-crisis situation, resources are limited. Time, money, and human resources can be stretched only so far, and are almost never sufficient to meet the needs of the affected population. There is a broad consensus that attention must be paid to the principles of "do no harm," and broad recognition that humanitarian actions can inadvertently exacerbate conflict. However, there is an optimal amount of conflict assessments, studies, and advising that is feasible before the resources (time, money, and staff) diminish the program's overall effectiveness.

The nature of providing lifesaving assistance requires making difficult choices with limited information. Few donors—public or private—would support a program if they believed there was a strong likelihood the program was "doing harm" and would require that humanitarian actors state their risk mitigation strategies as a condition for assistance. However, in emergency contexts, resource allocation is largely a zero-sum game, in the context of scarce money, overburdened staff, and the overarching need to provide assistance quickly.

Assessments and analysis take time, and a great deal of important information is not easily accessible. Every donor dollar spent on conflict experts is one less dollar spent on building houses, distributing food, or buying tarpaulins. The challenge is thus not the necessity of conflict sensitivity, but the degree to which it should be included in operational planning and budgeting. For organizations and humanitarian planners, overemphasizing conflict-sensitive program design risks diverting resources from the main mission, while underbudgeting might result in either unintentional harm or missed opportunities to contribute to the bigger picture of the crisis.

Integrating some conflict resolution and peacebuilding tools can also be low-cost. For example, programs that aim to build the capacity of humanitarian staff in conflict resolution skills (such as active communication, negotiation, and mediation) are typically less expensive than using specialized "conflict" personnel. Integrating conflict-related questions into other needs assessments might be feasible in some communities. Improved information sharing among humanitarian actors and between humanitarians and local communities might reduce misunderstandings and lead to greater self-awareness. However, nearly all of these interventions still require time and money and affect communities only indirectly (by targeting humanitarian personnel). Without a concerted strategy, dedicated staff, and specific peacebuilding activities, it is unlikely that the full potential will be achieved or that humanitarian action might "grow the pie."

CONCLUSION

As described in the UNICEF example cited above, each humanitarian agency and operation takes a deliberate decision as to how much to incorporate conflict sensitivity within its activities. As the current trends push the aims of traditional humanitarian response beyond the immediate provision of lifesaving assistance and encourage integration into the broader response to crises, the mission and mandate of humanitarian agencies is likely to move further into the field of addressing the causes of conflict and to integrate peacebuilding where possible. Just as the mantra following the Asian tsunami came to be "build back, better," and programs focused on building more resilient communities, it is likely that humanitarian agencies working in political crises will continue to look for ways to ensure that the humanitarian response after violent conflict also helps to prevent its recurrence, and overcome the technical and philosophical challenges.

QUESTIONS FOR FURTHER DISCUSSION

1. Maslow's hierarchy of needs features prominently, either explicitly or implicitly, in the prioritization of humanitarian response. To what extent should emergency response planners focus on "higher" levels of the pyramid?

2. What criteria should a humanitarian organization consider before deciding whether to participate in a "stabilization" operation?

3. The UNICEF statement of humanitarian principles, outlined above, contains a number of inherent contradictions. For example, balancing the need to respect local culture with the need to provide assistance in accordance with human rights principles might cause some challenges in providing aid in societies where women have few rights. To what extent should aid workers tailor their programs in societies where women's participation in public life is limited?

4. While "conflict sensitivity" is uncontroversial as an idea in the humanitarian community, there are disagreements on the extent. Minimalists argue that the principle is to ensure that interventions do not cause harm. Maximalists argue that humanitarian actions should be a tool for peacebuilding and contribute to an end to the crisis. Does integrating peacebuilding objectives into humanitarian projects dilute humanitarian organizations' mission? Does it compromise the principle of neutrality?

5. One of the key challenges in recruiting a diverse staff for humanitarian organizations is the need to balance "positive discrimination" in favor of the local population and marginalized groups, with the need for the most highly qualified experts capable of providing lifesaving assistance. How should organizations balance these two goals?

6. The section "Conflict Sensitivity in Practice" of this chapter has a story from a woman about some of the negative effects of rehabilitating a water source in her community. In your opinion, what could the NGO involved have done differently?

REFERENCES

Cluster Working Group on Early Recovery. n.d. Early Recovery Cluster Overview. One Response website. Retrieved October 10, 2012, from http://oneresponse.info/GLOBAL CLUSTERS/EARLY%20RECOVERY/Pages/default.aspx.

Conflict Sensitivity Consortium. 2010. Conflict-sensitive approaches to development, humanitarian assistance, and peacebuilding: Resource pack (pp. 15–40). Retrieved December 12, 2011, from www.conflictsensitivity.org/publications/conflict-sensitive-approaches -development-humanitarian-assistance-and-peacebuilding-res.

Crisp, J., H. Bowman, and N. Prokopchuk. 2011. *Lessons learned from UNHCR's response to the 2010 emergency in Kyrgyzstan and Uzbekistan.* Geneva, Switzerland: UNHCR.

Crisp, J., J. Riera, and R. Freitas. 2008. *Evaluation of UNHCR's returnee reintegration programme in Angola.* Geneva, Switzerland: UNHCR.

Do No Harm Project. 2004. *The Do No Harm handbook: The framework for analyzing the impact of assistance on conflict.* Cambridge, MA: Collaborative for Development Action and CDA Collaborative Learning Projects.

Duffield, M., K. Diagne, and V. Tennant. 2008. *Evaluation of UNHCR's returnee reintegration programme in Sudan.* Geneva, Switzerland: UNHCR.

Fitzpatrick, D. 2002. *Land policy in post-conflict circumstances: Some lessons from East Timor.* New Issues in Refugee Research, Working Paper #78, UNHCR.

Good Humanitarian Donorship. 2003, June 17. 23 principles and good practice of humanitarian donorship. Retrieved December 12, 2011, from www.goodhumanitarian donorship.org/gns/principles-good-practice-ghd/overview.aspx.

Goodhand, J. 2001. *Violent conflict, poverty, and chronic poverty*. Manchester, UK: Chronic Poverty Research Centre and Intrac.

Harvey, P., A. Stoddard, A. Harmer, K. Haver, and K. Taylor. 2012. *The state of the humanitarian system: Assessing performance and progress*. ALNAP. Retrieved October 30, 2012, from www.alnap.org/ourwork/current/sohs.aspx.

Harvey, P., A. Stoddard, A. Harmer, and G. Taylor. 2010. *The state of the humanitarian system: Assessing performance and progress*. London: ALNAP. Retrieved December 12, 2011, from www.alnap.org/pool/files/alnap-sohs-final.pdf.

Human Rights Watch. 2002. *Hidden in plain view: Refugees living without protection in Nairobi and Kampala*. New York: Human Rights Watch. Retrieved December 12, 2011, from www.hrw.org/reports/2002/kenyugan.

Humanitarian Practice Network. 1994, September 1. The upsurge of interest in the "relief-development continuum": What does it mean? *Humanitarian Exchange Magazine* 2: 8–10; www.odihpn.org/humanitarian-exchange-magazine/issue-02/the-upsurge-of -interest-in-the-relief-development-continuum-what-does-it-mean.

Izzi, V., and C. Kurz. 2009. *Etude sur la sensitivité aux conflits du Programme PEAR Plus*. Kinshasa, DRC: Search for Common Ground. Retrieved December 12, 2011, from www.alnap.org/pool/files/french-fullword-final.pdf.

Koddenbrock, K., and M. Büttner. 2009. The will to bridge? European Commission and U.S. approaches to linking relief, rehabilitation, and development. In J. Streets and D. S. Hamilton, eds. *Humanitarian assistance: Improving U.S.–European cooperation*. Washington, DC: Center for Transatlantic Relations, Johns Hopkins University/Global Public Policy Institute.

Lange, M., and M. Quinn. 2003. *Conflict, humanitarian assistance, and peacebuilding: Meeting the challenges*. London: International Alert; www.gsdrc.org/go/display&type =Document&id=1161.

Maslow, A. H. 1954. *Motivation and personality*. New York: Harper & Row.

Plaut, M. 2011, August 11. UN troops helped smuggle gold. *BBC News*. Retrieved December 12, 2011, from http://news.bbc.co.uk/2/hi/6941480.stm.

Telyukov, A., and M. Paterson. 2008. *Impact evaluation of PRM humanitarian assistance to the repatriation and reintegration of Burundi refugees*. Burundi: US Department of State. Retrieved from www.unhcr.org/refworld/docid/49ed70822.html.

UNICEF. 2003. *UNICEF's humanitarian principles*. New York: UNICEF.

Woodrow, P., and D. Chigas. 2009. *A distinction with a difference: Conflict sensitivity and peacebuilding*. Cambridge, MA: CDA Collaborative Learning Projects.

Zicherman, N., A. Khan, A. Street, H. Heyer, and O. Chevreau. 2011, October. Applying conflict sensitivity in emergency response. *HPN Network Paper 70*.

NOTES

1. The philosophical "humanitarian" concept of providing impartial assistance to civilians in wartime dates to the Enlightenment, with notions of the universality of humankind. The most recent Geneva Convention, of 1949, on the "Protection of Civilian Persons in Time of War" set out many of the principles that lay the foundation for modern humanitarian practice. From its creation, the United Nations gave itself a key role in overseeing

humanitarian affairs through its Third Committee on Social Cultural and Humanitarian Affairs at the General Assembly and through specialized agencies such as the UN High Commissioner for Refugees (UNHCR), the UN Children's Fund (UNICEF), and the World Food Program (WFP).

2. According to ALNAP (Harvey et. al, 2010), in 2008 the six largest international NGOs had a combined overseas operating budget of more than $4 billion, of which $1.7 billion went to humanitarian activities. The rest went to international development or other longer-term programs. Among them, these organizations—CARE, Catholic Relief Services (CRS), Médecins Sans Frontieres (MSF), Oxfam, Save the Children, and World Vision International—had more than 90,000 staff.

3. The UN Office of the Coordinator for Humanitarian Affairs maintains a real-time financial tracking system and interactive database of aid flows: http://fts.unocha.org.

4. The organization has since changed its name to CDA Collaborative Learning Projects; see www.cdainc.com.

5. For more info, see www.sphereproject.org.

6. These are: logistics, nutrition, shelter, camp management, health, protection, agriculture, telecoms, early recovery, education, and water and sanitation.

7. For example, the Darfur Peace Agreement in Sudan dedicated thirty-nine paragraphs to detailing the assistance and compensation to be given to displaced people, largely civilians perceived to be aligned with the rebel movements.

8. UNHCR outlined this policy for the German Foreign Ministry, writing, "The search for solutions has generally required UNHCR to promote . . . measures to establish conditions that would permit refugees to return safely and with dignity to their homes and to make a free and informed choice. Creating actual conditions for return, however, remains fundamentally a political process going well beyond the capacities of UNHCR. This process involves actors with different and often not necessarily converging interests"; "UNHCR Policy on Return to Burundi: List of Questions of the Ministry of Foreign Affairs of Germany"; www.unhcr.org/refworld/pdfid/3cd917cb4.pdf.

9. Agencies in the Conflict Sensitivity Consortium include ActionAid, CAFOD/Caritas, CARE, ENCISS, International Alert, Peace and Community Action Plan, Responding to Conflict, Saferworld, Save the Children, the Sierra Leone Red Cross, Skillshare International, SLANGO, and World Vision.

10. For more, see the Collaborative Development for Action, Reflecting on Peace Project, www.cdainc.com.

11. This and a number of the following examples come from programs on which the author worked or has direct knowledge. The names of the organizations involved have been edited out for confidentiality purposes.

12. Story is from the author's consultations with national NGOs in Niamey, Niger, December 2011.

13. Pareto-efficiency, named after Italian economist Vilfredo Pareto, refers to a relationship where the joint gain of both parties has been maximized, beyond which it is impossible to further increase the benefit to one party, except by disadvantaging the other.

chapter five

GENDER AND PEACEBUILDING

Evelyn Thornton and Tobie Whitman

*If you're hungry, keep walking. If you are thirsty, keep walking. If
you want a taste of freedom, keep walking. . . . We will keep walking
until peace, justice and the rights of women is not a dream, but is a
thing of the present.*

—2011 Nobel Peace Prize winner Leymah Gbowee's acceptance
speech for the John F. Kennedy Profile in Courage Award

Overview

THIS CHAPTER FOCUSES ON WOMEN'S contributions to integrated peacebuilding, as for most of the twentieth century, women and issues of gender
have been ignored or marginalized rather than mainstreamed.[1] Efforts at "gender
mainstreaming," ensuring that the different needs of women and men are taken
into account in all peacebuilding policies and interventions, have largely failed.
Practitioners have missed innumerable opportunities for peacebuilding and creating
sustainable peace (Reimann, 1999). According to Ambassador Donald Steinberg
(2007), who participated in negotiations to end the Angolan civil war, "A peace agreement that is gender neutral is, by definition, discriminatory against women and thus
far less likely to be successful." Yet women remain in the minority in formal peace
efforts, and gender analysis rarely informs initiatives. In the past two decades, women
comprised fewer than 8 percent of participants in more than a dozen key negotiations; and in the nearly six hundred agreements in that same period, only 16 percent
mentioned women or gender at all (UNIFEM, 2009a).

"Gender," the historical and societal construction of role differences between men and women, permeates all social institutions and practices. Socially constructed gender hierarchies create power asymmetries that normally place women at a disadvantage and may lead to conflict. Peacebuilding can change power dynamics into constructive relationships (Sampson et al., 2003), making attention to gender in peacebuilding essential (Tickner, 1992).[2] Including women and applying a gender lens are part of a broader transformation of social power relations toward positive peace.[3]

Studies are beginning to highlight the multiple and complex roles women play during conflict and the disproportionate burden they bear during war (Bouta and Frerks, 2002; Moser and Clark, 2001). Research shows that women suffer more and die in proportionally greater numbers than men from human rights abuses and sexual violence, the breakdown of social order, the lack of medical care, and the consequences of economic devastation (Kuehnast, de Jonge Oudraat, and Hernes, 2011, p. 7). As a result, conflict often redefines traditional roles and reconfigures gender relations. Women assume traditionally male roles, such as serving as the de facto head of household when men leave to fight, which creates opportunities for improved social equality that can help eliminate drivers of conflict (Kumar, 2001).

Women are often at the forefront of local peacebuilding initiatives. According to Johnson Sirleaf and Rehn (2002), "Women's leadership role is most visible in their communities; it is here that they organize to end conflict and build the skills necessary for peacebuilding and reconstruction" (p. 76). Women often act as nurturers in families and communities, and thereby play crucial roles in peacebuilding, typically in informal, unofficial capacity (Porter, 2007). Their marginalized status in many societies can provide them with a unique vantage point for conceptualizing conflict drivers and proposing approaches for reconciliation. For example, during negotiations in El Salvador over the reintegration of fighters, women leaders and negotiators of the Farabundo Marti National Liberation Front (FMLN) were critical in ensuring that programs included not only fighters but also men and women who had provided the FMLN support as cooks, as porters, and in other noncombat roles (Conway and Martinez, 2004).

Some researchers argue women have qualities (either biological or socially constructed) that uniquely equip them to address conflict, while others contend that women's alleged peacefulness results from their exclusion from power—that it is the outcome of their dependent and subordinate role in hierarchical gender relations (Ehrenreich, 1999; Fukuyama, 1998; Jaquette, 1999).[4] Causes aside, qualitative evidence indicates that women shape both the substance and process of reducing and transforming conflict. Women can help prevent conflict by identifying different early warning signals than men. For example, women often notice indicators such as an influx of weapons in a community, refugee migration, rapes, abductions, trafficking, hoarding of goods, rewards for "masculine" behavior related to the conflict, and increased propaganda before a conflict even begins (Makumi and Okello, 2006). When present in peace negotiations, women can broaden the set of issues addressed and expand debates beyond military action, power, and wealth-sharing to incorporate social and humanitarian matters (O'Neill and Vary, 2011). Research finds that peace processes with significant female involvement are more legitimate and sustainable compared to those with little or no participation from women (Potter, 2008).

Demands for women's participation in addressing conflict and mainstreaming gender grew in the period following the Cold War. During the 1990s, violent conflict took on a different and distinct character. Pankhurst (2007) writes that a key feature of these "new wars" is the lack of separation between the "war front" and the "home front" and that the increased vulnerability of civilians has become commonplace. It is widely cited that between 80 percent and 90 percent of twentieth-century war victims have been civilian.[5] Through the merging of the public and private spheres during conflict, women became visible as both victims of violence and as powerful agents of peacebuilding. This changed nature of conflict, along with recent civil society activism, has generated powerful momentum for women's participation in peace and security. Additionally, long-standing interest in gender mainstreaming within the development community has paved the way for peacebuilding organizations inclined to incorporate gender.

This chapter addresses the following topics:

- Key theories relevant to gender mainstreaming and women's inclusion in peacebuilding
- Skills and challenges for practitioners
- Current policy innovations
- Women's participation in different conflict contexts

Rather than examine the unique experiences of both men and women in integrated peacebuilding, this chapter focuses on women's participation.[6] Women's contributions to peacebuilding usually are ad hoc and rarely part of formal processes; thus decision makers around the world fail to maximize the conditions in which sustainable peace might take root. As noted above and in the sections that follow, activists and peacebuilders have made progress in changing the paradigm and increasing women's involvement. However, much work remains.

GENDER AND INTEGRATED PEACEBUILDING THEORIES

The growing field of women, peace, and security studies draws from a variety of disciplines and discourses, including political science, international relations, and sociology, but has no single home within academia. Most experts contend that theories on gender and the value of equitable participation linger at the margins of their respective disciplines.[7]

International Relations and Feminism

Arguments for women's inclusion and gender awareness in peacebuilding pull from feminist international relations discourse, which exposes the power dynamics and gendered assumptions of traditional state structures and mechanisms (Tickner, 1992). As Willett (2010) contends, "Gender hierarchies are socially constructed, and maintained, through power structures that work against women's participation in foreign and national security policymaking" (p. 145). Many theorists contend that unless societies reconcile unequal power relations between men and women, insecurities and violent conflict will persist. These perspectives provide a foundation for advocates who emphasize women's rights, and those who accentuate the positive outcomes of women's participation.

Women's Rights

Discourse on women in peace and security can be divided between arguments that stress women's right to participate, versus those that emphasize the impact and outcome of their participation. Put another way is Harders's (2011) question, "Should feminist peace politics be based on universal human rights or on politics of difference?" (p. 138).

Women's rights is the dominant subject within the movement for increasing inclusion and is often promoted under the larger umbrella of human rights. These rights-based arguments focus on advancing states' legal obligations to protect individuals. Supporters contend that these arguments are the most secure means of ensuring women's participation and freedom from oppression. As Anderlini and el-Bushra (2004) describe, "While women's human rights violations do not always involve state actors, in most cases, the state has either condoned existing practices, allowed the passage of discriminatory laws or instigated policies and programs that are inherently discriminatory again women" (p. 12).

This discourse draws from a host of international legal instruments, beginning with the 1948 Universal Declaration of Human Rights. In 1979, the Convention on the Elimination of Discrimination Against Women (CEDAW) emerged as a quasi-international bill of rights for women. By 2011, 186 countries had ratified it; controversially, the US is not a signatory. Women further garnered momentum around the 1995 Fourth World Conference on Women in Beijing. The conference's "Platform for Action" identified twelve critical areas of concern that remain obstacles to women's advancement. These areas include armed conflict, and power and decision-making, two factors that influence women's contributions to peacebuilding. While the Beijing Platform for Action and CEDAW address women's inequality across sectors, UN Security Council Resolution (UNSCR) 1325 specifically emphasizes women's right to participate in peace and security processes.

Human Security

The concept of "human security" also focuses on the primacy of the individual. Developed in 1994 by the UN Development Programme (UNDP) and later advanced by former Canadian foreign minister Lloyd Axworthy and UN Secretary-General Kofi Annan, the notion of human security challenges Cold War traditions of state-focused security (UNDP, 1994). Human security is created when individuals have "freedom from fear" and "freedom from want." In this paradigm, ameliorating insecurity requires increasing commitment to human and women's rights, rather than state or military security.

Diverse actors, from UN officials to theorists to female activists, have embraced the human security paradigm. If human security is the sum of all individuals' security, then women's security is essential. This discourse also resonates with advocates for women's inclusion because security issues addressed within the framework are often priorities for women, such as poverty and health (Anderlini, 2007). Yet, despite the growth in subnational actors, the international system and formal peace processes are still largely the domains of the state. The human security agenda is greatly challenged by the realpolitik of global relations (Baines, 2005). Additionally, while the linkages may appear obvious, human security approaches do not guarantee a gendered approach (Sarosi, 2007) and can be difficult to put into practice.

Democracy

As women's rights and human security activists focus on the right of the individual, some theorists make a case for women's inclusion based on the interests of the democratic state. The lack of participation and representation of women constitutes a democratic deficit (Harders, 2011). Additionally, liberal governments cannot tolerate excessive threats to women's well-being; as Harders (2011) explains, "No democratic state can accept high levels of individual or collective violence against some groups in that society" (p. 132). Implicit is that representatives of these communities will be advocates for the interests of their group. However, as discussed later in this chapter, this does not always transpire given the complexity of identity politics.

Conflict Transformation

Conflict transformation theorists are natural allies of those advocating for a gendered approach to addressing conflict. Conflict transformation is, according to Miall (2004), "a process of engaging with and transforming the relationships, interests, discourses, and, if necessary, the very constitution of society that supports the continuation of violent conflict" (p. 4); therefore, unjust gender relations need to be rearticulated to create positive peace. As Harders (2011) notes, "Even though it is quite possible to make formal peace without including women and looking at gender relations, the transformation of violent conflict is impossible without these gendered lenses" (p. 132).

Much of women's peace activism fits into this discourse and its assertion that multiple actors from a cross section of society, nationally and internationally, are needed to bring peace (Baksh-Sodeen, 2005; Francis, 2004). Theories that emphasize the importance of informal and multitrack peacebuilding and grassroots participation complement discourse on increasing attention to women and conflict (Lederach, 1997; Fischer, 2011). Marginalized groups, including women (e.g., youth, ethnic groups), draw from the discourse of inclusion to argue that underlying conflict drivers will be ameliorated by bringing their concerns into mainstream dialogue.

While the conflict transformation framework allows for incorporating women and attention to gender, it by no means guarantees their inclusion. Even as the fields of human security and conflict transformation claim to promote inclusivity and participation, there is still a tendency for women to be rendered invisible (Anderlini, 2007). For advocates of women's inclusion, gender must be front and center in all activities.

Inclusive Security

A subset of practitioners and thinkers argues for women's participation using evidence that women's direct involvement can transform the structures, methods, and outcomes of peace processes. Conflict prevention, negotiated agreements, nascent political structures, and reconstruction plans that are shaped by women's contributions better reflect broad social priorities and more public support. According to Hunt and Posa (2001), the concept of "inclusive security" is "a diverse citizen-driven approach to global stability, that emphasizes women's agency, not their vulnerability." The approach is "driven by efficiency. Women are crucial to inclusive security since they are often at the center of nongovernmental organizations, popular protests, electoral referendums, and other citizen-empowered movements whose influence has grown with the global spread of democracy" (p. 38).

This perspective draws on specific examples of women's participation providing tangible dividends for peace and security. For example, during talks between the Lord's Resistance Army and the government of Uganda from 2006 to 2008, women negotiators and civil society observers urged the parties to prioritize health and education for ex-combatants. They also expanded the definition of "cease-fire" to include the cessation of gender-based violence committed by combatants (Page, Whitman, and Anderson, 2009). Women in Northern Ireland in the 1990s led demands for the creation of a civic forum in which representatives of civil society organizations could provide input into Good Friday Agreement negotiations and stay updated on the process (Kilmurray and McWilliams, 2011). The agreement ultimately included references to achieving women's full political participation, provisions for the support of integrated education and mixed housing, and recognition of the rights of victims in the conflict (Page et al., 2009).

However, critics contend that by framing women as untapped resources, advocates risk creating unrealistic expectations that women's participation is the silver-bullet solution to each and every issue, no matter how difficult the circumstances (Sarosi, 2007). Additionally, as evidence to date is largely based on case-study inquiry, there is a need for macro-level assessment akin to the work of Wanis St. John and Kew (2008). After surveying a wide variety of peace processes, Wanis St. John and Kew identified a strong correlation between active civil society participation in negotiations and the durability of peace. The insufficient number of processes that have significantly involved women has prevented such quantitative studies of women's influence to date.

The aforementioned discourses are not necessarily mutually exclusive. Advocates for women's inclusion in peacebuilding may draw from various concepts to make their case. Despite the shared vision of more equitable participation for women, in practice these theories have implications for the prioritization of programs and policies, which modes of advocacy are employed, and which institutions are considered leverage points for change.

GENDER AND INTEGRATED PEACEBUILDING POLICIES/PRACTICE

A variety of skills and knowledge is required to mainstream gender and effectively promote women's participation in formal and informal peacebuilding processes.

Key Skills

Performing a gender-sensitive conflict analysis is the first step in designing peacebuilding initiatives that promote gender equality. Gender-neutral conflict analyses are by definition gender blind and can maintain entrenched power relations. Gender analysis can clarify the potential differential impact of external interventions on men and women. Comprehensive situational analyses can help identify the most important gender issues in conflict-affected communities, and therefore illuminate the most appropriate programmatic approaches. One method for situational analysis, used by the Office of the UN High Commissioner for Refugees, is People Oriented Planning (POP). POP uses simple matrices to diagram the evolution of gender roles in a community as a result of conflict or displacement. According to the US Agency for International Development (USAID, 2007), using such analytical techniques to understand local gender dynamics helps make interventions compatible with cultural norms. Practitioners need more planning instruments and methodologies that combine gender and conflict analysis (Bouta and Frerks, 2002).

While a solid understanding of gender is important, content expertise on topics within peace and security issues (e.g., technical knowledge of power sharing or disarmament, demobilization and reintegration) is critical. Practitioners with knowledge of specific topics as well as gender perspectives often are perceived as more credible than those with only the latter. Buchanan (2011), a woman peacebuilder from Nepal, explains that "having been a negotiator in a peace process, I recall being reluctant to bring out gender issues to avoid being marginalized. I thought, 'I am going to get known as "that gender person" and no one will listen to me.' So I developed expertise in other areas of peace processes and established my credibility in ceasefires which then enabled me to bring gender issues up across the board" (p. 8). Practitioners should develop content expertise in which to apply skills related to gender and women's inclusion.

Specific plans for outreach to women are paramount when designing an effective intervention. Practitioners can start by identifying and contacting the leadership of women's organizations in the area of planned engagement. Speaking with organizations and field staff about key individuals and locations where women congregate can provide a starting place. Often a female interpreter with knowledge of local culture and mores is helpful. Particularly in areas with high levels of illiteracy, word of mouth as well as radio messages can help mobilize both male and female participants.

Patience is essential to any outreach plan. Women are often pulled in many directions with diverse responsibilities in the home and the public sphere. They typically have household and child-care responsibilities, making time for seminars, workshops, and consultations difficult to find. Additionally, women with children may be unable to leave home for extended periods, particularly for residential trainings (Buchanan, 2011; Page et al., 2009). Some women may be unaccustomed to being asked for their opinions and may be confused or skeptical about a peacebuilding intervention. The personal toll of violence on the lives of women may make them reluctant to relive painful memories and may similarly dissuade them from participating. Threat of direct personal violence may also discourage women from getting involved. Yet program implementers can and should overcome these obstacles, as well as identify and collaborate with male allies.

Practitioners should also be aware of the threat of backlash. This can occur either because men feel that program implementers have disregarded their cultural mores or because they are envious of the direct support women are receiving. USAID (2007) notes that international agencies have not given adequate attention to this phenomenon. Involving men in the design and/or delivery of programming may be required and prudent for long-term impact.

Practitioners must use creativity and curiosity to identify and address the practical obstacles women face to participate in peacebuilding interventions. Consulting with women about how to encourage their participation in a practical manner is essential. For example, the UN-held consultations with women in the Democratic Republic of the Congo took into account their safety concerns about traveling in the evening; therefore, meetings were scheduled for the mornings. The women also felt most secure in an all-female environment, resulting in the exclusive use of female translators (Whitman, 2010). Had the UN not inquired about what was most practical, women's voices would have remained unheard in these local stabilization efforts.

Practitioners may need additional resources to facilitate women's participation. For example, providing appropriate security is crucial. As cited by Buchanan (2011), one female peacebuilder notes, "When I was negotiating in Aceh, my safety was under threat. This needs to be better addressed by mediators and third parties. If I had been living in Aceh at the time, I would have thought twice about joining the talks because of my family's safety" (p. 13).

Not every practitioner will be able to focus entirely on gender and women. Yet easy adaptations can be made to peace and security programming already under way. Practitioners may have to make extra efforts to ensure women's inclusion in mixed events at every level. Francis (2007) explains that a little bit of energy can ensure that women participate, such as "care by facilitators to encourage them to speak in plenary; chances to work in groups with other women if they want to; challenging male 'put-downs' and so on" (p. 10). While not a prerequisite, the presence of women facilitators can be important, both as role models and for psychological support.

While strong communication skills are generally critical to the practitioner's success, they are even more essential for those interested in working with women and on gender issues. A skilled ability to communicate effectively is beneficial for practitioners managing challenging emotional moments during peacebuilding activities. Those skills also help when implementers are defending the value of women's involvement to skeptics who might say, "We'll deal with the big issues first, then we'll get to the women" (Benard et al., 2008, p. 2). Working on women's inclusion often turns the practitioner her-/himself into a quasi advocate.

Impacting Policy/Systematic Change

Arguably the greatest catalytic policy instrument to advance women's participation in peacebuilding was the groundbreaking UNSCR 1325 (2000). The resolution provides a global framework for mainstreaming gender in all peace processes, including peacekeeping, peacebuilding, and postconflict reconstruction. UNSCR 1325 is simultaneously a demand for women's inclusion, a call for broader representation in peacebuilding, and an articulation that conflict prevention and resolution are integral to establishing human security in a post–Cold War world.

The UN Security Council (UNSC) supplemented this resolution with four others that strengthen and expand its provisions and secure implementation. The five resolutions together compose the women, peace, and security–themed agenda of the UNSC and have been part of creating a new normative framework within peace and security discourse (Tryggestad, 2010). Resolutions 1820, 1888, 1889, and 1960 specifically advance provisions for addressing sexual violence, as well as strengthen monitoring and reporting on UNSCR 1325 implementation, notably through reference to a set of performance-monitoring indicators. Twenty-six indicators launched in October 2010, the result of a comprehensive consultation process, will help to measure UN member states' execution of commitments to increase women's participation in peacebuilding, though data won't be generated for at least five years (UNSC, 2010).

UNSCR 1325 and its follow-on resolutions compose an internationally recognized legal framework. These tools are used worldwide to raise awareness about women's experiences of conflict as well as hold local authorities and governments accountable, including through civil society monitoring of commitments (Anderlini and Tirman, 2010). However, skeptics argue that because UNSCR 1325 was passed under Chapter VI of the UN Charter (not Chapter VII), the resolution is merely window dressing (Tryggestad, 2009); Chapter VII is the only manner through which the UN could invoke coercive enforcement and penalties for noncompliance.[8] Overall, according to Willett (2010), "implementation of 1325 has been erratic. . . . There has been a general lack of operational coherence for implementing the UN's 1325 commitments" (p. 142).

Though initially slow to act, many UN member states and regional institutions have or are developing plans to implement UNSCR 1325 in addition to broader gender-equality initiatives.[9] While national action plans (NAPs) have become the accepted modality of illustrating commitment to UNSCR 1325 implementation, their quality varies greatly. According to one assessment by the European Peacebuilding Liaison Office (2010), many NAPs "lack key elements that help ensure action, such as specific and realistic goals, objectives, and priority actions; clear timelines; a dedicated budget; indicators, benchmarks, and targets; clear lines of responsibility . . . and results-oriented and transparent monitoring and evaluation mechanisms" (p. 6). Dharmapuri (2011) explains that the top three troop-contributing countries to UN peacekeeping operations—India, Pakistan, and Bangladesh—do not have NAPs.

Just as many in the peace and security fields have acknowledged the critical role of women in advancing sustainable peace, so too has the development community identified the intersection of women, conflict, and sustainable development. For example, in 2007 UNDP endorsed an "Eight Point Agenda" to empower and protect women in crisis situations.[10] The development community has also been at the forefront of efforts to implement sex-disaggregated data collection, as well as monitoring and evaluation.

Gender mainstreaming is a key policy innovation for increasing women's inclusion in peacebuilding as well as in development initiatives. It aims to ensure that the different needs of women and men are taken into account in all policies, strategies, and interventions, both internal and external, to promote gender equality.[11] Coined as a concept in the early 1970s, gender mainstreaming has since been considered an appropriate method to advance gender equality in the international arena. Embraced initially by development practitioners, the peacebuilding community is starting to follow their early lead.[12]

In defining mainstreaming, it is helpful to identify what it is not. As Charlesworth (2005) writes, "The force of the term derives from its implied contrast with the notion of specializing in issues of gender, or what might be called 'gender sidestreaming.' The idea behind gender mainstreaming is that questions of gender must be taken seriously in central, mainstream, 'normal' institutional activities and not simply left in a marginalized peripheral backwater of peripheral women's institutions" (p. 1).

A variety of international and regional institutions, in addition to national agencies, have created gender-mainstreaming policies. The European Union was an early adopter of gender mainstreaming, particularly in regard to employment, as evidenced by the 1997 Treaty of Amsterdam. The Organization of American States was at the forefront of gender equality promotion, having begun work in the late 1990s to transform member states' political cultures and increase linkages between high-level officials and women peacebuilders. In July 2004, the African Union (AU) adopted the Solemn Declaration on Gender Equality in Africa after extensive collaboration with civil society organizations and government representatives, following the 2003 acceptance of the "Parity Principle," which ensures an equal number of male and female commissioners on its high-level secretariat. Additionally, many country-level foreign assistance agencies have gender-mainstreaming policies, such as the highly regarded British government's Department for International Development's policy (Watkins, 2004). As of 2010, "gender equality" had become one of the six core principles for aid effectiveness for US programs, as advanced in the State Department's Quadrennial Diplomacy and Development Review. Sex-disaggregated baseline data is a new component of all of USAID's project evaluations (Jalan, 2011), and a new 2012 gender equality policy frames gender as a strategic concern across the agency's programming.

A key component of gender mainstreaming includes gender budgeting or gender-responsive budgeting (GRB). Without specific allocation and tracking of funds related to gender, no mainstreaming policy can be successful. GRB seeks to ensure that the collection and allocation of public resources are effective and contribute to advancing gender equality and women's empowerment. At present, such spending levels are extremely low. For example, the UN Development Fund for Women (UNIFEM) analyzed five Poverty Reduction Strategy Papers of countries on the Security Council agenda in 2009. UNIFEM (2010b) found the inclusion of women's needs and issues was extremely scarce at the budget level, less than 2 percent.

Gender mainstreaming has been challenged by both a lack of clarity about what such an approach entails and the belief that gender mainstreaming is typically exclusively about women. The interchangeable usage of "gender" and "women" has therefore brought confusion as well as frustration. As Anderlini (2007) writes, "This conflation and expansion of terms has turned what should be obvious and fundamentally good practice into a seemingly incomprehensible set of issues. In practice, it has created confusion across institutions and has often gotten lost in translation across languages and cultures" (p. 201). Additionally, some claim that the concept detracts attention from the ways that inequalities are woven into the international system and that mainstreaming has drowned out the project of equality between women and men (Charlesworth, 2005; Willett, 2010).

Many organizations have attempted to successfully mainstream gender but lack the knowledge, capacity, and resources to implement effectively. Often a single office or individual will be tasked with redesigning internal and external systems for a whole organization. Instead of overhauling systems, a "gender focal point" will be a point person for one-off trainings and projects. Funds are often lacking and there is little institutional buy-in across departments. While the integration of gender into programming saw some successes, over time it was found to be insufficient in addressing the enormous challenges facing women. Thus, alongside mainstreaming exists specific gender programs. But creating stand-alone programming led many to see gender as a marginal or women's-only issue, and not as something central to all development work (Tiessen, 2007; UNDP, 2006). Over time, gender programming has expanded to include both stand-alone programming designed to advance opportunities for women and girls, and gender-sensitive mainstreaming that seeks to infuse a gender perspective into all aspects of development programming. Overall, neither the mainstreaming efforts nor the stand-alone programs have produced the gender equality they aim to achieve.

Key Policy Debates

One of the most significant policy debates related to women and peacebuilding is how to increase accountability for UNSCR 1325 implementation and ensure gender mainstreaming in peacebuilding. While the growing number of policies and NAPs is encouraging, without concrete changes in women's experience, they are simply words on paper. The most recent UNSC women, peace, and security resolutions mention sanctions against states for not enforcing aspects of the policies related to sexual violence. They are a step in the right direction, but true widespread implementation will be difficult to achieve given the large numbers of committed actors required to initiate change.

The use of quotas to encourage women's participation in peacebuilding is often mentioned in policy debates. Many who support their use recognize that quotas are simply one part of a complex equation to achieve lasting change. As Johnson Sirleaf and Rehn (2002) write, "We recognize that especially when numbers are small and cultural barriers enormous, quotas can only put women in power; they cannot guarantee that grassroots concerns will be addressed. . . . Certainly quotas alone cannot guarantee the emergence of a 'gender perspective' in the political process" (p. 181). Johnson Sirleaf and Rehn also contend, however, that individuals are more likely to develop gender awareness when a critical mass of women presides in decision-making positions.

The idea of a critical mass of women, that women exhibit styles of leadership and priorities different from those of men only when they achieve a certain proportion in an institution, has its roots in the late 1970s but picked up momentum a decade later.[13] Most supporters contend that critical mass is achieved at around 30 percent, a challenging target to achieve without relying on quotas (Wilber, 2011). For example, a constitutional provision establishing a 30 percent quota for women in all "decision-making organs" in Rwanda led women to make up 56 percent of the parliament in 2008 elections—the highest percentage in the world (Powley, 2008).[14]

Activists are often divided over whether to seek a "critical mass" of 30 percent female representation or an equal 50 percent presentation of men and women. Additionally, some skeptics argue that the long-term effect of quotas is unknown. They cite evidence suggesting that institutions, such as parliaments, do not notably evolve with a significant proportion of women (Neiva, 2008).

Many women themselves attest to the need for gender-sensitive processes and structures to complement female representation. As Buchanan (2011) writes, "The pressure to conform to the 'norm' . . . can be very strong, particularly when women are alone or few. For example, Shadia Marhaban, the only woman involved in the 2005 Aceh peace talks, cast doubt on the impact of her own presence. Women who have had this experience recall 'we had to fit into the process as men not as women'" (p. 11). The solution requires not simply including women but also creating an environment that enables new paradigms to develop: the two approaches together are essential.

Impact

Since the passage of UNSCR 1325 and subsequent resolutions, the women and peacebuilding movement has seen signs of success. As mentioned earlier, a growing number of NAPs and revisions to NAPs are being launched and implemented. Of the thirty-four NAPs that exist in 2012, 70 percent of these were created in the past three years. More accountability mechanisms, such as the UNSCR 1325 indicators, monitor implementation. Additionally, more multilateral organizations and government agencies have developed gender mainstreaming policies and structures by dedicating funding and staff to this effort. The Organisation for Economic Co-operation and Development reports that in 2009 donor nations and multilateral organizations dispersed $684 million in overseas development assistance with the objective of "gender and participatory development" within conflict, peace, and security programs; only $119 million was provided in 2006.[15] Reporting related to women and peacebuilding has also increased and been mainstreamed. For example, in 2010 90 percent of reports submitted to the UNSC from UN peacekeeping missions included coverage of women, peace, and security issues (UNSC, 2011). The many assessments of the field attest to the marked increase of actors focused on women in peacebuilding, which presents a refreshing challenge of coordination rather than scarcity. In 2011, three women leaders—President Ellen Johnson Sirleaf, Leymah Gbowee, and Tawakkul Karman—received the Nobel Peace Prize for their "non-violent struggle for the safety of women" and "women's rights to full participation in peace-building work" (Nobel, 2011). In bestowing this award, the Nobel Committee shined a light on the essential work women performed in preventing and ending war.

Despite the advancements women have made, many indicators reveal setbacks and ongoing challenges. While there have been peace negotiations with some representation of women and reference to gender-sensitive provisions since the passage of UNSCR 1325, most have not included women. According to the UN, since the passage of UNSCR 1325 there has been "little appreciable increase" in the number of women negotiators in peace processes, and no women have been appointed chief or lead peace mediators in UN-sponsored peace talks (UNIFEM, 2009a). Women are still advocating for a place in the Afghan peace process, fighting against rampant sexual violence in the Democratic Republic of the Congo, and waiting to see if the "Arab Spring" will offer new opportunities for participation.

The reality is many in the movement do not agree on how to define success. How will we know when gender has been effectively and consistently mainstreamed? Does success in the movement rise and fall with the percentage of women negotiators around the peace table? If so, what should that number be? For many, success is less quantifiable and related more to changes in the daily life of women in conflict-affected areas than to a tiny proportion of women involved in high-level peace processes. Even more challenging is incorporating the views of those focused not only on women's participation but also on creating fewer violent conflicts. If more women sit around the table but more wars occurs, is this success for the women-in-peacebuilding agenda? Additionally, what is the time frame for success? Does change need to happen immediately or can transformation take a generation? The movement has advanced considerably, but further progress is stymied by conflicting visions of success.

PROFILE OF A PRACTITIONER

For more than two decades, conflict in Sri Lanka has been "destroying our country and destroying our people," says Visaka Dharmadasa, a peace activist from the city of Kandy. Her son, a soldier in the Sri Lankan military, went missing after Tamil Tigers attacked a military base in 1998. The thought of her twenty-one-year-old son missing in action continues to trouble Dharmadasa today. "If you know your son is dead, you can at least mourn him," she says. "But now, for me, the issue is eternally pending."[16]

Dharmadasa designed and facilitated Track II dialogue processes, bringing together influential civil society leaders to work toward ending the civil war that gripped Sri Lanka for more than twenty-five years. When talks were foundering and leaders of the Liberation Tigers of Tamil Elam refused to speak with members of the Sri Lankan government and Norwegian negotiators, they asked Dharmadasa, founder of the Association of War-Affected Women and Parents of Servicemen Missing in Action (AWAW), to carry messages to the government. In January 2004, Dharmadasa wrote an analysis on the unraveling of the current peace efforts, which she presented to Yasushi Akashi, Japanese special envoy for the Sri Lankan peace process.

Although the Tamil Tigers were defeated in early 2009, the AWAW continues to work for peace by bringing communities together by providing peacebuilding training for women and assisting those affected by the 2004 tsunami. Recognizing that Sri Lankan women were still poorly represented in government—they hold only 5.9 percent of the seats in parliament and few senior government positions—in 2009 AWAW initiated a campaign to make the promise of UNSCR 1325 a reality. As Dharmadasa says, "You can't just say, 'Include women, include women.' You have to show the capacities of women." With this in mind, AWAW trained twenty-five women leaders on how to enable and encourage women to run for political office, through "Team 1325." So far, AWAW and Team 1325 have trained 1,250 women, with plans to train 375 more from across Sri Lanka.

Case Study: Guatemala

Throughout the 1970s and 1980s, the Guatemalan government and guerrilla groups waged a brutal civil war that victimized hundreds of thousands of civilians—particularly women and indigenous communities. With UN support, in 1991 the government began negotiations with the insurgent group, the Guatemalan National Revolutionary Unity, which led to a permanent cease-fire in 1996. To broaden participation in the negotiations, in 1994 the Assembly of Civil Society (ACS) brought together eleven interest groups, such as political parties, unions, indigenous groups, NGOs, and women's organizations. Although ACS did not have a formal seat at the table, many of the group's proposals were adopted in the final peace agreement.[17]

Women in particular played an important role in influencing the peace talks through the ACS. While only two women formerly participated in the negotiations, women's organizations and women civil society leaders largely shaped the ACS's agenda. The women's sector included representatives from thirty-two women's groups, which created alliances with women from other ACS sectors and from different political and ethnic backgrounds. Women successfully convinced negotiators to promote gender equality; almost half of the official accords included language calling for the recognition and protection of women's rights. The official accords acknowledged women's equal access to opportunity, including education, justice, health services, and political participation. The final settlement institutionalized women's role in implementing the actual agreements.

Not only did women ensure that gender-sensitive proposals were presented at the table, but they also pushed for the inclusion of marginalized sectors, such as displaced populations, in the Assembly. By working across divides and advocating for broader inclusion, women civil society leaders helped unify the ACS and mainstream an agenda that represented diverse groups' voices. Luz Mendez, the only woman negotiator for the Guatemalan National Revolutionary Unity, also helped ensure the peace agreement reflected women's concerns. Unfortunately, despite the gains made at the negotiating table in the 1990s, Guatemalan women today endure high rates of gender-based violence (Blanco and Hayes, 2007).

Case Study: Kenya

The Kenya National Dialogue and Reconciliation (KNDR) sought to resolve the violent dispute over the results of Kenya's presidential elections in December 2007. Under the auspices of Kofi Annan and the African Union Panel of Eminent African

Personalities, a power-sharing agreement brought an end to the violence, and a mediation process generated a series of agreements addressing the roots of the conflict. While the representation of women was notable, the agreement was not gender sensitive. The example illustrates the complex relationship between women's participation and gender equality.[18]

Relative to other formal negotiations, the KNDR process included a significant number of women. One in four of the members of each negotiating team was female, and women comprised a handful of senior advisers and technical staff. Graça Machel, long-time humanitarian, wife of Nelson Mandela, and former First Lady of Mozambique, was one of three eminent people on the panel. Two important factors helped promote women's concerns during the dialogue. First, the presence of Machel—whose seniority and long history with women's issues meant that she possessed the skills necessary to identify matters of enough importance and stature to advance the issues—was critical. Machel also helped build a coalition of women's civil society organizations previously divided by party affiliation and ethnic tensions, leading to a memorandum to the panel recommending UNSCR 1325 implementation and other constitutional reforms. Second, civil society mobilized to convene consultations with local women and then presented their priorities to the mediation team.

While the Kenyan process exemplifies the inclusion of women in mediation processes, it also illustrates how a focus only on numbers does not guarantee an inclusive and gender-sensitive agreement. While women were members of each negotiation delegation, they were appointed based on negotiating ability and party loyalty, and not because they were committed to gender equality and women's inclusion. As McGhie and Njoki Wamai (2011) explain, "Lessons should be drawn that political representation of women, while necessary, is not sufficient. Ensuring some form of participation by representatives who are specifically tasked and qualified to represent and advise on issues of women and gender within the peace process is also required at the mediation table" (p. 20). Because those involved in the mediation process lacked gender expertise, the process failed to turn broad recommendations by women in civil society into gender-responsive language in the agreement. Continued divisions within the women's movement, civil society's inability to engage on technical issues, and the panel's lack of a clear mandate to engage women formally restricted women's influence.

CHALLENGES IN THE FIELD

Women, peace, and security practitioners and theorists frequently wrestle with several unresolved questions and ethical challenges in their work. For example, advocates often have to respond to assertions that women's rights are a Western rather than a universal notion. Women activists in traditional societies may place themselves in physical harm. Some ask, "Who are we to impose our ideals on these societies, when our Western societies are not perfectly gender equal?" Policies and programs imposed without local support and interest, they say, are doomed to fail.

Many skeptics, however, are often unaware of the extent of women's historical involvement in society and politics. Arguments about what is "culturally appropriate" incorrectly assume culture is static rather than fluid. Moreover, women in traditional conflict-affected areas frequently are eager to have the space created for them to choose what works best in their community. As explained by Jacqueline O'Neill, director of the Institute for Inclusive Security (2010), "I have never encountered a culture in which women don't want at least the option to influence what happens to her, her family, or her community" (p. 4).

That is not to say that practitioners should take threats to physical security lightly. Intimidation and fear of violence can dissuade women's participation. From Afghan parliamentary candidates to Guatemalan female negotiators, the threat of violence can deter women from attempting to participate in peace and security processes. Practitioners must recognize the danger many female peacebuilders face and the risks they take by engaging in peacebuilding. They must respect the courage many women exhibit and develop the appropriate skills to handle difficult situations. Interveners can play a role in ensuring women understand the risks and provide them with the knowledge to decide whether to proceed.

Practitioners have another unresolved question to consider: How do they balance gender with other identity characteristics? Gender is often seen as more defining than other characteristics, such as race, class, and clan. According to Baines (2005), when activists call for "women to be brought to peace tables, we might well ask, 'which women?'" (p. 8). Those categories (and relationships among categories) are as important, if not more important, when it comes to inclusive representation. Women's views about a given conflict are never monolithic. That said, alongside difference lies great similarity among women's priorities for peacebuilding. The opportunity, and challenge, is harnessing the power of the similarities while recognizing, respecting, and integrating divergent experiences and perspectives. This often requires a greater degree of consultation with women built into the mediation process to draw out these diverse views.

Part of recognizing the heterogeneity of women's perspectives is accepting the vexing reality that not all women are advocates for women's inclusion, nor are they gender sensitive. Increasing women's involvement does not immediately or necessarily lead to peace processes' adequately addressing gender. Specific gender expertise, in addition to women's participation, is essential to create meaningful change (McGhie and Njoki Wamai, 2011). For example, in Bosnia, women parliamentarians would not support action to legislate parental leave because they believed in women's traditional role in the family (Johnson Sirleaf and Rehn, 2002). In turn, not all men are insensitive to gender. An essentialist view about the experiences of women is possible, and the practitioner should take care to not miss subtleties in perspectives and allegiances in peacebuilding work. Assumptions about women's gender sensitivity should not be made, nor should men's insensitivity to gender be taken as given.

Men are indeed resources for the women, peace, and security movement that should be further cultivated by practitioners. A key challenge is how to leverage the support of gender-sensitive men who value more equitable processes and want to mainstream gender in peacebuilding.[19] Practitioners cannot sustainably increase women's involvement and achieve gender parity without better engagement of male champions and persuading skeptical men and women about the significance of gender in conflict and peacebuilding. Neither men nor women can create peace and security without the other.

CONCLUSION

Conflict often upends traditional gender roles and creates a window in which peacebuilding practitioners can increase women's inclusion, a critical ingredient to realizing sustainable peace. As this chapter has articulated, activists have made important strides toward this goal, particularly in the form of new policies and practices at local, national, and international levels. UNSCR 1325 National Action Plans are proliferating, more financial resources are flowing, and the UN has appointed more women to senior positions than ever before. Nonetheless, much work remains to turn these policies and rhetorical commitments into meaningful change for women and men in conflict-affected areas. By better understanding the costs of inequity, the myriad ways women contribute to peacebuilding, and creative strategies for mainstreaming gender and including women, new practitioners and scholars will be better equipped to reap the dividends of inclusion.

QUESTIONS FOR FURTHER DISCUSSION

1. Which arguments are most compelling in advocating for women's inclusion in peacebuilding?

2. Are rights-based and efficacy arguments for women's inclusion mutually exclusive? Why or why not?

3. How can practitioners balance cultural mores and women's rights?

4. What examples can you cite of women's participation improving the process or outcomes of a peacebuilding initiative?

5. Do you believe gender equality and women's empowerment are equally important? Why or why not?

6. Do you support quotas for women's inclusion? Why or why not?

7. Which skills do practitioners need most to increase women's participation in peacebuilding?

8. What do you think is the biggest obstacle to increasing women's participation in peacebuilding? What needs to change and who can change it?

REFERENCES

Anderlini, S. 2007. *Women building peace.* Boulder, CO: Lynne Rienner.

Anderlini, S., and J. el-Bushra. 2004. The conceptual framework: Security, peace, accountability, and rights. In *Inclusive security, sustainable peace: A toolkit for advocacy and action* (pp. 1–44). Washington, DC: Hunt Alternatives Fund and International Alert.

Anderlini, S., and J. Tirman. 2010, October. What the women say: Participation and UNSCR 1325. Report, International Civil Society Action Network, MIT Center for International Studies, Cambridge, MA.

Baines, E. 2005, February. Rethinking women, peace, and security: A critique of gender in the Canadian human security agenda. Report, Liu Institute for Global Issues, University of British Columbia, Vancouver.

Baksh-Sodeen, R., ed. 2005. *Gender mainstreaming in conflict transformation*. London: Commonwealth Secretariat.

Bannon, I., and M. Correia, eds. 2006. *The other side of gender*. Washington, DC: World Bank Group.

Bell, C., and C. O'Rourke. 2010. Peace agreement or pieces of paper? The impact of UNSCR Resolution 1325 on peace processes and their agreements. *International & Comparative Law Quarterly* 59, no. 4: 941–980.

Benard, C., S. Jones, O. Oliker, C. Thurston, B. Stearns Lawson, and K. Cordell. 2008. *Women and nation-building*. Santa Monica, CA: Rand Corporation.

Blanco, B., and L. Hayes. 2007. The hidden challenge to development: Gender-based violence in Guatemala. *Trocaire Development Review*: 47–64. Retrieved January 5, 2012, from www.trocaire.org/resources.

Bouta, T. 2005. *Gender and disarmament, demobilization, and reintegration: Building blocs for Dutch policy*. The Hague: Netherlands Institute for International Relations.

Bouta, T., and G. Frerks. 2002. *Women's roles in conflict prevention, conflict resolution, and post-conflict reconstruction: Literature review and institutional analysis*. The Hague: Netherlands Institute of International Relations.

Bouta, T., G. Frerks, and I. Bannon. 2004. *Gender, conflict, and development*. Washington, DC: World Bank Group.

Buchanan, C. 2011. Peacemaking in Asia and the Pacific: Women's participation, perspectives, and priorities. Report, Centre for Humanitarian Dialogue, Geneva, Switzerland.

Charlesworth, H. 2005, Spring. Not waving but drowning: Gender mainstreaming and human rights in the UN. *Harvard Human Rights Journal* 18: 1–18.

Childs, S. and M. L. Krook. 2008. Critical Mass Theory and women's political representation. *Political Studies* 56, no. 3: 725–736.

Chowdhury, A. 2010, July 27. Doable fast-track indicators for turning 1325 promise into reality. Paper presented at working meeting, US Institute of Peace, Washington, DC. Retrieved January 5, 2012, from www.gnwp.org/doable-fast-track-indicators-for-turning-the-1325-promise-into-reality.

Conway, C., and S. Martinez. 2004. *Adding value: Women's contributions to reintegration and reconstruction in El Salvador*. Washington, DC: Hunt Alternatives Fund.

Dahlerup, D., and L. Freidenvall. 2005 Quotas as a "fast track" to equal political representation for women: Why Scandinavia is no longer the model. *International Feminist Journal of Politics* 7, no. 1: 26–48.

De Pauw, L. 1998. *Battle cries and lullabies: Women in war from prehistory to the present*. Norman: University of Oklahoma Press.

Dharmapuri, S. 2011. Just add women and stir. *Parameters* 41, no. 1: 56–70.

Ehrenreich, B. 1999. Men hate war too. *Foreign Affairs* 78, no. 1: 118–122.

European Peacebuilding Liaison Office. 2010, June. *UNSCR 1325 in Europe: 21 case studies of implementation*. Brussels, Belgium: Author.

Fischer, M. 2011. Civil society in conflict transformation: Strengths and limitations.

In B. Austin, M. Fischer, and H. Giessmann, eds. *Advancing conflict transformation: The Berghof handbook II* (pp. 131–156). Farmington Hills, MI: Barbara Budrich Publishers.

Francis, D. 2004, February. Gender and conflict transformation. *Committee for Conflict Transformation Support Review* 23: 1–11.

Fukuyama, F. 1998. Women and the evolution of world politics. *Foreign Affairs* 77, no. 5: 24–40.

Galtung, J. 1996. *Peace by peaceful means*. Oslo: International Peace Research Institute.

Greig, A., M. El Sanousi Omer, W. Tengey, and T. Calcut, eds. 2007. Engaging men in women's issues: Inclusive approaches to gender and development. *Critical Half* 5, no. 1.

Haq, K. 1999. Human security for women. In M. Tehranian, ed. *Worlds apart: Human security and global governance* (pp. 95–108). London: I. B. Tauris Publishers.

Harders, C. 2011. Gender relations, violence, and conflict transformation. In B. Austin, M. Fischer, and H. Giessmann, eds. *Advancing conflict transformation: The Berghof handbook II* (pp. 131–156). Farmington Hills, MI: Barbara Budrich Publishers.

Holvoet, N. 2006. Gender budgeting: Its usefulness in programme-based approaches to aid. Briefing note, EC Gender Help Desk, European Commission, Brussels, Belgium.

Hunt, S., and C. Posa. 2001. Women waging peace: Inclusive security. *Foreign Policy* 80, no. 3: 38–47.

Institute for Inclusive Security. 2010, April. Spotlight on Visaka Dharmadasa. Retrieved January 10, 2012, from www.huntalternatives.org/pages/8335_visaka_dharmadasa.cfm.

Jalan, S. 2011. No more silos. *Monday Developments* 29, no. 12: 14–16.

Jaquette, J. 1999. States make war. *Foreign Affairs* 78, no. 1: 128–129.

Johnson Sirleaf, E., and E. Rehn. 2002. *Women, war, and peace: The independent experts' assessment of the impact of armed conflict on women and women's role in peacebuilding*. New York: UNIFEM.

Kanter, R. M. 1977. Some effects of proportions on group life. *American Journal of Sociology* 82, no. 5: 965–990.

Kilmurray, A., and M. McWilliams. 2011. Struggling for peace: How women in Northern Ireland challenged the status quo. *Solutions* 2, no. 2. Retrieved January 5, 2012, from www.thesolutionsjournal.com/node/893.

Kuehnast, K., C. de Jonge Oudraat, and H. Hernes, eds. 2011. *Women and war*. Washington, DC: USIP Press Books.

Kumar, K. 2001. *Women and civil war: Impact, organizations, and actions*. Boulder, CO: Lynne Rienner.

Lederach, J. P. 1997. *Building peace: Sustainable reconciliation in divided societies*. Washington, DC: US Institute of Peace Press.

Makumi, M., and O. Okello, eds. 2006. *Rethinking global security: An African perspective*. Nairobi, Kenya: Heinrich Boll Foundation.

McGhie, M., and E. Njoki Wamai. 2011, March. Beyond the numbers: Women's participation in the Kenya National Dialogue and Reconciliation. Report, Centre for Humanitarian Dialogue, Geneva, Switzerland.

Miall, H. 2004. Conflict transformation: A multi-dimensional task. In A. Austin, M. Fischer, and N. Ropers, eds. *Transforming ethnopolitical conflict: The Berghof handbook* (pp. 67–89). Wiesbaden, Germany: VS-Verlag für Sozialwissenschaften.

Moser, C., and F. Clark, eds. 2001. *Victims, perpetrators, or actors? Gender, armed conflict, and political violence.* London: Zed Books.

National Police of Rwanda. South Sudanese MPs speak well of police for GBV guiding principle. Press release. Retrieved July 1, 2012, from www.police.gov.rw/spip.php?article162.

Neiva, P. 2008. Women in upper houses: A global perspective. *Brazilian Political Science Review* 1, no. 2, 77–95.

Nobel Peace Prize. 2011, October 7. Press release, Oslo. Retrieved from www.nobelprize .org/nobel_prizes/peace/laureates/2011/press.html.

Norris, P., and J. Lovenduski. 2001. Blair's babes: Critical Mass Theory, gender, and legislative life. Working Paper Series RWP01–039, Harvard University, John F. Kennedy School of Government. Retrieved March 10, 2012, from http://papers.ssrn.com/sol3 /papers.cfm?abstract_id=288548.

O'Neill, J., and J. Vary. 2011. Strengthening DDR and SSR through women's inclusion. In M. Civic and M. Miklaucic, eds. *The monopoly of force: The nexus of DDR and SSR* (pp. 77–108). Washington, DC: NDU Press.

Organisation for Economic Co-operation and Development. 2008. Development Assistance Committee guiding principles for aid effectiveness, gender equality, and women's empowerment. Retrieved January 5, 2012, from www.oecd.org/dataoecd/14/27 /42310124.pdf.

Page, M., T. Whitman, and C. Anderson. 2009. Strategies for policymakers: Bringing women into peace negotiations. Report, Institute for Inclusive Security, Hunt Alternatives Fund, Washington, DC.

Pankhurst, D. 2007. Gender issues in post-war contexts: A review of analysis and experience, and implications for policies. *Peace Studies Papers (fourth series) no. 9.* Bradford, UK: UN Research Institute for Social Development.

Porter, E. 2007. *Peacebuilding: Women in international perspective.* New York: Routledge.

Potter, A. 2008. Gender sensitivity: Nicety or necessity in peace process management? Centre for Humanitarian Dialogue, Geneva, Switzerland. Retrieved January 5, 2012, from www.hdcentre.org/files/Antonia%20Potter%20Gender%20sensitivity%20WEB.pdf.

Powley, E. 2008. *Engendering Rwanda's decentralization: Supporting women candidates for local office.* Washington, DC: Hunt Alternatives Fund and International Alert.

Puechguirbal, N. 2010. Discourses on gender, patriarchy, and Resolution 1325: A textual analysis of UN documents. *International Peacekeeping* 17, no. 2: 172–187.

Ramsbotham, O., T. Woodhouse, and H. Miall, eds. 2005. *Contemporary conflict resolution.* Cambridge, MA: Polity Press.

Reimann, C. 1999. *The field of conflict management: Why does gender matter?* AFB-Texte, 4/99. Bonn, Germany: Information Unit Peace Research.

Roberts, A. 2010. Lives and statistics: Are 90% of war victims civilians? *Survival* 52, no. 3: 115–136.

Sampson, C., M. Abu-Nimer, C. Liebler, and C. Whitney, eds. 2003. *Positive approaches to peacebuilding.* Washington, DC: Pact Publications.

Sarosi, D. 2007, October 4. Human security: Does gender matter? Paper presented at conference on Mainstreaming Human Security: The Asian Contribution, Bangkok, Thailand. Retrieved November 5, 2011, from http://humansecurityconf.polsci.chula.ac.th /Documents/Presentations/ Diana.pdf.

Steinberg, D. 2007, April 25. Failing to empower women peacebuilders: A cautionary tale from Angola. *PeaceWomen E-News*. Retrieved from www.crisisweb.org.

Tickner, A. 1992. *Gender in international relations*. New York: Columbia University Press.

Tiessen, R. 2007. *Everywhere/nowhere: Gender mainstreaming in development agencies*. Bloomfield, CT: Kumarian Press.

Tryggestad, T. 2009. Trick or treat? The UN implementation of Security Council Resolution 1325 on women, peace, and security. *Global Governance* 15, no. 4: 539–557.

————. 2010. The UN Peacebuilding Commission and gender: A case of norm reinforcement. *International Peacekeeping* 17, no. 2: 159–171.

United Nations Development Fund for Women (UNIFEM). 2009a. Women's participation in peace negotiations: Connections between presence and influence. Retrieved November 5, 2011, from www.unifem.org/attachments/products/0302_WomensParticipationInPeace Negotiations_en.pdf.

————. 2009b. Integrating gender responsive budgeting into the aid effectiveness agenda: Ten-country overview report. Retrieved August 15, 2011, from www.gendermatters.eu /resources_documents/UserFiles/File/Resourse/Budlender_unifemreport.pdf.

————. 2010a. Women count for peace: The 2010 open days on women, peace, and security. Retrieved from www.unifem.org/attachments/products/WomenCount4Peace _OpenDays_Report_en.pdf.

————. 2010b. What women want: Planning and financing for gender-responsive peacebuilding. Retrieved August 15, 2011, from www.unifem.org/attachments/products /0401_PlanningAndFinancingForGenderResponsivePeacebuilding_en.pdf.

United Nations Development Programme (UNDP). 1994. *Human development report*. New York: Oxford University Press. Retrieved from http://hdr.undp.org/en/reports /global/hdr1994.

————. 2006. *Evaluation of gender mainstreaming in UNDP*. New York: UNDP Evaluation Office.

United Nations Security Council (UNSC). 2010, April 6. Women and peace and security. Report of the Secretary-General (S/2010/173), New York.

————. 2011, September 29. Report of the Secretary-General on women, peace, and security (S/2011/598), New York.

United Nations Women. n.d. Gender responsive budgeting. Retrieved August 15, 2011, from www.unifem.org/gender_issues/women_poverty_economics/gender_budgets .php.

United States Agency for International Development (USAID). 2007. *Toolkit: Women and conflict*. Washington, DC: Author.

Wanis St. John, A., and D. Kew. 2008. Civil society and peace negotiations: Confronting exclusion. *International Negotiation* 13, no. 1: 11–36.

Watkins, F. 2004. DFID's experience of gender mainstreaming: 1995 to 2004. Report. Retrieved August 15, 2011, from www.oecd.org/dataoecd/47/52/35074862.pdf.

Whitman, T. 2010a. Joint protection teams: A model for enhancing civilian security. Report, Institute for Inclusive Security, Hunt Alternatives Fund, Washington, DC.

————. 2010b, January 28. Engaging women in the security sector. Speech, US Institute for Peace, Washington, DC. Retrieved August 15, 2011, from www.usip.org /newsroom/multimedia/video-gallery/engaging-women-in-the-security-sector.

Wilber, R. 2011. Lessons from Rwanda: How women transform governance. *Solutions* 2, no. 2. Retrieved January 5, 2012, from www.thesolutionsjournal.com/node/887.

Willett, S. 2010. Introduction: United Nations Security Council Resolution 1325: Assessing the impact on women, peace and security. *International Peacekeeping* 17, no. 2: 142–158.

NOTES

1. Lederach (1997) defines peacebuilding as efforts aimed at improving relationships and addressing root causes of conflict in order to prevent, reduce, or recover from violent conflict.

2. As described by Tickner (1992), "The achievement of peace, economic justice, and ecological sustainability is inseparable from overcoming social relations of domination and subordination; genuine security requires not only the absence of war but also the elimination of unjust social relations, including unequal gender relations" (p. 128).

3. Positive peace is defined by Galtung (1996) as "the presence of symbiosis and equity in human relations" as opposed to negative peace, which is the absence of direct violence (p. 14).

4. Others areas of debate in the field include the degree to which the aggressiveness in men that dominates much of geopolitics may be biological (Fukayama, 1999), while responses range from that of Barbara Ehrenreich (1999), who highlights that women can be aggressive and men can be passive, to Jane Jaquette's (1999) argument that our system of realpolitik socializes leaders, both male and female, toward aggression.

5. However, a strand of literature argues that this number is exaggerated and that inconsistent data collection makes broad estimates nearly impossible. See Roberts (2010).

6. For examination of gender, masculinity, and men's experiences in conflict, see Bannon and Correia (2006).

7. However, some theorists, such as Ramsbotham (2005), perceive that conflict resolution "has not been quite as gender-blind" as has been alleged (p. 268).

8. Chapter VI establishes peaceful methods of settling international disputes and the UNSC's powers in relation to them. Resolutions adopted under Chapter VI are advisory rather than binding.

9. Recent institutional women, peace, and security policies include NATO's Bi-Strategic Command Directive 40–1, "Integrating UNSCR 1325 and Gender Perspectives in the NATO Command Structures Including Measures for Protection During Armed Conflict," and the European Union's "Comprehensive Approach on UNSCR 1325 and 1820 on women, peace, and security (15671/1/08 REV 1).

10. Each of eight points, such as "Build peace with and for women: Involve women in all peace processes" (Point 4), is the foundation of programmatic work in countries around the world. Additionally, Goal 3 of the Millennium Development Goals (MDGs), "Promote gender equality and empower women," has recognized that women's participation is a component of long-term peace, stability, and development. The MDGs are eight international development goals all 193 UN member states and at least twenty-three international organizations agreed to achieve by 2015. Further, the Paris Declaration on Aid Effectiveness (2005) and the Accra Agenda for Action (2008) provide frameworks

and good-practice principles for fostering gender equality as a priority development issue. Additionally, many development and humanitarian organizations have mainstreamed gender, including organizations such as CARE.

11. Mainstreaming is defined by the UN Economic and Social Council, agreed conclusion, 1997/2, as "the process of assessing the implications for women and men of any planned action, including legislation, policies or programs, in all areas and at all levels. It is a strategy for making women's as well as men's concerns and experiences an integral dimension of the design, implementation, monitoring, and evaluation of policies and programs in all political, economic, and societal spheres so that women and men benefit equally, and inequality is not perpetuated. The ultimate goal is to achieve gender equality."

12. For example, many country-level foreign assistance agencies have gender-mainstreaming policies, such as that of the highly regarded British government's Department for International Development (Watkins, 2004).

13. For discussions of critical mass, please see works by Dahlerup and Freidenvall (2005); Childs and Krook (2008); Kanter (1977); and Norris and Lovenduski (2001).

14. An innovative system of decentralized elections has particularly assisted women seeking office. See the Inter-Parliamentary Union database for gender-disaggregated data on parliaments.

15. For statistics on funding, see OECD's database at http://stats.oecd.org/Index.aspx.

16. All information on Visaka Dharmadasa was taken from work by the Institute for Inclusive Security (2010).

17. All information on women's inclusion in Guatemala's peace processes was taken from work by Page, Whitman, and Anderson (2009).

18. All information about women's participation in the Kenyan negotiations was taken from McGhie and Njoki Wamai (2011).

19. See Greig, El Sanousi Omer, Tengey, and Calcut (2007) for case-study examples of men advancing the women, peace, and security agenda.

chapter six

PEACEBUILDING AND THE PRIVATE SECTOR

Shawn MacDonald

The role of business in society is this century's single most important and contentious public policy issue. Business is increasingly molding societal values and norms, and defining public policy and practice, as well as being the dominant route through which economic and financial wealth is created. How business is done will underpin how future local and global communities address social and environmental visions and imperatives. This is true whatever one believes to be critical in creating a just and sustainable world. Economic welfare, peace and security, global warming, human and animal welfare—just to name a few—are and will continue to be deeply informed by business in practice.

—SIMON ZADEK (2001, P. 29)

THIS CHAPTER COVERS A RANGE of topics associated with the role of private sector corporations in conflict as well as in peacebuilding and conflict resolution. It outlines the ways that the private sector contributes to social conflicts, while also describing the increased emphasis on holding corporations accountable for their conflict-related actions. Theories of corporate social responsibility and how they link to the theory and practice of peacebuilding are explored. Both conventional and emerging approaches by the private sector toward understanding its role in social conflict are analyzed, and trends in the field, such as the integration of corporate social responsibility initiatives with peacebuilding, are highlighted. Practical skills

127

needed to successfully integrate private-sector companies in peacebuilding are described, as are ethical and other challenges in this work. Several multi-stakeholder governed organizations dealing with the actions and responsibilities of companies in conflict-prone regions are profiled, and a case study is presented about innovative approaches to integrated peacebuilding and roles for companies in creating just, peaceful economies.

INTEGRATED PEACEBUILDING AND THE PRIVATE SECTOR

Corporations are a party to many of the social conflicts plaguing societies around the globe.[1] The conventional business model of externalizing costs (such as pollution) onto society while internalizing profits routinely leads to a wide range of conflicts. As business activity has grown in intensity and scope, there has been a concomitant globalization of dissent against corporate power. Recent calls for alternative approaches to business come from a global civil society sector and from a small (but growing) segment of the business sector itself. Even companies that might not take proactive steps to resolve conflict are likely to appreciate the value of avoiding negative publicity that comes from association with conflict.

Companies have long been directly or indirectly linked to broader social conflicts, including being accused of fomenting or abetting political conflicts to protect assets or effect regime change. Many conflicts labeled as "political" or "ethnic" are often more about control and exploitation of resources (such as oil, timber, and mineral wealth), where corporate interests are significant. With the rise of global media and corporate accountability activism, the role of business in conflict zones has been getting increased attention, and companies are finding it harder to claim a neutral stance. Sometimes attention is focused on a specific company role or action, such as assisting a government's counterinsurgency efforts. Other times it is on the corporate sector's link to, or responsibilities related to, human rights abuses and corrupt practices in a conflict or conflict-prone zone.

A number of companies have fueled tensions by exploiting natural resources, especially oil, gas, minerals, precious gems, and timber (Collier, 2007). The extraction of such valuable resources often enables parties to finance conflict. Companies may provide tax money or other resources to governments that fuel conflict. At other times, groups may directly control the site of production, then sell the resources to business actors, perpetuating the notion of the "resource curse," whereby nations possessing resources are accompanied by corruption, violent conflict, dislocation, and various market distortions (Ballentine and Nitzschke, 2005; Collier, 2000, 2007).

The links between companies and conflict go well beyond connection to the "resource curse." Companies' policies and practices tend to reflect the mores of the society in which they operate. In societies with deep conflicts over such issues as ethnicity or religion, companies routinely mirror and exacerbate the divisions in society by intensifying inequalities through actions that favor one side over another.

Where conflict is both the cause and the consequence of poor government, companies "gain" by avoiding labor or environmental regulation. Companies can also take advantage of corruption, chaos, and heavy state involvement in economic matters (and often ownership of key businesses by politicians). Mercenary companies and contractors that serve militaries and peacekeeping forces also play a role in conflicts. There is also much corporate activity related to weapons, human trafficking, and other illicit activities that flourish in conflict zones.

While companies can profit from conflict, it is important to emphasize that in general conflict is very bad for business. War destroys economies and hampers growth for years into the future; clearly, diminished markets are bad for business (Kunbar, 2007). For instance, a study determined that the existence of conflict is the most salient factor in determining whether a country's economy and social development advance (Milanovic, 2005), and the Global Peace Index shows that conflict has a tremendous impact on the global economy.[2] In the midst of conflict, companies and their employees are at great risk of violence and destruction of property. Being associated with conflict in one country can also mean diminished reputation for a company in other markets. Companies are understandably reluctant to invest in conflictual areas, even once hostilities have ended (Besley, Mueller, and Singh, 2011). Thus, it is not surprising that business communities focus more attention on reducing, resolving, or preventing conflicts rather than on waging conflict.

While the movement toward business contributing to peacebuilding grows, business leaders are often reluctant to change because it is often unclear what their role should be. While some business leaders have played constructive roles in ending conflicts, more role models and pathways are needed to encourage others to participate proactively (Iff et al., 2010).

HOW THE PRIVATE SECTOR LINKS WITH CONFLICT RESOLUTION

In the contemporary global conflict landscape, rapidly changing market conditions (including increased globalization, competition, technological change, and public awareness of social/environmental costs) mean that companies are facing new conflicts and new adversaries. While corporations appear to have more leverage and face fewer formal governmental restrictions than in the past, they do face an increasingly aware and empowered global civil society that seeks to hold them accountable.

Actions to influence companies can take place through advocacy campaigns and boycotts, as well as direct protests at the community, regional, and international level. All companies face the pressure to avoid negative publicity; the very threat of it can sometimes influence behavior. Therefore, the emergence of "socially responsible" companies has created a new model for private-sector actors. Those corporations that are not moving in this direction are increasingly subject to criticism.

In the traditional corporate worldview, success is defined as earning the most profit without necessarily considering the negative effects on society. This is a worldview best described by economist Milton Friedman (1970) in the following terms: "there is one and only one social responsibility of business—to use its resources and engage in activities designed to increase its profits so long as it stays within the rules of the game, which is to say, engages in open and free competition without deception or fraud" (para. 33). However, a more sophisticated, systems-based approach to conflicts both inside and outside the corporation is emerging: one that recognizes that long-term value for a company comes from engaging stakeholders and reorienting products, services, and business processes toward more sustainable and socially beneficial ends. This business worldview is in line with conventional wisdom in the conflict-studies field that holds that genuine resolution of conflict implies adequate and reasonably abiding satisfaction of all parties' needs and interests to the maximum degree (Fisher, Patton, and Ury, 1991; Moore, 2003).

There is a distinct movement within the corporate sector to improve companies' social (and long-term economic) performance by dealing more openly and creatively with their external stakeholders. More companies are specifically redesigning their management structures and processes (commonly known as dispute system design) to deal more strategically, equitably, and efficiently with conflicts both inside and outside the organization. Over the past several decades, with the rise of alternative dispute resolution processes, companies are increasingly trying to manage conflicts through the use of dialogue, mediation, regulatory negotiation, arbitration, special commissions and committees, and other conflict resolution processes (Kaye, 1996). Moreover, given the increasing role of civil society and business in international affairs, and changing roles of government in human rights and related areas, some companies are now also more explicitly seeking to play active peacebuilding roles in conflictual societies.

Partnership activity is increasing as all three sectors of society create new ways of working together. The growing use of codes of conduct, corporate–NGO partnerships, and multi-stakeholder initiatives to implement these agreements are all signs of a new approach by a portion of the corporate sector.

CORPORATIONS AND INTEGRATION OF CONFLICT RESOLUTION AND PEACEBUILDING

The mainstreaming of conflict resolution into the private sector has two dimensions. The first involves how corporations are integrating conflict resolution and/or peacebuilding approaches into their business practices or operations. The second looks at how the peacebuilding field engages with the private sector. Furthermore, other actors in the conflict system (governments, NGOs, international organizations) are reconsidering roles for the private sector.

Formerly, engaging the private sector was at best an add-on to the list of tracks described as possible routes to peace in a multi-track diplomacy approach articulated by Diamond and McDonald (1996). While the concept has since gained more attention, a clear and prominent role for business in conflict is still much less articulated and embraced than other tracks. Although examples of strong, effective engagement by business leaders in addressing conflicts exist from places as diverse as Kashmir, South Africa, and Sri Lanka, more efforts are needed.

Before integrated peacebuilding can even be considered, a key challenge for companies is developing sufficient awareness of the role(s) they play in conflict systems. Then companies (or a business leader in an individual capacity) need to decide what constructive roles in peacebuilding they can fulfill. Mainstreaming this role in a meaningful way with a critical mass of businesses requires a great deal of awareness-raising; ongoing encouragement and/or pressure from stakeholders; experimenting with roles;

and capacity-building within the business sector. This ensures that businesses "own" the process, while calibrating efforts to fit business prerogatives related to expenses and legal and image liabilities (Campbell, 2002). It is important to add that different types of mainstreaming processes are required for the major categories of social conflicts in which corporations find themselves: labor, environmental, and conflict-zone behavior. Organizations, such as International Alert and the Prince of Wales International Business Leaders Forum,[3] have pioneered new ways for companies to view their role in conflict zones, as discussed later in this chapter.

Yet, from a practical standpoint of trying to change these dynamics, one cannot underestimate the many challenges inherent in shifting from the status quo to building and sustaining a healthy, just economy and system of governance. It is important to recognize that the majority of companies in the world are still very much in the early stages of acknowledging their role in fueling environmental and labor conflicts in their operations. For mainstream companies a holistic integrated approach to social conflict is a long way off.

From the perspective of the peacebuilding field, integrating means adopting (to some extent) the language and methods of business so that the process is understood and accepted within the corporate system. For example, engaging in conflict-reducing activities needs to be framed not only as an ethical or moral matter, but as something good for the bottom line. To persuade business leaders, peacemakers must be prepared to discuss market dynamics and reputational risks.

From the company's perspective, new relationships are needed with civil society organizations based on genuine dialogue and substantive engagement around changes in policies and practices. Businesses must learn to engage with citizen and community groups that might be hostile toward the business and their pursuit of profit. For instance, some companies now communicate or even partner on projects with "radical" NGOs, such as Greenpeace, that they strenuously avoided in the past. Likewise, civil society groups need to learn how to engage with companies that have not previously embraced corporate responsibility.

To alter its relationship with conflict, the private sector also needs to change how businesses relate to each other, such as through joint efforts and associational initiatives to affect conflict patterns. For instance, in Sri Lanka the Business Community for Peace is an interesting example of leaders from across the private sector learning to work together for a pro-peace agenda.[4] They created a number of programs, such as BizPAct (Business-Peace-Action), which help local entrepreneurs imagine and plan new enterprises that are "conflict-sensitive and socially responsible" and that will form the basis of long-term development and sustainable peace. This organization has another pioneering program focused on reconciliation programs called Networking Regional Business for Conflict Transformation, which convenes leaders from business and other groups representing all ethnicities. These groups are trained in ways that enable them to be more sensitive to conflict and engage in crisis mediation and other initiatives.[5]

The first step many companies need to take is to avoid any actions that might be contributing to conflict. The principle of "do no harm" is important to keep in mind (Anderson, 1999). Yet, to be a positive force for peacebuilding, companies must perform an about-face in typical practices. For instance, companies need to cease direct financing of conflict parties and put their money behind peacebuilding efforts instead; they must avoid using their hiring process to favor one group over another in a fractured society and consider how to use workplace practices to bridge divides; and they must no longer exploit natural and human resources in a way that contributes to conflict dynamics. Instead, they must adopt practices that provide value and/or serve reconstruction, as well as peacebuilding. Companies need to increase their transparency in conflict-affected regions to show the nature and extent of their relationship with government (e.g., contract terms, taxes and royalties paid).

Civil society organizations that seek to integrate private-sector engagement as part of their peacebuilding efforts also face a number of challenges. Many such organizations are already strained programmatically and will find it difficult to create and sustain programs and staffing that focus on the private sector. They also may require new skills in such areas as communicating with the private sector; formulating programming options that include private-sector roles; negotiating complicated, high-profile partnerships; and mastering business and economic analysis.

Beyond those practical challenges, though, are the very real dilemmas activists and NGOs face in deciding whether, how, and which companies to engage. If NGOs take money from companies, they might be seen as compromised and accused of "peace-washing" in the sense that some NGOs have been accused of "green-washing" when they engage with companies without effecting real change in environmental practices. NGOs need to be careful not to sacrifice their work or values to pursue engagement with companies that might be focused on different objectives. NGOs also need to be very conscious of whether working with a company (such as partnering to create new corporate policies around conflict) might explicitly or implicitly deny them the opportunity to criticize the company on the implementation of those policies or any other matter. It is also important to consider that NGOs play a vital role in criticizing and changing the larger sociopolitical and economic systems that companies might tend to benefit from; so in terms of determining priorities, NGOs must weigh how much energy they put into critiques of the system in relation to how much they seek to change it "from the inside" by working with companies.

RELEVANT THEORY

There is a growing literature on corporate management of social conflict outside the labor relations and environmental fields, with a particular emphasis on linking business with sustainable peacebuilding efforts. Oetzel et al. (2010) recently published a comprehensive discussion of emerging scholarship in this field in the article "Business and Peace: Sketching the Terrain." The authors review recent literature on the role of business in resolving conflict and building peaceful economies, including many referenced throughout this chapter. Oetzel and her colleagues plot out the different roles for companies along a continuum of conflict intensity, with actions such as preventing conflict during the latent-conflict stage, conducting track-two diplomacy, and fostering economic development during and after hostilities. They describe how recent scholarship has sought to make the case for why peace is good for business and to describe how new expectations are emerging regarding how companies contribute to conflict and/or peace.

In addition to the growing number of publications concerning business and conflict and peace, research from other arenas is also germane to the topic. In particular, there are writings by academics and practitioners on corporate social responsibility and accountability (Bendell, 2004; Kuhn and Shriver, 1991), works on globalization (Korten, 2001; Sutton, 1993; Wood, 1995), studies of corporate code of conduct creation and use (Mamic, 2004; Parrett, 2004; Radin, 2004; Waddell, 1997), cross-sectoral partnerships (Argenti, 2004; Bendell, 2003), and stakeholder theory and practice (Andriof, 2003; Brynne and Mallet, 2005; Freeman, 1984; Hart and Sharma, 2004; Sachs, 2006a and 2006b). These works provide new perspectives on corporations, including various critiques and alternatives to corporate power, often in the context of governmental inability to control and regulate corporations. Although most of these do not directly address the role of companies in resolving conflicts or building peace per se, the concepts examined in these works certainly apply, including new notions of corporate responsibilities for social well-being; critiques of how corporations abuse power and cause conflict; and the promise of cross-sectoral partnerships with positive benefits for peace and social improvement.

Garriga and Mele (2004), for instance, provide an excellent overview of corporate social responsibility theories and approaches, describing how the theories break down into various categories, such as instrumental, political, integrative, and ethical. They argue that a truly useful theory and approach to corporate responsibility would integrate these strands. An instrumental theory would locate the corporate role based on what the entity is best suited to do and why: for instance, as a business is structured to build wealth, activities of a "social" nature, including participating in peacebuilding, should be viewed as means to the end of creating wealth. Political theories focus on the types and uses of corporate power in society and, therefore, are germane to determining what roles and responsibilities companies have in a political and social crisis, such as a violent conflict. Integrative theories describe how corporations are situated in society and have various social demands to meet.

Finally, Garriga and Mele (2004) analyze ethical theories that describe corporate responsibility to society in terms of ethical frameworks, conventional and aspirational values, and accepted business practices. For a company to understand and act upon its role in creating peace, it would need to be fully mindful not just of how that role might sustain wealth creation, but also how to appropriately and peacefully situate itself in relation to civil society and broader social and human values.

The connections are quite straightforward between these diverse bodies of work and the practical examples and topical issues discussed in this chapter. For example, management literature describes corporations as flexible entities that can be molded by charismatic leaders and by compelling visions (Hill and Jones, 2009). Thus, corporations can be viewed as capable of creative and flexible responses to conflict if such a goal is sincerely sought by leadership. This flexibility is particularly important with the call for new approaches in dealing with stakeholders. Literature on stakeholder theory and processes recommends ways to assimilate diverse viewpoints or build the capacity of underresourced stakeholders, which has a direct bearing on the concerns and needs of practitioners as they seek to consider the viewpoints of many different parties within a dynamic, complex conflict system (Phillips, 2002; 2003).

For instance, Freeman (1984) pioneered the concept of understanding the basic nature of the corporation as an entity that must strategically manage a wide variety of stakeholders. Hart and Sharma (2004) posit that corporations can gain much value from engaging even their most "fringe" stakeholders and that to avoid doing so has costly repercussions. Others help guide companies in specific ways to map out and engage stakeholders (Gray et al., 1997), including how to incorporate diverse stakeholders in creating codes of conduct and multi-stakeholder initiative standards (Brynne and Mallet, 2005). Jem Bendell (2003), an expert on stakeholder engagement and partnerships, provides guidance on how to use dialogue processes to bring about change in corporate behavior and relationships with stakeholders.

In practice, stakeholder consultation tends to happen along what Brynne and Mallet (2005) call the "consultation continuum" that "ranges from the provision of mere information at the minimal pole to full public control over the policy process at the maximum end. Intermediate points along the continuum are characterized as 'consultation,' 'partnership' and 'delegation'" (p. 1). The full array of such engagements are seen in the conflict resolution arena, though most seem to still be at the awareness-raising and dialogue stage that would fit under the label of "consultation."

The Center for Corporate Citizenship at Boston College (2005) published an interesting report, *Going Global: Managers' Experiences Working with Worldwide Stakeholders,* which cautioned companies that when they "step onto a global stage they face a far greater array of stakeholders whose expectations can appear contradictory and overwhelming." Companies "may see the value of listening to stakeholders and creating some kind of social dialogue yet not recognize that participation in such dialogues requires various skills and competencies these groups may not possess. In fact, one of the problems identified by experienced managers is that people only get recognized as an important stakeholder once they have these skills, which can create a false impression that everyone who needs to be involved is involved" (p. 41).

PROCESSES AND PROGRAM/POLICY INNOVATIONS

In the realm of corporations and conflict, a number of processes are being used to highlight problems, test solutions, and promote new approaches, particularly codes of conduct and multi-stakeholder initiatives (MSIs), including several specifically linked to conflict zones that will be discussed in this section: the Kimberley Process for Diamond Certification, the Voluntary Principles on Security and Human Rights, and the Extractive Industries Transparency Initiative. These initiatives are based on voluntary codes of conduct, which are policy documents that guide action, delineate priorities, help in choice-making, set standards, prohibit specific actions, or otherwise codify a corporation's approach to the social implications of its actions (International Federation of Accountants, 2007; Switzer and Ward, 2004). Some codes are implemented by MSIs, which are defined as organizations established and governed collaboratively between companies, civil society groups, and (sometimes) governments to implement a code of conduct to regulate corporate behavior in social conflict systems. MSIs represent a relatively sophisticated conception of corporate social responsibility because they place the corporate commitment into a framework for implementation that gives some control to external stakeholders.

One of the most significant policy innovations in the realm of corporations and conflict is the creation of several multi-stakeholder initiatives that seek to regulate corporate actions in conflict zones. These initiatives are bringing together NGOs, companies, and governments to create and implement solutions in ways they have never done before, building on the experience of numerous MSIs created to deal with corporate social conflicts in the environmental and labor realms. The MSIs discussed below are also dealing (however imperfectly) with some of the most vexing problems at the heart of the corporate-conflict nexus, including the "resource curse."

Using codes as a mechanism to hold companies accountable for their actions in conflict zones originated in South Africa. For decades, activists sought ways to hold companies accountable for their direct or indirect support of the apartheid regime. The most prominent corporate responsibility initiative related to South Africa was the Sullivan Principles program, which was a pioneering code-of-conduct system centered on pledges by signatory companies that were independently monitored and reported in part to the public (Sethi and Williams, 2000). The Sullivan Principles focused on the implementation of workplace and community relations policies and programs that presumably would ameliorate conditions of victims of apartheid.

While the Sullivan Principles had mixed results and were by no means universally supported, they were successful in demonstrating the possibilities inherent in private forms of corporate social regulation in conflict zones and more generally. It is fair to say that the Sullivan Principles were the real start of the corporate codes-of-conduct movement. However incomplete, the Sullivan system's emphasis on non-corporate-stakeholder engagement, monitoring, and reporting helped create the architecture of the multi-stakeholder initiative phenomenon that is now the most substantial policy approach in the arena of corporations and conflict.

In the past decade or so, despite any number of high-profile and controversial international conflicts or civil wars (e.g., Kosovo, Darfur, Iraq, Afghanistan), the trend in corporate accountability activism and multi-stakeholder activity around conflict-zone behavior is away from country-specific efforts, as was the case with the Sullivan Principles in South Africa. Instead, efforts focus more on the underlying dynamics and roles that corporations play in conflict zones more generally. Hence, the emergence of MSIs around the topics of corporate security forces policies and human rights in conflict zones; the role of companies in financing conflict; and the way that corporate contracts with governments contribute to the interplay of corruption and conflict in war-prone areas, particularly those with natural resources.

The Voluntary Principles on Security and Human Rights (created in 2000) are framed around three sets of issues: how companies should assess the risk of complicity in human rights abuses in connection with their security arrangements, including their relationships with local communities and other stakeholders; company relations with state security forces, both military and police; and company relations with private security forces.[6] The principles provide practical guidance to companies on how to incorporate international human rights standards and emerging best practices concerning policies and decisions around these topics.

The Voluntary Principles face a challenge: human rights and security challenges seem to multiply rather than diminish. More than a decade ago, when the Voluntary Principles were being negotiated, the focus was on Nigeria, Indonesia, and Colombia. Today, that list of hot spots has grown to include the Caspian Sea and Middle East regions, the Democratic Republic of the Congo, Equatorial Guinea, Angola, Peru, Ecuador, Bolivia, Venezuela, and Papua New Guinea.

It seems this MSI is more about maintaining a dialogue than about implementing specific, measurable outcomes. This is not surprising given that companies have only recently felt sufficient pressure from civil society to communicate about the problem, and there is no history of collaboration or a set of "reasonable" expectations for implementation. In the labor field, for instance, it is possible to set and monitor wage levels, but it is far more difficult to agree on an "acceptable" level of complicity with human rights abuses or draw the line between acceptable and unacceptable use of force by a company in protecting its assets in the midst of murky civil conflicts.

The range of human rights issues related to extractive companies is quite broad, yet this MSI focuses narrowly on the role of company security forces. Perhaps over time its mandate will expand. If it is successful, perhaps expanded standards that would apply to sectors in conflict zones other than highly visible extractive companies may be developed. The process does include some of the leading oil and mining companies, such as Exxon-Mobil, leading NGOs, including Amnesty International, and governments including the United States.[7]

The Kimberley Process for Diamond Certification is another conflict-zone-related MSI that has garnered sustained attention and a degree of commitment from a large and varied set of players, including governments, NGOs, the United Nations, and the leading diamond industry group. Formed in 2000, this MSI aims to ensure that the diamond industry is not complicit in the "blood diamond" trade, by which the highly valuable gems are used to finance horrendous conflicts in Africa.[8] This group operates a system by which the chain of custody of diamonds from mine to jeweler is verified to involve only legitimate companies. Today the Kimberley Process remains highly controversial, with concerns that governments have too much power and the initiative too little will or authority to tackle the toughest cases where its oversight is most needed. Global Witness, the key NGO in the Process, recently resigned from the system precisely because of ongoing concerns about effectiveness.

The Extractive Industries Transparency Initiative (EITI) is another creative initiative. Launched in 2002, the EITI focuses on the interplay of extractive industry revenues, corporate–government interactions, corruption, and conflict.[9] This nexus is seen in many of the world's conflict zones, where extractive-sector wealth is monopolized by corrupt ruling elites and becomes a significant source of conflict. The extractive wealth finances a vicious cycle of conflict aimed at controlling that very wealth, as seen between resource-rich provinces and the central governments in such places as Nigeria and Indonesia. Visser et al. (2010) explain the core problem the EITI was set up to solve: "Many countries are rich in oil, gas, and minerals and studies have shown that when governance is good, these can generate large revenues to foster economic growth and reduce poverty. However when governance is weak, they may instead cause poverty, corruption, and conflict—the so called 'resource curse.' The EITI aims to defeat this 'curse' by improving transparency and accountability" (p. 183). The EITI is structured as a signatory process by which countries and companies agree to "publish what they pay," thereby enabling citizens to know more about a fundamental part of their economy and government and hold parties accountable. As of early 2012, EITI has thirteen countries that have adhered to requirements over a period of several years and twenty that are "candidates," with several more signaling their intention to start the membership process.[10]

The three initiatives described above are emblematic of a global community struggling to find ways to regulate and hold accountable corporate power in conflict zones or conflict-prone areas while simultaneously harnessing that power to ameliorate or resolve conflicts. The "conflict system" in which they operate is relatively new as NGOs, governments, and businesses create norms and experiment with approaches to corporate responsibility in conflict zones and conflict-prone areas.

It is noteworthy that all of these MSIs focus on the extractive sector. The fact that extractive industries are very capital intensive helps explain why large, powerful multinational corporations tend to dominate this sector. This, in turn, means that the increasingly influential global media and civil society groups have a clear target or focus of attention and accountability for the myriad social conflicts connected to natural-resource extraction. Yet, there is a need to address the many other businesses working in conflict zones that are less likely to get attention or have a well-known name against which activists can campaign.

One notes the possibility of an inherent tendency toward frustration with these MSIs, as some might expect them to help settle conflicts when they are not really established to do this. The complicity of companies is certainly problematic, but it is not usually the main source of seemingly irreconcilable differences that often lead to violence and conflict. Furthermore, MSIs are totally dependent (as currently constituted) on the voluntary participation (and even funding) of companies (Switzer and Ward, 2004). Even if companies do not participate or do not follow the rules of a voluntary system in which they participate, they do not face governmental or public sanctions or other penalty. Another major problem to consider is that participation in MSIs and other corporate responsibility initiatives is very much a Western phenomenon and the market share of Western companies is decreasing. Companies from the BRIC countries (Brazil, Russia, India, and China) are increasingly investing and even dominating certain emerging markets and forging close ties to local governments without the "strings attached" that many Western companies and governments place on to human-rights and conflict concerns. Unless and until BRIC companies also embrace the values and activities of the MSIs and similar initiatives, the impact on the ground will remain limited.

More effort to engage business in actual peacebuilding is needed rather than only focusing on reducing their harmful complicity. Other forms of engagement besides MSIs are necessary to encourage peacebuilding by companies, as the MSI mechanism is essentially a regulatory (largely voluntary) process based on ending or improving negative behaviors or providing market incentives for positive behavior. It is also hard to imagine MSIs and other private forms of regulation emerging around conflicts that are not high profile or where there is not an obvious corporate link through high-value natural resources.

Another policy problem is the increase in the number and roles of private military contractors engaged in activities formerly reserved for militaries. It is interesting to note that the movement toward private codes of conduct discussed above has also been taken up by private security companies in the spotlight for their actions in Iraq and Afghanistan. For example, in 2010 in Switzerland, approximately sixty private security companies drafted and signed an international code of conduct that committed them to respect human rights and humanitarian law in their operations.[11] This initiative is difficult to evaluate because it is clearly in its formative stage. Yet, its existence undoubtedly reflects the fact that this link between profit-seeking enterprises and conflict is sufficiently problematic and acknowledged as such by various stakeholders, who are willing to work together to alter behavior.

Another policy innovation comes from the United Nations. The UN recently completed a process of codifying the responsibilities of companies in the arena of human rights. This in effect relates directly to conflictual situations, as human rights are often abused in the midst of conflicts, and various institutions have long been seeking more resources put toward codifying and somehow enforcing responsibilities of companies vis-à-vis human rights. The UN secretary-general appointed a special adviser (Harvard professor John Ruggie) to create and oversee a process to create a set of standards, which came to be known as the UN "Protect, Respect, and Remedy" Framework for Business and Human Rights.[12] The process of getting input from a variety of stakeholders around the world led to significant debate about the "sphere of influence" that companies do (or do not) have and their responsibilities within their sphere. The end product was a framework that emphasizes the imperative of going beyond simply respecting human rights laws to include affirmative protections for rights as well as commitments to remedy wrongs and violations. Now that the "Ruggie Framework" is completed, it remains to be seen whether and how various institutions—companies, NGOs, governments, the UN itself—will work with the standards to expand actual positive engagement by the private sector in human rights issues in conflict zones and elsewhere.

SKILLS PRACTITIONERS NEED TO BE EFFECTIVE

Practitioners in this arena need many of the same skills as those active in other conflict systems, yet with additional insight into the private sector that would preferably come from working closely with companies and/or within companies. Businesses and their employees have some unusual skills and resources that can enable them to play a potentially transformative role in peacebuilding and conflict resolution, such as high-stakes negotiating skills, strong communication abilities, and experience obtaining and efficiently utilizing resources. They often need, however, more aptitude in understanding community groups, politics, and the "messy" side of conflict.

Other skills are vital for both businesses and NGOs in efforts to boost business engagement in conflict regions. The ability to conduct a conflict assessment is important as parties explore how business may be linked to conflict. Knowledge and skill in stakeholder engagement is vital as groups and companies reach out to others. Furthermore, skill in convening groups to learn from each other and work together cannot be underestimated. Knowledge and experience in advocacy efforts are also very much needed as groups must engage and convince those from other sectors and from government to operate differently.

With a greater recognition of the crucial role of economic stability and opportunity as pillars of postconflict reconstruction, NGOs and businesses must become more knowledgeable, creative, and otherwise skilled in promoting, creating, and sustaining the sorts of jobs, finance, and business infrastructure that will enable people to have jobs and build prosperous communities.

KEY POLICY DEBATES IN THE BUSINESS SECTOR RELATED TO CONFLICT

A number of policy debates are relevant to this realm of conflict and peacebuilding. All institutions in this area face choices about how to work effectively with other actors that may fall outside their traditional areas. It is important to note that the major policy issue related to corporations in conflict is the general lack of enforcement of existing public policies (particularly laws and regulations) connected to corporate behavior. Even the most poorly governed countries often have laws that seek to reduce the "conflict" related to the impact of corporate behavior on workers, communities, and the environment. Certainly the specific actions and dynamics some companies are accused of when linked to sociopolitical conflict—including corruption, aiding insurgents, laundering money—are already outside the bounds of the law. It is imperative not to lose sight of the long-term structural need for competent governance by democratically elected officials who create and enforce laws and policies to ensure companies do not cause conflict.

With that in mind, citizens and civil society groups must be mindful that their efforts to facilitate new roles for business—such as private, voluntary regulatory schemes—might actually or figuratively weaken the authority of government, whose lack of will, resources, and legitimacy are both cause and consequence of so many conflicts.

Civil society groups need clear policies about taking corporate funds, to address matters such as establishing criteria for which companies are or are not acceptable donors and/or partners for projects. Some may assert that companies with poor records are not sufficiently trustworthy, while others may say that the "bad actors" are the ones most in need of engagement. Also, NGOs need a realistic sense of what "good enough" is in terms of amount and pace of change that they can expect from companies. NGOs primarily focused on one issue need to carefully consider whether they should broaden their scope of work to tackle related issues. NGOs also need sophisticated strategizing around effecting change at a systemic level and how working with one or a few companies might or might not lead to change across an industry. From the company perspective, business leaders also need careful consideration of their expectations of partnering with NGOs and government.

INTERNATIONAL ALERT

A leading institution in the arena of corporations and conflict is the globally active International Alert.[13] More than any other organization in the peacebuilding realm, International Alert has consistently highlighted the role of corporations—both positive and negative—in a variety of conflicts. Yet, in addition to building awareness of corporate roles in political conflicts, International Alert has also vigorously engaged in efforts to draw businesses and their leaders into playing constructive roles in conflict settings. For instance, International Alert has worked directly with businesses to promote practices that prevent companies from fueling conflict in places such as Nepal, Sri Lanka, and Colombia (Alexander, Gündüz, and Subedi, 2009).

International Alert has published numerous studies on the role of corporations in conflict. They also promote various tools and policy materials to the business and aid communities to encourage positive corporate roles in conflict zones. International Alert's work in this arena is based on the premise that economic health is a key foundation for sustainable peace: dysfunctional economies exacerbate societal tensions and lead to conflict, while postconflict peacebuilding is reinforced by economic opportunities for all parties. For instance, the organization engages international aid agencies and foreign investors on ways in which investments aimed at economic development can strengthen peace efforts. They also have partnerships and consultancies with private companies to help them institute new policies and approaches to operating in conflict zones. International Alert works with companies to craft and deliver advocacy messages to governments and others in the private sector to encourage positive roles in conflict prevention as well as peacebuilding.

Case Study: The Enough Project and Conflict Minerals

The link between minerals mining and the horrific war in the Democratic Republic of the Congo (DRC) presents one of the most interesting and consequential developments in the movement to hold corporations accountable for their role in conflicts. The Enough Project is a US-based civil society organization started in 2007 to mobilize action against crimes against humanity, genocide, and other atrocities.[14] The group has brought worldwide attention to the war in the DRC and specifically to the problem of "conflict minerals," whereby warring factions finance their fighting through controlling the mining and sale of highly valuable, relatively rare minerals that are integral to the manufacturing of computers, mobile phones, portable music players, and other electronic gadgets. The conflict minerals are the "3 T's"—tin, tantalum, and tungsten—and gold. While these minerals are mined elsewhere in the world, the DRC is a significant source country, so the strong, growing market for them means that the manufacturers cannot bypass the DRC altogether.[15]

The Enough Project estimates that armed groups operating in the eastern Congo earn hundreds of millions of dollars each year by trading in these minerals. In the process, further violence (including widespread and systematic rape and murder) is perpetrated in the course of fighting for control of the mineral trade, including the mines themselves and civilians coerced into operating them. This vicious cycle of violent conflict along with human and ecological exploitation has also engulfed neighboring countries, with the minerals going via multiple routes to enter the global processing and manufacturing chains of electronic products. Because those value chains are complicated and numerous, it has been challenging to trace which finished products (e.g., a Dell computer or an Apple iPhone) are made with metals that were mined in the horrific circumstances of eastern DRC or other similarly violent regions.

Yet, despite that challenge, the Enough Project successfully changed the dynamic by insisting that electronics companies find ways to take responsibility for their connections to the DRC conflict. The group conducted a massive advocacy campaign to expose the nature of the conflict-minerals dynamic, linking atrocities in the DRC with the enormously profitable electronics sector. They leveraged that outreach into a successful campaign to legislate responsibility by electronics companies for conflict minerals. The result was inclusion of a specific requirement in the Dodd-Frank Wall Street Reform Act (passed July 2010) to require American companies to ensure via tracing and auditing that raw materials in their products do not come from mines in the DRC caught up in the conflict (US Congress, 2010).

Under the law, companies must make an annual disclosure report of the country of origin of minerals they use in the manufacturing of their products, with specific reference to whether they come from the conflict-affected region of the DRC and surrounding areas. Several initiatives are under way by the two major electronics-company responsibility consortia: the Electronic Industry Citizenship Coalition (EICC) and the Global e-Sustainability Initiative (GeSI).[16] These efforts include a "bag and tag" program to isolate conflict-free minerals from other sources by keeping them separate in specially marked, secured containers. A multi-stakeholder process led to the creation of a "conflict-free smelter program" that verifies via audits which smelters have systems in place that properly track and verify sources of minerals before processing the ore for industrial purposes. GeSI and EICC are also working on a common reporting template for all companies.

In the midst of those efforts, the Enough Project is also proposing a system of certification (not yet in place) similar to that of Fair Trade that would enable manufacturers and eventually consumers to distinguish between those actors in the electronics supply chain that are verifiably excluding conflict diamonds from the DRC. The work of the Enough Project created a breakthrough in the use of a very specific legislative action by a powerful government to require specific actions on the part of companies to avoid complicity with conflict. What is particularly interesting is that companies are being held accountable for their relationship to a conflict via the commodities they use in manufacturing. Companies are being forced to acknowledge links to a country and situation with which they previously appeared to have had no relationship. It is one thing for a multinational company to pay attention to conditions in factories making its products in China or Guatemala, and quite another for it to trace and reform its links to the sources of the metals in yet another country.

This is indeed an important step in the quest for greater accountability for supply chains, but the drawback is that implementation is very complicated, as the conflict dynamics on the ground in the DRC change so rapidly. Moreover, tracing and securing the integrity of commodities all the way through to a finished product is very challenging. There is also a limit to the government's willingness to enforce such provisions. Some are critical of these new regulations, saying that the consequence has been a decrease in legitimate mining in the DRC and the loss of jobs for many desperate people in a time of crisis.[17] Increased transparency can also mean that illegal behaviors are forced farther behind the scenes, thereby exacerbating problems for the most vulnerable. Activists might also lose momentum or get pulled in other directions, thus decreasing pressure on companies. The world's voracious appetite for electronic products (not to mention the world's military need for products made with these rare minerals) means that the dilemma of sourcing from a highly conflictual region like the DRC will not be resolved easily or quickly because the demand by many will outweigh the concerns of a few. Other sources of these minerals (e.g., Bolivia) are also fraught with social problems and conflicts that may not receive as much attention as those in the DRC but could in the future.

Case Study: PeaceWorks

While much of the attention in the arena of corporations and conflict is on the role of massive multinational companies, there is a wellspring of creative entrepreneurial efforts that speaks to the need and opportunity for everyday business activity to serve as a positive peacebuilding force. Recent years have seen the advent of enterprises that in whole or in part deliberately focus on building peace through their very business activities. An example of this trend is the PeaceWorks Company, founded in 1994 by people who had been engaged otherwise in peacebuilding activities through more conventional channels.[18]

On its website, PeaceWorks describes itself as "a business that pursues both profit and peace. We pursue profit through our sales of healthful food products that are produced by neighbors on opposing sides of political or armed conflicts, whose cooperative business ventures we facilitate." By creating business ventures that literally bring together opposing sides to work together, PeaceWorks enables people to see profit from cooperation. Furthermore, well-run businesses serve to bring prosperity and stability to conflictual neighborhoods and regions. A portion of the profits from these businesses goes to support the PeaceWorks Foundation, which sponsors the One Voice Movement to advocate for peace between the Palestinians and Israeli through a two-state solution.

PeaceWorks has a conceptual underpinning called the Theory of Economic Cooperation, which is based on the value of interdependence that comes from bringing together presumed rivals and leveraging each other's strengths. As businesses are built and maintained, people get to know each other deeply while also seeing their future as linked at various levels with each other, not just in terms of future business success. PeaceWorks calls this "Our Cooperation Ecosystem," whereby joint ventures engaging both "sides" increasingly have a stake in maintaining the partnership across the divide.[19] At a higher level, such people and enterprises have a stake in building a society that is more stable, peaceful, and open to interaction among rivals. A key question is whether personal stakes in cooperation and personal transformations facilitated in the workplace through cooperative efforts can transcend other forces and dynamics that fuel conflict and division.

One of PeaceWorks' companies operates in Israel, creating food products such as tapenade and pesto sauces. Palestinians grow the olives, Egyptians make the glass jars, and Turks provide the sun-dried tomatoes, thus knitting together people and communities often in conflict with each other. In another business called Bali Spice, Christians, Buddhists, and Muslims work together in a conflictual part of Indonesia to build a profitable future.

Businesses like PeaceWorks can be seen in many conflict-ridden societies; indeed, they have always existed to some extent, as even the most conflicted societies have a modicum of economic, family, and other ties across the divide. It is the deliberate creation of such enterprises and the intentional marketing of them as peacebuilding efforts that marks this as a new and interesting phenomenon. Enormous challenges remain to grow these small-scale efforts so that they become a decisive market force in conflict regions.

Much innovation is occurring in the realm of business activities squarely linked to peace (Iff et al., 2010). A group called BPeace has created a network of business professionals who help build the capacity of local entrepreneurs in conflict-prone countries, such as Afghanistan and Rwanda, to expand their businesses and create jobs, especially for women. Their motto is: "more jobs mean less violence." Another innovative group, Building Markets, works in postconflict societies, particularly in places with peacekeeping operations, to link international spending (e.g., by militaries, United Nations, international NGOs) to local companies to promote economic recovery.[20] Building Markets has created or sustained more than 100,000 jobs in Afghanistan through promoting "host country first" procurement practices, whereby local businesses are given the opportunity to bid to provide goods and services to the many international groups operating there.[21] Similar programs are working in Haiti and Timor-Leste to provide substantial markets and investment for local businesses.

It is important to note that outside the creative work of such civil society groups, smaller, local companies are generally at the forefront of economic activity, including building and sustaining peace, but without fanfare; after all, even in stable societies, large multinational companies are only a part of an economy. After a conflict ends, the first investors are likely those with existing or previous roots in the region who, therefore, are familiar with both the challenges and the opportunities. Often people voluntarily or involuntarily exiled during previous regimes and during conflict will return to restart, expand, or create new businesses. Soon after cessation of conflict, certain types of businesses—such as mobile phone providers, construction, food processing, transportation, and basic banking—are among the first to invest, indeed are crucial in restarting basic economic life. Multinationals are more hesitant to invest substantially in capital-intensive ventures while the future is still uncertain and are also less likely to invest in marketing and distribution channels for foreign products while the economic outlook, policies, and confidence remain uncertain. Mashatt and Mendelson-Forman (2007) write of the "golden hour" (roughly the first year postconflict) when investment and economic stabilization and opportunity are as crucial to establish as physical security and when local business and micro-enterprise are particularly valuable and well positioned for success.

ETHICAL AND OTHER CHALLENGES AND UNRESOLVED QUESTIONS

A chief ethical concern for scholars and practitioners working at the interface of corporations and conflict relates to the potential for (and/or perception of) bias and even corruption that comes from accepting money from companies. The irony is that many actors, including civil society organizations, are calling for more engagement and funding by corporations for peacebuilding activities. In some cases, corporations are funding studies, conferences, and project activities.

One group, the CDA Collaborative Learning Projects, gets around this problem by working with companies to have a positive impact in communities while deliberately insisting that all project work be shared openly with other stakeholders.[22] This helps them to build and maintain trust in the community and avoid charges of co-optation.

An unresolved question in this area is the extent to which businesses should be involved in proactive roles in peacebuilding. It is not controversial to state that companies should not exacerbate conflict. It is challenging, however, to agree on roles for powerful business leaders in peace negotiations, designing postconflict systems, or setting the agenda for socioeconomic change. Very often business leaders and other elites in a society have long been part of the conflict; there might not be a high level of trust in their ability to play neutral or even constructive roles that go beyond their business interests. Furthermore, many of the companies likely to be engaged in conflict from a negative and/or positive perspective are likely to be multinational in scope and character, with leadership in Northern countries, far from the realities of the conflictual society.

Multi-stakeholder initiatives and various peacebuilding efforts sponsored by multinational companies and NGOs are sometimes criticized for being too focused on the ideas and strategies of Northern elites, perhaps thereby perpetuating global patterns of dominance. The challenge is to emphasize and empower local groups and businesses to take the lead in creating pro-peace business engagement, though these local companies are much less likely to face public, consumer, or media pressure to do so as well-known international companies are. Yet, it is also important to avoid romanticizing or relying only upon local leadership and business efforts, particularly as they might not have the financial means, psychological distance, or other resources to do all that is necessary.

Another challenge, particularly for civil society groups, is to conceptualize the issues in ways that focus on structural problems in economics and the business/government interface to get at deeper sources. Is it wrongheaded to focus on particular companies rather than the written and unwritten rules by which they operate? Does it undermine civil society to promote voluntary programs and self-regulation outside the structures of government? It is far easier and much more convenient to focus on a brand-name company while letting others go unchallenged and the structural underpinnings unaddressed.

A focus on corporations can help the peacebuilding field bridge the theoretical and practical debates about globalization and conflict. The dilemmas confronted by companies and by those seeking to change corporate behavior are very practical, topical issues in most contentious conflict systems linked to the globalization phenomenon. Furthermore, peacebuilding and corporate social responsibility fields are two of the most innovative, growing, and topical fields, both with a conscious emphasis on co-producing theory and practice.

CONCLUSION

This chapter has covered the wide range of issues associated with the role of the private sector in integrated peacebuilding. The goal of this chapter was to highlight the promise of major change in conflict dynamics that can come from engaging the private sector. The possibilities of innovation in practical approaches to peacebuilding are very real with companies as they face more scrutiny and come to understand how bad conflict is for business. The cursory review in this chapter underscores the reality that the issue of corporations and conflict is so large and complex that it merits being considered as a realm or schema of conflict classification in its own right. Hopefully, more scholars and students will come to think of corporate social conflict the way one thinks of environmental, religious, or ethnic conflict—not as an isolated phenomenon per se, but as a substantial focus of inquiry in its own right.

QUESTIONS FOR FURTHER DISCUSSION

1. Should companies be encouraged to continue operating in conflict zones or withdraw to avoid complicity?

2. What are the risks for companies that engage in peacebuilding?

3. Should there be different standards and approaches for companies and conflict based on the size, sector, nationality, or other attributes of the company?

4. Is peace sustainable without economic health? What does a peace-promoting economy look like and what role would corporations play in it?

5. What role can you play as a consumer to influence corporate behavior around conflict?

6. What can be done to break the "resource curse" that plagues so many countries with natural resources and implicates so many extractive companies in conflicts?

7. What obligations do technology companies have for the use of their products and services in the age of cyber-warfare, terrorism, surveillance and censorship by repressive regimes, and Facebook/Twitter revolutions?

References

Alexander, L., C. Gündüz, and D. B. Subedi. 2009. Strengthening the economic dimensions of peacebuilding (p. 2). International Alert. Retrieved December 15, 2011, from www.international-alert.org/sites/default/files/publications/LEO_Nepal.pdf.

Anderson, M. 1999. *Do no harm: How aid can support peace or war.* Boulder, CO: Lynne Rienner.

Andriof, J. R. 2003. *Unfolding stakeholder thinking.* Sheffield, UK: Greenleaf.

Argenti, P. A. 2004. Collaborating with activists: How Starbucks works with NGOs. *California Management Review* 47: 91–116.

Ballentine, K., and H. Nitzschke, eds. 2005. *Profiting from peace: Managing the resource dimensions of civil war* (Project of the International Peace Academy). Boulder, CO: Lynne Rienner.

Bendell, J. 2003. Talking for change? Reflections on effective stakeholder dialogue. In J. Andriof, S. Waddock, B. Husted, and S. Rahman, eds. *Reporting and performance.* Sheffield, UK: Greenleaf.

———. 2004. Barricades and boardrooms: A contemporary history of the corporate accountability movement (No. Programme Paper 13): UNRISD. Retrieved August 8, 2011, from www.unrisd.org/80256B3C005BCCF9/%28httpPublications%29/504AF359BB 33967FC1256EA9003CE20A?OpenDocument.

Besley, T., H. Mueller, and P. Singh. 2011, July 6. Conflict and investment. International Growth Centre. Retrieved March 5, 2012, from www.theigc.org/sites/default/files /presentation_slides/investment_-_background_paper.pdf.

Bray, J. 2005. *International companies and post-conflict reconstruction: Cross-sectoral comparisons.* Social Development Papers. Conflict Prevention and Reconstruction, Paper 22. Washington, DC: World Bank and International Alert. Retrieved April 3, 2012, from www2.gtz.de/wbf/lred/library/detail.asp?number=2951.

Brynne, A., and P. Mallet. 2005. *Stakeholder consultation practices in standards development.* Kaslo, Canada: ISEAL Alliance.

Campbell, A. 2002. *The private sector and conflict prevention mainstreaming* (p. 9). Ottawa, Ontario, Canada: Country Indicators for Foreign Policy.

Center for Corporate Citizenship. 2005. Going global: managers' experiences working with worldwide stakeholders. Boston College.

Collier, P. 2000. *Economic causes of civil war and their implications for policy.* Washington, DC: World Bank.

————. 2007. *The bottom billion: Why the poorest countries are failing and what can be done about it.* New York: Oxford University Press.

Costantino, C. A., and C. S. Merchant. 1996. *Designing conflict management systems: A guide to creating productive and healthy organizations* (1st ed.). San Francisco: Jossey-Bass.

Diamond, L., and J. W. McDonald. 1996. *Multi-track diplomacy: A systems approach to peace* (3rd ed.). West Hartford, CT: Kumarian Press.

Economic Recovery Strategies and Peacebuilding Process. 2008, November. *Private sector development and peacebuilding in peacebuilding initiative.* Peacebuilding Initiative Portal, HPCR International. Retrieved April 1, 2012, from www.peacebuildinginitiative .org/index.cfm?pageId=1903.

Fisher, R., B. Patton, and W. Ury. 1991. *Getting to yes: Negotiating agreement without giving in* (2nd ed.). New York: Penguin Books.

Freeman, R. E. 1984. *Strategic management: A stakeholder approach.* Boston: Pittman.

Friedman, M. 1970, September 13. The social responsibility of business is to increase its profits. *New York Times Magazine.*

Garriga, E., and D. Mele. 2004. Corporate social responsibility theories: Mapping the territory. *Journal of Business Ethics* 53, no. 1–2: 51–71.

Gray, R., C. Dey, D. Owen, R. Evans, and S. Zadek. 1997. Struggling with the praxis of social accounting: Stakeholders, accountability, audits, and procedures. *Accounting, Auditing & Accountability Journal* 10, no. 3: 325–364.

Guidance on Responsible Business in Conflict-Affected & High-Risk Areas: A Resource for Companies & Investors. 2010. New York: United Nations Global Compact and the Principles for Responsible Investing.

Hart, S., and S. Sharma. 2004. Engaging fringe stakeholders for competitive imagination. *Academy of Management Executive* 18, no. 1: 7–18.

Hemmati, M. 2001. *Multi-stakeholder processes for governance and sustainability—beyond deadlock and conflict.* London: Earthscan.

Iff, A., D. Sguaitamatti, R. M. Alluri, and D. Kohler. 2010, February. *Money makers as peace makers? Business actors in mediation processes.* Bern, Switzerland: Swisspeace. Retrieved April 3, 2012, from www.swisspeace.ch/topics/business-peace/publications.html.

Institute for Human Rights and Business. 2011, May. *From red to green flags: The corporate responsibility to respect human rights in high-risk countries.* Retrieved January 13, 2012, from www.ihrb.org/pdf/from_red_to_green_flags/complete_report.pdf.

International Alert. 2004. Promoting a conflict prevention approach to OECD companies and partnering with local business. Retrieved September 27, 2011, from www .international-alert.org/resources/publications/promoting-conflict-prevention-approach -oecd-companies-and-partnering-local-bu.

International Federation of Accountants. 2007. Key principles that are widely accepted features of good practice. In *Defining and developing an effective code of conduct for organizations* (p. 6). Professional Accountants in Business Committee. Retrieved September 27, 2011, from www.ifac.org/sites/default/files/publications/files/defining-and-developing-an.pdf.

Kanbur, R. 2007. Poverty and conflict: The inequality link. New York: International Peace Academy.

Kaye, J. D. 1996. Symposium on business dispute resolution—ADR and beyond: An opening statement. *Albany Law Review* 59: 839.

Kolk, A., R. v. Tulder, and C. Welters. 1999. International codes of conduct and corporate social responsibility: Can transnational corporations regulate themselves? *Transnational Corporations* 8, no. 1: 143–180.

Korten, D. C. 2001. *When corporations rule the world* (2nd ed.). San Francisco: Berrett-Koehler.

Kuhn, J. W., and D. W. Shriver Jr. 1991. *Beyond success: Corporations and their critics in the 1990s*. New York: Oxford University Press.

Lawhouse.dk. 2006. Business and human rights newsletter.

Mamic, I. 2004. *Implementing codes of conduct: How businesses manage social performance in global supply chains*. Austin, TX: International Labor Organization and Greenleaf.

Mashatt, M., and J. Mendelson-Forman. 2007. Employment generation and economic development in stabilization and reconstruction operations. Special report, Stabilization and Reconstruction Series #6, US Institute of Peace, Washington, DC.

Messick, D. M., and A. E. Tenbrunsel. 1996. *Codes of conduct: Behavioral research into business ethics*. New York: Russell Sage.

Milanovic, B. 2005. *Why did the poorest countries fail to catch up?* Carnegie Endowment Paper #62. Washington, DC: Carnegie Endowment for International Peace.

Moore, C. W. 2003. *The mediation process: Practical strategies for resolving conflict* (3rd ed.). San Francisco: Jossey-Bass.

Oetzel, J., M. Westermann-Behaylo, C. Koerber, T. Fort, and J. Rivera. 2010. Business and peace: Sketching the terrain. *Journal of Business Ethics* 89: 351–373.

Parrett, W. G. 2004. Globalization's next frontier—Principled codes of conduct that bolster the rule of law. *Business and Society Review* 109, no. 4: 577–582.

PeaceWorks. n.d. PeaceWorks, a not-only-for-profit company. Retrieved March 5, 2012, from www.peaceworks.com.

Phillips, R. 2002. Is corporate engagement an advocacy strategy for NGOs? The community aid abroad experience. *Nonprofit Management and Leadership* 13, no. 2: 123–137.

———. 2003. *Stakeholder theory and organizational ethics*. San Francisco: Berrett-Koehler.

Prince of Wales Business Leaders Forum, International Alert and Council on Economic Priorities. 1999. *The business of peace: The private sector as a partner in conflict prevention and resolution*. Retrieved April 2, 2012, from www.commdev.org/extractives/business-peace-private-sector-partner-conflict-prevention-and-resolution.

Radin, T. J. 2004. The effectiveness of global codes of conduct: Role models that make sense. *Business and Society Review* 109, no. 4: 415–447.

Rees, C. 2008. Corporations and human rights: Accountability mechanisms for resolving complaints and disputes. Report of Multi-stakeholder Workshop, Mossavar-Rahmani Center for Business and Government, Harvard University, April, 2007. Retrieved December 15, 2011, from http://baseswiki.org/w/images/en/a/a8/April_workshop_report_-_final.pdf.

Sachs, S. 2006a. Corporate social responsibility from a "stakeholder view" perspective. *Corporate Governance* 6, no. 4: 506–515.

Sachs, S. 2006b, November 8. Engaging stakeholders: CSR equals corporate stakeholder responsibility. *Ethical Corporation*. Retrieved April 1, 2012, from www.ethicalcorp.com/content/engaging-stakeholders-csr-equals-corporate-stakeholder-responsibility.

Sethi, S. P., and O. F. Williams. 2000. *Economic imperatives and ethical values in global business: The South African experience and international codes today.* Notre Dame, IN: University of Notre Dame Press.

Smith, G., and D. Feldman. 2003. *Company codes of conduct and international standards: An analytical comparison.* Washington, DC: World Bank Group.

Spar, D. L., and L. T. L. Mure. 2003. The power of activism: Assessing the impact of NGOs on global business. *California Management Review* 45, no. 3: 78–101.

Sutton, B., ed. 1993. *The legitimate corporation.* Cambridge, MA: Blackwell.

Switzer, J., and H. Ward. 2004. *Enabling corporate investment in peace: An assessment of voluntary initiatives addressing business and violent conflict, and a framework for policy decision-making.* Winnipeg, Canada: International Institute for Sustainable Development, Retrieved April 1, 2012, from www.eldis.org/assets/Docs/11831.html.

US Congress. 2010. *Wall Street reform and Consumer Protection Act* (pp. 838–846). US Securities and Exchange Commission. Retrieved December 15, 2011, from www.sec.gov/about/laws/wallstreetreform-cpa.pdf.

Visser, W., D. Matten, M. Pohl, and N. Tolhurst. 2010. *The A to Z of corporate social responsibility* (p. 183). New York: John Wiley and Sons.

Waddell, S., and L. D. Brown. 1997. Fostering intersectoral partnering: A guide to promoting cooperation among government, business, and civil society actors. *IDR Reports* 13, no. 3.

Williams, O. F., ed. 2008. *Peace through commerce—Responsible corporate citizenship and the ideals of the United Nations Global Compact.* Notre Dame, IN: University of Notre Dame Press.

Wood, E. M. 1995. *Democracy against capitalism: Renewing historical materialism.* New York: Cambridge University Press.

Zadek, S. 2001. *The civil corporation: The new economy of corporate citizenship.* Sterling, VA: Earthscan Publications Ltd.

Notes

1. Throughout this chapter, the terms "company," "corporation," "private sector," and "business" will be used mostly interchangeably to refer to profit-seeking enterprises: large and small, local and multinational, formally incorporated or not.

2. See www.visionofhumanity.org/gpi-data.

3. See www.international-alert.org and www.iblf.org.

4. See www.bpa-srilanka.com.

5. See www.bpa-srilanka.com/what-we-do.html.

6. See www.voluntaryprinciples.org.

7. See www.voluntaryprinciples.org/participants.

8. See www.kimberleyprocess.com/background/index_en.html.

9. See www.eiti.org/node/1164.

10. See www.eiti.org/countries.

11. See www.swissinfo.ch/eng/swiss_news/Security_firms_sign_code_of_conduct.html?cid=28748126.

12. See www.198.170.85.29/Ruggie-protect-respect-remedy-framework.pdf.

13. See www.international-alert.org.

14. See www.enoughproject.org.

15. See www.enoughproject.org/conflict_areas/eastern_congo.

16. See www.gesi.org/LinkClick.aspx?fileticket=E6I2mF17BAY%3d&tabid=75.

17. See "A Rule Aimed at Warlords Upends African Mines," *Bloomberg Businessweek,* August 4, 2011; www.businessweek.com/magazine/a-rule-aimed-at-warlords-upends-african-mines-08042011.html.

18. See www.peaceworks.com.

19. See www.peaceworks.com/Originals/mission.html.

20. For more on the field of economic recovery, see Economic Recovery (2008).

21. For more on Building Markets, see http://buildingmarkets.org (the organization was formerly called Peace Dividend Trust).

22. See www.cdainc.com.

chapter seven

RELIGION AND PEACEBUILDING

Qamar-ul Huda and Katherine Marshall

Peace is a gift of God and at the same time a task which is never fully completed. . . . Peace is the result of a process of purification and of cultural, moral and spiritual elevation involving each individual and people, a process in which human dignity is fully respected.
—POPE BENEDICT XVI, WORLD DAY OF PEACE, JANUARY 1, 2011

T HIS CHAPTER FOCUSES ON CONTEMPORARY ways in which religious institutions and actors foster peace through interventions in active conflict zones. It highlights the involvement of religious actors in conflict situations or tense social environments, and the ways in which they contribute to integrated peacebuilding, conflict prevention, and humanitarian relief. The discussion is set against the backdrop of a general tendency, especially in diplomacy, to neglect religious aspects of conflict in peacebuilding. While today's religious actors are far more often recognized as players in peacebuilding than two decades ago, they still tend to be sidelined at many levels. Especially in the world's most complex conflict situations, religious peacemaking rarely plays a central role.

This chapter starts by exploring the relationships between religion, conflict, peacebuilding, and development. A review of emerging theoretical approaches to religious peacebuilding follows, highlighting both academic and policy issues that aim to describe better practitioner roles. The field of peacebuilding is coming to recognize the multiple roles that religious communities play in the various phases of conflict. While literature on Christian and especially Catholic "peace churches" tends to be most abundant, Islamic peacebuilding highlights important and expanding work in different locales. Approaches and practical experience of faith traditions, such as Judaism and Buddhism, are coming into sharper focus. Appreciating these various religious traditions leads to richer and more sophisticated identification and integration of religiously inspired dimensions in peacebuilding. This chapter also highlights interfaith work and institutions. Contemporary peacebuilding challenges include the difficulties facing failing or weak states and the influence of religion in the "war on terrorism" or "countering violent extremism," likewise in debates about whether the world faces a "clash of civilizations." Women whose peace work is inspired by their religious beliefs and religious institutions (or proceeds despite the latter) present an especially important topic because religion and gender issues tend to be intertwined in policy debates and on-the-ground action. The chapter's final sections highlight specific examples of religious institutions that have been central to peacebuilding efforts.

Terminology is a complex dimension in considering religion. The definitions of commonly used terms, such as "religion," "faith," "spiritual," "secular," "transcendence," "faith-based," and "faith-inspired," are often contested. For the sake of simplicity, this chapter uses "religion," "religious," and "faith" with the understanding that such terms can be associated with a largely Western, institutional bias. Faith-inspired actors are defined here in broad terms, including formal and informal religious actors, individuals and institutions, which see themselves as motivated by and linked to a specific religious or spiritual dimension. Examples of religious actors include priests, rabbis, imams, gurus, Buddhist monks, women's and youth groups, and informal mediators, as well as international religious organizations, such as Religions for Peace, Pax Christi, Lutheran World Federation, the Mennonites, World Council of Churches, and the Muslim World Congress. "Religion," therefore, refers to the multitiered dimensions of all of these religious actors and communities.

RELIGION, CONFLICT RESOLUTION, AND PEACEBUILDING

The deep-rooted and ancient ideal that religious traditions seek peace for warring societies and troubled souls is well reflected both in the annual exhortation of Pope Benedict XVI on the Day of Peace (cited above); the Koranic counsel (8:62–63), "And if they incline towards peace, incline thou also towards it, and put thy trust in Allah"; and the New Testament teaching, "Blessed are the peacemakers, for they shall be called the children of God." Though religion is often associated with violence, faith and interfaith leaders stress the core ideal that religion fundamentally centers on peace. Faith can fuel deep and lasting anger even as it offers inspiration and persistence in work for peace, because religious beliefs speak to the deepest reservoirs of motivation and identity. Religion's roles in conflict and in peacebuilding are complex, varied, and often the subject of controversy. Is religion part of the problem or part of the solution? Are religious factors and actors sufficiently or even intelligently taken into account? In professional and academic theories and practical guidance materials for conflict resolution and peacebuilding, religious actors are often demonized or omitted entirely from the picture. Sophisticated understandings of religious actors in society, as both sources of conflict and potential partners in working for peace, are rare. Religion is a relatively recent entrant in thought about both humanitarian relief and international development. This is part of the general phenomenon of "religious illiteracy" that scholar Stephen Prothero (2007) has documented vividly, and is part of the broader intellectual and societal problem of appreciating how and why religion is integral to peacebuilding and development.

Religious actors play multilayered roles in conflict situations because religion is deeply embedded in the life of communities. Religious dimensions are invariably significant, whether a community enjoys fragile peace or outright violence. Religious actors may run the most lasting, sustainable social services, and keep schools and clinics operating in tense times. They have distinctive if not unique access to information. In various circumstances, they may also incite violence or, more commonly, respond to provocations with violent words. On the other hand, they may also work to actively negotiate peace settlements, bring parties together, and work to reconcile aggrieved parties.

Common understandings of the causes and course of conflict provide little space for culture, faith-based actors, women, and civil society actors. In many settings religious elements lurk in the far margins of conflict narratives, or are cast solely in negative roles. Religious actors and women may also share stereotypes of backwardness and innate conservatism, which further aggravate the gaps in understanding. The tendency to overlook or stereotype religious factors raises basic questions as to how far peacebuilding specialists and their development counterparts appreciate the fundamental complexities that characterize contemporary conflicts. For peacebuilding to be effective, the process needs to be grounded in supporting local institutions, empowering communities, and meeting people's needs and aspirations. This often means working in partnership with faith-based actors who in many regions of the world play a central role in community life and stability.

Peacebuilding reflects a set of beliefs and hypotheses that highlight the roots of conflict at the community level and views conflict management far more broadly than simply stopping violent conflict. As such, peacebuilding can be applied to any situation where there is potential or actual conflict. The key skills required include an interdisciplinary understanding of what causes social breakdown, participatory techniques that engage communities, a focus on process, and explicit efforts to address complex challenges like wounded memories, ethnic and religious tensions, as well as positive efforts to build thriving societies.

Religion is an essential element of peacebuilding. It belongs at the center of conflict resolution and transformation approaches, as well as in training for diplomats and policy makers. This begs the question, if religion has the potential to dramatically affect a conflict both positively and negatively, why has it not been sufficiently integrated into peacebuilding practices already?

RELIGION, PEACEMAKING, AND CONFLICT

In the decades following World War II, most social scientists, diplomats, and experts in the field of international affairs assumed that religion played less and less important roles in national identity, politics, law, and international relations. This perspective was shaped by the "secularization thesis," which advocated that secular liberal democracies should replace traditional patterns of governance and authority, including, and especially, those that were linked to religion (Stark, 1999). Indeed, as societies have modernized and moved toward postmodernity, the relationship between religion and society has changed in many ways. For instance, in many regions, religiously plural societies are becoming the complex norm. A widening variety of religious actors and tensions linked to religious identities play crucial roles in both conflicts and peacebuilding, as well as in building democracies. Religion is a factor in intercommunal violence in places as diverse as Pakistan, Afghanistan, Iraq, Egypt, Sri Lanka, Nigeria, India, Northern Ireland, Sudan, and Uganda. Negative perceptions of religion, such as religion's being used to motivate the violent conflicts that drive communities apart, have tended to predominate. Still, if driven by the influence of religious leaders who act as political or spiritual voices that resonate loudly within the society, religious values can play constructive roles in counteracting extremism and aiding in reconciliation. Some of the greatest peacemakers of our times—Archbishop Desmond Tutu, Mahatma Gandhi, and Martin Luther King Jr.—drew inspiration and practical approaches from their faith. Scholar Scott Appleby (2003) terms this dual role "the ambivalence of the sacred," alluding to religion's power to create spiritual commitments to both violence and peace.

As earlier chapters and the above discussion have highlighted, peacebuilding entails wide-ranging efforts to establish sustainable peace by addressing root causes of conflict through dialogue, institution-building, political and economic transformation, reconciliation, and empowering those who work on the ground. Peacebuilding also engages all actors working toward concrete structural transformations for peace and to prevent a relapse into conflict, going far beyond direct intervention to halt violent conflict, negotiate a peace agreement, or mediate among disputants from the international down to the community level (Lederach, 1997; Little and Appleby, 2004).

Religious or faith-based peacemaking shares these characteristics but involves distinctive ideas and roles. Religious actors are often the first to observe disturbing behavior and opinions on the ground before conflict erupts (Sampson and Lederach, 2000). They may be acutely sensitive to religious intolerance, ethnic hatred, tribalism, and communalism because these disrupt their communities. Faith leaders may contest bigotry, hatred, and dehumanization of any group as contrary to religious values. In times of crisis, religious leaders simultaneously serve as mediators, protectors, advocates, educators, peacebuilders, monitors, and agents of change (Steele, 2008).

This stands in contrast to the way many academics and media outlets portray modern religion. Especially since the Balkan genocide of the early 1990s, where religious differences were a significant factor and where religious leaders visibly inflamed conflict, religious actors have become associated with extremism and conflict. Other prominent cases include the Lebanese civil war, Northern Ireland, and Iran. Religion often tends to be portrayed as integral to belief systems belonging to a premodern, backward, irrational era.

Experience and analysis within the conflict resolution field, however, make it clear that religion is far more dynamic than this. Religion is commonly blamed for conflict when religious identities are falsely used and misappropriated. In some cases, Northern Ireland, for example, religion may not be the principal cause of conflict, even when the opposing actors have powerful religious identities. Religion within a conflict context, therefore, must be understood as a sacred veneer for political, economic, social, and historic battles among disputants instead of as the root cause of the conflict. Because religious affiliation is often central to an individual's or group's definition of who they are, when conflict does arise, religious differences can take on a heightened prominence and fuel emotions that are aroused when core beliefs and the very sense of a community's identity seem to be under threat.

A sharpened focus on religion as a factor in domestic and international conflicts is relatively recent in the scholarly field of conflict resolution, and within the larger social sciences. It is spurred by understandings that particular religious convictions contain essential sources of related danger. Theorists such as Holenstein (2005) and Haynes (1995) point to four fundamental areas of danger within religion. They suggest first that religion is often based upon absolute and unconditional principles that can lead to totalitarian characteristics: for instance, the claims by the Abrahamic religions— Christianity, Islam, and Judaism—of the absolutely divine and exclusive sense of existence. Second, they point out that an absolute and exclusive validity can fuel intolerance, overzealous missionary work, religious fragmentation, and sectarianism. Scholars cite the religious wars in medieval Europe to demonstrate religious exclusiveness that did not allow room for pluralism and tolerance. Today proselytizing or evangelizing work in non-Christian nations can generate tensions that at times erupt into violent conflict. Third, the passion that religion can arouse can increase aggressiveness and the willingness to use violence. By using symbolic values as an aspect of religious conviction, violence can be construed as a "holy" objective or obligation. And fourth, religious leaders within faith-inspired organizations may seek to legitimize abuses of power and violation of human rights in the name of their god or gods. Some scholars argue that both historically and currently, religious leaders use domination strategies of identity politics to harness real or perceived "ethnic-cultural" and "cultural-religious" differences that accentuate conflict. Misused religious motivation informs religious extremism, fundamentalism, and terrorist activities. Religious fundamentalist movements "lay claim to a single and absolutist religious interpretation at the cost of all others, and they link their interpretation to political power objectives" (Holenstein, 2005, p. 11). Others highlight "exclusive accounts of the nature of reality" in which believers accept religious beliefs that they regard as true beliefs (Kurtz, 1995). Since each faith claims authority that emanates principally from sacred texts, this sense of reality poses serious challenges to religious toleration and diversity, essential to coexistence in a globalized world, and often makes conflict more likely (Kurtz, 1995).

In contrast, many religious traditions have core beliefs that in both theory and practice can help develop a peaceful, multicultural world. Scholarship on religious peacemaking highlights the many cases where religious actors have transformed conflict peacefully and cultivated a "culture of peace" in war-torn societies. Religious leaders in Zamboanga City, Philippines, were outspoken about religious tensions between Muslims and Christians due to the Islamic extremist group Abu Sayyaf and they worked to forge a strategic plan to counteract violence and fundamentalism. In Cambodia, Buddhist monk Maha Ghossananda after 1992 led some 10,000 monks, nuns, and laity on daring monthlong marches from the northwest to the capital,

Phnom Penh. This "Pilgrimage of Truth March" traversed dangerous areas filled with land mines and active conflict and helped spur UN action and moves toward democracy (Maat, 1995; Weiner, 2003). In Jordan, the Royal Hashemite Kingdom assembled over 150 leading Muslim jurists from the Islamic world's eight most important law schools to discuss indiscriminate violence in the Middle East. They agreed to work together against the rise of extremism and the irresponsible, illegal act of calling other Muslims who disagree on certain positions apostates (*takfir*). The resulting "Amman Message" stated that "Islam honors every human being, without distinction of color, race or religion" (Royal Institute for Inter-Faith Studies, 2004). These examples illustrate the many ways in which world religious actors participate in peacebuilding and conflict prevention measures. From mass electoral participation to improving interfaith relations, from negotiating peace settlements in conflict zones to aiding refugee or internally displaced–person camps, religious actors can play invaluable roles on the ground.

Some of the world's most influential thinkers and actors for peace, past and present, drew their ideas and inspiration from their faith tradition, working through their faith networks to mobilize support to become agents of change. The best known are Mahatma Gandhi, whose writings and commitment to nonviolence and social activism serve as an example and inspiration (Ingram, 2003; Juergensmeyer, 2005), and Martin Luther King Jr., pastor and courageous social activist who inspired a generation of peacebuilders. Both died violently in struggles that were their life work.

Gandhi's life was a quest for peace and justice. Nonviolence and spirituality are, he argued, one and the same, as peace and justice are intertwined. Gandhi was a careful student of religion but also a skeptic, especially where organized religion was concerned. His philosophy drew on the religious principle of *ahimsa,* meaning to do no harm, a principle tenet of Buddhism, Hinduism, and Jainism alike. His beliefs sharpened as he worked against the injustices of apartheid in South Africa and colonial rule in India. Gandhi's peace philosophy—*Satyagraha,* or truth force—inspired such actions as marches and his constant advocacy against colonial rule, racial discrimination, and discrimination against the Dalit caste. For Gandhi, nonviolence went hand in hand with religion. "Non-violence is a power which can be wielded equally by all . . . provided they have a living faith in the God of Love" (Harijan, 1936, as cited in Chakrabarty, 2006, p. 133). Nonviolence "is an active force of the highest order. It is soul force or the power of Godhead within us" (British Broadcasting Corporation, 2012). Millions look to Gandhi's life and his violent death as symbolic of an independent and determined spirituality grounded in principles drawn from great religions, shaped by the demands of justice in his time.

Martin Luther King Jr. was a deeply spiritual leader. Known for his indomitable leadership of the civil rights movement, he was a powerful orator and preacher who came from a line of pastors. In 1955 he led the first large-scale nonviolent boycott to end bus segregation. As president of the Southern Christian Leadership Conference, he brought together his Christian theological training and his passion for civil rights. King's personal philosophy drew deeply on his Christian faith, but he also looked to different religious traditions. King described Gandhi, who inspired much of his nonviolent philosophy, as the "greatest Christian" (Blakely, 2001). "At the center of non-violence stands the principle of love" (King, 1957), he said. King was awarded the Nobel Peace Prize in 1964 (Gandhi never was—a striking omission).

Religious leaders, in times of crisis and in times of peace, offer more than religious guidance: equally important are traditions of spiritual enrichment, serving others, and being interconnected during difficult times. Religious communities are also a vital form of social capital. Churches, mosques, synagogues, and temples serve as places of worship and refuge but also as community centers. Religious institutions run schools, hospitals, and clinics with dense social networks and resources, both local and international. Their roles are especially critical where the state is weak or incapable of providing basic social and educational services. Peacebuilding work without the cooperation of religious actors may well lose legitimacy with the very people they are trying to help. Scholar Andrea Bartoli (2004) underscores the strengths of religious mediators, stressing four key factors: (1) religious actors possess intimate knowledge of the culture and language of peoples in conflict; (2) those deep roots provide negotiators with firsthand information as conflict changes on the ground; (3) leaders have access to a wide variety of political expertise, locally and internationally; and (4) some mediators develop long-term visions of peace adapted to the society in question. They can draw on a network of congregations and leaders, as well as direct friendships that develop over years of common experience. "Conflicts need to be 'seen' and 'read' properly, especially those that have major cultural, ethnic, and religious components" (Bartoli, 2004, p. 158). In sum, religious communities offer important insights and understandings of causes of conflict and possible avenues to solutions.

This suggests that to appreciate fully the root causes of any conflict, religious actors need to be included from the outset and should not be neglected at any stage of the process. The efforts of religious actors in conflict zones, such as in Mozambique, Algeria, Nepal, and the Philippines, demonstrate the many ways that religious actors contribute significantly to peacebuilding. These actors have been able to devise practical, long-term strategies not exclusively for any religious community but with a wider vision. In Mozambique, religious actors engaged rebel groups by listening to the concerns of those who had no land, resources, education, health care, or other basic necessities. Their complex and coherent approach to religious peacemaking allowed them to delegitimize violent behavior while emphasizing nonviolent peacebuilding.

Several Christian denominations broadly known as "peace churches" occupy a special place in the field of religious peacebuilding. The Quakers, Mennonites, and Church of the Brethren are renowned for their traditional opposition to war, principled objection to serving in the military, and constant advocacy for peace. These traditions, and others like them, stand for nonviolence and nonviolent resistance; Anabaptists, Shakers, and some among Pentecostal and Catholic communities share similar beliefs. Their traditions draw on the conviction that Jesus advocated for the use of nonviolence, which has led them to serve in many roles that include active mediators, leaders in global antinuclear and disarmament campaigns, and agents in conflict areas. Quaker communities, for example, work actively in many world regions. Groups trained in violence reduction works give public witness, demonstrate nonviolent intervention, accompany those affected by conflict, report on human rights, and negotiate. The American Friends

Service Committee and the Mennonite Central Committee provide relief, such as food and medicine. Established during the First World War, they have continued this service ever since. The American Friends Service Committee won the 1947 Nobel Peace Prize. In the 1980s and 1990s, the Mennonite Central Committee established peace centers, including the Conflict Transformation Program at Eastern Mennonite University, the Lombard Mennonite Peace Center in Illinois, and the Peace and Justice Network of the Mennonite Church. The Mennonite Conciliation Services, founded in 1979 to provide mediation services and training, was influential in leading mediation workshops in Northern Ireland in the 1980s. The examples cited here offer a glimpse of the rich experience and traditions of spiritual peacebuilding that take many different forms.

Common to them all is the spiritual conviction that religious communities can work holistically for social justice over the long term. Some methodologies frequently used in peacebuilding are forgiveness, recognition of pain, love for others, healing, trauma recovery, public confessions, joint prayers, use of narratives to create empathy, advocacy programs for victims, forums to explain misunderstandings, addressing the image of the "other" in the traditions, and the use of arts to express mutual respect. Analysis of the bonds that are formed in interfaith activities shows that they lead to a remarkable openness to dialogue that allows the parties involved to take risks to rebuild their lives. Religious peacebuilding efforts offer the promise of repairing broken relationships, healing damaged communities, reconciling conflicting parties, negotiating peace agreements, and re-creating a common vision of peace.

An Example of Theory and Praxis: Catholic Peacebuilding

The Catholic Church over many centuries has built a rich reservoir of teachings concerning war and justice (*jus ad bellum*—right to war), but until recently it lacked a "theology of peace," though Catholic hierarchies and individual Catholics (men and women) have commonly served as peace negotiators and advocates across the world. The Second Vatican Council in 1966 marked an important turning point. The Church, in its theology and praxis, has reoriented its vision of peace. The Catholic vision of peace highlights four elements: (1) human rights, (2) development, (3) solidarity, and (4) world order (United States Institute of Peace, 2001). The weak role of the Church in the face of Nazism and the Holocaust and instances where the Church hierarchy supported authoritarian and repressive regimes has contributed to a reflection on how the Church can better fulfill its missions of peace and social justice. The 1994 Rwanda genocide marked another important turning point. Religious leaders from all Christian denominations present there patently failed to halt the killings, while some were involved in inciting or even perpetrating them. Catholic Relief Services (CRS) has devoted major efforts to reflecting on how the genocide occurred, and what the organization might have done to prevent it. Its strategic focus shifted markedly as a result, and peacebuilding is a core part of its guiding philosophy. CRS has contributed to the Catholic Peacebuilding Network, whose mission is to deepen understanding of what constitutes a Catholic approach to peacebuilding (Schreiter, Appleby, and Powers, 2010) and to study practical implications for work on the ground.

Religious bodies, such as the Catholic Church, bring a transnational character to their work, combined with knowledge and intelligence linked to deep roots at the local level. They can be alert to looming conflict, gear social services (such as education and health) to conflict prevention, work to reconcile aggrieved parties or avert tension, and provide aid outside of multinational or state norms. Catholic University scholar Maryann Cusimano Love (Path to Peace Foundation, 2008) observes that "religious organizations in general and the Catholic Church in particular are not constrained by state sovereignty in their approaches to peacebuilding, but have rich social networks across societies available for use in building peace: schools, hospitals, international relief and development organizations, local community groups, etc." (p. 2). Through its international presence, influence on leaders or populations, and unique position as an observer at the UN, the Catholic Church has been able to facilitate peace talks between many warring groups. Catholics around the world have risked and lost their lives in peace efforts. Bishop Samuel Ruiz in Chiapas, who brought the Mexican government and the Mayan-based Zapatistas to the negotiating table in 1994, is an example of determined conflict resolution that drew on traditions of social justice and engagement. Using his authority as a representative of the pope in a very Catholic country, he bridged gaps between the indigenous peoples and the Mexican government (British Broadcasting Corporation, 2011).

INTERFAITH APPROACHES

In 1986, Pope John Paul II convened a large group of leading religious leaders in Assisi, Italy, to pray for peace side by side (making clear that the distinctiveness of each faith was not at issue). This meeting stands out among a wide array of efforts to bring together different traditions, to model peaceful engagement, and to counter violence. With religion tagged as a primary cause of conflict and the realities of deeply rooted, faith-driven tension among groups whose primary identity is their religion, the core idea was (and remains) that interfaith coupled with intrafaith dialogue and peacemaking efforts are needed to resolve conflicts and to build sustainable peace. Ambitious global interfaith institutions and alliances aim to translate common ideals for peace into concrete action.

Several ambitious global interfaith movements and institutions focus specifically on bringing together different religious traditions to demonstrate common concerns for human welfare and to perform practical work needed to address conflicts. The Parliament of the World's Religions convened in Chicago in 1893, with the goal of spreading a message of peace and promoting understanding of the diversity of world faiths. While the Parliament itself did not meet again until 1993 (again in Chicago), the idea took hold that in the interim leaders from different traditions would work together to make peace a common cause. In the 1970s, the World Conference of Religions for Peace (now called Religions for Peace) was created. With its headquarters today beside the New York UN headquarters, Religions for Peace, as its name suggests, works on both global advocacy and through regional councils to support peacebuilding. In West Africa, Religions for Peace worked actively to resolve the Liberia and Sierra Leone conflicts, supporting local peacemakers and enhancing their capacity to advocate together for practical change. The United Religions Initiative was born of the inspiration of the fiftieth anniversary of the UN and, with a philosophy of grassroots activism, also seeks to model an interfaith commitment to peace that builds on local "cooperation circles." Since some of the most vicious religious tensions are within faith traditions (e.g., Christianity or Islam), ecumenical efforts, for example, the World Council of Churches, are also part of this growing effort to work for peace through cooperation across theological and institutional frontiers. The World Council of Churches, for example, has been actively involved in working for a peaceful transition to peace for South Sudan and ensuing tensions there, as well as in northern Nigeria.

Creative interfaith dialogue is part of responses to overt interreligious tensions and to such worrying phenomena as rising Islamophobia and threats to minorities in different world regions. The Common Word initiative is an important example. In October 2007, 138 Muslim scholars, clerics, and intellectuals came together to declare their commitment to the common ground between Christianity and Islam. Signatories who support the resulting document, *A Common Word Between Us and You,* came from every denomination and school of thought in Islam and from every major Islamic country or world region. The message is addressed to the leaders of all the world's churches, appealing to the most fundamental common ground between Islam and Christianity. It asserts that the best basis for future dialogue and understanding is the love of God and the love of neighbor. Based on shared scriptural themes, Muslim scholars invited the Christian world to cooperate together and engage each other to build peace in their respective communities. Rather than engage in polemics, the signatories have adopted the traditional and mainstream Islamic position of respecting the Christian scripture, calling Christians to be more, not less, faithful to it. They committed themselves to more active interfaith dialogue, and the result is a series of meetings, engaging widening groups of scholars and practitioners.

Another initiative is a series of meetings of rabbis and imams that starting in 2005 have taken place in various cities: Brussels, Seville, and Paris. These ambitious gatherings of religious leaders from two contending faiths, coming from all over the world, have been marked by a willingness to engage. Peace and respect have been the guiding themes, looking to the teachings of both Judaism and Islam for common wisdom and new approaches.[1]

Interfaith movements and events at global or regional levels bring people together, offering venues where dialogue among disputing parties can occur and providing symbols of what interfaith harmony can look like. Annual Sant'Egidio Prayer for Peace gatherings are replete with symbolism, fine rhetoric, and person-to-person engagement. The annual Interfaith Harmony week that the UN General Assembly approved in 2010 likewise reinforces core messages about peace among religions. Equally important is grassroots interfaith work. This can involve local communities and women's and youth groups, either motivated by a wish to know their neighbors better or responding to specific incidents and tensions. Educational programs in schools are part of long-term solutions that introduce students to different faith traditions and encourage them to work together. The Interfaith Youth Core and the Faith Act Fellows promoted by the Tony Blair Faith Foundation are examples.

Interfaith harmony has an obvious appeal as an ideal, and the symbolism can be graphic as well as visible. The primary challenge facing these initiatives and organizations, however, is to find practical ways to resolve conflicts by the example of leaders and communities capable of building on common ground. Interfaith work must counter a considerable wall of cynicism about the true efficacy of these efforts, as they are often dismissed as largely ineffective endeavors, where everyone feels good but little is accomplished. Media reports of major interfaith events tend to be paltry at best. Increasingly, however, the interfaith movement has pursued a widening range of practical initiatives. Some focus on increasing understanding and knowledge about other faiths, on the premise that a peaceful, pluralistic world demands faith literacy at many levels and this can best be achieved through personal contact. Others focus on interfaith by praxis, cooperation that might center on education, community cleanliness, or postcrisis rebuilding. In some instances, interfaith groups are directly involved in conflict prevention or peacebuilding. An example is the interfaith effort termed the Alexandria Process, which brought together religious leaders from the Middle East. The leaders then formed "SWAT teams" where small groups from different religious traditions intervened where tensions flared up (say, a church or mosque was threatened). Other promising endeavors include the work of the "Imam and the Pastor," two Nigerian religious leaders, Mohammad Ashafa and James Wuye, who had been deeply involved in northern Nigeria's Muslim–Christian tensions, then came together determined to work for peace. Their Interfaith Mediation Centre in Kaduna, Nigeria, provides training and facilitates peacebuilding workshops. Their success has been captured in two films (*The Imam and the Pastor* and *An African Answer*), and their reputation as creative and determined peacebuilders has taken them to many countries, notably Kenya and South Sudan. Finally high-level interfaith advisory councils in places such as Liberia, Sierra Leone, and Nigeria advise governments on actions they need to take to dampen tensions and to build peace.

The arts offer another avenue where spiritual and religious understanding is used deliberately to foster peace. The Fes Festival of Global Sacred Music, held annually since 1992 in Morocco, is one example. The idea is that music reaches people at the emotional level far more effectively than simple words or exhortation, and world sacred music is an example without parallel of the marvels of the diversity of world cultures. Other ventures that build on the arts and often involve religion include soap operas, film, and creative ventures, such as the 99 Muslim comic book series. The latter features Muslim characters, male and female, who fight for justice and defeat evil forces. These various cultural diplomacy efforts aim to promote harmony through means other than formal dialogue and conflict resolution, bridging divides and awakening people to new ways of seeing "the other."

SHIFTING PARADIGMS: GOVERNANCE AND PEACE

The map of conflicts today shows increasing concentration in a few hot-spot regions that largely but not entirely coincide with very poor areas where development has failed to take root. The African Great Lakes and Horn regions and the Middle East are prime examples. Parts of Asia and Central America also are enmeshed in vicious conflict traps. Academic specialist and policy gurus increasingly appreciate that distinctive approaches are needed for these areas, both for analysis and for prescriptions. The classic proponent of this imperative is economist Paul Collier, whose 2008 book,

The Bottom Billion, and its 2009 sequel, *Wars, Guns, and Votes: Democracy in Dangerous Places,* press for different tactics. The troubled regions share several characteristics, with conflicts exhibiting complex links between cause and effect. Poverty is deeply entrenched, and weak governance (underpinning the common description "failing states"), the absence of rule of law, and shabby administration beset these areas. This witches' brew causes investors to shun the region, further perpetuating a poverty cycle. Where there are rich natural resources, governance weaknesses are tied to large-scale corruption that funnels off proceeds to elites. Inequality accentuates what are often bitter intergroup tensions that may have deep historic roots. In many hot spots a large youth bulge combines with unemployment to produce a glut of ready combatants.

In virtually all these situations, religious institutions are omnipresent. Where the state is weak or absent, religious institutions often de facto provide whatever public services and safety nets are available to populations (for example, church schools and clinics in central Africa, and Muslim education and health services in parts of the Middle East and the subcontinent). Religious institutions and leaders are integral parts of the societies and commonly have a profound appreciation for the character of conflict and capacity to look for ways out. Religious divisions, however, which often (as in the Balkans and in Nigeria) overlap with ethnic identities, also ignite tensions that boil over into violence given a trigger event. Proselytizing activities of faith groups seeking converts can also be a source of tension even where (as in India, Morocco, and Cambodia) nations pride themselves on tolerance and commitment to religious liberty. The tension occurs both because conversion work is seen as challenging core national identities, and because lines between delivery of humanitarian aid and evangelism are blurred.

The role of religious leadership for peace is especially important in these failing-state situations. All the tools of religious peacebuilding are called upon: healing wounded memories, reconciling estranged communities, rebuilding trust, and helping to restore a sense of meaning in lives. Above all in today's characteristically plural societies, faith literacy—understanding the traditions and beliefs that motivate others—is critically important for social harmony, which religious leaders can play important roles in promoting. Likewise, religious organizations, such as Catholic Relief Services, the Salvation Army, American Jewish World Services, and Islamic Relief, provide humanitarian relief as well as development services. Where they work together they can achieve remarkable results and avoid the perils that come with infighting and competition. Linking the vision and ethos of these institutions to the practical work they do on the ground is important. Challenges include lack of robust attention to religious factors in many diplomatic services and development agencies. Better tools are needed to demonstrate and identify, in practical ways, how religious actors can engage constructively in complex conflict situations, using their resources to point to potential conflicts, pinpointing causes and likely flashpoints, negotiating settlements, mediating in conflict, and pressing toward tangible and feasible postconflict scenarios. Prominent religious actors on successful truth and reconciliation efforts include examples of creative and constructive roles, with the prominent Archbishop of Capetown Desmond Tutu as a stellar example of inspiration and practical follow-through.

POST-9/11, ISLAM, AND THE WAR ON TERRORISM

No world religion is impervious to fomenting conflict, but in a post-9/11 world, Islam is often singled out as particularly violent. Critics associate it with extreme intolerance, arguing that Islam breeds radicalism. It is easy to see where the criticisms come from. With the combination of late twentieth-century fundamentalist movements, Islamist politics, al-Qaeda–style radicalism, Iran's theocratic revolution, and attacks by Islamist groups against civilians across the world, contemporary Islam is rarely discussed without referring to violence. Pope Benedict XVI's 2006 comments on Islam at the University of Regensburg referred to the religion as anti-rational, citing derogatory references to Islam by fourteenth-century Byzantine emperor Manuel II Paleologus (Vatican: The Holy See, 2006), epitomizing the images that fuel these tensions.[2]

Reasons for tensions involving Islam are actively debated. One perspective highlights the need for something resembling a reformation within the Islamic faith, essentially political, social, economic, and cultural, with religious doctrines reinterpreted to minimize conservative, orthodox, and traditional positions. Other ideas highlight promoting religious education, instituting political reforms, lessening the influence of religious law, and addressing social or cultural practices that appear to be obstacles to progress. Some policy makers advocate a "liberal" Western idealism—the values of freedom, justice, equality, democracy, and prosperity—as an alternative. The civil unrest movements of 2011–2012, commonly referred to as the "Arab Spring," clearly have a fundamental core of promoting human dignity, freedom of all types, and justice. But the assertions by some policy makers and scholars that Muslim societies are stagnant, irrational, and premodern and have failed to respond to the challenges of modernity are false. Even a cursory glance at Islamic history shows that these stereotypes are shallow and partial. Islamic history reveals extraordinary cultural and intellectual diversity: scientific and mathematical discoveries in the twelfth and thirteenth centuries; social and religious revivalist movements in the seventeenth century; nineteenth-century modernist reformation movements; pioneering work on religion, culture, and rationalism; and a massive amount of literature in twentieth-century Islamic thought on colonialism, political activism, peacemaking, governance, human rights, and democracy. Islam as a civilization and faith tradition has been anything but stagnant and intellectually dormant.

Initiatives in Islamic peacebuilding are occurring in all Muslim communities, every day, and throughout the world. From Muslim minorities in the West to majority Muslim societies in Africa, the Middle East, and South and Southeast Asia, peacebuilding activities are multiplying. Activities include high-ranking scholars, such as muftis and grand ayatollahs; regional and local politicians; imams, teachers, *qadi*s, lawyers, activists, religious educators, artists, musicians, women's groups, and others in civil society. In December 2005, the Mecca Al-Mukarramah Declaration united all heads of state from the Organization of the Islamic Conference (OIC) in affirming that "terrorism in all its forms and manifestations is a global phenomenon that is not confined to any particular religion, race, colour, or country, and that can in no way be justified or rationalized. . . . We are also called upon to redouble and orchestrate international efforts to combat terrorism" (bin Talal, 2006, p. 103). The conference highlighted that "the

Islamic civilization is an integral part of human civilization, based on the ideals of dialogue, moderation, justice, righteousness, and tolerance as noble human values that counteract bigotry, isolationism, tyranny, and exclusivism" (bin Talal, 2006, p. 104). The Second International Conference of the Assembly for Moderate Islamic Thought and Culture, sponsored by the Royal Hashemite Kingdom of Jordan in 2006, issued a twenty-five-point plan to support moderates in reforming and reviving all aspects of Islamic heritage, principles, and ethical values in the global Muslim community. It called for an international moderate movement with coordinated activities involving "all institutions and Islamic agencies, which adhere to the moderation programme." Point thirteen of the plan unequivocally endorsed "affirming a committee on dialogue with leading Western thinkers and politicians" (Amman Message, 2006, para. 13).

Since 9/11, Islamic peacebuilding efforts have increased at many levels and in many regions. Five basic principles underlie this work. First, all of humanity has a common origin, and human dignity must be recognized and respected, regardless of religion, ethnicity, or tribe. Second, the diversity among people encapsulates the richness of traditions. Third, Muslims striving to improve the world must cooperate, collaborate, and engage in dialogue with others as well as among themselves to foster peace. Fourth, to be actively involved with one's tradition means not to lead exclusivistic, hermetic lives, but to be engaged with others in a respectful manner. And fifth, practicing good deeds and striving toward justice must be present in everyday dealings with all human beings. These essential principles do not contradict Western approaches to conflict resolution; rather, the astounding similarities and overlapping themes among Islamic and Western peacebuilding efforts allow for more common ground in working toward ending conflict.

WOMEN, RELIGION, AND PEACE

As other sections of this book make abundantly clear, women's roles in both conflict and peacebuilding have been neglected in theoretical analysis as well as in practice. Women who have religious connections are often simply invisible. This is partly because, as many religious traditions exclude women from formal leadership, the leaders are most often men. The tendency not to look to or see religious women's roles is further accentuated by divides or tensions between secular women's groups and religious institutions.

This invisibility, however, obscures three important peacebuilding trends. First, women with ties to faith traditions are among the most active, determined, and creative activists for peace. Leaders include activist nuns in Central America and Colombia, pioneering Buddhist nuns in Asia, and missionary teachers and health workers in Africa. Religiously linked women, such as Sister Joan Chittister and Scilla Elworthy, are leaders in anti–nuclear weapon and anti–land mine movements. Jewish women such as Robi Damelin, a leading member of the Parents Circle/Families Forum, a group of bereaved Israeli and Palestinian families, work for reconciliation and peace (though not all operate with an explicit faith-based perspective). The late Egyptian scholar Zainab al-Ghazali used her television program to command millions of Arab speakers to better understanding culture, religion, and pressing societal issues. Indige-

nous Mayan leader Rosalina Tuyuc Velasquez stood up to military and civilian oppression against her people. All are dynamos determined to find peaceful solutions
for conflicts. Second, without ascribing common characteristics to all women, through
socialization or by nature, women tend to have practical skills in crossing divides and
healing. Many work within religious traditions or institutions in this spirit, even if
their roles are not formally recognized. Women often describe their motivation as including a spiritual element and draw upon their faith tradition in many ways. And
third, even where their formal roles are not recognized, many women are pillars of religious communities, whether through Mothers' Unions or simply by keeping the institutions going, especially in hard times. When women's voices are heard, the agendas
that they advance tend to differ from those presented by formal religious (or for that
matter political) leaders. Essentializing women is problematic given the vast diversities
involved, but a leader of such stature as Madeleine Albright does not hesitate to assert
that women are "simply better" at peacebuilding, including setting the agendas that
reconcile and build healthy societies (Marshall and Hayward, 2011). Awareness and
bridge-building are needed to end the exclusion of religious dimensions of gender
roles and women's engagement. Documenting the work is an important first step, and
exploring specific experience and skills that women bring is another.[3]

CONFLICT RESOLUTION PROCESSES/SKILLS

What skills and assets do religious leaders, religious actors, and religious communities
bring to conflict resolution? And what are the pitfalls that religious players may
encounter?

Looking first to the ideal, harking back to the core teachings of most faith traditions,
peace is an end as well as a means. Tradition and scripture offer exhortations, parables,
and ethical guidelines (do not kill, love thy neighbor as thyself). Leaders such as Mahatma Gandhi, Martin Luther King Jr., Desmond Tutu, Mother Teresa, and the Dalai
Lama offer both examples of commitment and wisdom and a capacity to convey their
teaching through the example of their lives. Among those honored by renowned
international peace prizes (Nobel, Niwano, Tanenbaum, and Coexist, for example),
many have religious callings or ascribe their actions to their religious teachings.

Looking to the hopeful example of conflicts deemed insoluble, such as those in
Northern Ireland and South Africa, religious leaders were integral in diverse and often
fragmented peace efforts. Roles played by inspirational individuals are difficult to
disentangle from the religious dimension per se, but clearly spiritual inspiration and
organization were part of peace processes in both instances. Spirituality's contribution
to the healing process after World War II was determined and creative. Pax Christi
and Moral Rearmament (now renamed Initiatives of Change) played roles in the complex history of what in retrospect seems something of a miracle that brought together
Germans and French still sore from the bitter war. Their approach to reconciliation
involved spiritual guidance, listening, apology, and visions of a better future.

A specific, distinctive feature ascribed to religious peacebuilders is their understanding of reconciliation and forgiveness. Secular in its official vision, South Africa's
Truth and Reconciliation Commission was infused with religious inspiration and

symbolism (Philpott and Powers, 2010). In Mozambique, traditional reconciliation practices, part of indigenous belief systems, are credited with the remarkably smooth postconflict transition (Cobban, 2007).

SUCCESSFUL RELIGIOUS PEACEBUILDING: THE COMMUNITY OF SANT'EGIDIO

Credited with extraordinary successes in negotiations in many different conflict situations, the Community of Sant'Egidio works without a formula or an explicit methodology. Veteran negotiator Mario Giro describes the Community's role as "track one and a half," meaning that they are independent but in most cases have relationships with governments. What is their secret?

The Community is sui generis, a global network that began as a student initiative inspired by the 1968 ethos of rebellion against authority and what a small group saw as the spiritual call to meet the needs of immigrant populations in Rome. After their work caught the attention of Pope John Paul II, they developed a special relationship with the Catholic Church as an independent lay community that focused on the poor and excluded, in Italian communities first and later in other regions, including Africa. They worked with street children and prisoners, immigrants and the destitute. In Mozambique, this knowledge and experience led to a call by both sides of a bitter conflict to be engaged. The ensuing process lasted for years and called on deep wells of patience and listening. Sant'Egidio offered a safe, welcoming place for adversaries to meet, encouraging persistence through the ups and downs of negotiations. The Community worked with governments but in retrospect was the main broker of a lasting peace settlement. Characteristic of Sant'Egidio's approach, their work continues, with the struggle against HIV and AIDS the next hurdle.

In short, the focus of Sant'Egidio on the poor, the nonprofessional character of the organization (everyone is a volunteer, and peace is their vocation, not their job), their flexibility and creativity (we are Italian, they remind us), and their spiritual commitment make for a remarkable alchemy. They are active in some of the world's most bitter conflicts, including the Balkans, Algeria, Côte d'Ivoire, Guinea, and northern Uganda.

Religion is part of what Sant'Egidio brings to conflict resolution and to the Community's self-motivated efforts to sound the alarm on brewing conflicts and to act to build peace. Spiritual inspiration and a close connection to Catholic institutions, both the formal hierarchy and the more decentralized orders, mark their work. The role of individual leadership and inspiration, however, is hard to disentangle from the spiritual. The Community is ultimately pragmatic.

CHALLENGES IN THE FIELD

The case for integrating religion in thinking and action for building sustainable peace is often neglected and sidelined. It derives from long traditions, both academic and within policy circles, that religion and politics are a combustible mix best left separated. Yet religion cannot be ignored in the face of intellectual challenges like Samuel Huntington's assertion that the world faces a clash of civilizations with strong religious dimensions, obvious realities of religiously framed wars or genocides, terrorists claiming religious motivations, and simmering or overt tensions and bitter conflicts among religious groups. Even so, the negative dimensions of religious impact in conflict zones have tended to dominate much analysis and discussion. The more positive impact, of both local work by religious leaders and transnational efforts that cross regional boundaries, needs to be better known to harness its potential.

Engaging religious actors can pose complex ethical and practical issues. Religious tensions commonly evoke powerful emotions, drawn from historical memories that may span many centuries. The challenges of Lebanon's long-lasting conflict and the bitter quality of the Arab–Israeli disputes illustrate well the deep roots and combustible dynamics of religious identities. The complex and shifting roles of religious authorities, witness Iran and Malaysia, also make engagement complex. Discernment and wisdom are called for.

The central challenge is to broaden and deepen the understanding of religion's part and to explore the specific ways in which religious actors contribute to resolving conflict. The forms and details will vary for each situation, as will the cast of actors: leaders and groups, men and women, young and old. The goal is to work toward ways that engage all in broader, mainstream conflict resolution and peacebuilding efforts.

QUESTIONS FOR FURTHER DISCUSSION

1. What are the challenges to integrating religion and peacebuilding?
2. What factors lead faith-based actors to advocate for peace versus exacerbating conflict?
3. How can policy makers work more effectively with faith-based actors?
4. What are likely to be the future trends in religion and peacebuilding?
5. How can faith-based actors work effectively with secular institutions in conflict regions?

REFERENCES

Abu Nimer, M. 2003. *Nonviolence and peace building in Islam: Theory and practice.* Tallahassee: University Press of Florida.

Amman Message. 2006. Recommendations of the Second International Conference. Retrieved June 1, 2012, from http://ammanmessage.com/index.php?option=com_content &task=view&id=30&Itemid=34.

An-Naim, A. 1996. *Toward an Islamic reformation: Civil liberties, human rights, and international law.* Syracuse, NY: Syracuse University Press.

Anderlini, S. N., C. Pampell, and L. Kays. n.d. Transitional justice and reconciliation. Hunt Alternatives Fund. Retrieved February 7, 2012, from www.huntalternatives.org /download/49_transitional_justice.pdf.

Appleby, S. 2003, September. Catholic peace building. *America* 189, no. 6: 12–15.

Arjomand, S. 2002. The reform movement and the debate of modernity and tradition in contemporary Iran. *International Journal of Middle East Studies* 34, no. 4.

Ashe, G. 1968. *Gandhi*. New York: Stein and Day.

Bacani, B. 2005. *The Mindanao peace talks: Another opportunity to resolve the Moro conflict in the Philippines*. Washington, DC: US Institute of Peace.

Bartoli, A. 1999. Mediating peace in Mozambique: The role of the community of Sant'Egido. In C. Crocker, F. O. Hampson, and P. Aall, eds. *Herding cats: Multiparty mediation in a complex world* (pp. 245–274). Washington, DC: US Institute of Peace.

———. 2004. Christianity and peacebuilding. In H. Coward and G. S. Smith, eds. *Religion and peacemaking* (pp. 147–169). Albany: State University of New York Press.

Bartoli, A., E. Giradet, and J. Carmel, eds. 1995. *Somalia, Rwanda, and beyond: The role of the international media in wars and humanitarian crises*. New York: Columbia University Press.

Bin Talal, G. M. 2006. *True Islam and the Islamic consensus on the Amman Message*. Amman, Hashemite Kingdom of Jordan: Royal Aal al-Bayt Institute for Islamic Thought. Retrieved July 2, 2012, from http://ammanmessage.com/index.php?option=com_content &task=view&id=116&Itemid=93.

Blakely, G. 2001, April. The formative influences on Dr. Martin Luther King, Jr. *Peace Magazine* 17, no. 2: 21.

British Broadcasting Corporation. 2011, January 24. Mexico bishop and indigenous champion Samuel Ruiz dies. *News: Latin America and Caribbean*. Retrieved February 19, 2012, from www.bbc.co.uk/news/world-latin-america-12270608.

———. 2012. Non-violence. *Ethics Guide*. Retrieved February 19, 2012, from www.bbc .co.uk/ethics/war/against/nonviolence.shtml.

Brock, J. G. 2001. *Sharpening conflict management: Religious leadership and the double-edged sword*. Westport, CT: Praeger.

Cady, L. E., and S. W. Simon, eds. 2007. *Religion and conflict in South and Southeast Asia: Disrupting violence*. London: Routledge.

Chakrabarty, B. 2006. *Social and political thought of Mahatma Gandhi*. New York: Routledge.

Cobban, H. 2007. *Amnesty after atrocity? Healing nations after genocide and war crimes*. Boulder, CO: Paradigm.

Coward, H., and G. S. Smith, eds. 2004. *Religion and peacemaking*. Albany: State University of New York Press.

Crocker, C., F. O. Hampson, and P. Aall, eds. 1999. *Herding cats: Multiparty mediation in a complex world*. Washington, DC: US Institute of Peace.

———. 2005. *Grasping the nettle: Analyzing cases of intractable conflict*. Washington, DC: US Institute of Peace.

Daftary, F., ed. 2000. *Intellectual traditions in Islam*. London: I. B. Tauris.

El Fadl, K. A. 2001. *Rebellion and violence in Islam law*. Cambridge: Cambridge University Press.

Ellul, J. 1970. *Violence: Reflections from a Christian perspective*. London: SCM Press Ltd.

Gandhi, R. 2008. *Gandhi: The man, his people, and the empire.* Berkeley: University of California Press.

Haynes, J. 1995. *Religion, fundamentalism, and identity. A global perspective.* Geneva, Switzerland: UN Research Institute for Social Development.

———. 2007. *An introduction to international relations and religion.* London: Pearson.

Helmick, R. G., and J. F. Keenan. 2010. *Living Catholic faith in a contentious age.* London: Continuum International Publishing Group.

Helmick, R., and R. Petersen, eds. 2001. *Forgiveness and reconciliation: Religion, public policy, and conflict transformation.* West Conshohocken, PA: Templeton Press.

Hodgson, M. 1974. *The venture of Islam: Conscience and history in a world civilization.* Chicago: University of Chicago Press.

Holenstein, A. M. 2005. *Role and significance of religion and spirituality in development.* Bern, Switzerland: Swiss Agency for Development and Co-operation.

Huda, Q. 2010. *Crescent and dove: Peace and conflict resolution in Islam.* Washington, DC: US Institute of Peace.

Ingram, C. 2003. *In the footsteps of Gandhi: Conversations with spiritual social activists.* Berkeley, CA: Parallax Press.

Jeffrey, P. 1998. *Recovering memory: Guatemalan churches and the challenge of peacemaking.* Uppsala, Sweden: Life and Peace Institute.

Johnston, D., and C. Sampson, eds. 1994. *Religion: The missing dimension of statecraft.* New York: Oxford University Press.

Juergensmeyer, M. 2005. *Gandhi's way: A handbook of conflict resolution.* Berkeley: University of California Press.

Kakar, S. 1996. *The colors of violence: Cultural identities, religion, and conflict.* Chicago: University of Chicago Press.

Kamali, M. H. 1997. *Freedom of expression in Islam.* Cambridge: Islamic Texts Society.

King, M. L. Jr. 1957, February 6. Non-violence and racial justice. *Christian Century* 74, no. 6: 165–167.

Kraybill, R. 1994. Transition from Rhodesia to Zimbabwe: The role of religious actors. In D. Johnston and C. Sampson, eds. *Religion: The missing dimension of statecraft* (pp. 208–257). New York: Oxford University Press.

Kurtz, L. 1995. *Gods in the global village: The world's religions in sociological perspective.* Pine Forge, PA: Sage.

Lai, B. 2006. An empirical examination of religion and conflict in the Middle East, 1950–1992. *Foreign Policy Analysis* 2, no. 1: 21–35.

Lederach, J. P. 1997. *Building peace: Sustainable reconciliation in divided societies.* Washington, DC: US Institute of Peace.

———. 2005. *Moral imagination: The art and soul of peacebuilding.* New York: Oxford University Press.

Little, D., ed. 2007. *Peacemakers in action: Profiles of religion in conflict resolution.* New York: Cambridge University Press.

Little, D., and S. Appleby. 2004. A moment of opportunity. In H. Coward and G. S. Smith, eds. *Religion and peacemaking* (pp. 1–26). Albany: State University of New York Press.

Lubbe, G. 1994. *A decade of interfaith dialogue: Ten Desmond Tutu lectures and responses.* Johannesburg: South African Chapter of the World Conference on Religion and Peace.

Maat, B. 1995, May. Dhammayietra, walk of peace. *Catholic Worker,* p. 22.

MacQuarrie, J. 1973. *The concept of peace.* New York: Harper & Row.

Marshall, K. 2011. Bringing intercommunal cooperation and religious voices into humanitarian development policy. Working Paper, UN Alliance of Civilizations. Retrieved July 2, 2012, from http://repository.berkleycenter.georgetown.edu/1111MarshallUNAOC PolicyBriefFINAL.pdf.

———. 2013. *Global institutions of religion: Ancient movers, modern shakers.* New York: Routledge.

Marshall, K., and S. Hayward. 2011. Women in religious peacebuilding. *United States Institute of Peace Peaceworks,* 7.

Morewedge, P., ed. 1979. *Islamic philosophical theology.* Albany: State University of New York Press.

Moyser, G., ed. 1991. *Politics and religion in the modern world.* London: Routledge.

Nasr, S. H., and O. Leaman, eds. 1996. *History of Islamic philosophy.* London: I. B. Tauris.

Niyonzima, D., and L. Fendall. 2001. *Unlocking horns: Forgiveness and reconciliation in Burundi.* Newberg, OR: Barclay Press.

Path to Peace Foundation. 2008, October 7. Peacebuilding: A role for religion. *Catholic Peacebuilding and Emerging International Norms and Practices of the UN and Other International and Governmental Bodies.* Retrieved February 19, 2012, from www.thepathtopeacefoundation.org/images/Side%20events/Cusimano%20Love%20FINAL.pdf.

Philpott, D., ed. 2006. *The politics of evil: Religion, reconciliation, and the dilemmas of transitional justice.* Notre Dame, IN: University of Notre Press.

Philpott, D., and G. Powers, eds. 2010. *Strategies of peace: Transforming conflict in a violent world.* New York: Oxford University Press.

Prothero, S. 2007. *Religious literacy: What every American needs to know—And doesn't.* New York: HarperOne.

Rosenthal, F. 1990. *Muslim intellectual and social history.* Aldershot, UK: Ashgate.

Royal Institute for Inter-Faith Studies. 2004, November. Amman Message. Retrieved February 19, 2012, from www.riifs.org/nashra/Ammanmessage_e.htm.

Rupesinghe, K., and S. N. Anderlini. 1998. *Civil wars, civil peace: An introduction to conflict resolution.* London: Pluto.

Sachedina, A. 2007. *The Islamic roots of democratic pluralism.* Oxford: Oxford University Press.

Said, A. A., A. N. Funk, and A. S. Kadayifici, eds. 2001. *Peace and conflict resolution in Islam: Precept and practice.* Lanham, MD: University Press of America.

Sampson, C., and J. P. Lederach. 2000. *From the ground up: Mennonite contributions to international peacebuilding.* New York: Oxford University Press.

Schreiter, R. J., R. S. Appleby, and G. F. Powers, eds. 2010. *Peacebuilding: Catholic theology, ethics, and praxis.* Maryknoll, NY: Orbis.

Smock, D. 2006. *Religious contributions to peacemaking: When religion brings peace, not war.* Washington, DC: US Institute of Peace.

Smock, D., and Q. Huda. 2009. *Islamic peacemaking since 9/11*. Washington, DC: US Institute of Peace.

Stark, R. 1999. Secularization, R.I.P. *Sociology of Religion*, 60, no. 3: 249–273.

Steele, D. 2008. An introductory overview to faith-based peacebuilding. In M. Rogers, T. Bamat, and J. Ideh, eds. *Pursuing just peace: An overview and case studies for faith-based peacebuilders* (pp. 5–41). Baltimore, MD: Catholic Relief Services.

Thistlethwaite, S., ed. 1987. *A just peace church: The Peace Theology Development Team*. New York: United Church.

———. 2011. *Interfaith just peacemaking: Jewish, Christian, and Muslim perspectives on the new paradigm of peace and war*. New York: Palgrave Macmillan.

United States Institute of Peace. 2001, April 9. Catholic contributions to international peace. Special report. Retrieved February 19, 2012, from http://permanent.access.gpo.gov /websites/usip/www.usip.org/pubs/specialreports/sr69.pdf.

Vatican: The Holy See. 2006, September 12. Faith, reason, and the university memories and reflections. Apostolic Journey of His Holiness Benedict XVI to München, Altötting, and Regensburg. Retrieved February 19, 2012, from www.vatican.va/holy_father /benedict_xvi/speeches/2006/september/documents/hf_ben-xvi_spe_20060912_university -regensburg_en.html.

Weiner, M. 2003. Maha Ghosananda as a contemplative social activist. In D. Keown, C. S. Prebish, and C. Queen, eds. *Action dharma: New studies in engaged Buddhism* (pp. 110–127). New York: Routledge.

Williams, S., and S. Williams. 1994. *Being in the middle by being at the edge: Quaker experience of non-official political mediation*. London: Quaker Peace & Service.

World Council of Churches, Pontifical Council for Interreligious Dialogue, World Evangelical Alliance. 2011. Cambodia Report. In *Christian witness in a multi-religious world: Recommendations for conduct*. World Faiths Development Dialogue. Retrieved July 2, 2012, from www.oikoumene.org/fileadmin/files/wcc-main/2011pdfs/ChristianWitness recommendations.pdf.

Zayd, N. 2004. *Rethinking the Qur'an: Towards a humanistic hermeneutics*. Utrecht, The Netherlands: Humanistics University Press.

Zehr, H. 1995. *Changing lenses: A new focus for crime and justice*. Scottsdale, PA: Herald Press.

NOTES

1. For more info see www.imamsetrabbins.org.

2. See also Organization of Islamic Conference (OIC) response, www.oic-oci.org /press/English/2006.

3. For work from the US Institute of Peace/Berkley Center and World Faiths Development Dialogue to this end, see http://berkleycenter.georgetown.edu/programs/religion -and-global-development.

chapter eight

ENVIRONMENTAL CHANGE AND PEACEBUILDING

Ashley Laura McArthur

If these resources are very valuable, if these resources are scarce, if these resources are degraded, there is going to be competition. And it is over that competition that we get conflict. . . . The time has come for us to realize that to work for peace, we need to manage our resources in a responsible way, in an accountable way so that people—so people don't feel like they're marginalized.
—NOBEL PEACE PRIZE LAUREATE WANGARI MAATHAI (1940–2011)
ON WHY THE NOBEL COMMITTEE CHOSE TO HONOR
HER ENVIRONMENTAL ACTIVISM (MAATHAI, 2009)

THIS CHAPTER EXPLORES THE RELATIONSHIP between environmental changes and integrated peacebuilding. Environmental changes around the world, both natural and human-induced, are occurring at alarming rates and are expected by specialists from a range of fields to aggravate conflicts in the future. In regions like sub-Saharan Africa and much of the Middle East, where armed conflict is already prevalent, further spikes in conflict occur as life-sustaining resources including arable land and potable water become increasingly scarce. As such, a major challenge facing peacebuilding efforts is how to respond effectively to such environmental changes and assess the implications for achieving and maintaining peace. This chapter considers the following questions: (1) What are the consequences of environmental change for peacebuilding and conflict resolution? (2) How can peacebuilding and its core principles shape and improve societies' responses to the effects of environmental change?

Integrated Peacebuilding and the Environment

Recent scholarship posits that as human-induced environmental change intensifies, tensions over already overburdened natural resources, such as land, water, biofuels, fisheries, and precious minerals, will also heighten. According to climate model projections generated by the International Panel on Climate Change (IPCC),[1] global temperatures will likely rise approximately 3 degrees Celsius by the year 2100. This figure may appear minimal, but the resulting intensification of the global hydrologic cycle spells a variety of dismal implications for the biosphere, including an overall increase in natural disasters, such as severe droughts, floods, forest fires, hurricanes, and mass extinctions. Other human-induced environmental changes, including deforestation, soil nutrient depletion, and the exhaustion of fisheries across the globe, also severely compromise water availability and food production.

These and other environmental shifts are expected to dramatically undermine ongoing efforts to reduce poverty, foster stable economies, and improve global standards of living. Such pressures threaten to weaken social institutions and stoke societal tensions by placing significant pressures on the relationships, institutions, and governmental programs upon which the peaceful conduct of societies rely, and without which the possibility of armed conflict escalates.

Historically, violent conflict has had destructive consequences for the natural environment as well. The already heavy toll that warfare imposes on local populations is exacerbated by the acceleration of environmental changes. Given the cyclical relationship between armed conflict and environmental decline, disentangling the mechanisms of environment-related conflict has become increasingly important. The pursuit of peace depends on our ability to understand and overcome environmental challenges in the coming decades. This chapter examines the theoretical underpinnings of the relationship between environmental change and armed conflict; the current mechanisms in place that attempt to address the issue; and the challenges increasingly faced by peacebuilding efforts in a context of environmental flux.

Peace and Conflict Theory
Relevant to Environmental Change

The Environment–Conflict Connection

Extensive study has been conducted to explore the causal pathways between environmental decline and armed conflict. Thomas Homer-Dixon stirred interest in this issue in 1991 when he hypothesized that increasing rates of environmental change would likely lead to increased frequency and intensity of conflict, and later conducted analysis on several case studies of allegedly environmentally induced conflicts, including the Rwandan genocide and the civil war in Chiapas, Mexico. One of his early papers concludes, "Our research shows that environmental scarcity causes violent conflict" (Homer-Dixon, 1994). He proposes a series of causal frameworks for predicting and explaining the environment–conflict connection, which several theorists have since reworked and expanded upon. His explanations center primarily on finding a link between environmental scarcity and social effects, such as forced migration and economic strain, both of which have since been affirmed by advocates of the environment–conflict hypothesis. Under this framework, climate change initiates a complicated series of cause-and-effect relationships that aggravate key factors—poverty, institutional failure, and other more complex mechanisms—leading to insecurity, instability, and an increased risk of armed conflict. Weak institutions and poor responses to environmental hardship further exacerbate the potential for violence and the eruption of armed conflict.

Critics of Homer-Dixon's assessment and other similar studies note that they are not fully representative, and object to his decision not to address instances when environmental changes did not lead to conflict, or when conflict was not attributable to environmental factors (de Soysa and Gleditsch, 2006; Levy, 1995). Conflict-resolution and security theorists have since debated the issue extensively, generating a flurry of theories, case studies, and research that attempts to answer the question as to whether a causal relationship exists between environmental factors and conflict. Some critics have disparaged scholarship on environmental conflict as a ploy to attract the interest and resources of high-level politics (Kalyvas, 2001). This argument states that by elevating environmental decline to the status of a security issue, environmentalists aim to alarm powerful policy makers into taking action and dedicating resources that benefit the environment. Regardless of the motivation, however, it is generally accepted that environmental factors complicate, if not contribute to, societal distress in many instances. It is therefore necessary to examine the potential ties between environmental change and conflict.

Pathways to Conflict

Homer-Dixon, along with his initial hypothesis about the environment–conflict connection, proposes three types of environmental scarcity that might contribute to violent conflict: supply-induced scarcity, demand-induced scarcity, and structural scarcity (Homer-Dixon and Percival, 1998). Supply-induced scarcity occurs as certain key resources diminish until there is not enough to support the population, as in the case of Somalia, where lasting drought has created extreme scarcity of food and potable water. Rising populations and increased per capita use of those resources increase demand, leading to demand-induced scarcity, as in the case of India and Pakistan's simultaneously increasing use of freshwater from the same river contributing to water stress for both countries. Socioeconomic inequities lead to structural scarcity experienced in the form of poverty and unmet basic needs by disadvantaged groups (Homer-Dixon, 1994). This effect is seen in the Gaza Strip, for example, where the ample supplies of freshwater are allocated primarily to supporting the commerce and citizens of Israel, leaving very little potable water for Palestinians to pursue their livelihoods.

Leif Ohlsson (2000) proposes that the "missing link" between environmental decline, poverty, and increases in violent conflict is livelihood destruction: the loss of the means to provide for oneself and family. Overlooking this connection, Ohlsson maintains, has led to confusion and disagreement in scholarly analysis over whether poverty or environmental decline was really to blame for many cases of instability. Ohlsson (2000) theorizes that in cases when one or more already marginalized groups lose their livelihood, conflict mechanisms are put in motion including "relative deprivation and the strengthening of bonds along . . . fault lines prevalent in almost all societies, but not gaining full salience until livelihoods are threatened" (p. 1).

Forced migration is also widely considered a potential causal pathway from environmental change to violent conflict. Hardships including severe drought, agricultural failure, or change in land use can generate devastating famines and droughts that prevent people in affected regions from meeting their basic needs (Homer-Dixon, 1994). These effects threaten to ignite large-scale migrations and force indigenous populations from their homelands and into neighboring territories that may also be experiencing resource scarcity. This additional pressure on already strained resources can fuel resentment toward those encroaching populations and incite additional conflicts.

The failure of civil institutions is considered another pathway between conflict and rising poverty levels, which can be induced by environmental decline or misuse. As governmental and civil institutions fail to provide the structure and security necessary to respond to unrest and maintain stability, conflict becomes increasingly likely (Goldstone et al., 2010). Institution-building is a staple strategy of the peacebuilding field and is more frequently employed as a means of bolstering peace in environmentally compromised regions. The United Nations Environment Programme (UNEP) has responded to the environment–conflict nexus by promoting the institutional capacity of conflict-affected countries to effectively restore and manage their natural environment. UNEP (2009) efforts in Afghanistan have built upon this understanding that peacebuilding, environment, and development are interrelated, by aiding Afghanistan's National Environmental Protection Agency, which equips the country with the means to manage its natural resources more effectively. Although conditions in Afghanistan are still highly unstable, such efforts represent a step toward development, security, and a more solid foundation undergirding the welfare of Afghanis and Afghan society.

As James Lee (2009a) of American University notes, environmental changes must occur at a manageable pace for societies to successfully adapt. While humans are capable of enduring brief shortages of essential resources and changes in their environment—particularly if they have the means and foresight to accumulate emergency reserves of vital resources required for survival—the long-term hardships expected to result from climatic changes leave no time for societies to recover from the depletion of stored supplies. Conversely, sudden natural disasters often occur without warning and make adaptation and recovery difficult.

Conflict, in turn, may hasten environmental decline and generate a cyclical, self-perpetuating pattern of social and environmental destruction. This dynamic is particularly problematic in postconflict situations where the environmental effects of conflict have degraded natural resources, thereby further compromising the population's ability to meet its basic needs. Darfur serves as a tragic example. This conflict was the outcome of several contributing factors, not the least of which was a severe, long-term drought and a paucity of arable land. When conflict erupted across ethnic divides over scarce resources, the already stressed environment became increasingly uninhabitable. In fact, the same environmental factors that initially contributed to the conflict "have worsened as a result of the current crisis" (Bromwich, 2008, p. 22). For example, the conflict's demand for timber and fuel wood, combined with the breakdown of governance structures, has led to rampant deforestation.

The Changing Nature of Conflict

Today, new theories suggest that environmental change may alter the very landscape of conflict and the patterns by which it emerges and operates. As James Lee (2009a) notes, "The past is a good guide, but new types and modes of conflict emerging from climate change are to be expected" (para. 20). Lee's vision of future conflict and its ties to environmental change is based in part on Michael Klare's (2001) "New Geography of Conflict" concept, which predicts the emergence of "a global landscape in which competition over vital resources is becoming the governing principle behind the disposition and use of military power" (p. 214).

Klare (2001) identifies a virtual band situated geographically around the earth's equator wherein a concentration of resources—oil and coal, diamonds and precious gems, timber, water, and key metals and minerals—markedly correlates with a high incidence of conflict. Klare predicts that this pattern will likely worsen and intensify with rising temperatures and diminishing water resources in future decades. Lee (2009b) takes this theory a step further, contending that rising temperatures will expand the "equatorial tension belt," citing projections by the IPCC that lateral zones directly north and south of the equator will be especially hard hit by declines in precipitation, diminishing food production, and frequent natural disasters, the result of which may yield an intensified correlation between resource scarcity and conflict.

The Special Status of Water

Many expect water to influence future politics more than any other natural resource. Whereas in recent decades geopolitics have been driven in large part by the pursuit of increasingly scarce oil supplies, the availability of potable water is now dangerously limited across nearly the entire African and Asian continents, including such populous countries as India, China, and Nigeria. Many conflict specialists argue that as water scarcity worsens, societies will become more inclined to engage in armed conflict over water access and control. More than 263 transboundary water basins on Earth together compose more than 45 percent of its land surface, meaning that many countries rely on and potentially compete for shared water resources, which may lead to significant conflict as supplies dwindle (Wolf, 2002).

Yemen has seen its ecological stability entirely unravel in recent years. With insufficient rainfall negatively affecting crop yield and limited groundwater being swiftly depleted, the population is becoming increasingly desperate, and the leadership anticipates social unrest if the drought continues. As one Yemini cabinet minister observed several years ago, before the recent onset of conflict, "This is a very dangerous time. . . . Economic strife can lead to radicalization" (Kenyon, 2008). Yemen has been among the first to suffer devastation related to fluctuations in climate-dependent systems, and many fear that its trajectory toward environment-related social and political instability could become a global pattern.

Considerable debate has evolved in the conflict and security fields over whether water will play a central role in future conflicts. Scholars Peter Gleick (2010) and Aaron T. Wolf (2002) have argued that the severity of water scarcity may prompt intense competition for survival that could culminate directly in armed conflict. Conversely, critics of this theory have maintained that water scarcity is historically inclined to yield increased cooperation and strengthen diplomatic interdependence (Deudney, 1990). Water has frequently inspired peaceful initiatives to manage jointly held resources. Even tumultuous relations, such as those between India and Pakistan, have been significantly soothed and normalized thanks to collaborative water management of the Indus River. Still, disputes over water typically have been caused by distribution problems that can be alleviated by agreements about allocation; absolute water scarcity may prove more resistant to the pacifying effect of a joint user agreement.

This chapter is not intended to offer definitive answers as to the question of causality. Today most experts in peacebuilding and security generally agree that environmental factors and natural resources play a significant role in many armed conflicts, though they still differ on the strength of that relationship and how best to respond. As new research and study continue to bolster and debate the prediction of environmentally driven armed conflict, other discussions center on more practice-oriented questions—specifically, which intervention efforts stand the best chance of preventing the environment–conflict dynamic from manifesting?

Applying Conflict Resolution Theory to Environment-Related Conflict

Among conflict resolution theorists and practitioners, initiatives have emerged to integrate conflict sensitivity into environmental programming and, conversely, to instill conflict resolution efforts with an understanding of environmental vulnerabilities. A resurgence of interest in the nexus between environment and conflict gives ample reason for revisiting key theories and concepts that attempt to explain why conflict emerges.

Resource conflicts: Johan Galtung (1982), considered the father of Peace Studies, once predicted, "The destruction of the environment may lead to more wars over resources" (p. 99). Scholarship in the field of conflict resolution has since posited multiple theories about the relationship between natural resource scarcity and violence. Conflict resolution scholars, however, have at times questioned the concept of resource conflicts, calling them simplistic and shortsighted. A scarcity of resources does not alone account for violent conflict, even when parties themselves point to resource disputes as the source of conflict. There are usually other conditions and coinciding events—such as religious differences, power vacuums, or attempted rebellion—that contribute to the manifestation of resource-related disputes. The concept of environment as "threat multiplier"—an exacerbating factor rather than the sole cause in conflict scenarios—seems to at least partially satisfy this criticism.

Materialist theory of conflict: Materialist theories of conflict posit that, rhetoric and values aside, the underlying reason societies engage in violent conflict is that people are motivated by material interests (Moghaddam, 2008). For this reason, materialist theories are quite easily linked to the environmental conflict hypothesis. A basic expression of materialism is the theory of simple resource scarcity, which posits that the scarcity of resources alone is enough to trigger and perpetuate armed conflict. Under this framework, societies that face increased scarcity of vital resources will more likely engage in armed conflict than endure ongoing resource-related hardship (Homer-Dixon, 1994). Similarly, the "abundance curse" or "resource curse" theory proposed by Paul Collier (2007) posits that nations whose economies are 25 percent or more dependent upon primary commodity exports are more prone to conflict because dominant groups are inspired to use violent force to acquire those resources. These include oil, minerals, precious gems, and drug crops, all of which have played a central role in recent conflicts.

Resource mobilization theory: This theory (McCarthy and Zald, 1977) lends support to the "abundance curse" concept by targeting the availability of surplus resources as the key predictor of violent conflict. It provides some explanation as to how environment-related violent conflict is sustained over time. When rebel groups capture control of natural resources, such as water or diamonds, they tend to exploit that control to generate the funds they need to recruit soldiers, sustain their armies, and amass deadly weapons, further increasing their capacity to control additional resources.

Greed versus grievance: This economic framework, proposed by Collier and Hoeffler (2000), distinguishes between conflict inspired by grievance due to a perception of unmet basic human needs, and conflict inspired by greed and the pursuit of control over precious resources. According to the realist perspective on conflict and basic human needs, societies will declare war on their neighbors before resigning themselves to starvation and death, lending some support to the "grievance" concept of conflict.

Social identity theory: Identity-related theories of conflict can also help explain the environmental conflict hypothesis. Social identity theory, proposed by Tajfel and Turner (1979), suggests that most people seek a positive and distinct identity from collective forms of identity, such as ethnicity, religious affiliation, and language. In instances of large-scale migration, ethnic or religious groups that would otherwise have little reason to interact could come to share land and resources within a relatively short time frame. The results may include a perceived identity threat by either side, which can push people to respond violently to one another.

Relative deprivation theory: Runciman's (1966) justice-oriented theory of conflict also lends support to the environmental conflict hypothesis. Relative deprivation theory posits that poverty and hardship alone do not inspire armed conflict, but rather that the perception of hardship relative to other individuals and groups evokes a sense of injustice that fuels a violent reaction. Climate change and other forms of environmental transformation will inevitably burden societies unevenly in the future, creating a scenario for relative deprivation to instigate violence.

Structural violence: Another key concept that informs the conversation about environmental security is Galtung's theory of structural violence, which expands the definition of violence to include structures that generate societal conditions in which others suffer. Within this framework, the extraction of certain resources, such as oil and diamonds, by foreign companies can have devastating effects on local economies and communities. Similarly, climate change could be considered an act of structural violence caused by the energy-intensive industrialized world that increases its wealth at the expense of the more vulnerable developing world. This conception of climate change raises questions of liability and justice, and has inspired some consideration of "climate courts," wherein countries accused of polluting the atmosphere would be tried for inflicting harm upon other countries.

Environment as an Intervening Variable or "Threat Multiplier"

Taken to the extreme, materialist theories of conflict suggest that all reasons for engaging in violence are merely excuses contrived to disguise materialistic interests, and all conflicts should be explained in material terms. In this way, materialist theory can be extrapolated to suggest that environmental decline and diminishing resources will mean more conflict in the future.

At the opposite extreme, it has been argued that environmental change and conflict have never been definitively linked, and the resource conflict concept may be entirely misguided (Gleditsch, 1998). Certain quantitative assessments of historical conflict and environmental data suggest that the environment–conflict link is deeply flawed and that environmental challenges more often lead to cooperation than to conflict. One such analysis conducted by researchers at Oregon State University examined 1,700 state-to-state interactions related to water in transboundary water basins from 1946 through 1999 (Wolf, Yoffe, and Giordano, 2003). The study concluded that in circumstances of water sharing, expressions of verbal support and nonmilitary agreements were significantly more likely to occur than armed conflict or even mild verbal hostility. Proponents of the environmental conflict hypothesis argue, however, that (1) a hundred peaceful exchanges cannot undo the consequences of a single violent encounter, and (2) the past is not necessarily a good predictor of the future in terms of societal responses to environmental changes. For example, whereas conflict in the past could have been resolved by one group's choice to migrate to another tract of land, humanity does not have nearly the same amount of freedom to expand into unoccupied territory as it once did (Lee, 2009a).

The historical overlap between conflict hot spots and regions vulnerable to environmental upset also does not suggest or prove causation; pinning down exactly where a given conflict originated, or what exactly caused it, is in most cases difficult if not impossible. Conflicts typically have multiple contributing causes, which typically do not instigate violence separately but can combine to foster violence and predation. Environmental pressure is likely just one among several factors that ultimately lead to the outbreak and perpetuation of violence. As such, the environment is considered a threat multiplier (CNA Corporation, 2007) or an intervening variable—one of a few key contributing factors fueling a conflict or pattern of conflict. It is between these extremes that scholarship, research, and practice have developed most abundantly in recent years to address the nexus between conflict and the environment.

Environmental Security

The security field has undergone reassessment in recent years in response to growing concerns about the implications of factors not traditionally considered security threats. Part of the debate has centered on whether a revised definition of security should include the study of threats posed by environmental degradation. The term "environmental security" has quickly become a buzzword among proponents of a more inclusive concept of security (Mathews, 1989; Myers, 1986). Environmental security has since been the subject of ongoing and at times contentious dialogue over whether environmental degradation is a legitimate security concern.

The value of the concept of environmental security for peacebuilding and security studies and the legitimacy of its claims have both come under repeated scrutiny (Barnett, 2000; Levy, 1995). Critics of the environmental security concept have claimed that the term is ambiguous and that it may be mistaken for the protection of the environment from potential threats, just as "national security" refers to the protection of the nation-state and "human security" refers to the protection of human safety. Others object that the term positions the environment itself as a security threat and masks the role of human activity in instigating destructive environmental changes. Subsequent iterations by advocates of environmental security have framed it as the stability of peaceful societal and human conditions partly or fully dependent on environmental factors, and their protection from a range of possible environmental threats, whether natural or caused by human activity.

PROCESSES AND SKILLS RELEVANT TO ENVIRONMENTALLY INTEGRATED PEACEBUILDING

Processes Applicable to Environment-Related Conflict

While both theoretical and empirical studies have yielded conflicting predictions about the possibility of future environmentally induced conflict, many practitioners in a range of disciplines have moved beyond the question of causation and begun addressing the business of managing and mitigating the environment–conflict connection.

International treaties: Most manifestations of traditional negotiations strategy are competitive, are adversarial in nature, and do not depend on the satisfaction of all parties. They may, however, be sources of stability if the interested parties are willing to honor the established terms, or if one party is strong enough to enforce compliance. Numerous environmental challenges and disputes have been resolved, or at least managed, via international or subnational treaties. The Nile River Basin Cooperative Framework, for example, has governed the relatively peaceful management of the river since its forging in 1929, although with increased difficulty as the availability of water changes. Moreover, part of the success is attributable to the amount of power Egypt yields in the region (Solomon, 2010). Nevertheless, due to the prominent role water plays in interstate politics, the presence of a governing agreement on its use has influenced the relationships between the involved parties for decades. The overall success of environmental negotiations, however, is unique in that it relies heavily on the stability of the agreement, which in turn depends largely on the agreement's acceptability to all parties involved. As the ecology of the Nile River changes, and as upstream states bump against the limits of their share of the water according to the treaty, its legitimacy gets called into question. As Ethiopia, Kenya, Burundi, and neighboring countries agree to override the treaty in the interest of developing with the Nile waters, the potential for dissolution of the treaty may leave a vacuum of communication and cooperation and may lead to increased conflict over water distribution.

Negotiated rule-making: As in the case of the Nile River, environmental factors and fluctuations can lead to international and domestic policy changes, including re-definition of existing boundaries, economic diversification, manufacturing, power generation, and land-use regulations, and climate adaptation measures. Many policies, laws, agreements, and other structures will be undermined by environmental change and will require revision to reflect new conditions and resource availability. Negotiated rule-making, the process by which interested parties jointly negotiate the terms of an administrative rule or policy, presents one option for managing policy formation in an inclusive, collaborative manner aimed at building consensus, mutual trust, and universal acceptance of policy decisions. The US Department of the Interior, the US Environmental Protection Agency, and other federal agencies have all employed this method with reputed success. While the upfront cost of negotiations can be greater than that of traditional forms of rule-making, the benefits include improvements in stakeholder satisfaction, timeliness, accuracy, and shared responsibility. The platform can work especially well in cases where parties have differing areas of expertise but a shared interest in new regulation. Although the name formally applies to negotiations at the federal level in the US, the World Trade Organization serves as an example of an international, multilateral body engaged in negotiated rule-making.

Transparency initiatives: Environmental changes can also present new opportunities for the private sector to profit, inviting extractive industries and investors to pursue newly available or newly valuable resources. Failing to consider the consequences of extraction and the resulting environmental degradation may have devastating effects. Incorporating innovative mechanisms into trade systems can help minimize such negative effects and safeguard against corrupt forms of resource extraction and trade and contribute to more sustainable economic development. The Kimberley Process, the internationally recognized (but not universally accepted or implemented) certification scheme for distinguishing conflict-free diamonds from those obtained illegally, is one such mechanism. Another is the Extractives Industry Transparency Initiative (EITI), which established a global standard requiring transactions between companies and governments to be made publicly visible. Participation in EITI is voluntary, but partners and supporters of EITI must commit to divulging the necessary information in the interest of accountability to the public.

Environmental peacebuilding: To a large extent, peacebuilding and successful environmental sustainability efforts go hand in hand and are mutually enhancing. Fostering the peaceful and stable operation of society requires strengthening its capacity for effective governance, which also better prepares the society to respond to and cope with environmental changes (International Alert, 2010). It is critical for peacebuilding efforts to also address the natural landscape of a conflict situation, particularly when hostile groups stand to gain materially from the continued exploitation of natural resources without the added restraints and regulations of a peacetime society. History has shown that while environmental factors can contribute to conflict, they can also contribute to peace. Environmental peacebuilding convenes the parties in conflict to address a common environmental challenge through working toward superordinate goals, with the intent of fostering a sense of common purpose, as well as mutual understanding and concern, and providing all parties a reason to improve their communications and working relationships. The Declaration of Goma, signed in 2005, yielded transboundary, joint management of natural resources between Uganda, Rwanda, and the Democratic Republic of the Congo, thereby signifying major progress toward a sustained peace in the once war-torn country of Rwanda. Unfortunately, the declaration yielded the difficult lesson that such agreements must be regional and widely encompassing, as exploitation simply shifted to a neighboring area in the Democratic Republic of the Congo. Despite its shortfall, the cooperative agreement at least created space for increased communication and trust between the parties involved (UNEP, 2009).

Collaborative resource management: Collaboration is an increasingly critical part of an effective resource management strategy, particularly when vital resources are on the decline or become threatened. Because geopolitical boundaries do not mirror natural boundaries or equally distribute natural resources, communities must work together to decide how best to manage limited resources. Failing to work cooperatively with surrounding communities to establish rules of appropriate use can lead to wasteful use, mutual distrust, and potentially violent encounters. In northern Canada, for instance, native wildlife including caribou, geese, and certain species of whale are comanaged according to regionally negotiated agreements between indigenous peoples, hunters and fishers, and provincial governments. This collaborative management process takes advantage of the regulatory and enforcement power of the government, as well as the expertise of indigenous groups and hunters and their ability to easily monitor the species, provided authority is divided equitably among invested groups.

Natural-disaster diplomacy: This innovative concept is similar to environmental peacebuilding in its attempt to find opportunities for dialogue in otherwise bleak environmental challenges. The 1999 earthquakes that sparked cooperation and joint response efforts by Greece and Turkey serve as an example of this method of peacebuilding (Ganapti, Kelman, and Koukis, 2010). Supporting theorists argue that "the cooperative spirit generated from common efforts to deal with disasters" can gain traction through shared concerns, joint successes, and emerging relationships and networks developed to focus on the problem at hand (Kelman and Koukis, 2000, p. 214). Eventually such newfound commonalities can override existing political, ideological, and other barriers, and eventually supersede them. A peaceful new dynamic in the wake of a natural disaster may be short-lived; divisions can reemerge as time passes and as society recovers from the disaster. But the instance of cooperation still remains in the collective memory of the parties and can create connections that last, even if conflict reignites (Kelman and Koukis, 2000).

Gender-based intervention and the empowerment of women: Women tend to bear the brunt of both violent conflict and environmental decline. They are also frequently the sole providers for their families in developing regions of the world, and thus deeply rely on consistent agricultural yields and the availability of safe and accessible drinking water to ensure their families' survival. Approximately 80 percent of farmers living on the African continent are women (World Food, n.d.). WaterAid (n.d.) reports that women in rural Africa frequently trek ten or more miles per day to fetch water, and the distance often doubles during dry seasons. They are also vulnerable to violence in conditions of armed conflict and guerrilla warfare. When these two hardships coincide, women and their dependents are at tremendous risk.

Due in part to these vulnerabilities, women are also likely to appreciate the value of environmental sustainability and social stability. Socially, politically, economically, or otherwise, empowered women can positively and thoroughly impact their communities by prioritizing policies and institutions that support peace and environmental stewardship. Social and economic reform can further empower women to become advocates for sustainability and responsible, forward-thinking environmental stewardship—principles that inspire strides toward ensuring a smoother transition to a changing climate and its many effects. By enabling women to launch "green" businesses, promote sustainable farming and resource use, and participate in decision-making that affects their communities, women's empowerment contributes profoundly to a healthy environment capable of supporting a stable society.

Peacebuilding Skills Necessitated by Environmental Change

Just as economies, industries, and disaster response mechanisms must evolve to suit new conditions, conflict management systems must also adapt to remain relevant. If theories such as Homer-Dixon's are correct, and conflict in the future will be increasingly linked to and exacerbated by environmental problems, a familiarity with environmental problems and sources of conflict will become highly valuable, and perhaps necessary, to successful interventions. Environmental factors can be highly technical and rapidly evolving, and conflict intervention may become a more complex undertaking with more factors to consider, terminology to understand, and interest groups to involve.

Similarly, practitioners will benefit from an understanding of both policy formation processes and enforcement practices, as well as sensitivity to indigenous perceptions regarding environmental management. Finding ways to broker more effective relationships and communications between government officials and stakeholders can have a lasting impact on environmental management practices. These efforts may require the empowerment of citizens and advocacy groups, as well as capacity-building for those responsible for governance.

Peacebuilding and conflict resolution practitioners will also do well to foster relationships with officials working to plan and implement local and national natural disaster response mechanisms. The anticipated increase in natural disasters, particularly if they are not handled in an organized or equitable manner, may trigger additional conflict. Incorporating conflict sensitivity into natural-disaster response efforts can ensure that such efforts are socially equitable and do not stoke existing grievances or tensions.

Methods of Intervention

Societies today harbor diverse opinions on how best to implement policy mandating environmental conservation. Some types of intervention include:

Voluntary programs and social engagement: Certain national and local initiatives aimed at providing publicly available resources for improving the ecological impact of one's home, business, and community, and to incentivize those efforts, have had a significant impact on greenhouse gas emissions and freshwater consumption. Several popular movements have emerged in recent years with the goal of promoting voluntary changes, making those government-backed resources incredibly valuable. Corporate social responsibility, for example, has also gained significant traction among companies and trade associations interested in maintaining a positive public image, preventing internal corruption, or abiding by founding organizational principles.

Voluntary reproductive health services are widely considered a potential boon for environmental conservation by helping families avoid unintended pregnancies and in turn curbing population growth, which limits human impact on resources. At times, however, vehement opposition from religious and political groups has yielded policy that either limits or eliminates these services and their funding. One such example is the US Mexico City Policy, which at times has limited US funding to safe reproductive health services in developing countries. Providing voluntary resources such as reproductive health services could potentially minimize the rate at which societies deplete their natural resources and come to face increased social turmoil.

Intervention through mandatory policy enactment: Multiple attempts have been made to arrive at internationally and nationally recognized agreements to reduce greenhouse gas emissions in the interest of limiting global climate change and its impacts on societies. While voluntary programs are in place all over the world, major emitters, such as China and the United States—and increasingly Brazil and India—have yet to implement mandatory emissions reduction measures. It is, however, more than likely that some form of policy initiative requiring emissions to be cut drastically will be necessary in future decades to stabilize atmospheric carbon dioxide (CO_2) levels and limit the extent to which resultant climatic changes drive conflict. Mandatory policies like greenhouse gas emissions reductions could, in a very real sense, help limit future related conflict.

The most promising and arguably the most widely disappointing attempt to forge such a mandatory policy at an international level has been the UN Framework Convention on Climate Change Conference of the Parties, which as of 2012 has convened eighteen times since 1994. Attempts to foster consensus have yielded little ground between developed and developing countries, in part because negotiations have fallen to heads of state accustomed to power-based negotiations, and teams of climate negotiators with varying levels of authority to enact new policies in their home countries. Many countries, particularly those regions and countries vulnerable to the effects of climate change, have already self-imposed mandatory limits under the Kyoto Protocol and individual national commitments. Until the major emitters agree to cut their own contributions to atmospheric warming, however, there is little by way of policy to regulate the steady flow of greenhouse gas emissions contributing to the phenomenon.

Efforts to establish a means for developing countries to receive aid for climate adaptation have provided some hope but have had limited success. When representatives from over 190 countries convened in Durban, South Africa, for the 17th Conference of the Parties in December 2011, the insistence by some developed countries that negotiations over the Green Climate Fund's management should be reopened and reconfigured discouraged many developing countries in need of immediate aid.

Technological interventions: Advances in current technology could potentially help minimize the negative consequences of environmental degradation. For example, desalination technology will need to become significantly more financially viable and less resource-intensive to be deployed widely enough to meet global water demands. Alternative energy sources and advances in energy efficiency will be necessary to slow the occurrence of global climate change. Some technological interventions may require the abandonment of current technologies, such as hydroelectric power, which can severely disable and even eradicate entire wetland ecosystems upon which animals and human societies rely, and coal, which is responsible for much of the carbon dioxide emitted into the atmosphere by industrialized countries. National and local policy can help encourage research and development into how technology impacts the environment, and how it can contribute to more sustainable economies.

Whatever policy initiatives nations and communities choose to undertake, it is important that those policies be integrative, mutually compatible, and suited for sustaining working relationships between neighbors and across levels of authority and power. No single community or country can secure itself entirely against environmental distress or social conflict. But cooperation between neighboring locales, regions, and nations to coordinate their policies can help parties respond to threats preemptively and effectively.

Policy and Systematic Changes

Key institutions: Until recently, there has been limited funding allocated to activity and research on the environment–conflict nexus, in part because it is a frontier area of research and theory, and in part because of the controversial nature of discussions about climate change and environmental conservation. Additionally, the regions most vulnerable to environmental hardships are the ones that rely heavily on agriculture and subsistence livelihoods, where flood or drought can equate to famine when crops are destroyed. Primarily agrarian communities generally lack the robust economy needed to attract large investments in research on what adaptation measures are needed. Exceptions include places of particular strategic interest to the US and other wealthy countries, including such areas as the Democratic Republic of the Congo that are rich in natural resources, such as oil, diamonds, coltan, tin, and tungsten; key choke points in the extraction and transmission of oil, such as Angola and the Nile Delta; or those countries considered potential havens for terrorist recruitment, as in the case of Afghanistan.

Nevertheless, an increasing number of organizations are initiating efforts to address environmental security. Several institutions concerned with environmental issues, such as the United Nations Environment Programme, the World Resources Institute, and the UN Intergovernmental Panel on Climate Change (IPCC), now incorporate integrated peacebuilding into their ongoing work. All three of these major organizations now have divisions, projects, or research teams devoted to addressing the social impact of environmental decline or change. The African Centre for the Constructive Resolution of Disputes in South Africa has hosted multiple events focusing on the links between environment, conflict, and peacebuilding.

Likewise, many organizations that traditionally focused on peace, conflict, and security are now becoming increasingly attentive to environmental concerns, such as climate change and water scarcity. These organizations include the Stimson Center, the Brookings Institution, and International Alert. Africa's University for Peace has also introduced a program for the study of environment and peace. The African Union, intended to unite African countries in the pursuit of common goals, has made a strong, collective effort to promote climate protection at the UN Framework Convention on Climate Change negotiations.

Several conflict resolution organizations have begun specializing in environmental conflict resolution and environmental peacebuilding, emergent subdisciplines to the conflict resolution field. Organizations focused specifically on this type of work include CONCUR Inc., RESOLVE, CDR Associates, the Meridian Institute, and Peace Parks International.

Notable research initiatives on the environment–conflict nexus include the Uppsala Conflict Data Project; the International Peace Research Institute, Oslo; the Environment and Conflicts Project at the Center for Security Studies at ETH Zurich; and the Environmental Change and Security Program at the Woodrow Wilson International Center for Scholars.

The IPCC is, in theory, meant to provide a platform for collaboratively addressing the issues of climate mitigation and adaptation. In practice, however, it looks more like negotiations: severe power imbalances between developed and developing countries have severely undermined efforts to approach these problems cooperatively. Economic concerns at the national level have prevented many developed countries from supporting an international agreement to reduce emissions reduction, and vulnerable developing countries do not individually have the clout to pressure developed countries to act. Following the 16th Conference of the Parties in 2010, the World People's Conference on Climate Change and the Rights of Mother Earth took place in Bolivia, representing an effort among developing and small island countries to unite for their cause in hopes of collectively presenting a more formidable force in the ongoing climate negotiations. It is unclear how effective this convention was at affecting the actions of developing countries, but it does represent a noteworthy effort to level the power imbalance currently hindering negotiations.

Policy Innovations

Improved governance: Ensuring that a society or community can survive future environmental changes requires effective governance and assurance that existing institutions such as law enforcement, social services, emergency services, and education services will remain operational in times of crisis. Anticorruption laws may limit the extent to which extractive industries and individuals in power benefit at the expense of uncompensated and underserved groups, which may in turn deepen grievances, perpetuate structural violence, and lead to armed conflict. Additionally, committing governance structures to support affordable or no-cost mediation services for environmental disputes can provide an outlet for parties to address their differences peacefully and constructively. Many consider improved governance, particularly in the agricultural sector, "a central condition for development, reducing poverty, preventing environmental destruction—and for reducing violence" (de Soysa, Gleditsch, and Sollenberg, 1999).

Corporate social responsibility and transparency: Transparency initiatives such as the Kimberley Process and EITI, both referenced above, can be incorporated into policy intended to improve governance and trade patterns by requiring disclosure of certain information. The International Monetary Fund (2011) has a transparency policy in place to ensure member countries' uses of Fund resources, as well as the Fund's own organizational information and documentation, are made available to global audiences in order to promote "greater openness and clarity by the IMF."

Reproductive health services: Concerns about the impact of an overburdened environment, both globally and regionally in places experiencing rapid population growth, have spurred controversy around the already sensitive topics of reproductive health education and family planning services. Advocates maintain that limiting population growth can minimize the strain placed on already limited natural resources, such as water. Whereas technical advances have enhanced the potential benefits of family planning services and resources for stabilizing population, they are difficult to implement in religious and conservative societies, or in places dependent on aid from other countries and organizations in places where reproductive health is controversial.

Economic diversification: Economies entirely dependent on the natural environment, and particularly those that rely on a single commodity, are at greater risk of conflict than those that rely on sectors such as manufacturing and international commerce. Several countries expecting environmental decline have undertaken plans to diversify their economies to bolster against potential economic maladies, which would otherwise strain public resources and increase the likelihood of a violent incident (Collier and Hoeffler, 2000). Botswana, for example, is politically stable and has a thriving economy. Although its economy is based in very large part on the availability of diamonds, the government has proactively instated diversification policies with mining revenues and the help of foreign aid. As such, Botswana has avoided the kind of environmental collapse that could otherwise destabilize the country given fluctuations in both the diamond industry and the global economy (Solomon, 2000).

Key Policy Debate: Rights Versus Duties

The concept of rights versus duties is at the heart of policy debates associated with environmental change and related conflict. The communities most vulnerable to and least responsible for environmental decline assert their legitimate *rights* to their land, livelihoods, and basic resources, all of which are increasingly threatened by natural disasters, such as floods, droughts, extreme weather events, and so on. Meanwhile, the entities most responsible for global environmental change—resource-intensive countries, such as the United States, China, and those in the European Union, as well as large companies profiting from the swift consumption of fossil fuels, freshwater, and other resources—insist that they have a *right* to continue exploiting the earth's natural bounty for the sake of profit and sustaining their ways of life. There is much less acknowledgment of basic human duties, such as the duty to limit the impact of one's actions and behaviors on others, or the duty to refrain from squandering communal resources, such as global water supplies and the earth's atmosphere. The failure of high-emitting and -consuming countries to acknowledge their own duties and respect others' rights has contributed to their failure to implement effective environmental policies.

INSTITUTIONAL PROFILE: UNDP

The United Nations Development Programme (UNDP) is committed to incorporating conflict and other crisis prevention into its development initiatives. The program gives special attention to the importance of environmental sustainability in the seventh of its Millennium Development Goals (MDGs), a systematic framework for deeply reducing poverty and other forms of deprivation by 2015. Among the benefits of the MDGs for many countries and regions is a more resilient society capable of sustaining peace and resisting violent conflict. Each target for Goal 7, improving environmental sustainability, has a widely ranging set of indicators, including carbon emissions reduced, fish and wildlife sanctuaries protected, consumption of ozone-depleting substances, and proportion of drinking water used versus the amount available (United Nations Interagency Framework Team for Preventative Action, n.d.). Improving performance under these metrics is understood to have positive repercussions for global development and the reduction and prevention of poverty-driven crises and conflicts.

UNDP is responsible in large part for "[working] with Least Developed Countries (LDCs) to achieve sustainable human development focused on inclusive growth in order to alleviate poverty and reduce vulnerability to shocks, such as natural disasters and conflict"(UNDP, n.d., para. 8). One such instance is in South Sudan, where UNDP established a new reservoir providing potable water in the El Ganaya district. The effect has been an alleviation of local tensions and competition in the wake of the recent civil war in the former Sudan. The first of its kind in South Sudan, the project was part of a recovery program put in place by UNDP, the Sudan's Government of National Unity, and its government of South Sudan, in the wake of the conflict. Other contributors include Save the Children Sweden, Danish Church Aid, the Roman Catholic Diocese of El Obeid, and other nongovernmental organizations, demonstrating the power of collaboration for environmentally oriented peacebuilding.

Case Studies: Good Water Neighbors Middle East[2]

In 2001, Eco Peace and Friends of the Earth Middle East initiated the Good Water Neighbors (GWN) project to foster dialogue between Jordanians, Palestinians, and Israelis in communities mutually dependent on shared water resources. The initiative has spurred improvements in water management practices by providing a basis for collaborative problem solving and newfound trust and understanding on individual, communal, and regional levels. Education, dialogue, and joint projects focused on safe, sustainable, and cooperative water management have resulted in improved water allocation and the implementation of new technology.

Despite the obvious challenges of working on the vitally contentious issue of water in the region, the GWN project has met with great success. A mayor's network emerged from ongoing public stakeholder meetings, uniting government officials from all around the Jordan River and Dead Sea in ongoing efforts to jointly address shared environmental concerns, such as the presence of sewage in the Jordan River and rapidly declining water levels in the Dead Sea. The GWN project received Time magazine's "Heroes of the Environment" award in 2008, recognizing the project as a leader in environmental activism and peacebuilding in the historically turbulent region. The project also leveraged an impressive $75 million in less than a decade for potential infrastructure upgrades in the region, particularly in Palestinian communities. Youth, government officials, and adults have engaged extensively in numerous projects coordinated by the GWN project with admirable success.

Case Study: Condor-Kutuku Conservation Corridor

The Cordillera del Condor region became the object of contention between Ecuador and Peru in 1995 due to imprecise and disputed borderlines. When tensions reached a boiling point and the two countries engaged in armed conflict for about three weeks, Argentina, Brazil, Chile, and the US swiftly initiated a peace agreement committing both countries to withdraw and demobilize their embattled troops. Lingering disagreement over the demarcation of land borders undermined efforts in 1997 to normalize border relations between the two countries, leading to the remilitarization of the region in 1998. Soon thereafter, with the help of US satellite mapping, Peru and Ecuador were able to agree upon a new border demarcation and decided jointly that the area should be devoted to conservation purposes. Each country established a national park on either side of the border, until local conservation groups, indigenous communities, and the international conservation groups Conservation International and the International Tropical Timbers Organization partnered to establish a bioregional management regime. The 2004 creation of the Condor-Kutuku conservation corridor served as one of the earliest models for the international peace park movement and evidenced the potential success of such a mechanism (Ali, 2007).

CHALLENGES IN THE FIELD

Several challenges and unresolved questions linger at the crossroads between environmental change and peacebuilding.

Zero-sum Versus Win-win

Thomas Malthus observed that although food production increases arithmetically, human growth increases geometrically. The modern Malthusian school of thought argues that current growth rates are certain to exhaust finite natural resources in the near future, leading to absolute resource scarcity and chaotic struggles for conflict over what limited resources remain. Conflict resolution tends to regard the zero-sum approach of traditional negotiations as overly fatalistic and lacking in creativity, and focuses instead on "expanding the pie" to create value out of creative solutions. Admittedly, on a very broad scale, resource scarcity is not a zero-sum problem, and a more balanced distribution of global resources, such as food and water, could meet the material needs of all people on Earth. However, as countries such as India and China strive to attain a standard of living akin to that in the US, concern spreads that a broadly adopted high consumption rate will deplete the planet's resources in mere decades. In fact, the New Economics Foundation predicted in 2008 that if the entire human population had a rate of consumption equal to that of the average American, we would require 5.3 Earths to remain sustainable (Lovell, 2007).

At a very local level, an increasing number of societies face absolute scarcity, and finding new resources is in some cases unrealistic. This problem may be because the total sum of a given resource falls short of the total daily requirements of the community, or because the community lacks the capital or technology to make the most of the available resource in question. The most difficult conditions for conflict resolution to face, and perhaps the most in need of intervention, are the genuinely zero-sum conflict situations that may become increasingly prevalent as the environment changes. What can be done in cases when resources are so limited that conflicts truly are zero-sum?

Climate-related impacts in particular may defy all local solutions aside from simply managing conflict and minimizing its destructive impacts. International efforts will likely be required to restore the ecologies of many vulnerable regions and prevent environmental distress from compounding existing risk of conflict. As such, advocacy for more responsible energy and environmental policies at an international level should be considered a priority for addressing environment-related conflict.

Oversimplifying the Environment–Conflict Connection

Scholars including Geoff Dabelko, director of the Environmental Change and Security Program at the Woodrow Wilson International Center for Scholars, stress the importance of not overstating the link between environmental decline and the emergence of conflict. "Hyperbole and oversimplification" serve only to polarize the issue, disrupt progress toward a balanced and inclusive perspective, and ignite fear that could lead to rash reactions. Finding a balanced, reasonable, and constructive approach to raising these issues for discussion and action is a popular and worthwhile pursuit.

Risk of "Securitization"

Some scholars in the peace and conflict studies field have expressed concern over the possible militarization of environmental issues that could result from its securitization. Conflict resolution tends to approach conflict in a more nuanced manner than other power-based forms of dispute resolution, with careful consideration of the possible repercussions and long-term consequences for the surrounding community. The concern has been raised that the military community is ill-equipped to handle the challenges posed by environmental factors, and a more refined approach through conflict resolution may be overlooked if powerful states choose military solutions to solve increasingly urgent environmental problems. Despite this criticism, peace activists and conflict specialists who actively engage with military officials find them well aware of the utility of nonmilitary approaches and are more familiar than anybody with the destructive consequences of warfare. Dialogue and coordination between peacebuilders and military professionals show great promise for mutual support in capacity-building and other intervention efforts.

Is Environmental Security Part of a Northern Agenda?

Jon Barnett (2001) maintains that predictions about a global future of environmentally induced warfare are presumptuous and discriminatory against communities vulnerable to climate-related disasters. The water wars hypothesis, for example, "can be read as a case of 'civilised' Europeans constructing a barbaric Other" (p. 57). According to his assessment, predicting that the global South will spiral into chaos assumes that developing countries and their populations will deal with problems with brute violence—which, coincidentally, he notes, is how the industrialized global North has historically responded to challenges.

Cultural Sensitivity

All communities arguably have methods for managing and resolving conflicts, and it is critical that third parties bear this in mind when considering or planning an intervention. Communities vulnerable to environmental change and its effects have unique cultures and characteristics that must be acknowledged and respected in order for interventions to be integrated into the cultural fabric, and for change to persist after the third party departs.

CONCLUSION

Many questions still linger about the role of environmental changes and their effect on armed conflict, as well as the mechanisms behind such a contribution. Yet as the consequences of modernization continue to disrupt natural ecosystems, undermine precious resources, and lead to suffering and societal instability, all sources of information and knowledge must be considered about a possible resolution. Both historical patterns and scientific predictions have wisdom to share with regard to the environmental conflict hypothesis and how best to address it. Integrating an understanding of the relationship between environment, conflict, and peace into the conflict resolution field, and integrating conflict resolution principles into initiatives focused on environmental conservation and restoration, will strengthen the capacity of practitioners and environmental specialists alike to respond effectively to emerging challenges.

QUESTIONS FOR FURTHER DISCUSSION

1. How might environmental changes affect or possibly complicate existing major conflicts?

2. Could environmental degradation create zero-sum conflicts? If so, what is the solution?

3. What aspects of peacebuilding are well suited for addressing environmentally induced conflict? What aspects are not?

4. What obstacles might exist to effectively integrate peacebuilding practices into the environmental arena?

5. What is the most important step toward preventing or eliminating the risk of environment-related conflict?

Further research: What evidence exists for and against the "environmental conflict" hypothesis?

REFERENCES

Ali, S. H. 2007. *Peace parks: Conservation and conflict resolution.* Cambridge, MA: MIT Press.

Bannon, I., and P. Collier. 2003. *Natural resources and violent conflict: Options and actions.* Washington, DC: World Bank.

Barnett, J. 2000. Destabilizing the environment–conflict thesis. *Review of International Studies* 26, no. 2: 271–288.

———. 2001. *The meaning of environmental security: Ecological politics and policy in the New Security Era.* London: Zed Books.

Barnett, J., and W. N. Adger. 2007. Climate change, human security, and violent conflict. *Political Geography* 26: 639–655. Retrieved January 15, 2012, from www.gsdrc.org/go /display&type=Document&id=3409.

Binningsbø, H. M., I. de Soysa, and N. P. Gleditsch. 2007. Green giant or straw man? Environmental pressure and civil conflict, 1961–99. *Population and Environment* 28, no. 6: 337–353.

Brady, C. 2011, June/July. The specter of "climate wars." *USAID Frontlines.* Retrieved April 1, 2012, from http://transition.usaid.gov/press/frontlines/fl_jun11/FL_jun11_CONFLICT .html.

Bromwich, B. U. 2008. Environmental degradation and conflict in Darfur: Implications for peace and recovery. *Humanitarian Exchange Magazine* 39. Retrieved March 15, 2012, from www.odihpn.org/humanitarian-exchange-magazine/issue-39/environmental-degradation -and-conflict-in-darfur-implications-for-peace-and-recovery.

Brown, O., A. Hammill, and R. McLeman. 2007. Climate change as the "new" security threat: Implications for Africa. *International Affairs* 83, no. 6: 1141–1154.

Buhaug, H., N. P. Gleditsch, and O. M. Theisen. 2008. Implications of climate change for armed conflict. In R. Mearns and A. Norton, eds. *Social dimensions of climate change: Equity and vulnerability in a warming world* (pp. 75–102). Washington, DC: World Bank.

Burke, M. A., E. Miguel, S. Satyanath, J. A. Dykema, and D. B. Lobell. 2009. Warming increases the risk of civil war in Africa. *Proceedings of the National Academy of Sciences* 106, no. 49: 20671–20674.

Catholic Relief Services. 2009. *Water and conflict: Incorporating peacebuilding into water development*. Baltimore, MD: Author.

CNA Corporation. 2007. *National security and the threat of climate change*. Alexandria, VA: Author.

Collier, P. 2000. *Economic causes of civil conflict and their implications for policy*. Washington, DC: World Bank.

———. 2007. *The bottom billion*. New York: Oxford University Press.

Collier, P., and A. Hoeffler. 2000. Greed and grievance in civil war. Policy Research Working Paper No. 2355. Washington, DC: World Bank.

Crowfoot, J. E., and J. M. Wondolleck. 1990. *Environmental disputes: Community involvement in conflict resolution*. Washington, DC: Island Press.

Dabelko, G. D. 2009, August 24. Avoid hyperbole, oversimplification when climate and security meet. *The Bulletin*. Retrieved June 24, 2011, from www.thebulletin.org/web-edition/op-eds/avoid-hyperbole-oversimplification-when-climate-and-security-meet.

de Soysa, I., N. P. Gleditsch, and M. Sollenberg. 1999. To cultivate peace: Agriculture in a world of conflict. *Environmental Change and Security Project Report* 5: 15–25.

Deudney, D. 1990, December. The case against linking environmental degradation and national security. *Journal of International Studies* 19, no. 3: 461–476.

Dietz, T., E. Ostrom, and P. C. Stern. 2003. The struggle to govern the commons. *Science* 302, no. 5652: 1907–1912.

Environmental Change and Security Program. 2008–2009. *ECSP Report, Issue 13*. Washington, DC: Woodrow Wilson International Center for Scholars.

Evans, A. 2010, September 9. Resource scarcity, climate change, and the risk of violent conflict. World Development Report 2011: Background Paper. New York: World Bank.

Galtung, J. 1982. *Environment, development, and military activity: Towards alternative security doctrines*. Oslo: Norwegian University Press.

Ganapti, E., I. Kelman, and T. Koukis. 2010. Analyzing Greek-Turkish disaster-related cooperation: A disaster diplomacy perspective. *Cooperation and Conflict* 45, no. 2: 162–185. Retrieved March 17, 2012, from www.disasterdiplomacy.org.

Giordano, M. F., M. A. Giordano, and T. A. Wolf. 2005. International resource conflict and mitigation. *Journal of Peace Research* 41, no. 1: 47–65.

Gleditsch, N. P. 1998. Armed conflict and the environment: A critique of the literature. *Journal of Peace Research* 35, no. 3: 381–400.

Gleick, P. 2010, January 10. Water, climate change, and international security. *Circle of Blue*. Retrieved March 1, 2012, from www.circleofblue.org/waternews/2010/world/peter-gleick-water-climate-change-and-international-security.

Goldstone, J. A. 2002. Population and security: How demographic change can lead to violent conflict. *Journal of International Affairs* 56, no. 1: 3–21.

Goldstone, J., et al. 2010. A global model for forecasting political instability. *American Journal of Political Science* 54, no. 1: 190–208.

Hauge, W., and T. Ellingsen. 1998. Beyond environmental security: Causal pathways to conflict. *Journal of Peace Research* 35, no. 3: 299–317.

Homer-Dixon, T. F. 1991. On the threshold: Environmental changes as causes of acute conflict. *International Security* 16, no. 2: 76–116.

———. 1994. Environmental scarcities and violent conflict: Evidence from cases. *International Security* 19, no. 1: 5–40.

Homer-Dixon, T. F., and J. Blitt, eds. 1998. *Ecoviolence: Links among environment, population, and security.* Lanham, MD: Rowman & Littlefield.

Homer-Dixon, T. F., and V. Percival. 1998. Environmental scarcity and violent conflict: The case of South Africa. *Journal of Peace Research* 35, no. 3: 279–298.

Institute for Environmental Security. 2006, October. *Inventory of environment and security policies and practices.* The Hague, The Netherlands: Author.

International Alert. 2010, April 29. International Alert co-hosts "South Asia Climate and Security Expert Roundtable" in Dhaka. Retrieved December 8, 2011, from www.international-alert.org/news/international-alert-co-hosts-south-asia-climate-and-security-expert-roundtable-dhaka.

International Monetary Fund. 2011, September 14. Transparency at the IMF. Retrieved January 1, 2012, from www.imf.org.

Kalyvas, S. 2001. "New" and "old" civil wars: A valid distinction? *World Politics* 54, no. 1: 99–118.

Kelman, I., and T. Koukis. 2000. Disaster diplomacy. *Cambridge Review of International Affairs* 14, no. 1: 214.

Kenyon, P. 2008, June 3. Water, food shortages squeeze Yemen. National Public Radio. Retrieved November 10, 2012, from www.npr.org/templates/story/story.php?storyId=90328214.

Klare, M. T. 2001. The new geography of conflict. *Foreign Affairs* 80, no. 3: 49–61.

Le Billon, P. 2001. The political ecology of war: Natural resources and armed conflicts. *Political Geography* 20: 561–584.

Lee, J. R. 2009a, August 14. A brief history of climate change and conflict. *The Bulletin.* Retrieved June 17, 2011, from www.thebulletin.org/web-edition/features/brief-history-of-climate-change-and-conflict.

———. 2009b. Climate change and armed conflict: Hot and cold wars. New York: Routledge.

Levy, M. A. 1995. Is the environment a national security issue? *International Security* 20, no. 2: 35–62.

Lovell, J. 2007, October 5. World moves into the ecological red. *Reuters.* Retrieved January 3, 2012, from www.reuters.com.

Maathai, W. 2009, October 7. *Tell me more.* M. Martin, interviewer. National Public Radio. Retrieved January 3, 2012, from www.npr.org/templates/story/story.php?storyId=113572748.

Mathews, J. 1989. Redefining security. *Foreign Affairs* 68, no. 2: 162–177.

Maxwell, J. W., and R. Reuveny. 2000. Resource scarcity and conflict in developing countries. *Journal of Peace Research* 37, no. 3: 301–322.

Mazo, J. 2010. *Climate conflict: How global warming threatens security and what to do about it.* New York: Routledge.

McCarthy, T. D., and M. N. Zald. 1977. Resource mobilization and social movements: A partial theory. *American Journal of Sociology* 82: 1212–1241.

Michael, D., and A. Pandya, eds. 2009. *Troubled waters: Climate change, hydropolitics, and transboundary resources.* Washington, DC: Henry L. Stimson Center.

Moghaddam, F. 2008. *Multiculturalism and intergroup relations.* Washington, DC: American Psychological Association Press.

Myers, N. 1986. The environmental dimension to security issues. *Environmentalist* 6, no. 4: 251–257.

———. 2002. *Environmental refugees: A growing phenomenon of the 21st century.* Philosophical *Transactions of the Royal Society* 357: 609–613.

Ohlsson, L. 2000. *Livelihood conflicts: Linking poverty and environment as causes of conflict.* Department for Natural Resource and the Environment. Stockholm: Swedish International Development Agency.

Omolo, N. 2010. Gender and climate change–induced conflict in pastoral communities: Case study of Turkana in northwestern Kenya. *African Journal on Conflict Resolution* 10, no. 2: 81–102. Retrieved August 7, 2011, from www.accord.org.za.

Perry, E. C., C. Potgieter, and U. Bob. 2010. Environmental conflicts and women's vulnerability in Africa. *African Journal on Conflict Resolution* 10, no. 2: 121–136.

Renner, M. 2002, October. *The anatomy of resource wars.* Washington, DC: Worldwatch Institute. Retrieved January 5, 2012, from www.worldwatch.org/node/828.

Reuveny, R. 2007. Climate change–induced migration and violent conflict. *Political Geography* 26: 656–673.

Reuveny, R., J. W. Maxwell, and J. Davis. 2011. On conflict over natural resources. *Ecological Economics* 70: 698–712.

Ross, M. L. 1999. The political economy of the resource curse. *World Politics* 51, no. 2: 297–322.

———. 2004. What do we know about natural resources and civil war? *Journal of Peace Research* 41, no. 3: 337–356.

Runciman, W. G. 1966. *Relative deprivation and social justice: A study of attitudes to social inequity in twentieth-century England.* Berkeley: University of California Press.

Shaw, B. 1996, Spring. When are environmental issues security issues? *Environmental Change and Security Project Report* 2. Washington, DC: Woodrow Wilson International Center for Scholars.

Smith, D., and J. Vivekananda. 2007, November. *A climate of conflict: The links between climate change, peace, and war.* London: International Alert.

Solomon, M. 2000. *Growth and diversification in mineral economies: Planning and incentives for diversification.* Mineral Corporation. Presented to the UN Conference on Trade and Development.

Solomon, S. 2010 *Water: The epic struggle for wealth, power, and civilization.* New York: HarperCollins.

Solomon, S., D. Qin, M. Manning, Z. Chen, M. Marquis, K. Averyt et al. 2010. *Contribution of Working Group I to the Fourth Assessment Report of the Intergovernmental Panel on Climate Change.* Cambridge and New York: Cambridge University Press.

Sultana, F. 2011. Suffering for water, suffering from water: Emotional geographies of resource access, control, and conflict. *Geoforum* 42: 163–172. Retrieved January 7, 2012, from www.elsevier.com.

Tajfel, H., and J. C. Turner. 1979. *An integrative theory of intergroup conflict: The social psychology of intergroup relations* (pp. 33–47). W. G. Austin and S. Worchel, eds. Monterey, CA: Brooks/Cole.

United Nations. n.d. MDG Goal 7: Ensure environmental sustainability. Retrieved August 1, 2012, from www.un.org/millenniumgoals/environ.shtml.

United Nations Development Programme (UNDP). n.d. Thousands get clean water in Sudan. Retrieved August 15, 2012, from www.undp.org/content/undp/en/home/ourwork /environmentandenergy/successstories/southsudanreservoir.html.

United Nations Environment Programme (UNEP). 2009. *From conflict to peacebuilding: The role of natural resources and the environment*. Nairobi, Kenya: Author.

United Nations Interagency Framework Team for Preventative Action. n.d. Environmental scarcity and conflict: Guidance note for practitioners. New York: United Nations Environment Programme. Retrieved April 1, 2012, from www.unep.org /conflictsanddisasters/Policy/EnvironmentalCooperationforPeacebuilding/UNEU Partnership/tabid/29405/Default.aspx.

Urdal, H. 2005. People vs. Malthus: Population pressure, environmental degradation, and armed conflict. *Journal of Peace Research* 42, no. 4: 417–434. Retrieved June 7, 2011, from www.jstor.org.

Urdal, H., and C. Raleigh. 2007. Climate change, environmental degradation, and armed conflict. *Political Geography* 26, no. 6: 674–694.

Walton, B. 2010, November 30. Pakistan and India in dam building race: Interpreting the Indus Water Treaty. *Circle of Blue*. Retrieved November 8, 2012, from www.circleofblue .org/waternews/2010/world/pakistan-and-india-in-dam-building-race-interpreting-the -indus-water-treaty.

Water Aid. n.d. Problems for women. Retrieved November 10, 2012, from www.wateraid .org/uk/what_we_do/the_need/206.asp.

Westing, A. H. 1995. Environmental approaches to the avoidance of regional violent conflict. Environment and Conflicts Project. *ENCOP Occasional Papers* 14, no. 1: 148–153.

Wolf, A. T. 1998. Conflict and cooperation along international waterways. *Water Policy* 1, no. 2: 251–265.

———. 2002. *Conflict prevention and resolution in water systems*.

Wolf, A., S. Yoffe, and M. Giordano. 2003, February. International waters: Identifying basins at risk. *Water Policy*, 29–60.

World Food Programme. n.d. Our work, overview. Retrieved November 10, 2012, from www.wfp.org/Our%20work/Preventing%20Hunger/Focus%20on%20women/Women4 Women%20overview.

Notes

1. The IPCC is a committee of scientists appointed by countries across the globe, convening under the auspices of the UN Framework Convention on Climate Change to address the issue of climate change.

2. Case from *Friends of the Earth*, http://foeme.org.

chapter nine

SECURITY AND PEACEBUILDING

Sam Feigenbaum, Rachel Goldberg, and Rhea Vance-Cheng

Making peace, I have found, is much harder than making war.

—GERRY ADAMS

W HILE THE FIELDS OF PEACEBUILDING and security may at first appear to have contradictory goals, both strive to achieve peace, security, and the establishment of a safer world. Although cooperation between the two areas has grown over the past decade, peacebuilding and security largely remain distinct and separate areas. This chapter explores how peacebuilding and security can be better integrated to address the new security threats of the twenty-first century. In contrast to that of the past century, today's security threats are intricate and multifaceted, and include a diverse array of dangers, from terrorism to environmental degradation, pandemics, cyber threats, global financial crises, and natural disasters (Moghaddam, 2010).

These new types of security threats emerged from two main sources: the end of the Cold War and the rise of globalization. After the end of the Cold War and breakup of the Soviet Union, the world witnessed a change in the nature of conflicts from primarily interstate conflicts (such as World War II) to largely intrastate conflicts and civil wars (such as Rwanda and the former Yugoslavia). In addition, globalization and technological advancement have increased the shape, scope, and speed of security threats. Today, conflict in one corner of the globe can rapidly create insecurity in geographically distant regions. As a result, terrorism, nuclear proliferation, hacking of computer networks, and epidemics are now high-level concerns for security practitioners. These new threats have prompted many policy makers and security practitioners to shift their thinking and begin to employ integrated approaches to address security threats.

The main purpose of this chapter is to inform students and practitioners about efforts to integrate security and peacebuilding, both in theory and in practice. This will be accomplished by focusing on four goals. The first is to review three main security theories that have traditionally underpinned security practices: realism, liberalism, and constructivism. Each theory's respective explanation for conflict and insecurity, along with recommendations for mitigating conflict and security threats, is explored.

The second aim of the chapter is to explore the main integrated frameworks that fuse ideas from peacebuilding and security. The models discussed are the hard–soft power continuum, human security, responsibility to protect (R2P), and development-diplomacy-defense security (3D).

The chapter's third goal is to explain integrated *practices* that incorporate tools and strategies from peacebuilding and security. The chapter discusses several integrated practices including counterterrorism, human terrain systems (HTSs), provincial reconstruction teams (PRTs), security sector reform (SSR), disarmament-demobilization-reintegration (DDR), and nonviolent observation.

The final goal is to discuss the ethical dilemmas and challenges of integrating these two fields. This discussion weaves throughout the chapter and concludes by presenting key challenges in the field.

INTRODUCTION TO THE SECURITY SECTOR

The emergence of new security threats in the new millennium has had profound effects on the security field. As the world's only superpower, the US and its security-sector institutions offer an excellent perspective into the evolving nature of the field—and set the trend for global security. It is clear that in recent years, despite its unsurpassed military dominance, the US is finding it difficult to defeat modern security threats solely through the use of military means.

The primary US security institution was originally called the War Department but was renamed the Department of Defense (DoD) after the passage of the National Security Act of 1947 consolidated the major branches of the military. The DoD is responsible for international security threats[1] and is charged with several tasks including the maintenance of a modern military, procurement, research and development, housing, atomic defense, national defense, base and equipment maintenance, and veterans' benefits (OMB, 2012). The main bureaucratic hub of this operation is the Pentagon, which oversees "approximately 1,431,400 men and women on Active Duty, 848,040 Reserve and National Guard, and 790,400 civilians" in nearly every country in the world (Department of Defense, 2012, para. 4). The scope of US involvement in military affairs literally extends the world over, maintaining 662 bases worldwide, two-thirds of which are in Germany (218), Japan (115), and South Korea (Department of Defense, 2010, p. 9).

While the United States is unrivaled in quality of forces and ability to project its power on a global scale, this influence comes at a considerable cost, a reflection on the global security field at large. Defense expenditures account for nearly a quarter of the nation's budget. In 2011 the DoD spent just over $705 billion, more than doubling its total outlays in the decade since September 11, 2001 (OMB, n.d., Table 3.2). This reflects a global trend, most notably in the five permanent members of the Security Council,[2] all of which increased military spending in the past decade, with 2010 global military spending reaching almost $1.6 trillion (SIPRI, 2010). To put this in perspective, Global Issues (2011) cites that "the UN's entire budget is ... approximately 1.8%" of global military spending.

The United States' domestic security figures stand in notable contrast to the forces of international peacekeeping, which receive far less personnel and funding. The UN's peacekeeping force totals around 98,900 and is composed of police, troops, and observers. While the number of deployed peacekeepers is on the rise, it still represents only around an eighth of the US reserve force alone (United Nations, 2012). These figures suggest that the world's nations continue to prioritize spending on national security through military channels versus allocating resources for international security through the further development of peacebuilding and development programs. It is important to note that global development spending is approximately $129 billion per year and that there are increasing efforts to strengthen regional political and security organizations, such as the African Union (AU) and the Association of Southeast Nation States (ASEAN).

TRADITIONAL SECURITY THEORIES

To understand the foundations of the security sector, it is important to first look at key theories that help shape foreign policy and security responses. This section briefly delineates the three major schools of thought as they pertain to security. It discusses each theory's explanation of insecurity and policy prescriptions while also denoting the major shifts in the field, which have occurred in the past century.

Realism

In the past millennium, realist ideologies have been prominent in guiding much of global security policy. Modern realist thinkers, such as Jervis, Waltz, and Mearsheimer (Donnelly, 1992), evolved traditional theories of realism that were first crafted by Hobbes, Machiavelli, and Thucididyes (Forde, 1992). Each thinker's conception of realism varies, but they have a common view that the prime source of insecurity is human nature, which is viewed as inherently violent and aggressive (Glaser, 2010). Realists argue that power is the basic currency in the international system and that more powerful states should maintain order and protect their own interests. Realist theory holds that the primary means of state security is hard power, which includes population, territory, resources, and weapons (Glaser, 2010). Realism also suggests each nation's threat level should be calculated based solely on the nation's power and capability.

In the past, many policy makers adopted a realist approach to security—the Cold War being a prime example. During the Cold War, while policy makers worked to improve relations between the superpowers using dialogue and diplomacy, they dedicated the majority of their time and resources to containing the Soviet Union by building hard power to deter a Soviet attack. US efforts to maintain security included stockpiling nuclear arms, innovating tracks to store and deploy nuclear missiles, and creating protective defense shields while also planning for the possibility of conventional war with the USSR (Spanier and Hook, 2009).

Liberalism

Following the Cold War, security thinkers began reducing their reliance on traditional realist theories and incorporating liberalist and constructivist theories, as well as new tools to deal with new types of security threats. Although liberalism is often misinterpreted as the key opponent of realism, both theories share crucial assumptions. Realism and liberalism each view nations as the key actors in international relations, but unlike realism, liberalism suggests that additional parties, such as nongovernmental organizations (NGOs), international organizations, corporations, and international institutions, influence the behaviors of nation-states (Morgan, 2010). As a result, liberalists strive to understand the motives and interests of a multitude of actors and explain their roles in creating and mitigating security threats (Navari, 2008). In general, liberalists believe that international institutions are the best remedy for insecurity and that the international system is evolving into a system of cooperation and collaboration that will help mitigate conflict (Morgan, 2010).

As liberalist theory has predicted, the capacity of international institutions is indeed evolving and their role is expanding. Global security institutions, such as the United Nations, and regional security institutions, including the North Atlantic Treaty Organization, European Union, African Union, and Association of South East Nations, are increasing their efforts to tackle security threats collectively and collaboratively. Still, many nations are hesitant to put their full faith (and resources) into collective security models.

Constructivism

Like liberalism, constructivist theory is slowly gaining recognition in the security world and has even played a role in the formation of the peacebuilding field. Within the wider social constructionist movement, constructivists argue that ideas, identity, and interactions influence nations' behavior (Moghaddam, 2005). Unlike realists, constructivists do not believe that conflict erupts primarily from a struggle for material goods, but rather from a clash of identities, ideas, cultures, norms, and belief systems (Agius, 2010).

In practice, constructivist theory calls for a wide range of soft-power tools—such as trust-building, development, democratization, education, and dialogue—to help defuse the diverse and dynamic sources of conflict. Some of these tools are being integrated into modern security practices (notably in operations in Afghanistan and

Iraq) to help reduce conflict and terrorism, and to stabilize at-risk nations. Most of the constructivist policy tools largely reflect a soft approach to power.

Integrated Frameworks

The integrated frameworks discussed in this section—the hard-soft power continuum, human security, responsibility to protect, and development-diplomacy-defense security (3D)—are a marriage of peacebuilding and security theories, and offer new theoretical designs to better suit the changing global security environment. The focus is each model's main theoretical contribution, remedies for insecurity, and challenges.

Hard-Soft Power Continuum

This chapter relies on the hard-soft power continuum to frame the linkages of security and peacebuilding (Nye, 1990a). This continuum provides a broad conceptualization of integrated security approaches that fuse hard and soft power. As an example, policy makers often use diplomatic power—backed up by material (hard) power—to defuse security threats and create peace. When a security threat arises, however, disagreements over the efficacy of hard-power or soft-power solutions are common.

Hard power is exerted primarily in the form of the military; however, sources of hard power vary and include natural resources, economic dominance, territory and geography, technology, and political stability. Ultimately these factors allow nations to maintain powerful and adept armies that can use the threat of force to eliminate threats and achieve security objectives (Nye, 1990b). Many practitioners consider hard power more effective and politically feasible in the face of an imminent attack, but there are also significant challenges. Hard power approaches can be expensive and largely focus on addressing surface-level threats, while often ignoring and possibly aggravating the root causes of insecurity.

On the other hand, soft power influences and entices nations to act peacefully. Sources of soft power tend to be more difficult to measure and include education, empowerment, economic development, and culture (Nye, 1990a). Soft power approaches can reduce threats by increasing jobs, education, gender equality, and overall quality of life. Many practitioners consider soft power a more effective long-term strategy to dealing with potential security challenges, given the focus on deep-rooted sources and motivations for conflict, such as identity, religion, empowerment, and perceptions (Moghaddam, 2010).

It is essential to integrate hard and soft power to deflect surface-level threats as well as defuse the deep-rooted sources of conflict. The challenge is striking the ideal balance between the two approaches. One way to conceptualize this hybrid approach is characterized by a continuum of power, which ranges from soft-power influence-based approaches to hard-power coercion- and military-based approaches. The following chart is an aid to conceptualizing political power as a continuum and shows the varying ways in which actors, theories, approaches, and methods change depending on the type of power exerted.

FIGURE 9.1. Continuum of Power: Integrating Peacebuilding and Security Approaches

	SOFT POWER				INTEGRATED				HARD POWER	
	1	2	3	4	5	6	7	8	9	10
Actors:	NGOs/local actors				Cooperation				Military	
Theories:	Constructivism				Liberalism				Realism	
Approach:	Peacebuilding				Hybrid				Military intervention	
Methods:	Dialogue				Capacity-building				Force	
Examples:	Education programs				Security sector reform				Military attack	
Targets:	Deep-rooted causes				Hybrid				Surface-level threats	
Time Frame:	Long-term				Both				Short-term	

For example, the US is using both a hybrid hard-soft power approach to deflect the Iranian nuclear threat. Soft power programs aim to defuse the threat's root causes: anti-Americanism and a belligerent Iranian regime. An example of a soft power–based program is Voice of America, which broadcasts pro-American radio and news programs to Iran to build relations with the Iranian population and spread US influence. One of their programs is the satirical Iranian television program *Parazait*, which is similar to Jon Stewart's *The Daily Show* and humorously critiques religious and political leaders in the Islamic republic. The goal of the program is to influence Iranians and undermine the legitimacy of the current Iranian regime (Bahrampour, 2011). The US uses this soft power tactic to complement more dominant hard power approaches. In the case of Iran, the US predominantly relies on economic sanctions (and the possible threat of military action by the US or Israel) to coerce the government to halt nuclear development, while programs such as *Parazait* are designed to defuse the deeper root causes of the Iranian nuclear threat.

Human Security

Another hybrid framework that integrates ideas from peacebuilding and security is the human security model. Human security places individual security over a state-centered focus and has two main components, according to the foundational definition published in the UN Development Report of 1994. First is "freedom from fear," which includes tangible problems such as "safety from chronic threats such as hunger, disease, and repression" (UNDP, 1994, p. 3). Second is "freedom from want," which incorporates intangible problems such as "protection from sudden and hurtful disruptions in patterns of daily life—whether in homes, in jobs or in communities" (UNDP, 1994, p. 3). In addition, there are seven dimensions of human security: "economic security, food security, health security, environmental security, personal security, community security, and political security" (UNDP, 1994, pp. 23–24).

Significant controversy surrounds the concept of human security. Scholars find it difficult to completely agree on a definition, partially because the concept is so broad.

Some contend that human security should include both "freedom from fear" and "freedom from want," whereas other scholars think that human security is only "freedom from want." In addition, critics argue that broad definitions with several dimensions of human security make it difficult to operationalize (MacFarlane and Khong, 2006).

Nonetheless, there have been attempts to integrate human security into practice. The UN Trust Fund for Human Security (2009) explains that in practice human security approaches are people-centered, context-specific, comprehensive, multi-sectoral, and prevention oriented. They consist of three main phases: (1) analysis, mapping, and planning, (2) implementation, and (3) impact assessment. Human security approaches are suggested for a wide range of tasks including postconflict reconstruction (UN Trust Fund for Human Security, 2009).

There are still many challenges to putting human security into practice. For one, creating human security is a long-term process and tends to be incompatible with the short-term nature of most military interventions. When the political will for an intervention dies down, politicians and military actors (if there are any) are frequently pressured to develop quick exit strategies, which can create a security vacuum. In many cases military interventions may even reduce human security. For human security to be effective in practice, it seems essential to foster strong local security institutions and if necessary the political will for the types of long-term interventions needed to create human security.

Responsibility to Protect (R2P)

Another integrated framework is the Responsibility to Protect (R2P), which shares many commonalities with human security. The International Commission on Intervention and State Sovereignty (ICISS) conceived of R2P in 2001. It has since been incorporated into various international documents, including the African Union's 2005 Founding Charter and the 2006 UN Security Council Resolution 1674.

This framework's main theoretical contribution is the reconceptualization of the notion of sovereignty. It diverges from traditional theories, which assume that state sovereignty is a universal, unchangeable organizing principle of the international system. Instead, R2P radically redefines sovereignty as a *privilege*, not a *right* (ICISS, 2001).

To earn this privilege, nations must protect their citizens from four types of mass atrocities: genocide, war crimes, crimes against humanity, and ethnic cleansing. To do this, nations should be accountable and transparent, respect human rights, promote social and economic well-being, and establish nonviolent, democratic avenues for change (ICISS, 2001). While the framework does not explicitly state that nations should be democratic, it suggests that certain democratic characteristics and institutions allow nations to effectively protect their citizens.

R2P is increasingly useful in today's shifting international climate and provides a platform for confronting intrastate conflicts, which threaten regional and global security. In addition to providing a legal and theoretical justification for intervention in intrastate conflicts, the R2P framework provides multiple tools and practices for dealing with intrastate conflicts. The framework draws from the fields of conflict prevention, humanitarian intervention, and postconflict reconstruction and classifies recommended actions into three areas: responsibility to prevent, responsibility to react, and responsibility to rebuild (ICISS, 2001). Responsibility to prevent incorporates early warning systems, and detection and amelioration of root causes of conflict. Unfortunately, as the 2001 ICISS report points out, decisive preventative action is lacking. The report lists three prerequisites for successful conflict prevention: early warning, a preventive toolbox, and political will (ICISS, 2001).

An obstacle to incorporating responsibility to protect into practice is the weak capacity of evolving international institutions, which often lack the funding, the resources, and the consent from more powerful members to intervene to protect other nations. Still, the most substantial challenge is building consensus about the circumstances in which intervention is appropriate and what might be the appropriate form of engagement. This is extremely difficult, as several nations do not subscribe to R2P and those who do often disagree on the circumstances in which it is acceptable. A number of critics view R2P as being selectively applied and used only to intervene in conflicts on a selective basis that fits the interests of more powerful states.

The current debate over a possible international intervention in Syria illustrates this challenge. As of the date of this publication, Syria has been embroiled in conflict for more than a year. Thousands have been killed as the government under the leadership of Bashar al-Assad continues to attack several civilian population areas and an emerging Free Syria Army begins to take shape. Despite several attempts at intervention and overwhelming international support to do so, Russia and China, two countries that have veto power on the UN Security Council, remain steadfastly committed to traditional principles of sovereignty and refuse to support an international intervention in Syria. Without their votes, little can be done, and the international community cannot uphold the responsibility to protect (MacFarquhar and Shadid, 2012).

Another model that is similar to R2P is development-diplomacy-defense (3D), which emphasizes the importance of using diplomatic, economic, and social incentives prior to any military intervention. Both R2P and the 3D model emphasize that the international community should intervene only if the state is incapable of protecting its citizens. The challenging part is knowing who has the power to decide when this is the case and building consensus within existing international institutions on appropriate actions.

Development, Diplomacy, and Defense (3D Security)

The 3D security framework is one of the most comprehensive and widely recognized security frameworks to integrate ideas from peacebuilding. Many nations including Canada and the US are beginning to acknowledge the value of this approach. US Secretary of State Hillary Clinton (2010) has spoken about these efforts:

> We are elevating development and diplomacy as core elements of our foreign policy, alongside defense. We're doing so with strong support from Secretary Gates, the Chairman of the Joint Chiefs Mike Mullen, who have really become believers in the necessity for us to be activists in diplomacy and development to try to prevent conflict, to try to ameliorate and resolve conflict, to try to go into post-conflict situations to begin to help rebuild. (para. 4)

Many of the ideas in this framework have been used in the past, but the peace-building organization 3P Human Security (formerly 3D Security) is a key organization helping to integrate these ideas into the development-diplomacy-defense (3D) framework and educating policy makers and academics on the effectiveness of this model. The organization emphasizes that security policy needs to move away from one-dimensional, hard power–focused security strategies and employ multiple tools such as soft power and conflict prevention to inoculate against security threats (3D Security Initiative, 2011).

The 3D framework suggests that the go-to security strategies should be development and diplomacy and the hard security strategy (defense) should be used only as a last resort. The approach suggests that a large toolbox is necessary for policy makers to deflect security threats. These tools are split into the three categories of development, diplomacy, and defense (3D Security Initiative, 2011).

The first category, development, includes the creation of economic, social, and political infrastructure. This includes a large array of activities such as building schools, digging wells, paving roads, and supporting civil society organizations. These types of projects may assist in ameliorating several global security threats. For instance, development projects can help reduce terrorism by creating legitimate governments and helping a population have their basic needs satisfied (and therefore be less likely to support terrorist activities).

The second category is diplomacy, which is communication and negotiation through political and legal channels to resolve conflicts. There are two main types of diplomacy—Track I and Track II. Track I diplomacy is formal dialogue and negotiations between political leaders. Track II diplomacy is unofficial interaction between civil society, businesses, and religious leaders (3D Security Initiative, 2011).

The third category of security tools is defense, which includes a wide range of military tasks coordinated by the government. The framework stresses that relying only on military defense is inadequate protection against burgeoning security threats such as terrorism, ecological disasters, and disease (3D Security Initiative, 2011).

There are several challenges to putting the 3D model into practice. For one, there is disagreement over how to effectively use diplomacy and development to protect US security. Some policy makers and academics believe that the US should direct development aid based on US national interest, which in many cases already occurs. Others believe that development aid should go where it is needed most to prevent conflict and reduce risks to US security in the future. For instance, Oxfam International (2011) found that since 2001, the Democratic Republic of the Congo, home to one of the world's worst humanitarian crises, received at most $10 per person in international humanitarian aid, whereas Iraq received up to $120 per person.

In addition, there is disagreement over whether the three prongs of this approach should be coequal pillars or whether more resources should be dedicated to defense. In practice, defense receives the majority of funding. In 2011, the US budgeted $773 billion for national security and defense and only US $55.8 billion to foreign affairs, which includes the development and diplomacy budget (Feldstein, 2010). Surprisingly, many prominent security practitioners, including former US Defense Secretary Robert

Gates and current US Defense Secretary Leon Panetta, have advocated for money to be redirected from defense to diplomacy (Clinton, 2010; Kaufman, 2012). Overall, the 3D model emphasizes that it is essential for the three sectors to coordinate their efforts in conflict situations, thus ensuring they are efficiently working toward the same goal. Still, the challenges of collaboration across diverse sectors pose obstacles to implementing the 3D model.

INTEGRATED PRACTICES

The practices described in this section combine hard-power, security-based approaches with soft-power, peacebuilding tools to defuse security threats and create more peaceful societies. The practices discussed include counterterrorism, human terrain systems, provincial reconstruction teams, security sector reform, disarmament, demobilization, reintegration, and nonviolent observation. This section discusses the goals, strategies, examples, and challenges for each practice.

Counterterrorism

Counterterrorism practices and policies are evolving, incorporating hard and soft power tools such as development, diplomacy, and defense to confront nontraditional security threats. In today's security climate, terrorism is the primary threat identified by many security practitioners. Whether terrorism deserves this status is debatable[3]— other global phenomena such as epidemics, interstate wars, and refugees/internally displaced people represent significant security threats. In 2010, 9,823 individuals were killed in terrorist attacks worldwide (National Counterterrorism Center, 2011) compared to 1.75 million deaths worldwide from HIV and AIDS (World Health Organization, 2011). Nevertheless, terrorism is at the top of the security agenda, and some counterterrorism activities may benefit from increased collaboration with the peacebuilding field, from both the theoretical and operational standpoints.

Counterterrorism includes methods, tactics, and strategies used to respond to violent, subnational, organized groups that use terrorism as a tactic to achieve their political goals. Peacebuilding tools can be critical in understanding the sources of terrorism, designing processes to help engage armed actors in dialogue, and creating a constructive, fruitful peace process free from spoilers. Critically, for peace to be sustainable, peace processes in conflict-affected societies must address underlying motivations for social change through violence—for example, encouraging armed actors seeking regime change to choose to work within a fairer political framework and participate in elections and disarm.

Dozens of US government agencies and organizations perform tasks within President Barack Obama's National Strategy for Counterterrorism, which incorporates the "whole-of-government" for "balancing near- and long-term counterterrorism considerations."[4] President Obama stresses that "the exercise of American power against terrorist threats must be done in a thoughtful, reasoned, and proportionate way that both enhances U.S. security and delegitimizes the actions of those who use terrorism," and that aims to, among other goals, "protect the American people, homeland, and American interests . . . disrupt, degrade, dismantle, and defeat al-Qa'ida and its affiliates and adherents, prevent terrorist development, acquisition, and use of weapons of mass destruction" (White House, 2011, p. 7).

The United Nations and its members also seek to coordinate terrorism efforts. For example, in its Global Counterterrorism Strategy the UN (2006) suggests that in order to defuse the root causes of terrorism, it is important to "continue to strengthen and make best possible use of the capacities of the United Nations in areas such as conflict prevention, negotiation, mediation, conciliation, judicial settlement, rule of law, peacekeeping and peacebuilding, in order to contribute to the successful prevention and peaceful resolution of prolonged unresolved conflicts. We recognize that the peaceful resolution of such conflicts would contribute to strengthening the global fight against terrorism" (United Nations, 2006, lines 131–135). One of the challenges that the UN (and other institutions) faces is developing a clear definition of terrorism. This has proven to be very difficult given the diverse composition of the UN member states. For example, what some states would label as terrorism is seen by others as fighting oppression or for liberation. Instead the UN works to identify and limit financing for certain types of terrorist activity such as taking hostages, or hijacking aircraft and spreading chemical or biological weapons.[5] For example, the UN has taken steps to limit the movement and financing of a select group of al-Qaeda and Taliban entities and individuals.[6]

International recognition of the use of peacebuilding in conjunction with security as a measure of prevention against international terrorism is an important step in beginning to address these often intractable conflicts. However, there are significant ethical and practical concerns. For one, peacebuilding and security practitioners are likely to disagree about which measures are justified to identify, catch, and punish terrorists or even on who should be classified as a terrorist. For instance, the counterterrorism tactics of illegal detentions, lengthy interrogations, and waterboarding violate the peacebuilding principle of "do no harm," and peacebuilders are unlikely to collaborate with counterterrorism experts in these areas. Because of the *Holder vs. Humanitarian Law* ruling, it has also become increasingly difficult for US-based peacebuilding organizations to engage with armed groups that have been classified as terrorists by the US government.[7] While most peacebuilders wouldn't condone the violent acts of such organizations, they would emphasize that to increase chances of peace, it is necessary to engage with them. Furthermore, there are often challenges and significant differences in the organizational cultures and practices of hard security approaches to prevent terrorist attacks, policing and intelligence activities, and soft power approaches. Finally, security actors may be uncomfortable with the reintegration of terrorists into society through processes such as disarmament, demobilization, and reintegration (DDR).

It is clear that to date, there has been an overwhelming emphasis on hard power approaches to dealing with terrorist threats and insufficient resources devoted to soft power approaches, such as peacebuilding. A hybrid approach to counterterrorism, using hard and soft power strategies including policing, patrols, and partnering with local forces to improve the rule of law, in conjunction with dialogue and development from peacebuilding, can likely help tackle both the immediate repercussions of terrorism as well as the more systemic causes of terrorism. The combination of hard power and soft power may ultimately prove to be the most efficient and sustainable long-term counterterrorism strategy.

Provincial Reconstruction Teams and Human Terrain Systems
As one component of the grand counterterrorism strategy, US and coalition forces strive to eliminate insurgencies in nations such as Iraq and Afghanistan. While security actors in these nations initially focused their attention on hard power approaches, the failure of the initial military campaign to quell insurgencies prompted security actors to focus some attention on the more deep-rooted sources of insurgency and incorporate soft power tools to defuse them. Two controversial programs that embody US efforts are provincial reconstruction teams (PRTs) and human terrain systems (HTS).

PRTs in Afghanistan and Iraq attempt to link security, development, and peacebuilding actors to develop more effective approaches to winning the hearts and minds in local communities and reducing the support for insurgencies and terrorism. Team members come from several sectors including development, peacebuilding, diplomacy, defense, and agriculture and aim to change social conditions likely to breed insurgency, such as illiteracy, unemployment, and deprivation of basic needs. To remedy these potential sources of insurgency, they strive to improve literacy rates, create jobs, and establish sources of food, water, and shelter. PRTs undertake a wide range of projects to achieve these objectives, including building roads, clinics, wells, schools, dams, and power grids, and employing locals on development projects and other related actions (Bebber, 2008). These projects use soft power–based approaches to reduce support for insurgency.

Another process that combines both hard and soft power to fight insurgency is human terrain systems (HTSs), which strive to use knowledge of local cultures to build stronger links between security forces and locals, ultimately to improve military efficiency. The first HTS was implemented in 2005. This controversial program, designed and run by the US Army and the Department of Defense, consists of teams of social scientists in Iraq and Afghanistan that conduct research on cultural norms, tribal structures, and tribal power relationships. Many dispute the efficacy of HTSs' ultimate goal, which is improving the military's understanding of the local population and applying this cultural literacy to the Military Decision-Making Process (Gonzalez, 2008).

The tasks of HTSs include first recruiting, training, deploying, and supporting an embedded, operationally focused sociocultural capability; second, conducting operationally relevant research and analysis; and third, developing and maintaining a sociocultural knowledge base to add into a comprehensive database known as MAP-HT (Gonzalez, 2008). McFate and Fondacaro (2011) suggest that the teams provided information that helped military leaders solve problems using nonlethal methods. McFate and Fondacaro (2011) cite the example of an Afghani cultural norm: celebratory fire. As a Special Forces officer explains:

> Had we understood the cultural role of celebratory gunfire, more than one wedding party would have been spared from fires conducted in self-defense against a perceived threat. While downrange, I tried to impress upon my crew the importance

of cultural intelligence in the tactical environment. . . . The knowledge enabled us to "retract the fangs" on several occasions, allowing us to identify the behavior of potential threat groups to our own party as benign. (p. 66)

In addition, HTSs dispelled the myth commonly held among soldiers in Iraq that a black flag signaled belligerence. In fact, the flag is a religious symbol that many Shi'a Muslims fly from their homes. After HTSs corrected this misunderstanding, many lives were spared and needless hostility was reduced (McFate and Fondacaro, 2011). HTSs' nontraditional approach to security stresses cultural fluency as a means to increasing soft power and reducing violence and security threats.

Despite the successes of the HTSs, there are still many challenges and ethical dilemmas concerned with collecting cultural information on the battlefield. For instance, military recruiters find it difficult to enlist qualified social scientists credentialed with essential knowledge of local cultures and languages. One reason is that anthropologists employed by the HTSs receive a significant negative stigma from the anthropological community and in some cases are blacklisted from jobs in academic institutions and anthropology organizations (Caryl, 2009). Another significant obstacle is ensuring the safety of the team members. Conducting interviews in war zones is extremely dangerous, and to date three HTSs members have died in the field (Caryl, 2009). A third challenge is gathering accurate information. Informants may be unreliable, as they are likely to receive threats from insurgent groups and may be motivated to falsify information. Likewise, cultural communication differences and language barriers threaten the validity of the information.

Overall, HTSs represent a critical partnership between the social sciences and the military, and work to incorporate notions of intangible security threats into traditional security operations. Long regarded as insignificant, culture is becoming a vast new source of insight for security actors. Cultural misunderstandings, on a large scale, often throw unwanted fuel onto an already tense conflict (see Avruch and Black, 1993). Human terrain teams represent an attempt to address cultural problems before they arise.

Security Sector Reform (SSR)

Another hybrid process used in counterinsurgency efforts in Afghanistan and many other parts of the world affected by conflict is security sector reform (SSR). The main purpose of SSR is to establish a basic, functioning security infrastructure in conflict-ravaged nations. A key aspect is creating a strong civilian institution to allow citizen-led, transparent control over security forces and institutions, which is a prerequisite to peace, security, and stability (Hänggi, 2004).

Many parties take part in the process of security sector reform, including all institutions and parties mandated to protect citizens against violence or coercion. This includes the military, intelligence agencies, police, paramilitary forces, and even judicial institutions. Furthermore, even non-state-endorsed security parties, such as guerrilla or rebel forces and private military contractors, are sometimes considered part of this sector, especially when these groups exert significant leverage and control over territory. In some cases, after demobilization these groups are integrated into the state security forces (Hänggi, 2004). For instance, a number of Maoist forces have been integrated into the security sector in Nepal following a decade-long conflict started by the Maoist groups as they sought to end the monarchy and establish a socialist government. This has made it extremely difficult to create a stable and effective security sector in Nepal, but is still considered a vital part of the SSR process (Halperin, 2010).

While SSR can take place in any state in which security forces jeopardize democratic rule, SSR tends to occur in "failed states," which lack a basic government, security, and social infrastructure, often due to internal conflict (Hänggi, 2004). As with the implementation of other processes mentioned in this chapter, SSR has had mixed results. The case of Afghanistan illustrates the challenges and ethical dilemmas of SSR.

In Afghanistan, SSR has been a key focus of the overall reconstruction strategy. However, this instance exposed a vital vulnerability of SSR; it requires a certain level of base security to operate. This usually entails an outside security force, such as NATO or UN peacekeepers, to maintain security conditions until the domestic security sector is developed and ready to take over.

Mark Sedra (2004) lists several additional challenges of SSR in Afghanistan. For one, various armed groups including al-Qaeda, the Taliban, and the Hizb-i-Isami destabilize the Afghani government and undermine the SSR process. Similarly, the culture of warlordism resists regional governmental rule, and the pervasive narcotics trade exacerbates insecurity and instability (Sedra, 2004). Furthermore, the international coalition's lack of cultural understanding cripples essential elements of SSR, including the creation of a strong and functioning national army and police force and of accountable and transparent defense and judicial ministries. A cultural specificity the coalition ignored in the initial SSR strategy in Afghanistan was the attention to ethnic demographics within the army, police, and defense ministry. Often a majority of a certain ethnic group in an institution would delegitimize that institution for the remainder of Afghani citizens, or deter the participation of other ethnic groups (Sedra, 2004). Afghanistan also suffers from general SSR challenges, including lack of funding and poor coordination among agencies and coalition members. SSR is also difficult to implement in weak states, which usually lack a strong government capable of supporting a security sector.

The requirement of a security buffer for SSR to operate successfully is itself an ethical dilemma. In which situations is it appropriate to use multinational forces to suppress conflict and instability long enough for SSR to take hold? In addition, when are local security forces deemed capable of controlling the security sector independently without help from multinational forces?

The inherent bias in SSR toward democracy also poses an ethical question. Can and should SSR be performed without changing a country's political system? While the overall world trend seems to be moving toward democratic systems, many parts of the world operate on different models. Additionally, as the push for democracy is largely associated with the West, SSR could carry a connotation of cultural imperialism when applied in non-Western nations.

Looking to the future, it is clear that SSR is a work in progress. Perhaps the largest contribution peacebuilding has to this model is a greater attention to context and culture-specific norms. Incorporating input into the general SSR model from non-Western countries might also be beneficial.

Disarmament, Demobilization, and Reintegration (DDR)

DDR is another process that fuses hard and soft power and incorporates peacebuilding and security ideas to ideally create greater stability and reduce security threats. The goal of DDR is to dismantle conflict infrastructure (weapons, armies, camps, etc.) that make societies primed and vulnerable for the resurgence of violence (United Nations, 2010). DDR is commonly stipulated in a peace accord and carried out by international actors including the UN, Organization of American States, or European Union (Anderlini and Conaway, 2004). Other actors also take part, including bilateral donors and civil society.

DDR consists of three phases. The first two steps deal with hard threats to security, while the third step is influenced by peacebuilding and attempts to end militants' *motivations* for fighting. The first step, *disarmament*, consists of confiscating guns and weapons from former belligerent groups, storing them safely, and ultimately destroying them. *Demobilization* is dismantling armed groups, shutting down militant camps, and separating former combatants from belligerent groups. The final (and arguably the most difficult) step is reintegration. During this phase, combatants attempt to return to their former homes or new locations and slowly reenter society. They receive jobs, trauma counseling, and education in order to return to their previous lives and reintegrate into the community (United Nations, 2010). While implementation and funding have proven to be constant obstacles, DDR strives to stabilize postconflict nations to make them less likely to produce new security threats, such as terrorists, disease epidemics, and economic instability.

One large DDR effort took place following the war in Bosnia-Herzegovina. The World Bank and the International Organization for Migration implemented DDR and SSR programs with the goal of dismantling Bosnia-Herzegovina's ethnically stratified armies and created a single ethnically unified security sector. During the first phase, DDR implementers directed former combatants to cantonment sites, confiscated their weapons, registered individuals for DDR programs, and administered questionnaires with personal information and questions about their socioeconomic status and skills. Ex-combatants later received livestock, business entrepreneur kits, job training, or employment. The program successfully graduated thousands of participants, and follow-up evaluations found that participants who completed the program earned about double the income of individuals on the waiting list for services (Moratti and El-Rayess, 2009). Many practitioners deem this outcome successful and hope that ex-combatants making an adequate living in mainstream society will be less likely to engage in crime, violence, and conflict.

Still, there are several challenges to DDR. The Achilles' heel of DDR often is providing a sufficient number of stable, sustainable jobs for ex-combatants in weak postconflict economies (Meek and Malan, 2004). In addition, the success of DDR is tied to the overall progress in postwar stabilization, peace agreements, and the creation of a strong security sector. If stability is not restored postconflict, then violence may reemerge and even ex-combatants who went through DDR may be drawn to the profitability of reentering armed groups (Hanson, 2007). As a result, it is essential that DDR occur in conjunction with security sector reform and other stabilization programs.

NONVIOLENT OBSERVATION

The processes above highlight the incorporation of peacebuilding into security studies, but the reverse is also occurring. Many peacebuilding practitioners are recognizing that providing security for humanitarian workers and human rights activists can help them to work more safely, efficiently, and effectively. While it raises numerous ethical issues and practical concerns, in some cases humanitarian aid workers are using security details to perform their work in regions that are otherwise difficult to enter because of safety concerns.

However, hard power–based armed security details are not always the most effective or practical method to provide security for at-risk activists. Rather, in many cases, soft power–based nonviolent observation can efficiently and effectively provide security to at-risk individuals. Pioneered by Peace Brigades International (PBI) in 1981, this strategy provides unarmed volunteer protective accompaniment for human rights workers and communities at risk of political attacks (PBI, 2012). For instance, from 1989 to 1998 in Sri Lanka PBI volunteers supported nonviolent actions such as accompanying Buddhist monks on a peace march and observing nonviolent street demonstrations and pickets (PBI, 2012).

Nonviolent observers can influence decision makers and prevent attacks by creating repercussions for belligerent actions including damaging their image, negative media coverage, straining relationships with other nations, and in some cases applying international pressure (PBI, 2012). Nonviolent observers are backed by an extensive international support network, which they can quickly and easily mobilize to pressure attackers if necessary (PBI, 2012). Several organizations emulated this method including Christian Peacemakers and the Nonviolent Peace Force. With this approach, Peace Brigades International successfully protected many lives without losing a single volunteer.

The success of Peace Brigades International shows that soft power strategies such as unarmed security details can sometimes be more effective than armed protection units. Furthermore, in the case of politically motivated violence, the political costs of attacks in the presence of a nonviolent observer could deter decision makers more effectively than the possibility of having a hit man killed by armed security details.

Of course, there are significant challenges for nonviolent observers. For instance, protective accompaniment seems more effective at deterring politically motivated attacks, but is likely ineffective in certain situations, such as terrorism and religiously motivated violence. A nonviolent observer will influence the behavior only of a rational, morally attuned attacker, who recognizes the drawbacks of attacking while a nonviolent observer is watching. This and other factors, such as a shortage of volunteers and the high cost of protective accompaniment, make nonviolent observation extremely difficult to implement on a large scale. A final serious concern is the safety of nonviolent observers. In many cases, including the case of Christian Peacemakers in Iraq, nonviolent observers become targets for violence.

Case Study: Christian Peacemakers in Iraq

In 2002, six months prior to the US invasion of Iraq, Christian Peacemakers traveled to the region to document human rights abuses and nonviolently observe the conflict. In 2005, their work was disrupted when four Christian Peacemakers from the United Kingdom were abducted by the Iraqi group known as the Swords of Righteousness Brigade. The group demanded the release of all Iraqi hostages detained by the US in exchange for the release of the Christian Peacemakers. The resulting crisis left one hostage dead and prompted a rescue operation by multinational forces to retrieve the remaining three (Brown, 2008). The mission ultimately succeeded on March 23, 2006, but stirred significant controversy when the former hostages remained firmly committed to principles of nonviolence and refused to testify or seek retribution against their captors for their offenses (Campbell, 2006). Even more controversy arose when the rescued hostages initially refused to thank the security forces that rescued them. Instead, they released a statement giving thanks that no shots were fired during their rescue (McGrory, Evans, and Meo, 2006).

This case illustrates several of the broader challenges and ethical dilemmas that result from integrating peacebuilding and security. The Christian Peacemaker commitment to nonviolence (a notion coveted by many peacebuilders) rendered them unwilling to engage with military forces, even when their lives were at risk.

THE CHALLENGES OF INTEGRATION

The Christian Peacemaker case elicits broader questions, which should be carefully considered before integrating peacebuilding into security: To what extent can/should security practitioners and peacebuilders work together? Are there certain irreconcilable differences between the two approaches? While both the security and the peacebuilding fields are committed to providing security, they may go about this using fundamentally different means.

One significant challenge presented by integrated peacebuilding is protecting the humanitarian space. Most peacebuilders and humanitarian aid workers strive to remain neutral during their work and attempt to resolve conflict without favoring one side or another. In contrast, military personnel usually enter complex conflict dynamics seeking to support actors that further military goals and objectives. In some cases, humanitarian aid workers seek to deliver supplies to actors deemed belligerent by the military. As a result, peacebuilders are faced with an ethical dilemma of whether to pursue security objectives or maintain neutrality.

If humanitarians choose to aid solely parties approved by the military, then they may be perceived as taking sides. This would jeopardize the "humanitarian space," and thereby delegitimize the safety zone that may protect neutral aid workers from hostilities (Dziedzic and Siedl, 2005). Practitioners are also working to reconcile security force collaboration with maintaining the essence of humanitarianism. For instance, Larissa Fast (2011) found that an "acceptance approach" in which aid workers develop strong relationships with locals could significantly improve their safety.

Another similar problem is the politicization of humanitarian aid. Oxfam's 2011 report on this subject documents several instances of nations aiding certain countries to achieve specific security goals. As a result, many nations including the US continue to spend much of their aid budget on countries of interest, while countries in desperate need of aid are forced to go with less. In many cases, this marriage of humanitarian aid with national interests is ultimately ineffective. Oxfam (2011) discusses how humanitarian aid to Afghanistan failed to achieve military objectives, was costly, and risked the lives of humanitarian aid workers.

Another significant ethical concern is the safety of local populations. Many of the peacebuilding/security hybrid processes risk the safety of local populations. For instance, HTSs put local informants at risk to acquire information. Informants may then become targets for insurgents for "collaborating with the enemy." In general, when military forces withdraw, local populations who interacted or received protection from security forces are left vulnerable.

In particular, locals employed by NGOs collaborating with the military may be at high risk. Peacebuilders frequently work with local partners to ensure that their projects are sustainable and contain a degree of local ownership. Working with security forces may attach a stigma to these peacebuilding programs and create resentment in local communities, creating security risks for local employees. As a result, peacebuilding professionals must seriously consider whether collaboration with security forces creates unnecessary and unethical levels of risk for local partners, employees, and populations.

There is also the critical issue that the military in many areas has increasingly become involved in providing humanitarian relief and in some cases short-term development. This has led to a blurring of lines in some cases and has raised many strong concerns from humanitarian and development organizations working in such environments.

Finally, many peacebuilding and security practitioners question whether the two fields should collaborate at all. Practitioners grapple with questions such as: Do military interventions themselves cause future insecurity? Can guns create peace? Is it possible or advisable to attempt to improve a security situation without using security forces at all? These questions stem from a fundamental debate in the peacebuilding field regarding whether military actions are a peacebuilding tool, or simply suppress violence and ultimately perpetuate a conflict. In particular, Mary Anderson's (1999) principle of "do no harm" questions whether a basic motivation to help or to do good actually means that a subsequent intervention by outsiders is justified and results in positive gains. Her work encourages practitioners to question whether the fundamental act of intervention could worsen the conflict. In other words, peacebuilding professionals must ask how they are impacting the conflict simply with their presence—and whether it is negative or positive.

It is important to acknowledge that external intervention can prolong or exacerbate conflicts. As a result, some argue that the best way to improve security is without security forces. This does not mean, however, that nonsecurity actors must do the work. Security actors may assist in noncombat missions, two of which are peacekeeping missions and disaster relief. The critical dilemma, therefore, is how to decide when to deploy armed security forces and when to choose alternatives, such as supporting diplomatic peace efforts, development, or indigenous methods of resolving disputes.

Overall several ethical dilemmas result from the union of peacebuilding and security. Each practitioner must grapple with these issues and decide how and when it is worthwhile to work with security forces and when it is unethical.

CONCLUSION

Looking forward, in order to collaborate, peacebuilding and security practitioners clearly must overcome significant challenges. They must work together to find common principles, language, and goals. Collaboration between security and peacebuilding should help to defuse new security threats caused by globalization and the post–Cold War world order. Fortunately, integration has already begun in a number of areas. Shifts in security ideology from primarily realism toward liberalism and constructivism indicate an evolving security paradigm. New schools of thought are applying traditional security principles in innovative ways. For instance, human security advocates strive to make individuals rather than states the basic element in need of security; responsibility-to-protect supporters argue that sovereignty is a privilege, and not a right; and the 3D model suggests that diplomacy and development efforts should be exhausted before defense is employed.

As this chapter has demonstrated, integration is beginning to occur not just in theory, but also in practice. Some security actors are slowly adopting peacebuilding theories, which highlight the importance of addressing the root causes and perpetuators of conflict. To address these root causes, security actors are beginning to employ hybrid processes, which use hard power to achieve short-term objectives and address the symptoms of insecurity, and soft power to achieve long-term goals and focus on the deeper sources of insecurity. Some of the hybrid approaches discussed in this chapter are counterterrorism, HTSs, DDR, SSR, and nonviolent observers. Still, there are many challenges and ethical dilemmas to integrated peacebuilding. For successful and sustainable collaboration to occur, a shared operational language, linked channels of communication, and a unified institutional structure are of paramount importance.

QUESTIONS FOR FURTHER DISCUSSION

1. How can practitioners improve security sector reform? What about counterterrorism, DDR, nonviolent observer groups, and human terrain systems?

2. What are the benefits of peacebuilding and security practitioners' working together? What are the pitfalls?

3. Should the peacebuilding and security fields continue to work together in the future?

4. When is it counterproductive for the fields to work together?

5. Which theory provides the best remedy for insecurity: realism, liberalism, or constructivism? Why?

6. How do hard power and soft power address security differently?

7. Which hybrid framework will most effectively create peace and security: responsibility to protect, human security, or the 3D framework? Why?

REFERENCES

3D Security Initiative. 2011. A new vision for U.S. and global security. Retrieved April 15, 2012, from www.3dsecurity.org.

Agius, C. 2010. Contemporary security studies. New York: Oxford University Press.

Aid, M. M. 2010. The secret sentry: The untold history of the National Security Agency. Bloomsbury Publishing.

Anderlini, S., and C. Conaway. 2004. Disarmament, demobilisation, and reintegration. In *Inclusive security, sustainable peace: A toolkit for advocacy and action.* Washington, DC: Institute for Inclusive Security and International Alert. Retrieved January 15, 2012, from www.inclusivesecurity.org/explore-resources/toolkit-for-advocacy-and-action.

Anderson, M. 1999. *Do no harm: How aid can support peace—Or war.* Boulder, CO: Lynne Rienner.

Avruch, K. 2009. Culture theory, culture clash, and the practice of conflict resolution. In D. J. Sandole, S. Byrne, I. Sandole-Staroste, and J. Senehi, eds. *Handbook of conflict analysis and resolution* (pp. 241–255). London and New York: Routledge.

Avruch, K., and P. W. Black. 1993. Conflict resolution in intercultural settings: Problems and prospects. In D. Sandole and H. van der Merwe, eds. *Conflict resolution theory and practice* (pp. 131–145). Manchester, UK: Manchester University Press.

Bahrampour, T. 2011, January 22. Iranian daily show, meet *The Daily Show. Washington Post.* Retrieved March 30, 2012, from www.washingtonpost.com/wp-dyn/content/article/2011/01/21/AR2011012103880_3.html?sid=ST2011012103765.

Bebber, R. 2008. The role of provincial reconstruction teams in counterinsurgency operations. *Small Wars Journal.* Retrieved October 25, 2012, from http://smallwars.org/jrnl/art/the-role-of-provincial-reconstruction-teams-in-counterinsurgency-operations.

Brown, T. 2008. *118 days: Christian Peacemakers team held hostage.* Chicago: Christian Peacemakers Teams.

Burton, J. W. 1998. Conflict resolution: The human dimension. *International Journal of Peace Studies* 3, no. 1. Retrieved April 20, 2012, from www.gmu.edu/academic/ijps/vol3_1/burton.htm.

Campbell, D. 2006, December 8. Former Iraq hostages refuse to give evidence against captors in trial. *The Guardian.* Retrieved March 14, 2012, from www.guardian.co.uk/uk/2006/dec/09/iraq.iraqtimeline.

Caryl, C. 2009, September 8. Human terrain teams. *Foreign Policy Online.* Retrieved from http://www.foreignpolicy.com/articles/2009/09/08/reality_check_human_terrain_teams.

Clinton, H. 2010, May 7. Secretary Clinton: Development and diplomacy core elements of foreign policy, alongside defense. Retrieved March 14, 2012, from http://geneva.usmission.gov/2010/05/09/clinton-foreign-affairs-day.

Collier, P., and A. Hoeffler. 1998. On economic causes of civil war. *Oxford Economic Papers* 50, no. 4: 563–573.

Collins, A. 2007. *Contemporary security studies.* New York: Oxford University Press.

Cooper, M. A. 2011, October 26. Medical aspects of lightning. National Weather Service. Retrieved March 15, 2012, from www.lightningsafety.noaa.gov/medical.htm.

CSIS. 2008, January. Integrating 21st-century development and security assistance. Retrieved March 11, 2012, from http://csis.org/files/media/csis/pubs/080118-andrews -integrating21stcentury.pdf.

Department of Defense. 2010. Base structure report. AT&L Leaders. Retrieved March 10, 2012, from www.acq.osd.mil/ie/download/bsr/BSR2010Baseline.pdf.

————. 2012. About the Department of Defense. Retrieved August 14, 2012, from www.defense.gov/about.

Donnelly, J. 1992. Twentieth-century realism. In T. Nardin and D. Mapel, eds. *Traditions of international ethics* (pp. 85–111) Cambridge: Cambridge University Press.

————. 2000. *Realism in international relations.* Cambridge: Cambridge University Press.

Doyle, M. 2005. Three pillars of liberal peace theory. *American Political Science Review* 99, no. 3: 463–466.

Dziedzic, M., and M. Siedl. 2005. Provincial reconstruction teams: Military relations with international and nongovernmental organizations in Afghanistan. US Institute of Peace. Retrieved March 2, 2012, from www.usip.org/publications/provincial-reconstruction -teams-military-relations-international-and-nongovernmental-organ.

Fast, L., C. Finucane, F. Freeman, M. O'Neill, and E. Rowley. 2011. *The acceptance toolkit.* USAID & Save the Children.

Feldstein, S. 2010. *The 3 Ds: "Co-equal pillars"?* Hauser Center for Nonprofit Organizations, Harvard University, Cambridge, MA.

Forde, S. 1992. Classical realism. In T. Nardin and D. Mapel, eds. *Traditions of international ethics* (pp. 62–84). Cambridge: Cambridge University Press.

Galtung, J. 1969. Violence, peace, and peace research. *Journal of Peace Research* 6, no. 3: 167–191.

Gillon, S. M. 2011. *Pearl Harbor: FDR leads the nation into war* (1st ed.). New York: Basic Books.

Glaser, C. 2010. Contemporary security studies. New York: Oxford University Press.

Global Issues. 2011, May 2. Spending for peace vs. spending for war. *World Military Spending.* Retrieved March 12, 2012, from www.globalissues.org/article/75/world-military -spending#Spendingforpeacevsspendingforwar.

Gonzalez, R. 2008. Human terrain: Past, present, and future application. *Anthropology Today* 24, no. 1: 21–28.

Halperin, G. 2010. *Nepal's SSR process "essential" if fragile peace is to hold.* Security Sector Reform Resource Centre. Retrieved March 10, 2012, from www.ssrresourcecentre.org /2010/05/14/nepal%E2%80%99s-ssr-process-not-just-desirable-but-essential-if-fragile- peace-is-to-hold.

Hänggi, H. 2004. Conceptualising security sector reform and reconstruction. In A. Bryden and H. Hanngi, eds. *Reform and reconstruction of the security sector* (pp. 1–11). Geneva Centre for the Democratic Control of Armed Forces.

Hanson, S. 2007, February 16. Disarmament, demobilization, and reintegration (DDR) in Africa. Council on Foreign Relations. Retrieved April 20, 2012, from www.cfr.org /africa/disarmament-demobilization-reintegration-ddr-africa/p12650.

International Commission on Intervention and State Sovereignty (ICISS). 2001. Responsibility to protect. International Development Research Centre, Ottawa, Canada. Retrieved March 10, 2012, from http://responsibilitytoprotect.org/ICISS%20Report.pdf.

Jones, S. G. 2008. Counterinsurgency in Afghanistan (vol. 4). Rand Corporation.

Kaufman, T. 2012. US needs to better use its "soft power." *News Journal*. Retrieved April 15, 2012, from www.tedkaufman.com/ted_kaufman_on/us-needs-to-better-use-its-soft -power.

Kilcullen, D. 2006. Counter-insurgency redux. *Survival* 48, no. 4: 111–130.

———. 2009. "The crazies will kill them": Afghanistan, 2006–2008. In *The accidental guerrilla: Fighting small wars in the midst of a big one* (1st ed.). New York: Oxford University Press.

Korb, L. 2009. *Assessing the debates: Development, diplomacy, and defense as a policy framework*. Africom Conference. Retrieved April 11, 2012, from www.americanprogress.org /issues/2009/03/korb_africom.html.

Kyazze, A. B., and V. Kudrat. 2011, October 12. NGO–Military Contact Group Conference: Civil-military relations in natural disasters. Retrieved March 10, 2012, from http://reliefweb.int/sites/reliefweb.int/files/resources/Full_Report_3072.pdf.

Lederach, J. P. 1997. *Building peace: Sustainable reconciliation in divided societies*. Washington, DC: US Institute of Peace.

———. 2003. *The little book of conflict transformation*. Intercourse, PA: Good Books.

MacFarlane, S. N., and Y. F. Khong. 2006. Human security and the UN: A critical history. Bloomington: Indiana University Press.

Macfarquhar, N., and A. Shadid. 2012, February 4. Russia and China block UN action on Syrian crisis. *New York Times Online*. Retrieved May 1, 2012, from www.nytimes .com/2012/02/05/world/middleeast/syria-homs-death-toll-said-to-rise.html.

Malkasian, C., and G. Meyerle. 2009. Provincial reconstruction teams: How do we know they work? Carlisle, PA: Strategic Studies Institute, US Army War College. Retrieved January 10, 2012, from www.strategicstudiesinstitute.army.mil/pubs/display.cfm ?pubid=911.

McFate, M., and S. Fondacaro. 2011. Reflections on the human terrain systems during the first 4 years. *Prism* 2, no. 4: 63–82.

McGrory, D., M. Evans, and N. Meo. 2006, March 26. Army's top general attacks Kember for failing to thank SAS rescue team. *The Times* (London). Retrieved March 20, 2012, from www.thetimes.co.uk/tto/news/world/middleeast/iraq/article1994100.ece.

Meek, S., and M. Malan. 2004. *Trends in DDR in peacekeeping in Africa*. ISS Monograph: No. 106. Pretoria: Institute for Security Studies; www.iss.co.za/pubs/monographs /no106/Sec1.htm.

Moghaddam, F. M. 2005. The staircase to terrorism. *American Psychologist* 60, no. 2: 161–169. doi:10.1037/0003-066X.60.2.161 Retrieved April 5, 2012, from http:// fathalimoghaddam.com/upload/doc/1256627851.pdf.

———. 2008. *Multiculturalism and intergroup relations: Psychological implications for democracy in global context*. Washington, DC: American Psychological Association Press.

———. 2010. *The new global insecurity*. Westport, CT: Praeger Security International.

Morgan, P. 2010. Contemporary security studies. New York: Oxford University Press.

Moratti, M., and A. S. El-Rayess. 2009. Transition justice and DDR: The case of Bosnia-Herzegovina. International Center for Transitional Justice. Retrieved January 15, 2012, from www.ictj.org/publication/transitional-justice-and-ddr-case-bosnia-and -herzegovina-0.

Muggah, R. 2010. Innovations in disarmament, demobilization, and reintegration policy and research: Reflections on the last decade. Small Arms Survey, Norwegian Institute of International Affairs (NUPI) Working Paper 774. Retrieved March 15, 2012, from www.english.nupi.no/content/download/13642/128894/version/6/file/WP-774 -Muggah.pdf.

National Counterterrorism Center. 2011. *2010 report on terrorism*. Retrieved April 5, 2012, from www.nctc.gov.

Navari, C. 2008. Liberalism. In P. D. Williams, ed. *Security studies: An introduction*. New York: Routledge.

Northrup, T. A. 1989. The dynamic of identity in personal and social conflict. In L. Kriesberg et al., eds. *Intractable conflicts and their transformation* (pp. 55–82). Syracuse, NY: Syracuse University Press.

Nye, J. 1990a, Autumn. Soft power. *Foreign Policy* 80: 153–171. Retrieved March 10, 2012, from www.jstor.org/stable/2151022.

———. 1990b. The changing nature of world power. *Political Science Quarterly* 105, no. 2: 177–192. Retrieved March 10, 2012, from www.jstor.org/stable/2151022.

Obama, B. 2010. National security strategy. Washington, DC: White House.

Office of Management and Budget (OMB). n.d. Table 3.1. Retrieved April 10, 2012, from www.whitehouse.gov/omb/budget/Historicals.

———. 2012. Budget of the United States government. Retrieved April 20, 2012, from www.gpo.gov/fdsys/browse/collection.action?collectionCode=BUDGET&browse Path=Fiscal+Year+2012&searchPath=Fiscal+Year+2012&leafLevelBrowse=false &isCollapsed=false&isOpen=true&packageid=BUDGET-2012-BUD&ycord=257.

Oxfam International. 2011. *Whose aid is it anyway? Politicizing aid in conflict and crisis*. Oxford: Oxfam International.

Peace Brigades International (PBI). n.d. About protective accompaniment. Retrieved March 3, 2012, from www.peacebrigades.org/about-pbi/about-protective-accompaniment /?L=oqbwjvalwgqx.

———. 2012. Sri Lanka. Retrieved March 3, 2012, from www.peacebrigades.org /?id=2261.

Peace Building Initiative. 2008, December 19. History. PeaceBuildingInitiative.org. Retrieved January 4, 2012, from www.peacebuildinginitiative.org/index.cfm?fuseaction=cmc _printall.print&pageId=1764&printview=true.

Rosecrance, R. 1974. Kissinger, Bismarck, and the balance of power. *Millennium: Journal of International Studies* 3, no. 1: 45–52.

Ross, M. 2004, Winter. How do natural resources influence civil war? Evidence from thirteen cases. *International Organization* 58: 35–67.

Rubenstein, R. 2001. Basic human needs theory: The next step in theory development. *International Journal of Peace Studies* 6, no. 1.

Runciman, W. G. 1966. Relative deprivation and social justice. Harmondsworth, UK: Penguin.

Sambanis, N. 2004. Using case studies to expand economic models of civil war. *Perspectives on Politics* 2, no. 2: 259–279.

Sedra, M. 2004. Consolidating an elusive peace: Security sector reform in Afghanistan. In A. Bryden and H. Hänggi, eds. *Reform and reconstruction of the security sector* (pp. 207–230). New Brunswick: Transaction Publishers.

Shane, S. 2011, September 8. Al Qaeda's Outsize Shadow. *New York Times*. Retrieved March 15, 2012, from www.nytimes.com/2011/09/08/us/sept-11-reckoning/qaeda.html.

Slocombe, W. B. 2004. Iraq's special challenges: Security sector reform "under fire." In A. Bryden and H. Hänggi, eds. *Reform and reconstruction of the security sector* (pp. 231–255). New Brunswick, NJ: Transaction Publishers.

Spanier, J., and S. W. Hook. 2009. *American foreign policy since World War II* (18th ed.). CQ Press.

Spini, D., and W. Doise. 2005. Universal rights and duties as normative social representations. In N. Finkel and F. M. Moghaddam, eds. *The psychology of rights and duties: Empirical contributions and normative commentaries* (pp. 21–48). Washington, DC: American Psychological Association Press.

Stockholm International Peace Research Institute (SIPRI). 2010, April 11. Military expenditure SIPRI factsheet. Retrieved March 10, 2012, from www.sipri.org/research/armaments/milex.

Tyler, T. R., and P. Degoey. 1995. Collective restraint in a social dilemma situation: The influence of procedural justice and community identification on the empowerment and legitimacy of authority. *Journal of Personality and Social Psychology* 69: 482–497.

Tyler, T. R., and Y. J. Huo. 2002. *Trust in the law*. New York: Russell Sage Foundation.

United Nations. 2003. Commission on Human Security. Human Security Now. Retrieved March 15, 2012, from www.ochaonline.un.org/humansecurity/CHS.

———. 2006. United Nations General Assembly adopts global counter-terrorism strategy. UN Action to Counter Terrorism. Retrieved March 15, 2012, from www.un.org/terrorism/strategy-counter-terrorism.shtml.

———. 2007, June 12–14. DDR and transitional justice. Second International Conference on DDR and Stability in Africa. Kinshasa, Democratic Republic of the Congo. Retrieved March 10, 2012, www.un.org/africa/osaa/speeches/ddr%20and%20tj%20in%20africa%20-%20english.pdf.

———. 2012, February. Monthly summary of military and police contribution to UN operations. Troop and police contributors. Retrieved March 10, 2012, from www.un.org/en/peacekeeping/contributors/documents/Yearly.pdf.

United Nations, Department of Peacekeeping Operations. 2010. *DDR in peace operations: A retrospective*. Retrieved May 3, 2012, from www.un.org/en/peacekeeping/resources/publications.shtml.

United Nations Development Programme (UNDP). 1994. Human development report. Retrieved March 10, 2012, from http://hdr.undp.org/en/reports/global/hdr1994/chapters.

United Nations Security Council. 2006. 63rd session. Resolution S-RES-1674 (Responsibility to Protect).

United Nations Trust Fund for Human Security. 2009. Human security in theory and practice. Retrieved March 10, 2012, from http://hdr.undp.org/en/media/HS_Handbook_2009.pdf.

United States Department of Defense. 2011, November. Agency financial report. Undersecretary of Defense. Retrieved March 16, 2012, from http://comptroller.defense.gov/afr/fy2011/DoD_FY11_Agency_Financial_Report.pdf.

Waltz, K. N. 1979. *Theory of international politics.* New York: McGraw-Hill.

Weggeland, D. 2011. Less boom for the buck: Projects for COIN effects and transition. Counter Insurgency Advisory & Assistance Team. Retrieved January 15, 2012, from www.isaf.nato.int/article/coin/less-boom-for-the-buck.html.

White House. 2011, June. National strategy for counterterrorism. Retrieved March 15, 2012, from www.whitehouse.gov/sites/default/files/counterterrorism_strategy.pdf.

Williams, P. 2008. Security studies: An introduction. New York: Routledge. Taylor & Francis.

World Health Organization. 2011. The top 10 causes of death. Retrieved January 10, 2012, from http://www.who.int/mediacentre/factsheets/fs310/en/index.html.

NOTES

1. The primary security institution dealing with domestic threats is the FBI.

2. The 2012 Security Council members include the United States, the United Kingdom, France, China, and Russia.

3. For instance, evidence by John Mueller suggests that the likelihood of an American being killed in a terrorist attack from anywhere in the world is around 1 in 3.5 million (Shane, 2011). According to the National Weather Service, the odds of being struck by lightning are 1 in 10,000 (Cooper, 2011).

4. American counterterrorism agencies include the National Counterterrorism Center, the State Department, the Department of Defense, the Department of Homeland Security, the Federal Bureau of Investigation, and the Central Intelligence Agency, as well as indirectly by the US Agency for International Development (USAID).

5. For more details, see www.un.org/en/sc/ctc/laws.html.

6. For more info, see /www.un.org/sc/committees/1267/aq_sanctions_list.shtml.

7. For more details, see the Charity and Security Network, www.charityandsecurity.org.

chapter ten

MEDIA AND PEACEBUILDING

J. P. Singh

Media-related peacebuilding goes beyond the traditional disengaged journalistic role. It is designed to have an intended outcome: a reduction of conflict among citizens. Rather than merely informing, material is selected for its potential in transforming conflict, by shifting attitudes of the parties involved in conflict, by providing essential information. This approach also extends from traditional journalism media into avenues such as popular music, soap operas and call-in shows, community radio and video projects, and street theatre, wall posters, or concerts.

—Ross Howard[1]

THE VIOLENT WAYS IN WHICH the Syrian state has responded to protests in 2011–2012 can be watched and heard almost in real time over social media. A YouTube video of secret police shootings in Homs, Syria, from April 2011 has the following caption: "Thanks to mobile phone cameras and YouTube we can tell our stories. The protesters gathered after the funeral of 8 protesters got killed last day [*sic*], and they decided to sleep in the city center to show the secret police that they are not afraid of their guns."[2]

The global media create and circulate representations at Internet speeds, from various perspectives and in many languages. The sounds, words, and images seek to communicate messages about human interactions and natural or material phenomena. It should, therefore, not surprise us that these media representations should be contested or marred with debates. Communication is about storytelling, and it is hard to find agreement when stories are told from diverse perspectives.

Integrated peacebuilding as applied to media is Janus-faced: it applies to how professional media handle conflict within their own ranks, and also how media contribute to or alleviate human conflict. At times, both facets attend to the same conflict. In general, peace media, deploying various types of technological platforms, have developed alternative forms of storytelling that engender or strengthen processes of peace in societies. There is also the emerging field of peace journalism, which is dedicated to using media tools to build an understanding of diverse perspectives and advance peace in conflicted regions. Peace journalism employs terminology that builds and reports on peace rather than only on conflict. For example, one of the important global North–South debates in the 1970s and 1980s was over the way media represented the global South. Subsequently, this debate itself was the cause of a major North–South confrontation at the UN Educational, Scientific, and Cultural Organization (UNESCO) from the mid-1970s to the mid-1980s, which contributed to the departure of the US and the UK from this organization at that time.

This chapter first discusses the main issues and theories about media and peacebuilding before moving on to their implications for policy debates and presenting case studies. At a macro level, media and peacebuilding theories speak to the "what" or the content of representation in general, but also explain specifically how media may facilitate or create an "us versus them" context during conflicts. At a micro level, media and peacebuilding theories focus on the "how," or the process of media representations. These cover everything from the heuristic devices known as frames that media employ to present stories, to the ideological and political biases that these devices carry.

THEORIES

It is important to start with an acknowledgment that the term "media" carries a multiplicity of meanings. As a plural of "medium," it can imply channels or conduits of communication including printing presses, telecommunication lines, broadcasting, Internet, and social media such as YouTube, Twitter, and Facebook. However, such a definition is incomplete without discussing the types of communication content that transmit over the medium in question. References to newspapers, television news, or blogging, therefore, carry the connotation of encompassing both the medium and the content of communication. The evolutionary dynamic in media is that they continue to bring in voices that challenge authority, starting from the day when the "Fourth Estate" of newspapers came into being, to the current period of social and Internet-based media.[3] Citizen journalism and blogging are examples of these phenomena. On the other hand, the media are often also criticized for biases and for engendering them, rather than merely reporting or representing conflicts. The double movements between medium and content and between voice and bias are important markers for understanding the multiple meanings of media.

Beyond the definition of media, concerns regarding media, representations, and conflict can be traced to macro or general concerns about propaganda, elite bias, and lack of empathy, or concern with "otherness"—the "what" of media referred to above.

Since its foundation, print media has been charged with distributing propaganda, a term that can be traced back to the Counter Reformation and the Roman Catholic Church's attempts to deal with its detractors (Nichols, 2003). During the Cold War, Western media characterized communist media agencies as mouthpieces of the state, which to a great extent they were, while state-run media characterized Western media as beholden to their capitalist owners. The difference between Western and communist media has been freedom of the press and free-speech laws that existed in many democratic societies that also allowed for critiques of the government. Nevertheless, as writers such as Herman and Chomsky (2002) have argued, the media can be vehicles for manufacturing consent: the authors cite instances of US military and foreign trade policies to illustrate how media are propagandistic in the way they defend institutions of power, such as the government or big business. The most forceful case at the broadest level is made in literary theorist Edward Said's Orientalism (1979). Building on philosopher Michel Foucault's work, Said links representations with power: all knowledge is informed with the perspective of power holders, and domination means that the dominated are presented as weak. "The Oriental is irrational, depraved (fallen), childlike, 'different'; thus the European is rational, virtuous, mature, 'normal'" (p. 40). Such an ideology provided a justification for colonialism, and as many have argued, for the ongoing "clash of civilization" such as that put forward in Samuel Huntington's (1993) famous thesis in which the Islamic-Confucian "civilization" is presented as hostile and almost barbaric. Huntington's thesis found resonance in media, especially after the attacks on September 11, 2001.

Media theorization has connected production of such otherness with conflict. Kenneth Boulding (1959), one of the founders of the conflict resolution field, noted that national images are formed during childhood and not imposed just by the elite. Collective memories sustain the images. He calculates system-level security through a matrix of each state's friendliness or hostility toward other states that is contingent upon the national images it holds. This leads to a simple but telling conclusion: "It is hard for an ardent patriot to realize that his country is a mental, rather than a physical phenomenon, but such indeed is the truth!" (p. 52). Such thinking was easily transported to the role of media. Mirror-image theories showed, for example, how American and Soviet citizens held similarly distorted images of each other, believing the other side to be hostile and aggressive (Bronfrenner, 1961). Cees Hamelink (2011) has argued that media can increase the lack of empathy with others, leading to anxiety and at worst resulting in dehumanization and violence. Media can thus be directly linked to perpetuating violence. For example, Hutu-dominated print media and radio in Rwanda contributed significantly to the Tutsi genocide in 1994.[4]

The work of Johan Galtung (1980; 2000) has called for positive and peace journalism to counteract the negative and warmongering effects of conflict media.[5] Galtung was the first to highlight the need for peace journalism, to counteract conflict reporting and journalism (Lynch and Galtung, 2010). Violence or war-oriented journalism focuses on the conflict as it unfolds and can often lead to dehumanization through "us versus them" rhetoric and posing the "other" as the problem. Peace journalism highlights the possibilities for peacebuilding. Not surprisingly, peace journalism is often critiqued for being activist-oriented and, in the case of social and new media, encouraging social mobilization. It may also be impractical to implement. Nevertheless, Galtung and others point to how journalists from one side often incriminate the other side for bias and negative framing, to argue that the only way forward is for journalists to develop rich context that explores the causes of conflict. Galtung's TRANSCEND approach (Galtung and Tschudi, 2001) seeks to stimulate journalistic creativity toward finding solutions for conflict after rich explorations of each party's interests and the associated contexts.

Having examined the "what" of representations at the macro level, we can turn to the micro level or the "how" of media—the ways in which media produce representations that might be biased. Communication theorists have put forward a variety of concepts and empirical studies to understand the ways in which media operate either to produce particular forms of bias or, conversely, lead to accountability and transparency.

The dominant ways in which media construct their narratives may be understood via frames, agenda-setting, and indexing. Frames refer to the angle or heuristic devices used to present a subject. Its roots lie in psychology (Kahneman, 2011). Agenda-setting refers to issues and the ways that they get covered (Entman, 1991). Indexing refers to the ways in which media reflect opinions within dominant institutions, such as government (Bennett, 1990; Mermin, 1999). Studies of US foreign policy find that reporters tend to reflect the government's point of view in their coverage, especially as media tend to get their information from government sources, such as press briefings or, in the case of war, from journalists embedded with troops (Mermin, 1999). For example, the case that the George W. Bush administration constructed against Iraq in 2002 at the UN Security Council was later found to be spurious, but only after the media had faithfully reported it. Earlier, news media tended to reflect the prerogatives of the US government in the Vietnam War. News coverage became more divided only when these divisions began to appear in Washington (Bennett, 1990; Hallin, 1986). This has led some to note that media have the most influence when there is policy plurality and elite opinion is divided (Robinson, 2001).

War coverage has attracted the most attention in examining news media biases linked to indexing and agenda-setting. Related topics have included decisions by some news media not to show graphic war violence, as it valorizes it or produces emotional, rather than reason-based, responses. Although media, especially in the US, are reluctant to show bodily violence and dismemberment in war, they are quite willing to show violence in general or, as Johan Galtung and other theorists of peace journalism have argued, focus on the conflict rather than existing or possible peace processes. However, others have argued that showing human casualties is important for humanizing the costs of war. Still other scholars have argued that war in the information age is already dehumanized when represented on television, where its images often appear to be like those of video games (Der Derian, 1991). Harkening back to cultural theorist Jean Baudrillard, this is the world of hyperrealism in which the signifying images float in a hyperreality, divorced from the original signifying event.

The idea of the "CNN Effect" captures best the influence the twenty-four-hour news cycle has on governmental and institutional decisions and policy making. It also provides an antidote, to some extent, to the indexing and framing hypotheses that posit media conformity to institutional politics. The CNN Effect points to how media itself has emerged as a major and independent actor in world politics. Livingston (1997) has further divided the CNN Effect into three types of functions: setting policy agendas, accelerating decision-making, and hindering or impeding particular policy decisions. The findings on the CNN Effect have been mixed (Gilboa, 2005): while coverage of global events points toward the attention policy makers pay to them, it is unclear how this link is made and what policy makers decide. The decision of the US government to intervene in Somalia is often attributed to television coverage showing widespread starvation, but Livingston (1997) and Mermin (1999) have argued that this coverage followed, rather than led, decision-making in Washington. Similarly, the Rwandan massacre has been attributed to the lack of attention global media gave to the fate of the Tutsis. However, subsequent research shows that the US government had satellite imagery and other information that showed Hutu movement toward carrying out genocide but that it chose not to act (Litfin, 2002). One might conjecture the government would have acted sooner if its internal intelligence had been supplemented with outside news reports.

There is some evidence that media do play a significant role in mobilizing support for humanitarian crises. The role of social media and mobile telephony for organizing support and donations for the 2010 Haitian earthquake is an example. A CBS study found that of the $14.9 billion raised internationally, $4 billion was raised by NGOs and charities, with $66 million raised by the Hope for Haiti Now telethon (Attkisson, 2010).[6] For example, the International Red Cross worked with telecommunication carriers to enable donations via SMS texts, raising $8 million, which generated donation charges on users' monthly bills.

Media indexing, or the ways that the traditional media provide information by relying mostly on government sources, may play a role even in the positive cases recounted above. Mobilization of support may depend on feelings of paternalism toward those in need or that their needs resonate with a population's internal discourse about aiding others. Wilson (2011), for example, shows that the images of NGOs conducting development work tend to exaggerate agency and empowerment to potential donors when asking for donations. Skonieczny (2002) demonstrates with content analysis that US media generated support for the North American Free Trade Agreement largely through an Orientalist paternalistic discourse, which showed Mexico in need of US assistance. Similarly, Steele (2007) shows how media helped to generate enhanced foreign aid commitments to the 2004 Asian tsunami after UN humanitarian official Jan Egeland's remark calling the initial US aid "stingy" was widely reported: this played into a reflexive discourse in the US—most Americans like to view themselves as generous toward those in need. Even the anti–foreign aid Senator Jesse Helms was moved to promise more help.

On the other hand, various forms of new media are also credited with producing accountability and transparency in global politics, especially within elite global institutions and decision-making. Such accountability could come from media playing a watchdog role or from an international organization's internal communication strategy to make its decision-making transparent. Of course, the external scrutiny and internal transparency may be linked. Thus, Smythe and Smith (2006) note that successive critiques of the World Trade Organization have made the organization more transparent to the point that most of the organization's historical documents and minutes can now be found online. O'Brien et al. (2000) show how global social movements in general have challenged global governance organizations. Keck and Sikkink (1998) and Sikkink (2009) detail information networks underlying global social movements for gendered violence, human rights, and the environment.

The larger context within which these "new media" issues must be debated is that of online or web-based media activism, alternatively termed "digital activism," "e-advocacy," and "cyber-politics." There is a great deal of scholarship on how online activists are now connected to each other and the ways that they use a variety of multimedia devices to influence others (Joyce, 2010; McCaughey and Ayers, 2003). Most scholarship on these issues is rich with case studies of how activists are able to use SMS, bulk texts, videos/photos, ringtones, Twitter, and location-ware to organize "smart mobs," monitor politics, and conduct citizen reporting (Cullum, 2010). Nevertheless, others doubt that these case studies all point in as positive directions as these technologies suggest. A subtle analysis of three cases of "online insurgency" leads Dartnell (2006) to conclude that our politics are now transformed into mostly image- and identity-based politics that might engender more, rather than less, conflict through strengthening nationalist and religious movements. Dartnell (2006) writes that "contemporary global politics is a transnational '24/7' exchange of text, photos, audio and videoclips, blogs, and chat rooms that constantly transmits and retransmits the emotional and moral content of our politics" (p. 5).

The value of specifying techniques for measuring the impact of digital politics has, therefore, become important. The case studies themselves are being analyzed through techniques mentioned earlier. The ways in which the activists frame and propagate their messages is, for example, quite central to most case study analysis. Beyond cases, Karpf (2010) distinguishes between tactical and strategic measures of impact. Tactical measures provide data on, for example, how many people receive a Twitter feed, or how many subscribe to a political blog or read it daily. Strategic measures go a step further to analyze the influence of the media. A few strategic measures might be quite simple, such as the top twenty political advocacy blogs or the number of people who rely on a particular medium as a primary source for their political values.

There is often caution placed on this increased media scrutiny of global decision-making, especially through instant relays of messages. Hedley Bull (1977/1995) first called attention to "loudspeaker diplomacy," in which decision-makers become increasingly populist and media-dependent, rather than solving problems behind closed doors. Bull mostly posited diplomacy as an elite realm, responding to power politics, but effective in producing a "global order." Overall, the role of media in defusing conflict is mixed: while the CNN Effect points to the ubiquitous presence of media, other concepts have highlighted areas in which the media follow rather than lead policy makers. In the new media environment, positive cases are matched with negative ones. At the international level, the media's role has been heavily debated and has generated a set of normative concerns and policy prescriptions.

POLICY DEBATES AND PEACEBUILDING SKILLS

The major policy debates in the media sector at the international level have arisen from efforts to highlight and correct media propaganda and biases. Nazi propaganda, especially as related to the so-called racial supremacy, brought forth the need to address false and inflammatory information. This was reflected in the debates that led toward the creation and subsequent workings of UNESCO.

At the root of the policy debates have been the sources of conflict that may be traced back to the Hobbesian view of the world in which its participants are mutually suspicious of each other or in a perpetual state of war. Whereas for Thomas Hobbes the only way to end war was through a preponderant authority (or a Leviathan) that produced discipline, policy debates in the postwar era have sought to address sources of conflict through mutually acceptable patterns of global governance; in the case of the media, through deliberations and research on the sources of conflict. Although not limited to UNESCO, this subsection refracts these debates through this organization's lens, because UNESCO remains the most important organization providing normative guidance on media and communication issues, especially as the organization's explicit aim is to foster a culture of peace (Singh, 2011). As mentioned earlier, prominent theorists such as Johan Galtung and Cees Hamelink developed their theses regarding peace journalism and media in the context of UNESCO debates and ideals.

Three periods in these global policy debates are examined, and they are directly linked to the prerogatives of those in power that were theorized in the last section. The three periods are: the creation and beginnings of UNESCO, the New World Information and Communication Order, and the current debates on the digital divide and the World Summit on Information Society. Each section also addresses the peacebuilding skills that were practiced or developed as a result of these debates.

UNESCO: Original Debates

The discussion for UNESCO arose out of the Conference for Allied Ministers for Education that began to meet in London in 1942. The idea was to counteract Nazi propaganda through education. Racism, at that time understood within the Nazi anti-Semitic project, was one of the chief targets. UNESCO would draw inspiration from Enlightenment beliefs in education and virtue to assert that science and information would produce a new ethic and culture of peace. UNESCO's preamble states, "That since wars begin in the minds of men, it is in the minds of men that the defences of peace must be constructed."

UNESCO came into being in November 1945, and one of its first tasks was a series of studies that unraveled the spurious science of race and spoke to the social formation of ideas concerning race. Claude Levi-Strauss's (1958) work on race, for example, arose from these studies. He emphasized that cultural origins of the ideas of race arise from the ways that societies foster inequalities, and proposed that the solution was to foster reciprocal exchanges among societies rather than allow one to dominate the other.

Communication is UNESCO's fifth sector of competence, and although the "C" in UNESCO stands for "culture," media debates have featured prominently in the organization's functioning. In 1946 the UN General Assembly established a Sub-Commission on Freedom of Information and of the Press as part of the UN Commission on Human Rights. The resolution also called for the UN to convene a Conference on Freedom of Information, which took place in Geneva in 1948 and was attended by fifty-four states (Wells, 1987). Carroll Binder, a member of the American Society of Newspaper Editors and later also of the subcommission, noted that efforts to commit the UN to the concept of freedom of information "were successful beyond expectations" (Wells, 1987, p. 61). The Eastern Bloc countries, however, viewed the subcommission and the US push for media freedoms as capitalist propaganda and, therefore, hesitated to join UNESCO. It was clear from the beginning that questions of media freedom or propaganda would be sensitive at the international level.

UNESCO: The NWICO Debates

The most spectacular media and conflict issue at the global level may be the New World Information and Communication Order (NWICO) debate representing developing countries' efforts during the 1970s and the early 1980s to call attention to information flow and communication imbalances between the North and the South. The NWICO movement was part of growing assertiveness among the developing world in the post-colonial era. While uniting the developing world with a common cause and producing heated confrontations with the developed Western world, these countries extracted few substantial concessions. However, NWICO represents an acknowledgment of the importance of communication to peacebuilding and development, and can be linked directly to the theoretical issues pointed out earlier.

There was intellectual support for the developing world's cause in disciplines within and beyond communication and in forums beyond UNESCO. One of the intellectual founders of NWICO, Kaarle Nordenstreng (1983), traced NWICO concerns back to the nationalist movement in the colonies and wrote of the four "Ds" of NWICO: decolonization, democratization, demonopolization, and development. The developing world was also emboldened with the postcolonial world's advocacy at the UN in general, which resulted in a broader and parallel movement for a New International Economic Order (NIEO). The UN General Assembly formally adopted the Declaration of Establishment of NIEO in 1974. The idea of an NWICO was launched formally after the 1976 Colombo Summit of the Non-Aligned Countries in Sri Lanka, an independent bloc of developing countries formed to counter US or Soviet influence, and the 1976 Nairobi 19th General Conference of UNESCO. The Non-Aligned Movement meeting in Colombo called for self-reliance in communications across developing countries. The NWICO agenda was also endorsed by a resolution in the 31st UN General Assembly the same year.

Initially, NWICO laid importance on correcting the one-way flow of negative news and information from the developing world to developed countries. UNESCO carried out several authoritative studies on the imbalance in these information flows and also appointed a high-level commission headed by the Nobel Peace Laureate Sean MacBride to analyze these issues. But by the time of the MacBride Commission Report and its influential work, *Many Voices, One World* (1980), developing self-reliant communication infrastructures within the developing world became important.

The MacBride Commission (1980) thus wrote that

> communication be no longer regarded merely as an incidental service and its development left to chance. Recognition of its potential warrants the formulation by all nations, and particularly developing countries, of comprehensive communication policies linked to overall social, cultural, economic and political goals. Such policies should be based upon inter-ministerial and inter-disciplinary consultations with broad public participation. The object must be to utilize the unique capacities of each form of communication, from interpersonal and traditional to the most modern, to make men and societies aware of their rights, harmonize unity and diversity, and foster the growth of individuals and communities within the wider frame of national development in an interdependent world. (pp. 254–255)

The immediate international demand in the late 1970s consisted of the developing world's trying to regulate journalistic activities, which was reflected in the 1978 "Declaration of Fundamental Principles Concerning the Contribution of the Mass Media to Strengthening Peace and International Understanding, to the Promotion of Human Rights and to Countering Racialism, Apartheid and Incitement to War." The UNESCO Declaration on the Mass Media, as it came to be known, was originally introduced in 1970 by the Soviet Union and became the first attempt to provide guidelines for journalists working in the developing world, after over eight years of negotiations. Attempts by developing countries to actually regulate the activities of media firms within their borders were defeated because of pressure from Western nations.

Next, many developing countries sought to license and, therefore, reduce the number of foreign journalists within their borders. Other conferences began to express similar concerns, including a conference of 30,000 journalists in Mexico City that tried to propose a code for journalistic ethics. The issue flared up in 1981 when UNESCO sponsored a meeting on the protection of journalists, an issue of importance to many international journalists' unions. Instead, the meeting's focus became governmental jurisdiction. The North accused the South of wanting not only to reduce foreign journalists but also to permit only government-blessed news stories (McPhail, 1981). Nothing but heated exchanges emerged from the meetings. Western journalists, even in liberal newspapers such as the *New York Times*, were not sympathetic to NWICO or regulation of journalistic activities through ethical codes and published articles opposing UNESCO.[7]

The MacBride Commission submitted its report in 1980 to the UNESCO General Conference in Belgrade, and a couple of positive developments followed after the adoption of this report at the General Conference. Amid the heated polemics of the other debates, the commission's report was a sobering reflection on the needs of the developing world and was a clarion call for improvement of information infrastructures in these countries. It also called attention to the lack of communication technology (as opposed to merely flows) governing North–South communication relations. On the technology count, the West was more willing to help. Accordingly, at the initiative of the US, the International Program for the Development of Communication was established, which would, among other things, facilitate transfers of communication technologies for print and broadcast media. However, the program languished due to lack of funding, and after the US and the UK pulled out of UNESCO, it all but died.

British Prime Minister Margaret Thatcher and US President Ronald Reagan would find UNESCO's demands to be unacceptable. The conservative constituencies supported Thatcher and Reagan, of course, but they also received journalistic support from the relatively independent or liberal media firms in their countries. Reagan's coming to office would be an especially welcome development. Reagan endorsed the Talloires Declaration from France in 1981 by the World Press Freedom Committee with delegates from twenty-one countries, which asked UNESCO to abandon its demands. In July 1981, Senator Dan Quayle introduced a resolution in the Senate for the US to withdraw from UNESCO altogether. By the end of 1983, the US had withdrawn from UNESCO, following congressional and media support for the action. Soon after, the UK and Singapore followed suit. NWICO continued to be supported by UNESCO and the Non-Aligned Movement, but it slowly fizzled out.

Information Societies

The current state of global media issues offers a perspective on integrated peacebuilding across tensions and conflicts in various ways. First, issues of representation have mainstreamed from the East–West or North–South dimensions discussed earlier in this section to globalized dimensions. Issues of representation encompassing media bias, framing, or propaganda are now as important within societies as across them. Second, global media issues continue to become increasingly participatory as they bring in voices and rights of peoples who had been marginalized earlier. Social media and citizen journalism assist with this participation. Third, media and information policy issues have moved from being a limited few to much broader participation via several global organizations and civil society. It may not be an exaggeration to note that these issues can be found on one forum or the other in just about every global organization these days. Fourth, media issues and theories have integrated related issues: media needs are related to information infrastructures in general; types of media continue to broaden with social media and the Internet; and understandings applied to media are now relevant for understanding various forms of communication.

These seemingly disparate issues can be understood within the common rubric of the so-called information societies or knowledge societies, which underscore the importance of information infrastructures, access, and use to societies around the world. UNESCO was one of the international organizations in the World Summit for an Information Society (WSIS), which began in 1998 as an International Telecommunication Union initiative to examine "digital divide" issues and to consider information society ideas as broadly as possible. The union asked the UN secretary-general to convene WSIS and received the authorization through UN General Assembly Resolution 56/183. The digital divide issues, or the unequal levels of access to information networks and content, had become prominent on the international agenda.

WSIS deliberations included multiple stakeholders—businesses, governments, civil society, international organizations, and experts—as part of a global movement toward what is being termed "Mush," or multiple stakeholder diplomacy. WSIS convened two major global summits apart from numerous other forums: in 2003 in Geneva and in 2005 in Tunis. One of the transnational civil society campaigns that made it to the Tunis agenda was the Communication Rights for an Information Society campaign. The campaign resulted from the Platform for Communication Rights, a worldwide group of civil society NGOs including the powerful Association for Progressive Communication, working on human rights and communication issues. However, instead of communication rights or the digital divide, issues of Internet governance dominated Tunis and the successive deliberations that resulted from WSIS.

PEACEBUILDING PROCESSES/SKILLS

Five conflict resolution processes can be distilled from the policy discussion above, all of which suggest how media conflicts have been deliberated at the international level and the skills that a practitioner must learn. First, as this chapter turns to processes, global deliberation and governance have helped to resolve communication conflicts or suggest particular processes. The foundation of the UN system set the pace, and with UNESCO, there was an early acknowledgment or reality that communication issues were important, as evidenced in the Cold War debates. Later, while NWICO issues remained unresolved, they prefaced the fact that communication conflicts would be resolved through global deliberations, a trend that continues with WSIS. Global deliberations have led to framing norms for media representations and have led to similar moves at regional and national levels. In April 1989, European NGOs adopted a Code of Conduct on Images and Messages Relating to the Third World, revised in June 2007 to Code of Conduct on Messages and Images. However, there are also difficulties in this task. Given the variety of practices, UNESCO has, for example, found it hard to frame a universal code of ethics for journalists. These efforts get even more complicated than before with the rise of citizen journalism and availability of "news" through social media platforms such as blogs, wikis, YouTube, and Twitter. The growth in the number of people reporting news and the platforms over which it is circulated make it hard to define the boundaries of journalism.

Second, global deliberations are supplemented with importance given to developing media training and capacities. The tradition of a healthy press in the Western world was coupled with the importance of nationalized media in the Eastern Bloc, and the modernization aims of the postcolonial world also endorsed national media development. While UN agencies, such as UNESCO, have provided training to journalists, so have national agencies, such as the BBC and, in the past, the Soviet news agency Tass. More recently NGOs, such as Intermedia and Internews, have also stepped in, with funding from private donors and national development agencies such as the UK's Department for International Development (DFID) and the US Agency for International Development (USAID). Proliferation of regional television networks, such as Al-Jazeera and Teleglobo, or globalized non-English language channels, such as Telemundo, have also brought diversity to the production of content.

TABLE 10.1. Growth Rates of Information Infrastructure

Category	Income Levels	1995	2000	2005	2009
Internet users per 100	High Income	3.75	30.55	59.43	72.20
	Middle Income	0.42	1.71	8.27	20.72
	Low Income		0.13	0.93	2.57
Mobiles per 100	High Income	7.76	49.84	84.79	111.07
	Middle Income	0.29	4.88	27.19	66.63
	Low Income	0.01	0.26	4.56	25.07
Telephone lines per 100	High Income	48.66	55.34	51.29	45.04
	Middle Income	4.68	8.92	14.97	14.54
	Low Income	0.49	0.59	0.89	1.16

Source: World Bank, World Databank: World Development Indicators and Global Development Finance. Available at http://databank.worldbank.org. Accessed August 10, 2011.

Third, there is much-needed convergence between content and conduit issues to outline the importance of infrastructural provision. The term "digital divide" in the 1990s began to capture this element, and infrastructural access is now an important topic for agencies that support and track progress, such as the World Bank and the International Telecommunication Union, and the World Economic Forum, which prepares a Network Readiness Index. With the importance of social media and content delivery via the Internet, infrastructural provision impacts various forms of media, and its prioritization from local to global levels is an important process. Table 10.1 provides summary statistics on global information infrastructures. While middle- and low-income countries have narrowed the digital divide with exponential growth rates in mobile telephony, Internet growth and usage (the latter contingent on a technical skill set) remain low. The growth in infrastructures has come from mostly market-driven and privatized or liberalized forms of telecommunication firms; however, the peace media applications discussed in this chapter have been the work primarily of civil society organizations.

Fourth, research and methodologies are preparing media better to represent the increasingly complex world. Worldwide media organizations deploy sophisticated methodologies to gauge audience feedback, and, with the Internet, most online content providers create space for feedback and reader-generated critique and content.

Fifth, there is increasing advocacy for balanced and professional media coverage. The Association for Professional Communication (apc.org), which provides networking and capacity-building support, now lists over fifty members from thirty-five countries. The Women's Feature Service (wfsnews.org), which began with a UNESCO initiative in 1978, provides media content from a gender perspective.

Following these processes, successful skills for practitioners of integrated peacebuilding would include the following:

Professional training for reporting with sensitivity on issues of exclusion/inclusion, marginalization, stereotyping, bias, and propaganda.

Empathic listening: While this skill cannot be easily taught, it is not hard to imagine that it can be cultivated through detailed knowledge of local circumstances and the complexity of people's lives. Most representations that cause conflict are, after all, those that simplify, stereotype, and caricature from an arm's-length perspective.

Technical training is necessary for using media technologies, including cameras, computers, and editing technologies. Empowering local communities and citizen journalists is an especially powerful way to reduce marginalization.

Professional negotiation and deliberation at the global level are needed. Many civil society organizations participating in WSIS noted that they did not possess the technical skills necessary to participate effectively in such forums.

Further research dissemination and deliberation among media professionals is also necessary to enable them to report from diverse perspectives and develop a sense of ethics and the impact of peace media.

Case Studies

In outlining cases of the connection to media, conflict, and peacebuilding, this section uses a strategy that varies by type of media and geographic region. However, special attention is paid to the case of the Danish newspaper *Jyllands-Posten* to speak to the role that traditional media have played in conflict escalation and de-escalation.

Jyllands-Posten and Newspapers

The publication of twelve cartoons depicting the Prophet Muhammad in the Danish newspaper *Jyllands-Posten* on September 30, 2005, triggered one of the biggest protests in Europe around Islamic cultural expressions or, in this case, prohibitions on particular expressions in Islam. Iconic depiction of the prophet is generally prohibited in Islam. Initially, neither *Jyllands-Posten* nor the Danish government, both of which came under fire, apologized or issued any regrets. While 5,000 people, organized by the Islamic Society of Denmark, protested outside the newspaper offices on October 14, touching off debates in Danish media, the protests from moderate Muslims were muted. However, the protests became heated after a delegation of Danish Muslims, including two radical imams, toured the Middle East and showed the twelve published images and other incendiary fabricated cartoons to Muslim and government leaders.

The courts in Denmark ruled in favor of *Jyllands-Posten,* which offers some evidence that the case the newspaper made for publishing the cartoons must be accepted at face value. On March 15, 2006, the director of public prosecutions in Denmark also ruled that the publication of cartoons did not violate any freedom of speech laws or prohibitions. The republication of the cartoons across Europe in solidarity with *Jyllands-Posten* also, to some extent, shows that European newspapers in general understood that no laws were being broken.

While the cartoons withstand the free-speech test, it is also easy to argue that the *Jyllands-Posten* cartoons were meant to be offensive. As the American humorist P. J. O'Rourke (2006) pointed out:

> What sort of reaction did *Jyllands-Posten* expect to its comic strip? Europeans consider Americans stupid, but if the *Washington Post* printed a cartoon showing Martin Luther King in a Sambo get-up being chased around a palm tree by the tiger of identity politics, Don Graham would know what happens next. . . . That the Europeans didn't think anything would happen illustrates the state of European thought. Ideas have consequences, as Europeans, of all people, should know. (p. 13)

In February 2006 news stories also emerged that *Jyllands-Posten* had rejected cartoons of Jesus Christ from illustrator Christoffer Zieler in April 2003 with an e-mail from the Sunday editor, which noted: "I don't think *Jyllands-Posten*'s readers will enjoy the drawings. As a matter of fact, I think that they will provoke an outcry. Therefore, I will not use them" (quoted in Fouche, 2006).

Jyllands-Posten has also argued that it received widespread support from moderate Muslim populations for its stance. In particular, editor Fleming Rose (2006) has called attention to the number of e-mails he received from moderate Muslims, and in January 2006 the paper ran photos and interviews with moderate Muslims, many of whom objected to being represented by radical imams. Much of this is ipso facto: *Jyllands-Posten* has a history of causing offense to Muslims and did not publish views of "moderate" Muslims before the cartoon episode.

Nevertheless, the contours of the cartoon controversy were never defined solely by an exclusive concern for free speech that might point to moderation on the part of *Jyllands-Posten* or the appeals to moderate Muslims. As the episode's unraveling demonstrates below, the controversy gathered steam precisely because it was framed in provocative terms from European non-Muslims and received due resonance and escalation from its interlocutors, the radical Islamists.

Both the Danish government and *Jyllands-Posten* apologized in early 2006 after initially refusing to do so. This followed the ways in which the cartoon controversy spilled over into protests in the Islamic world. Analyses of the cartoon affair reveal two factors that are relevant for this chapter. First, most of the framing of the Muslims from the non-Muslim European perspectives in the media was increasingly negative and carried out in terms of portraying the conflict as a clash of civilizations. Powers (2008) cites studies, based in content analysis and other techniques, that *Jyllands-Posten* had a history of making disparaging comments about Muslims in Europe. Studies also show that the media framed the cartoon conflict in terms of violence rather than any form of moderation or an intercultural dialogue, despite Fleming Rose's frequent mention of the printing of moderate voices ipso facto. Mónica Codina and Jordi Rodriguez-Virgili (2007) note, "These cartoons were offensive for three reasons. Islam prohibits any depiction of the Prophet; the Sunnis in fact, do not permit any depiction of human beings. The second is that they are mocking and satirical. And finally, they link Islam and terrorism" (p. 33).

Nevertheless, the case also illustrates the typical cycle of how media escalated the latent conflict about Islamic identity in Europe, which reached a peak with protests in the Islamic world, followed by de-escalation marked by official apologies and reflection on how the situation got out of hand.

New Media Cases

The two cases analyzed here from January 2008—the use of Internet-based platform Ushahidi to report on ethnic violence following the December 2007 Kenyan elections and the use of Facebook to organize protests against paramilitary groups in Colombia—offer insights into how media can be used to diffuse latent or existing conflicts. In general, they speak to burgeoning domains of crisis mapping, and media activism and slacktivism (Morozov, 2009).

The software platform Ushahidi, named after the Swahili word for testimony or witness, was first made public in the December 2007 Kenyan elections (Vericat, 2010). The election had resulted in a political stalemate, with incumbent president Mwai Kibaki, of Kikuyu ethnicity, declared victorious—a result that challenger and opposition leader Raila Odinaga, of Luo origin, contested. Voter fraud and manipulation were reported in media, and ethnic riots began in Kenya. Within a week of the election, over one hundred people had been reported killed. In total, over 300,000 people were forced to leave their homes during the violence and 1,200 were killed (Wadhams, 2008).

A small group of Kenyan software developers assembled and launched the Ushahidi platform in a few days. It allowed citizens to use a variety of media, such as mobile phones, land lines, radio, or Internet, to monitor elections and report cases of violence, which were then centrally collected and reported on Google maps. These maps allowed people to avoid areas of violence, and journalists also picked up eyewitness accounts being reported on Ushahidi. Eventually a power-sharing arrangement was worked out between the two electoral contenders. Ushahidi contributed to conflict de-escalation and helped to create conditions for peace. Since then the Ushahidi platform, a form of citizen journalism, peace media, and participation, has had a variety of applications, including reporting from conflict and disaster zones, such as anti-immigrant violence in South Africa in mid-2008 and the Haiti earthquake in 2010. It was even deployed in the 2010 winter snowstorm in Washington, D.C., and during the severe Russian winter of 2011–2012.[8]

The success with Ushahidi has led to development of other similar platforms and generated a whole new field of crisis mapping, even though many of the practitioners may not identify themselves with this name.[9] The platforms have a common emphasis on information-sharing through networks, crowd sourcing, and some form of satellite surveillance. Apart from Ushahidi, similar platforms include ArcGIS.com, Sahana, and Google Crisis Response. Harvard's Satellite Sentinel Project—in part funded by actor George Clooney—is well known for analyzing violence between Sudan and South Sudan with images and data collected through DigitalGlobe's satellites (Raymond, Howarth, and Hutson, 2012). The United Nations has also developed crisis-mapping platforms for its humanitarian response in various forms including the secretary-general's innovative Global Pulse project, which enables information exchanges on crises and disasters among organizations and individuals.[10] While crisis mapping is largely a bottom-up phenomenon relying on crowd sourcing, policy institutions can use it effectively to enable information sharing. This was the case with enabling the government to create transparency on tsunami relief in Japan in April 2010, or for the United Nations Office for the Coordination of Humanitarian Affairs to respond to and track the political crisis in Libya in spring/summer 2011. (Cavelty, 2011).[11]

Media activism has also taken on new dimensions, many of which also link to crowd sourcing. Most agencies for peacebuilding, humanitarian aid, or social advocacy now offer some form of social media platform for activists.[12] These platforms help facilitate activities ranging from fund-raising, letter-writing, and petitions, to mobilizing support for sit-ins and demonstrations. Media professionals themselves are indulging in new and old forms of activism. For example, the International League for Conservation Photographers mobilizes for collective action on the environment (Eilperin, 2012).

A powerful example of the use of social media activism comes from thirty-three-year old civil engineer Oscar Morales Guevara's Facebook group "One Million Voices Against the FARC," created in January 2008 to protest the paramilitary kidnappings and killings that the Marxist-inspired terrorist organization Revolutionary Armed Forces of Colombia (FARC) have carried out since the 1960s. Although the kidnappings subsided to 393 in 2007 from over 3,500 in 2000 (Lapper and Schipani, 2008), the hostage talks in late 2007 were held up as Colombian President Álvaro Uribe withdrew support for mediator Venezuelan President Hugo Chavez, and a number of FARC lies were also exposed in the media. Morales's Facebook group soon enabled over 250,000 users to endorse a protest against FARC. On February 4, 2008, the protest took place around the world in nearly two hundred cities and forty countries. The estimates range from hundreds of thousands of protesters up to 12 million. It was one of the biggest protests in Colombia and may have brought out nearly 2 million people in Bogotá alone (Brodzinsky, 2008). The slogan of the protesters, which can be interpreted as a framing device, was "No more kidnapping, no more lies, no more deaths, no more FARC."

The year 2011 also featured heavy use of social and new media in the protests against authoritarian rule that came to be known as the "Arab Spring." Twitter feeds, SMS texts, Facebook, Ushahidi, blogging, and YouTube were all used for social mobilization in the uprising against Egyptian President Hosni Mubarak that led to the eighteen-day occupation of Cairo's Tahrir Square starting on January 25, 2011. While the protest obviously resulted from widespread dissatisfaction with the Mubarak regime, social media helped to end the isolation people felt and resulted in widespread mobilization. In this case, the Egyptian government's partial shutdown of the Internet or mobile telephony only led to more fears and mobilization. More recently, a similar role is attributed to social and new media in the ongoing protests, at the time of this writing in June 2012, against the harsh regime of Syrian President Bashar al-Assad. YouTube videos filmed by mobile devices have mobilized global opposition to the regime and led to condemnations of the regime's actions, including from the Arab League.

Social media have especially added another dimension to the politicization of conflict that goes beyond the CNN Effect to mobilize almost immediate opposition to particular actions. Two examples from the US presence in Afghanistan since December 2001 and the invasions of Iraq since 2002 are illustrative. Starting in April 2004, photographs taken by US soldiers of inmates at the Abu Ghraib prison outside of Baghdad quickly circulated over media channels and the Internet, and highlighted the inhumane treatment and torture being meted out to prisoners of war at the hands of the military. Prior to the Abu Ghraib incident, US President George W. Bush's administration had sought to build a legal case for certain forms of torture being admissible under the Geneva Convention Against Torture. The circulation of the Abu Ghraib pictures was embarrassing and spoke tragically against the US case for torture. In January 2012, a YouTube video showed four US Marines in combat uniform urinating over three dead bodies, purportedly those of Taliban fighters, in Afghanistan, while making inhumane comments and jokes. Although immediate denunciation followed from the US administration and the four marines were quickly identified, the video nevertheless revived memories of Abu Ghraib and questionable US actions abroad. The video complicated US moves toward negotiating with the Taliban and exchanging prisoners of war, with the goal of making way for an eventual withdrawal of US forces from Afghanistan in 2014.

These "success" stories notwithstanding, there is also increasing concern among media activists that "slacktivism," or online activism—often limited to joining Facebook groups or sending and receiving Twitter feeds—is not only a less viable alternative to traditional "in-person" activism, such as call-ins and protests, but that it may be detracting from much-needed activism. The click-based "nano-activism" is an example of "feel-good online activism," as Morozov (2009) terms it, and he calls for comprehensive surveys to counter the pros and cons of online activism. One such study shows that slacktivists—or "social champions," as this study calls them—are more likely than their offline counterparts to donate to charity, to boycott or champion products based on firms' support for social causes, and to take part in physical protests (Center for Social Impact Communication, 2011). Anecdotal evidence cannot be easily dismissed as demonstrated through the amazing work of many activist platforms.[13]

JOURNALISTIC ETHICS AND PEACE MEDIA

Lack of empathy and dehumanization can cause or exacerbate conflict. Media frames and content, as shown above, can be powerful devices in the conflict cycle. Efforts to de-escalate conflicts using media have, therefore, focused on professional training to emphasize ethics and responsibility. More recently, powerful storytelling techniques are being propagated through a variety of media to engender peace.

The basic problem regarding ethics is that they vary from society to society, as evident in the NWICO debate. However, there seems to be some consensus that press freedoms are correlated to peace and development (Guseva et al., 2008).

Lacking universal ethics, most journalistic training now includes emphasis on the need to report the truth, present multiple viewpoints on controversial subjects, and use noninflammatory language. Many news agencies, such as BBC, or media agencies, such as Internews and Intermedia, now regularly impart such training to local and international journalists, while UNESCO continues to promote the cause of developing professional curricula for journalism, for example, through its series on journalism education. A December 2005 meeting resulted in the Model Curriculum for Journalism Education (UNESCO, 2007).

Galtung's work on peace journalism, highlighted earlier, also seeks to move beyond negative journalism. An extreme case of the latter is the role that Radio Télévision Libre des Mille Collines played in 1994 in inciting hatred against the Tutsis during the Rwandan genocide. The story of *Jyllands-Posten* above also qualifies as negative journalism. On the other hand, peace journalism is rich in historical context and humanization, and portrays war or violence itself as causing further conflict. The use of the Ushahidi platform or the Facebook protests in Colombia can be taken as examples of peace media, although they are not journalist-centered. Cees Hamelink (2011) has recently called for an International Media Alert System to monitor media content in war or conflict zones. He sees this as an extension of the "responsibility to protect" principle that has arisen in humanitarian interventions.

Peace media have now moved beyond "reporting" issues to explore "soap operas" or storytelling as formats to present narratives that explore peace, especially through image- and context-rich story lines, often based on local issues. Such narratives can be dated to the early years of "entertainment-education," which started with socially progressive messages being inserted in Mexican and Indian soap operas (Singhal and Rogers, 1999). In 1995, the NGO Search for Common Ground (SFCG) opened a radio station in Burundi. Studio Ijambo pioneered SFCG's soap opera for peace approach with *Umubanyi niwe Muryango* (*Our Neighbors, Our Family*). This soap opera followed the lives of a Hutu and a Tutsi family, which was widely credited with fostering an empathic understanding. In 1999, SFCG pioneered another successful format: *In Inkingi y'ubuntu* (*Heroes*), which tracked characters who had undertaken enormous risk to help save the life of someone in an entirely different ethnic group. More recently the SFCG has carried out particularly noteworthy work through similar soap operas. Its award-winning show *The Team* uses sports imagery and metaphors, specifically in soccer (football), to explore processes of peace in over fifteen African, Asian, and Middle Eastern countries. Each show "follows the characters on a football team who must overcome their differences—be they cultural, ethnic, religious, tribal, racial or socio-economic—in order to work together to win the game."[14]

CONCLUSION

Our current media-rich environments are as conducive to escalating conflict as they are to de-escalating it. Media content is increasingly under scrutiny, and social media is dispersed in real time throughout the world. While we grapple with the "old" issues of media objectivity, bias, framing, and dehumanization, new issues dealing with the CNN Effect and the hyperspeed of communication and media flows make the challenges even more insuperable. On the more positive side, new media are also well suited for social mobilization and advocacy for conflict reduction, and professional journalists now work alongside citizen journalists in gathering and disseminating news. It is clear that integrating peacebuilding into new and traditional media has significant potential to contribute to reducing conflict, changing attitudes, and effecting change.

QUESTIONS FOR FURTHER DISCUSSION

1. Under which contexts do media contribute to or decrease conflict?
2. What sort of professional training can journalists receive to correct against bias and negative framing?
3. Will citizen journalism and social media platforms increase or decrease conflict in the future?
4. Do we need an International Media Alert System in a world of social media, Internet, and the CNN Effect?
5. How can we measure the impact of peace journalism?
6. How can peace journalism thrive in a market-based economy?
7. Despite rigorous training, US journalists are often critiqued for their biases and pro-US reporting. Are these critiques fair? What do you think are the causes of this bias?

REFERENCES

Attkisson, S. 2010, April 22. Haiti earthquake aid: Nearly \$15 billion in donations. CBS News. Retrieved June 5, 2011, from www.cbsnews.com/8301-31727_162-20003180-10391695.html.

Bennett, L. W. 1990. Toward a theory of press–state relations in the United States. *Journal of Communication* 40, no. 2: 103–125.

Boulding, K. 1959, June. National images and international systems. *Journal of Conflict Resolution* 3, no. 2: 120–131.

Brodzinsky, S. 2008, February 4. Facebook used against Colombia FARC with global rally. *Christian Science Monitor.* Retrieved February 1, 2012, from www.csmonitor.com /World/Americas/2008/0204/p04s02-woam.html.

Bronfrenner, U. 1961. The mirror image in Soviet–American relations: A social psychologist's report. *Journal of Social Issues* 16, no. 3: 45–56.

Bull, H. 1977/1995. The anarchical society: A study of order in world politics. New York: Columbia University Press.

Cavelty, M. D. 2011, November. *Crisis mapping: A phenomena and tool in emergencies.* Report No. 103, Center for Security Studies, ETH Zurich.

Center for Social Impact Communication. 2011, November. Dynamics of cause engagement. Georgetown University and Ogilvy Public Relations Worldwide, Washington, DC. Retrieved February 5, 2012, from http://csic.georgetown.edu/research/215767.html.

Codina, M., and Rodriguez-Virgili, J. 2007. Journalism for integration: The Muhammad cartoons. *Javnost—The Public* 14, no. 2: 31–46.

Cullum, B. 2010. Devices: The power of mobile phones. In M. Joyce, ed. *Digital activism decoded: The new mechanics of change* (pp. 47–70). New York: International Debate Education Association.

Dartnell, M. Y. 2006. *Insurgency online: Web activism and global conflict.* Toronto: University of Toronto Press.

Der Derian, J. 1991. The (s)pace of international relations: Simulation, surveillance, and speed. *International Studies Quarterly* 44: 295–310.

Dutton, W. H. 2007, October 15. Through the network (of networks)—The Fifth Estate. Inaugural lecture, Examination Schools, Oxford University.

Eilperin, J. 2012, February 16. Wildlife photographers turn their cameras toward conservation. *Washington Post.* Retrieved March 10, 2012, from www.washingtonpost.com /lifestyle/style/wildlife-photographers-turn-their-cameras-toward-conservation/2012 /02/16/gIQAnNdiPR_story.html.

Entman, R. 1991. Framing US coverage of international news: Contrasts in narratives of the KAL and Iran Air incidents. *Journal of Communication* 33, no. 3: 419–449.

Fouche, G. 2006, February 6. Danish paper rejected Jesus cartoons. *The Guardian.* Retrieved February 15, 2012, from www.guardian.co.uk/media/2006/feb/06/pressandpublishing .politics.

Galtung, J. 1980. *The true world: A transnational perspective.* New York: Free Press.

———. 2000. Conflict transformation by peaceful means: The Transcend Method. United Nations Disaster Management Training Program. Retrieved June 5, 2012, from www.transcend.org/pctrcluj2004/TRANSCEND_manual.pdf.

Galtung, J., and M. Ruge. 1965. The structure of foreign news. *Journal of Peace Research* 2, no. 1: 64–91.

Galtung, J., and F. Tschudi. 2001. Crafting peace: On the psychology of the TRANSCEND approach. In D. J. Christie, R. V. Wagner, and D. D. Winter, eds. *Peace, conflict, and violence* (pp. 210–222). Upper Saddle River, NJ: Prentice Hall.

Gilboa, E. 2005. The CNN Effect: The search for a communication theory of international relations. *Political Communication* 22: 27–44.

Guseva, M., et al. 2008. *Press freedom and development.* Paris: UNESCO.

Hallin, D. 1986. *The uncensored war.* Berkeley; University of California Press.

Hamelink, C. J. 2011. *Media and conflict: Escalating evil.* Boulder, CO: Paradigm Publishers.

Herman, E., and N. Chomsky. 1988/2002. Manufacturing consent: The political economy of the mass media. New York: Pantheon.

Huntington, S. 1993, Summer. A clash of civilizations. *Foreign Affairs* 72, no. 3: 22–49.

Joyce, M., ed. 2010. *Digital activism decoded: The new mechanics of change.* New York: International Debate Education Association.

Kahneman, D. 2011. *Thinking, fast and slow.* New York: Farrar, Straus & Giroux.

Karpf, D. 2010. Measuring success of digital campaigns. In M. Joyce, ed. *Digital activism decoded: The new mechanics of change* (pp. 151–164). New York: International Debate Education Association.

Keck, M. E., and K. Sikkink. 1998. *Activists beyond borders: Advocacy networks in international politics.* Ithaca, NY: Cornell University Press.

Lapper, R., and A. Schipani. 2008, February 4. Bogota to rise against abductions. *Financial Times.* Retrieved February 2, 2012, from www.ft.com/intl/cms/s/0/c91e4c44-d2c2 -11dc-8636-0000779fd2ac.html#axzz1jyHJkiOu.

Levi-Strauss, C. 1958. *Race and history.* Paris: UNESCO.

Litfin, K. 2002. Public eyes: Satellite imagery, the globalization of transparency, and new networks of surveillance. In J. P. Singh and J. Rosenau, eds. *Information technology and global politics: The scope of power and governance* (pp. 65–90). Albany: State University of New York Press.

Livingston, S. 1997 Beyond the CNN Effect: The media–foreign policy dynamic. In P. Norris, ed. *Politics and the press: The news media and the influences* (pp. 291–318). Boulder, CO: Lynne Rienner.

Lynch, J., and J. Galtung. 2010. *Reporting conflict: New directions in peace journalism.* Brisbane, Australia: University of Queensland Press.

MacBride Commission. 1980. *Many voices, one world: Towards a new, more just, and more efficient World Information and Communication Order.* Lanham, MD; Rowman & Littlefield.

McCaughey, M., and M. D. Ayers. 2003. *Cyberactivism: Online activism in theory and practice.* New York: Routledge.

McPhail, T. L. 1981. *Electronic colonialism: The future of international broadcasting and communication.* Beverly Hills, CA: Sage Publications.

Mermin, J. 1999. *Debating war and peace.* Princeton, NJ: Princeton University Press.

Morozov, E. 2009, May 19. The brave new world of slacktivism. *Foreign Policy.* Retrieved February 1, 2012, from http://neteffect.foreignpolicy.com/posts/2009/05/19/the_brave _new_world_of_slacktivism.

Nichols, J. S. 2003. Propaganda. In D. H. Johnson, ed. *Encyclopedia of international media and communications* (pp. 597–606). San Diego, CA: Elsevier.

Nordenstreng, K. 1983. *The Mass Media Declaration of UNESCO.* Norwood, NJ: Ablex Publishing.

O'Brien, R., A. M. Goetz, J. A. Scholte, and M. Williams. 2000. Contesting global governance: Multilateralism and global social movements. In *Contesting global governance: Multilateral economic institutions and global social movements* (pp. 1–23). Cambridge: Cambridge University Press.

O'Rourke, P. J. 2006, February 20. Laugh riot: Fun and games in Europe. *Weekly Standard,* pp. 13–14.

Powers, S. 2008. Examining the Danish cartoons affair: Mediatised cross-cultural tensions? *Media, war, and conflict* 1, no. 3: 339–359.

Raymond, N., C. Howarth, and J. Hutson. 2012, February 7. Crisis mapping needs an ethical compass. Globalbrief. Retrieved March 7, 2012, from http://globalbrief.ca/blog/features/crisis-mapping-needs-an-ethical-compass/4744.

Robinson, P. 2001. Theorizing the influence of media on world politics: Models of media influence on foreign policy. *European Journal of Communication* 16, no. 4: 523–544.

Rose, F. 2006, February 19. Why I published those cartoons. *Washington Post.*

Said, E. 1979. *Orientalism.* New York: Vintage.

Singh, J. P. 2011. *United Nations Educational, Scientific, and Cultural Organization (UNESCO): Creating norms for a complex world.* London: Routledge.

Sikkink, K. 2009. The power of networks in international politics. In M. Kahler, ed. *Networked politics: Agency, power, and governance* (pp. 228–247). Ithaca, NY: Cornell University Press.

Singhal, A., and E. M. Rogers. 1999. *Entertainment-education: A communication strategy for social change.* New York: Routledge.

Skonieczny, A. 2002, December. Constructing NAFTA: Myth, representation, and the discursive construction of U.S. foreign policy. *International Studies Quarterly* 45, no. 3: 435–454.

Smythe, E., and P. J. Smith. 2006, January–March. Legitimacy, transparency, and information technology: The World Trade Organization in an era of contentious trade politics. *Global Governance* 12, no. 1: 31–53.

Steele, B. J. 2007, November. Making words matter: The Asian tsunami, Darfur, and "reflexive discourse" in international politics. *International Studies Quarterly* 51, no. 4: 901–925.

United Nations Educational, Scientific, and Cultural Organization (UNESCO). 2007. *Model curricula for journalism education.* UNESCO Series on Journalism Education. Paris: Author.

Vericat, J. 2010. Open source mapping as liberation technology: An interview with David Kobia. *Journal of International Affairs* 64, no. 1: 195–201.

Wadhams, M. 2008, December 3. Will Kenya's election violence recur? *Time.* Retrieved February 1, 2012, from www.time.com/time/world/article/0,8599,1869113,00.html.

Wells, C. 1987. *The UN, UNESCO, and the politics of knowledge.* New York: St. Martin's Press.

Wilson, K. 2011. "Race," gender, and neoliberalism: Changing visual representations in development. *Third World Quarterly* 32, no. 2: 317–331.

ACKNOWLEDGMENTS

Thanks to Erin Gamble, Katherine Saulpaugh, and Stephanie Vineyard for research assistance, and to Craig Zelizer for detailed feedback.

Notes

1. From Institute for Media, Policy, and Civil Society, *An Operational Framework for Media and Peacebuilding*, 2002, p. 9. www.mediosparalapaz.org/downloads/MEDIA_AND _PEACEBUILDING.pdf. New Media should also be included in this quote, but this report was issued in 2002.

2. "Syria, Homs—Secret Police Shooting Peaceful Protesters"; www.youtube.com/watch ?v=4moi9vt6qWk&skipcontrinter=1, accessed February 7, 2012.

3. The term "Fourth Estate" comes from Edmund Burke's observation that the press members covering the Parliament's three realms (clergy, commons, and aristocrats) now composed another vital estate. More recently, Dutton (2007) writes of a "Fifth Estate" of information and communication technologies, including the Internet, producing accountability in governance through interlinked digital networks.

4. Estimates for the total number of people killed range between 500,000 and 1 million. Most of the killings took place between April and June 1994 and were triggered by the assassination of President Juvenal Habyarimana, who was Hutu. The Tutsi monarchy, which had been favored under Belgian colonists, had been overthrown in 1959–1962, and a civil war began in the 1980s when the Tutsis organized in Uganda. For more information on the role of the media in the conflict, see Hamelik (2011, pp. 49–52).

5. See also Galtung and Ruge (1965). The authors begin to discuss key concepts that would later form the basis of peace journalism.

6. As of the date of the article (April 2010), in addition to the above amounts, $1.019 billion was funded by US tax dollars through USAID, $1.15 billion came from US tax dollars, and an additional $8.75 billion for redevelopment came from countries besides the US and world bodies.

7. To this day, UNESCO is careful not to mention any issues that pertain to regulating journalistic activities or ethics.

8. Ushahidi practices are well documented. Please see, for example, http://blog.ushahidi .com and http://community.ushahidi.com.

9. For more information, see the International Network of Crisis Mappers, with nearly 5,000 members worldwide: http://crisismappers.net.

10. www.unisdr.org/archive/24223, accessed March 7, 2012.

11. For tsunami relief, see www.sinsai.info, and for the Libya crisis, see http:// libyacrisismap.net.

12. See, for example, NOW (www.now.org/issues/media), the SPIN Project (www .spinproject.org/section.php?id=42), War Is a Crime (http://warisacrime.org/media), and Fairness and Accuracy in Reporting (FAIR) (www.fair.org/index.php?page=119).

13. See, for example, activist platforms such as change.org, purpose.org, and avazz.org, which crowd-source and mobilize activism for global issues, sometimes instantaneously.

14. See Search for Common Ground's TEAM program: www.sfcg.org/programmes /cgp/the-team.html. The countries are Angola, Burundi (radio only), Côte d'Ivoire, Democratic Republic of the Congo, Ethiopia (radio only), Indonesia, Kenya, Lebanon, Liberia, Morocco, Nepal, Pakistan, Palestine, Sierra Leone, and Zimbabwe. Building on the need to make the program sensitive to local context and culture, in Pakistan the team plays cricket, while in all other countries football (soccer) is the sport used in the program.

chapter eleven

HEALTH AND PEACEBUILDING

Paul Charlton

The role of physicians and other health workers in the preservation and promotion of peace is the most significant factor for the attainment of health for all.
—WORLD HEALTH ASSEMBLY, RESOLUTION 34.38, 1981

THIS CHAPTER WILL FOCUS ON the relationship between the health field and peacebuilding. First I discuss the connections between health and conflict, and introduce three approaches to integrating health and peacebuilding activities. Next I cover possible roles for health workers in peacebuilding, and the conflict resolution theory and skills that underpin effective engagement. Finally I discuss key policy debates in the field and central questions for practitioners moving forward.

The health professions share a long history in mitigating the effects of conflict. The Geneva Conventions, Médecins Sans Frontières surgeons operating in war zones, and International Committee of the Red Cross (ICRC) teams that visit prisoners of war are iconic examples of the importance of health actors in conflict settings. Groups are increasingly utilizing the health field as a resource to foster peacebuilding and conflict resolution beyond the traditional instances of battlefield medicine and humanitarian relief. Pan American Health Organization (PAHO) interventions in Central American conflicts in the 1980s heralded new visions of utilizing health activities as a bridge for peace. PAHO's successful facilitation of cease-fires to allow mass children's vaccination has helped lead to new points of access for the positive impact of health-based programming in conflict areas. They have also generated contentious debate.

While the capacity for health activities to influence peace should not be oversold, a growing body of evidence suggests that it holds a great deal of value for the field.

249

Today's complex conflict environments directly involve health actors and are potential terrain for the integration of health and peacebuilding interventions.[1] As this remains a relatively new field, many aspects of the health field's relationship with peacebuilding are still being shaped. What are proper goals for health peacebuilding? What works, and in what circumstances? What are the risks? How much impact can these interactions have? How should critically reflective practitioners proceed? These are some of the questions that must be addressed by those who wish to integrate peacebuilding with health activities.

INTRODUCTION TO THE FIELDS OF HEALTH AND CONFLICT

Although the fields of health and conflict have a long history of interaction, they are often framed as activities operating in two fundamentally different domains. Increasingly such assumptions are being challenged. Grove and Zwi (2008) suggest three reasons for devoting attention to the links between health and peace:

> First, humanitarian interventions in the presence of violent political conflict typically include a major health component. Second, the health sector and health services more generally are increasingly recognized as helping to secure lives and livelihoods and demonstrating the commitment of government to meeting the needs of its people. Third, health is seen in some situations as an entry-point for more overt and explicit efforts to build peace, and may be used instrumentally to promote these objectives. (pp. 67–68)

Two of the most prominent discourses that permeate the health–conflict–peace nexus are health diplomacy and peace through health. Both terms are still used rather interchangeably[2] and are in many ways different faces of the same endeavor. Nonetheless, each discourse has gained traction with its own audience and often sounds as a distinct voice within the field.

The discourse on health diplomacy (also termed "medical diplomacy" or "global health diplomacy") assumes a focus on international relations and explores the interactions between global health and foreign policy. Fidler (2005) offers three perspectives through which actors approach this global health and foreign policy relationship. The first "rejects the idea that health is merely a technical, non-political activity and argues that health has become a preeminent *political value* for 21st century humanity," a goal that foreign policy should pursue "as an end in itself" (p. 183). Supporters argue that health interventions can change people's attitudes, and thereby yield desirable political effects. The second perspective depicts health as a tool, "an instrument of statecraft the value of which extends no farther than its utility in serving the material interests and capabilities of the state" (p. 185). In this view, although health may be a form of soft power, strategic foreign policy goals should drive the funding and provision of global health activities, not the other way around. The third perspective posits a middle ground between the ideology of the first and the realpolitik of the second, in which the health sciences (especially epidemiology) and politics are interdependent. This perspective suggests that while influence runs both ways, the scientific principles of epidemiology serve to "channel action on health in specific directions that neither ideology nor power politics can alter" (p. 186). Advocates for each of these positions exist within both the health and political spheres. The burgeoning literature on health and foreign policy suggests that the core conceptual grounding of this relationship has yet to be realized.[3]

As the health diplomacy discourse tends to focus more on the international relations dimensions of health, Peace Through Health movements tend to adopt more of a peacebuilding discourse. Often used interchangeably with the terms "health peacebuilding" or "health as a bridge for peace," the Peace Through Health movements assert that health workers have a role to play in the prevention and mitigation of war and violence. Three claims underpin this view: first, that "peace is a prerequisite to health (and therefore that peace is the business of all health sector actors)" (McInnes and Rushton, 2010, p. 5); second, that health interventions can change people's attitudes, which may have desirable political effects; and third, that health workers have certain attributes that uniquely position them for building peace.

The first claim emerges from health providers' ethical and professional commitment to improving the well-being of their patients. The health field is explicitly oriented around reducing the pain and suffering of the patients and populations it serves. To most effectively achieve this, health providers must strive to identify and act on prior causes of illness and injury: "Not only cure, but also prevention, becomes the imperative" (Santa Barbara and Arya, 2008, p. 3). Given that war and other violence is an important cause of illness, injury, and death, it follows that health professionals have an ethical and professional duty to help prevent war and other violence.

The notion that peace and violence are fundamental aspects of health is now widely recognized. The opening declaration of the Constitution of the World Health Organization defines health as "a state of complete physical, mental and social well-being and not merely the absence of disease or infirmity" (WHO, 1946, para. 2). Forty years later, the 1986 WHO Ottawa Charter outlined the critical resources and conditions for health as peace, shelter, education, food, income, a stable ecosystem, sustainable resources, social justice, and equity (WHO, 1986).

Violence, on the other hand, is widely discussed as a driver of poor health. Santa Barbara and Arya (2008) outline six primary determinants correlated with lower levels of population health: poverty; war and other violence; environmental degradation; disintegration of community; poor governance; poor human rights observance (p. 10). As the authors note, "War . . . brings the other five lethal factors in its wake" (p. 10).

Epidemiological data seems to support this. Estimates suggest 170 million to 230 million people died in the twentieth century as a direct or indirect result of conflict, with an estimated 5 percent of *all* deaths during the twentieth century resulting from the impact of collective violence (Levy and Sidel, 2008, p. 25). In some conflicts there is evidence that 90 percent of the fatalities were civilians (Levy and Sidel, 2008, p. 4). The mortality rate in the general population during war may increase up to tenfold the preconflict rate (Garfield, 2008, p. 24). Beyond fatalities, conflicts inflict direct injuries upon combatants and noncombatants from bullets and bombs, land mines, sexual violence, and intentional maiming. The indirect costs ripple even wider. Conflicts often create humanitarian crises, such as population displacement, malnutrition, and the destruction of shelter, health facilities, and water-sanitation infrastructure, which in turn increases the spread of infectious diseases, such as HIV and other sexually transmitted diseases, malaria, tuberculosis, diarrheal illnesses, and pneumonia. The use of systematic, mass sexual violence as a weapon of war can result in appalling physical and psychological trauma, including debilitating incontinence from gynecological fistulas (ACQUIRE Project, 2006).

Psychological trauma alone can lead to devastating long-term repercussions. Rape, enslavement, torture, forced participation in killings, combat, fear, and insecurity are just some aspects of conflict that often leave deep marks on combatants and noncombatants, perpetrators and survivors alike. The impacts are often less visible and harder to diagnose than overt physical destruction, but no less significant. They include life-altering levels of anxiety, depression, substance abuse, hostility, social withdrawal, estrangement, isolation, feelings of meaninglessness, anticipation of betrayal, hypervigilance, and an inability to trust (Kanter, 2008; Zelizer, 2008). A meta-analysis of studies on post-traumatic stress disorder (PTSD)[4] rates in conflict-affected populations suggests a prevalence from 13 percent to 25 percent, with rates often much higher in some conflicts depending on exposures (Steel et al., 2009, p. 548). These psychological impacts on survivors of trauma can ruin lives and families, predispose communities to recurrent cycles of violence, and result in the transmission of destructive behavior and beliefs from one generation to the next (Barsalou, 2001; Leaning, 2008; Pearrow and Cosgrove, 2009).

A deep relationship clearly exists between health and conflict. Given the duty of health workers to heal and save lives, acknowledging this entails a moral call to action for the health field. Yet encouraging health workers to engage with conflicts is problematic. There are concerns that health peacebuilding can be used manipulatively or be imposed from the outside with little internal legitimacy (Various Palestinian NGOs, 2005). Skeptics note little empirical correlation between a group's health status and its disposition for violence and war, which suggests that efforts to improve health may have minimal ability to prevent conflict (Fidler, 2005). The connections between conflict and health are not uniform. While war may negatively impact physical wellness in the short term, the long-term effects of conflict could result in reduced oppression and increased justice that may positively impact well-being. Nevertheless, while legitimate conceptual concerns remain, increasing numbers of scholars and practitioners are tentatively accepting this argument that peace is a prerequisite to health and is therefore an appropriate domain of health actors.

The claim that well-planned health interventions can improve health outcomes *and* at the same time contribute to achieving wider political goals is proving more controversial (McInnes and Rushton, 2010). Is there evidence to substantiate this claim? Do advocates understand the consequences of linking political and health interventions? Is it ever possible to achieve both health and peace outcomes without sacrificing one for the other? Answers to these questions are important because this claim is increasingly being used to justify a wide variety of health interventions that focus on different political targets, from building peace to "winning hearts and minds" (Thompson, 2005). The veracity of the underlying assumptions deserves critical analysis, as do the risks and benefits of adopting this orientation. Even if health activities are shown to yield political impact, clarity on foundational principles and wisdom in deciding how best to enact those principles are important.

THREE MAIN PARADIGMS LINK THE HEALTH SECTOR WITH PEACEBUILDING

To understand how peacebuilding integrates with health activities, it is helpful to examine three ways in which health professionals already reach out to the peacebuilding field for assistance. Each orientation is structured around a distinct goal and thus engages with conflict differently.

Conflict Resolution Skills for Better Health Programming

The first orientation utilizes conflict resolution skills and processes to deliver more effective health activities in conflict settings. The goal is explicitly and solely a health-based one (with health narrowly defined): *to best address the health needs of populations in a particular conflict setting.* In this context, conflict resolution skills and processes help health workers achieve their targeted health goals while ensuring that these activities do not cause inadvertent harm. This aspect of integrated peacebuilding is the least controversial linkage between the health and peacebuilding fields.

Delivering health services in conflict settings can be challenging. Effectiveness often requires conflict resolution skills and a level of political understanding of the community's conflict dynamics that are outside health workers' expertise. For example, in the early stages of a humanitarian crisis, medical teams frequently must negotiate with various power holders over access to populations affected by the fighting, where to establish medical facilities, who will be treated, and how to ensure the medical team's safety. They often negotiate with militaries and armed groups about weapons policies on hospital premises, interact with government agencies, and investigate reports of human rights abuses and massacres. These tasks involve challenging decisions about the principles guiding health work in conflict zones, how to implement those principles in context, and how to navigate the political and social complexities of the conflict. While such tasks are fundamental for success, they are rarely within the traditional skill set of many health workers.

Mary B. Anderson's influential 1999 text *Do No Harm* raised expectations for the humanitarian relief and development fields by arguing that even well-meaning interventions may cause undesirable effects. Every intervention in a conflict can become a driver of conflict. Anderson points out that humanitarian aid can have the unintended consequence of benefiting warring parties and prolonging a conflict to the detriment of the civilian populations whose suffering the aid is intended to relieve. For example, when a southern Sudanese movement split into two factions, an aid agency redesigned its health-training program to include two separate training centers, one for each faction (Anderson, 1999). In hindsight, a staff member noted this decision had inadvertently rewarded the split and missed an opportunity to create a safe space where people from both sides could legitimately meet and work together.

In contemporary conflicts, it is not enough to deliver health services and assume that the net impact will be positive. The bare minimum is to ensure that the intervention does no harm. Although the "do no harm" ethic is widely accepted within the health field, in complex and often chaotic conflict settings it remains difficult to achieve in practice. The difficulty of avoiding harm in conflicts points to the value of placing peacebuilding specialists on health teams and training health field teams in conflict resolution skills such as conflict analysis, conflict impact assessment, mediation, and negotiation. The use of conflict resolution skills for better health programming is perhaps the most straightforward way in which health actors are integrating peacebuilding into the field.[5]

Leveraging Health Programming for Peace

The second orientation moves beyond doing no harm to focus on a new goal: *leveraging on-the-ground health work to promote peace in communities affected by conflict*. The distinction between working "in" conflict versus working "on" conflict is important. Not content to only deliver health services "in" conflict settings, this approach explicitly seeks to meet the health needs of populations *and* have a positive impact on the conflict.[6]

This is the realm of some of the more innovative approaches to health and peace. In the 1980s and early 1990s PAHO facilitated collaboration between guerrilla groups and governments on "days of tranquility" for polio vaccination campaigns in El Salvador and Peru that eventually achieved the eradication of polio from the Americas. In addition to attaining the eradication goals, collaboration by conflicting parties on these health issues was cited as a factor that helped to raise the level of trust between groups (de Quadros and Epstein, 2002). In the 1990s and early 2000s the World Health Organization's Health as a Bridge for Peace (HBP) program drew from the PAHO experience as it sought to integrate health initiatives with conflict management, social reconstruction, and sustainable community reconciliation (WHO, 2002). The concept was implemented in a variety of WHO interventions in the late 1990s and early 2000s, including in Haiti, Angola, Mozambique, Sri Lanka, Indonesia, and the Balkans, though it has been much less prominent in WHO literature in recent years.[7]

Current health-peacebuilding paradigms expand on this foundation and continue to evolve more robust theoretical visions for how health professionals can (and should) contribute to peacebuilding and violence prevention. Increasing numbers of programs put these frameworks into practice, from postconflict peacebuilding with schoolchildren in Croatia to conflict-resolution training of community health promoters in Cambodia and culturally sensitive health delivery in the Solomon Islands (see, respectively, Woodside, Santa Barbara, and Benner, 1999; Ui, Leng, and Aoyama, 2007; and Zwi et al., 2004).[8] The following table adapted from Rodriguez-Garcia, Schlesser, and Bernstein (2001) highlights the wide range of health-peacebuilding activities being attempted.

These activities often involve nontraditional roles for health actors, who may find themselves engaged with issues less widely viewed as health terrain. Critical skepticism can be appropriate here. Not all approaches to peacebuilding in the health field are likely to be fruitful, and some bring with them risks to the legitimacy of the underlying

TABLE 11.1. Health-Peacebuilding Actions and Stages of Conflict

Stage of Conflict	Health-Peacebuilding Actions

I. Stable Peace	• Promote:
	    Health for all, equity
	    Human development
	    Human rights
	• Prevent inhumane weapons/warfare

II. Impending Crisis	• Predict areas/sources of future conflict • Develop decision-making and capacity-building tools • Health and human rights monitoring
III. Outbreak of Violence	• Conflict-resolution training • Problem-solving workshops • Establishment of Health Humanitarian Assistance Programs • Special envoys, mediation, arbitration
IV. Warfare	• Promote/initiate confidence-building measures • Provision of health and humanitarian services • Technical cooperation in health (control of epidemics), water, and sanitation • Monitor health effects of sanctions and other diplomatic efforts • Immunization cease-fires • Ministry of Health cooperation
V. Postcrisis	• Facilitation of dialogue among health workers from both sides of the conflict • Cooperative health projects • Peacebuilding awareness and capacity-building • Rehabilitation of health services and training of personnel • Development of programs to integrate military health personnel • Joint programs addressing issues of mental health/disabilities • Design of common protocols for collaboration between groups

Adapted from Rodriguez-Garcia, Schlesser, and Bernstein, 2001.

health activities. These programs also seek outcomes and impacts that are notoriously difficult to measure, which can be a particular challenge for donors. Nonetheless, this is a domain in which the peacebuilding and conflict resolution field can make many beneficial contributions, especially by helping health partners navigate the opportunities and potential pitfalls of treading the health-peacebuilding path.

Reframing Destructive Conflict as a Health Problem to Bring About Political Change

A third orientation asserts that peace and conflict are central components *of the health domain*. As health problems, war and violence fall squarely within health actors' sphere of expertise. Health workers in this orientation attempt to record the impacts of violence, examine its causal relationships, perform their diagnoses, and publicize their results. They use this information to work through political channels and effect change. Addressing violence and conflict as a public health problem is thus not significantly different from the type of public health campaigns that tackled smallpox, air pollution, or tobacco use.

The International Physicians for the Prevention of Nuclear War, an international organization of physicians and scientists, was awarded the 1985 Nobel Peace Prize for its work in the establishment of political discourse about the realities of nuclear war. Using their knowledge, expertise, and influence, they alerted societies and political leaders to the looming health catastrophe should nuclear war ever occur. They altered political discourses on the feasibility of ever deploying nuclear weapons and argued against the enormous resource expenditures on the nuclear arms race, highlighting the significant negative impact this resource diversion was having on other important global needs (MacQueen et al., 1997). Articulating both a peace message and a health message, the organization highlights the strengths health workers can bring to political advocacy.

Utilizing health data to move public opinion and instigate political change is central to this approach. Information collection/dissemination and advocacy are the two major activities for actors in this paradigm. This third orientation differs from the first two in that it is frequently not connected with on-the-ground delivery of health services in any particular conflict setting. Instead, health professionals act as advocates who enable wider audiences of health supporters to contribute to peacebuilding efforts. From a distance, networks of clinicians, epidemiologists, public health specialists, health advocacy organizations, and politicians can take information—data, stories, examples—of how violence and conflict affect individuals' or populations' well-being, then make the case for adopting concrete interventions to change the situation.

There are many ways for peacebuilders to help health actors shape and leverage these issues. Crafting advocacy campaigns and situating health-peacebuilding interventions within broader approaches to building peace are two examples. To help integrate programming, peacebuilding specialists can gain public health expertise (through a master's degree in public health, for instance). Additionally, innovative organizations such as CeaseFire, which approaches urban US gun violence through the lens of epidemiology, utilize the expertise of community members, hospital partners, and filmmakers as they develop effective data-driven, evidence-based interventions to reduce violence.[9] The breadth of potential collaboration on such activities is just beginning to be explored.

Roles for Health Workers in Peacebuilding

These three paradigms—using conflict resolution skills to make a health program more effective; using a health program to build peace; and reframing conflict as a public health problem—are ways in which health workers are already seeking out assistance from peacebuilders and conflict resolution specialists. Not all health workers or health donors view their relationship with conflict in this manner. Many, in fact, may never have been exposed to these ideas. Advocates will need to inform reticent health donors and health practitioners about how conflict is relevant to their field and how they might engage with the conflicts around them to better integrate peacebuilding into health activities.

Toward this end, MacQueen and Santa Barbara (2008) suggest ten common mechanisms through which health sector actors can influence peace:

- Redefinition of the situation
- Articulation of superordinate goals
- Mediation and conflict transformation
- Dissent and noncooperation
- Discovery and dissemination of knowledge
- Rebuilding the fabric of society
- Solidarity and support
- Social healing
- Evocation and extension of altruism
- Limiting the destructiveness of war (p. 27)

Whether the conflict is domestic or international in scope, most health actors can find their existing activities aligned with at least one of these mechanisms. Through greater familiarity with these roles, many skeptical health workers may discover that the health-peacebuilding field is not as foreign as initially perceived.[10]

IS THE RELATIONSHIP BETWEEN HEALTH, AND CONFLICT AND PEACEBUILDING UNIQUE?

Health offers a unique perspective that can be leveraged to reduce conflict and build peace. While every sector active in conflict settings brings strengths and weaknesses for conflict resolution and peacebuilding, health offers some particularly valuable attributes. Drawing from MacQueen (2008), strengths the health field brings to peacebuilding include:

Trust

Health activities, as traditionally conceived, are undertaken fundamentally not to benefit the provider but to benefit the patient and community. With generally high moral expectations for the behavior of these professionals, communities frequently bestow a significant degree of trust on health workers. This is important because trust is a particularly valued commodity in conflict settings.

Impartiality

Many health organizations, especially those active in conflict-related humanitarian relief, strive to remain impartial between parties within the conflict. The International Committee of the Red Cross (ICRC) is a prime example of this. Organizations seek to serve all competing parties and maintain relationships with all sides while maintaining some distance from each party. The extent, and success, of this distancing varies. The concept of humanitarian space relies heavily on these factors. Health activities are often a core element of creating such humanitarian space.

Superordinate Goals

Health, like peace and justice, is a widely accepted human good, if not fundamental human right. In the midst of conflict, the goal of health often carries broad social legitimacy. It has the potential to transcend the immediate interests of conflicting parties and orient them around a common goal, a focal point that can be utilized in peace-building. US–Soviet cooperation (under the auspices of the WHO) on smallpox erad-ication at the height of the Cold War is an example of health's potential as a superordinate goal (Manela, 2010).

Access

Through the above qualities and with the ability to deliver tangible services to meet concrete human needs, health workers often have unparalleled access to war and con-flict zones (MacQueen, 2008). Access, open communication channels, and ongoing relationships are invaluable in times of conflict and can open bridges toward peace. Access can also allow the uncovering of information about the impacts of violence, including human rights violations such as torture and massacres. The question of how best to utilize this information leads to challenging questions for health workers as to their ethical responsibilities and the most appropriate way to discharge those responsibilities.

Strong Foundational Principles

Health is guided by the principle of altruism (MacQueen, 2008). A professional com-mitment to serving patients, along with a pragmatic expectation that health workers intervene when possible to make things better, resonates with core principles of peace-building and conflict resolution. As seen in the language of the WHO commitments mentioned above, the peacebuilding principles of justice, equity, and peace are central to the health field.

Commitment to Scientific Principles

The robust scientific grounding of health helps contribute expectations for objective standards, measurements, and facts (MacQueen, 2008). Such standards can be in short supply in conflict environments, which are often plagued by misinformation, mistrust, and propaganda. There is also a relatively well-integrated global health community, oriented around measuring its impacts, improving its practices, disseminating ideas, and adopting best practices from other settings. Such a network can serve as a platform for peacebuilding including in the arena of evaluation.

Violence Is a Public Health Problem

While some fields may struggle to establish how their activities relate to conflict or peace, the causal links between violence and poor health outcomes are clear. As the impacts of conflict often fall within the sphere of expertise of health workers, it is reasonable to maintain that health workers have a role to play in aspects of conflict engagement.

With those strengths come potential drawbacks. MacQueen (2008) suggests that potential challenges to integrating health and peacebuilding activities include the per-ception that health workers engaged in peacebuilding may be extending beyond their area of expertise, and the concern that health workers without the necessary training in the skills of peacebuilding may attempt interventions and fail. Such scenarios risk damaging health actors' legitimacy and can put health workers and health programs at risk of being targeted in active conflict settings. Finally, health teams are often already overburdened in conflict settings and lack the time, energy, and resources to engage in any additional activities. This concern is particularly acute for health care providers, who often find that demands for their time far outstrip anything they can reasonably provide (MacQueen, 2008).

Such challenges are not unique to the health sector. Indeed, they may be faced by almost all sectors seeking innovative, interdisciplinary integration. MacQueen (2008) suggests that "time, patience, adequate training and standards, building institutional support, gradual growth of understanding and respect from other organizations, and the demonstrated effectiveness of the method" can help minimize these risks (p. 25). Ways to effectively mitigate these drawbacks are needed.

RELEVANT THEORY

Prevention

The public health concepts of primary, secondary, and tertiary prevention are fundamental to the goal of integrating peacebuilding into health activities (Santa Barbara and Arya, 2008; Vass, 2001). Primary prevention aims to mitigate violence by acting on its causes. While this is the most effective form of prevention, it is also typically the most difficult to achieve. Secondary prevention aims to minimize harm once violence has occurred, through shortening the course of a war or mitigating its effects on populations. Delivering medical aid in active conflict zones is a common example of secondary prevention. Tertiary prevention aims to rehabilitate the population and society in the aftermath of conflict. Examples include reintegration efforts and attempts to lessen the long-term impacts of trauma. This tiered prevention paradigm is widely applied to the design and evaluation of health-peacebuilding programs (see Gordon, 2011).

Galtung Violence and Peace

Johan Galtung's (1990) delineation of direct violence (people are murdered), structural violence (people die through lack of access to resources), and cultural violence (the attitudes and beliefs that justify this) resonates with the health sector, as do his definitions of negative peace (halting direct violence) and positive peace (overcoming structural and cultural violence as well). These concepts deepen the substance of health peacebuilding, pushing it from merely attempting to reduce the impacts of war, to instead advocating for justice, equity, and holistic well-being.

Conflict Stages

Even within a single conflict environment, health-peacebuilding interventions often must adapt to the stage of the conflict cycle.[11] For instance, during times of war, health actors may elect to focus their entire energies on meeting the acute health needs of a population while striving to maintain access across the conflict, keep communication channels open, and gather accurate information about the war's impacts. In contrast, before the outbreak of violence (and following its cessation), health actors may instead intentionally dedicate more time and energy to their peacebuilding activities to mitigate risk factors for conflict, facilitate relationships, and promote social rehabilitation. Peace-building specialists can be valuable in helping health actors accurately analyze the context and tailor their activities for maximum positive impact.

Peacebuilding Levels

The idea of multi-track peacebuilding is a cornerstone of health actors' engagement in conflict settings (Diamond and McDonald, 1993; Lederach, 1997). Rarely do health workers serve in the role of elite-level political actors in the context of international armed conflicts (at least not in their capacity as a health worker). Instead, health actors often operate as middle-level peacebuilders, functioning in leadership positions within a setting of protracted conflict, but with authority typically situated outside the structures of formal government or opposition movements. Their position derives largely from relationships and respect rather than from political or military power. Notably, middle-level health leaders are connected to both the top and the grassroots levels, offering important channels for communication and trust-building. Their preexisting relationships with counterparts often cut across the conflict divide. All of these factors help midlevel leaders share perspectives and link parties in ways that might otherwise be impossible.

Realistic Expectations

Multi-track diplomacy also helps to establish realistic expectations for what health in isolation can contribute to peace. Peacebuilding on the grassroots and middle levels is important for creating conditions conducive to achieving and sustaining peace. Successful peacebuilding, however, often still depends upon coordinated peace processes at the top levels. In the absence of high-level peace efforts, grassroots and midlevel peacebuilding are less effective.

Case Study 1: HEAL Africa in the Democratic Republic of the Congo

Case taken from D'Errico, Wake, & Wake, 2010.

HEAL Africa, a Congolese health NGO based in eastern Democratic Republic of the Congo (DRC), formed in 2000 with a focus on providing health care through the education of medical doctors. Noting the spread of HIV due partly to the use of rape as a tool of war, the organization later expanded its goals to include preventing, mitigating, and reversing the impacts of conflict on the populations it serves. Through incorporating community education and empowerment into health outreach programs delivered by health professionals, these activities have engaged primary, secondary, and tertiary levels of conflict prevention. Multidisciplinary teams that include medical professionals design all of its programs. The context of this region of the DRC, where high-level political accords have struggled to resolve many of the drivers of local conflict (issues over land, resources, and ethnic identity), is significant, as it suggests the types of complex conflicts in which multi-track efforts may be most valued.

Primary Prevention: Reducing the Likelihood of Conflict

The community-level projects (such as agricultural trainings and the formation of representative district committees to mediate in local disputes and select vulnerable participants for HEAL programs) are implemented "in order to reduce common risk factors for conflict—notably the lack of access to meaningful employment opportunities, gender inequality and inter-ethnic tensions" (p. 151).

Secondary Prevention: Treating the Immediate Effects of War

HEAL's core activity remains providing emergency and long-term medical care to patients in internally displaced–person camps, its rural health centers, and its hospital in Goma. This includes large numbers of gynecologic fistulae surgeries, "a direct consequence of sexual violence as a weapon of war" (p. 151). Its Safe Motherhood program helps create maternity insurance groups to provide support for pregnancy, delivery, and neonatal care. These funds help reduce gender imbalances exacerbated by conflict and protect women who give birth to children conceived through rape, who might otherwise be ostracized.

Tertiary Prevention: Postconflict Rehabilitation of Individuals and Society

Economic security, gender equality, and interethnic conciliation are primary foci at this level as well. The Heal My People program provides psychological and social support to survivors of rape through "locally appointed women in counselling, providing husband–wife mediation and conducting community education classes on reintegration" (p. 151). It provides micro-credit support for women involved in the program, offering financial security that was found to make participants feel "more physically secure and personally confident to partake in community discussions" (p. 153). Owning goats even helped to provide some protection from rebel groups, as the resource could be traded to limit violence (Zwank [2008], as cited in D'Errico et al., 2010). The Gender and Justice project also aided rape survivors with legal assistance to prosecute cases where appropriate, which is a critical factor in restoring some trust in the legal and judicial system.

Key Lessons

HEAL's emphasis on treating the immediate health effects of war gives it the opportunity to engage on these other levels. HEAL's experience highlights the time constraints facing many health workers. Because all HEAL outreach activities directly involve health workers, the organization must balance trade-offs "between emergency and hospital treatment and its other prevention priorities" (p. 156). During periods of overwhelming medical need, outreach programs are often delayed, canceled, or understaffed. To date, engaging on political issues outside traditional medical roles does not appear to have damaged HEAL's legitimacy or trust in the community. Moreover, the interethnic composition of HEAL's staff may have discouraged the perception that HEAL activities are politically motivated.

CONFLICT RESOLUTION PROCESSES AND SKILLS

Health peacebuilding often requires skills not taught in traditional health-care education tracks. There is a wide scope to increase interdisciplinary training, using conflict resolution specialists to help educate and train health actors. In addition, there are opportunities for peacebuilders to gain more expertise in health. Building cross-sectoral teams is an especially promising approach. People with stronger conflict resolution backgrounds can be valuable members of health teams, just as health workers can be valuable members of peacebuilding teams.

Integrating peacebuilding with health activities frequently involves processes and skills such as the following:

Conflict analysis. Conflict-sensitive health activities require political and social mapping of the stakeholders, conflict dynamics, stages and levels of violence, underlying issues, and opportunities for change. Such analyses help health actors assess their position within the conflict, select what role to adopt in relation to other actors, and choose appropriate interventions. While in certain contexts conflict specialists working on a health team may conduct such analyses, health workers themselves may require training to complete these on their own. Conflict analyses are complementary to the health needs assessments routinely administered in humanitarian relief and development activities. Increasingly, health workers in such contexts must be prepared to produce both.

Additionally, large health agencies may use conflict specialists to inform global-level planning. For instance, field delegates for the ICRC conduct conflict analyses as part of the process of generating annual budget projections (Forsythe, 2007). Political analyses are used to predict refugee flows, displaced persons, scope of political detention, and the likelihood of major armed conflict. These analyses are later fed into the community through various channels, constituting an early warning system for many humanitarian crises.

Negotiation, mediation, and facilitation. Health actors in conflict settings frequently have long-term relationships with the conflict parties and firsthand knowledge of the conflict issues. Especially in local- and midlevel conflicts, trusted health actors may find themselves in the role of negotiator, mediator, or facilitator between parties (Anderson, 2006). Health professionals can benefit from additional training in this arena.

Dialogue on conflict issues. Due to their professional role, health workers are often able to initiate public discussions—through the media, community forums, youth groups, and schools, to name just a few—on sensitive conflict topics, such as sexual violence, HIV/AIDS, and psychological trauma otherwise seen as socially taboo. Health workers can provide a level of scientific objectivity on health and conflict issues that allows them significant influence when reaching out to other peacebuilders (including politicians and religious leaders; see Kaufmann and Feldbaum, 2009).

Giving voice to marginalized communities. Because of their access to communities in conflict, broad social legitimacy, and trusted relationships, health workers can serve as key supporters and advocates for marginalized communities. Beyond assessing impacts and raising awareness about a community's plight, health workers may also help communities establish linkages with other entities that can help the community improve its condition.

Advocacy. Often health workers are some of the few present to witness and report on the suffering and trauma of conflict. When these firsthand stories and data on the impacts of a conflict are integrated into broader advocacy efforts, health actors can use this information to influence public opinion and political action. Input from the peacebuilding field is helpful here, as the training of most health workers does not prepare them to engage effectively in advocacy.

Establishing relationships across the divide. Relationships are foundational to conflict resolution and peacebuilding. Establishing relationships is an element of most health activities, and something that the health-care field is often successful in achieving. This includes creating opportunities for health professionals and governmental entities to connect across the conflict divide.

Trust-building. Health activities have been used as trust-building measures. Examples include humanitarian cease-fires for vaccination campaigns, health worker exchanges, and joint trainings for health workers from different sides of the conflict.

Peacebuilding and conflict resolution training. The audiences for these trainings may include health workers and the communities with whom they work. These trainings may be conducted by health workers or by other peacebuilders through integrated health-peace programming. Health issues such as HIV and sexual trauma can provide a unique platform for discussing the impacts of structural and cultural violence and can help orient people to the concepts of positive peace. Health education networks are another venue for training students and professionals on these skills, which forge widespread academic and professional linkages between the fields of peacebuilding and health.

Responding to psychosocial trauma. Addressing psychosocial trauma is a key challenge for postconflict rehabilitation and reconciliation efforts. Mental health professionals can play important roles working with communities to develop appropriate, effective activities to help rebuild societies after the fighting has stopped.

Monitoring and evaluation. The health field brings to its peacebuilding partnerships a robust tradition of measuring impacts of interventions. This is particularly valuable for the notoriously difficult to measure fields of conflict resolution and peacebuilding.

IMPACTING POLICY/SYSTEMATIC CHANGE
Key Policy Debates in the Sector Related to Conflict

Health Politicized

Health actors have expressed concern that linking health aims with peacebuilding activities overtly politicizes the role of health activities, threatening their ability to be effective in conflict settings by undermining trust and legitimacy. Many contest this claim, arguing that health interventions have never been as apolitical as some made them out to be (McInnes and Rushton, 2010). Indeed, almost all activities in a conflict setting have political impacts.

Rather than denying the political dimension of health activities, some health professionals are being explicit about their moral and political goals of helping communities build positive peace and acknowledging the inherently political nature of work in conflict settings. Even though such a position may align with core health commitments, the aim of building peace can directly threaten parties who benefit from the conflict. Health interventions may grow even more politicized through health diplomacy activities that are designed to win hearts and minds. The dilemmas associated with all of these stances enter uncomfortable ethical and policy terrain. The most appropriate way for health actors to frame the political dimensions of their work remains hotly debated.

Health Instrumentalized

The traditional humanitarian principle of independence aims to help humanitarian institutions like the ICRC (1996) "resist any interference, whether political, ideological or economic, capable of diverting them from the course of action laid down by the requirements of humanity, impartiality, and neutrality" (p. 10). While the economic independence of humanitarian actors from donor states has long been a contentious issue, recent movements to overtly instrumentalize health as a form of soft power bring these debates to the fore.

When, if ever, is it appropriate to instrumentalize health? Integrating peacebuilding perspectives into health programming for the purpose of achieving peace, particularly positive peace as envisioned by Galtung, seems to be a political goal aligned with fundamental principles of the health field. The argument is strengthened by the claim that working with communities to help achieve positive peace is at its core an attempt to achieve holistic health. Yet if this is so, the important question arises: Is this the case for other forms of health diplomacy, which may explicitly seek to use health to achieve "ulterior" foreign policy goals? Health diplomacy advocates (including within the military) may explicitly fund or deliver health services in an attempt to win hearts and minds, improve relationships between local communities and occupying forces, bolster a population's perceptions of the legitimacy of their government, or promote reconciliation between antagonistic communities within a state (McInnes and Rushton, 2010.). This overt political instrumentalization of health activities alarms many health actors, yet conceptual confusion remains as to why health peacebuilding is palatable while other forms of health diplomacy are not.

Debates over the proper role for the military in health activities in conflict zones highlight this tension. For example, US Marine Female Engagement Teams deployed in Afghanistan have used the provision of health services as an opportunity to access and build relationships with Afghan women in order to collect intelligence from those women, which men would not provide (Boyd, 2011). This information is then passed along to combat units to act on. Civilian health actors have articulated qualms about such activities, claiming they are antithetical to the health field's core ethics and noting they may destroy trust, the legitimacy of health workers, and perceptions of future health activities. Debates over military involvement in the health sector are likely to remain for the foreseeable future (Gordon, 2011). One example was the use of a disingenuous vaccination program to obtain genetic material from Osama bin

Laden's children in an effort to secure an additional means to identify him. One author claims that this mission both was a failure in its primary aim and that it further jeopardized relations between the US and Pakistan.[12] The impact on future legitimate vaccination campaigns in Pakistan has yet to be seen.

When health programs are designed (or funded) to achieve both health and political aims, there can be disagreement on which takes priority when tensions arise. Most health-peacebuilding ventures tend to place health outcomes first, while for military medicine and other forms of health diplomacy, political aims may take precedence. Actors prioritizing health outcomes over political aims risk losing crucial funding and missing opportunities to leverage their health activities for positive, population-level impacts. Conversely, prioritizing political aims over health outcomes risks losing trust and compromising moral principles central to the health field; and attempting to do both equally can lead to achieving neither (McInnes and Rushton, 2010). Successfully navigating these risks requires significant foresight and critical reflection during implementation.

Is Change Sustainable?

The theoretical argument for why the health field should engage with violence and conflict is strengthening. Many now suggest that there is sufficient evidence to justify the claim that health interventions can impact peace and conflict. The rigorous impact evaluations needed to ground this theory have been slow to materialize. One reason is that the overall number of intentionally designed, systematic health-peacebuilding initiatives undertaken is still quite small. Local health organizations and smaller international actors are engaging in these activities, but these experiences have not produced the types of large-scale impact analyses the field needs.

It is rather surprising that one of the more comprehensive impact evaluations of a health-peacebuilding initiative remains the early WHO/Department for International Development (1999) Health as a Bridge for Peace assessment from Bosnia-Herzegovina in 1999. Even a decade after a sympathetic appeal went out in the prominent *British Medical Journal* for "evidence, not just ideology" (Vass, 2001), a lack of rigorous data endures. The low levels of quantitative data have been cited as one of the reasons for the program's failure to gain a wider audience (Rushton and McInnes, 2006). More recent impact assessments are trickling in,[13] but far more are needed.

As a result, many questions remain unanswered: How much impact can health peacebuilding have? What are the conditions required for success? Are health-peacebuilding efforts best restricted to certain contexts, such as postconflict settings? Answering these questions is crucial because integrating health and peacebuilding programming involves costs: it requires donors to divert resources from other projects, asks health workers to reallocate their time and energy, and potentially endangers trust, access, and the legitimacy of the health field.

Given the inherent difficulty in measuring peacebuilding and conflict impacts, even the proper way to evaluate health-peacebuilding programs remains unresolved. Many health-peacebuilding initiatives define success using both health and conflict outcomes. Since further mainstreaming peacebuilding into health activities requires convincing both those focused on health and those focused on conflict that this is a worthwhile investment, defining success in terms of health and political impacts may be unavoidable. Nonetheless, measuring both sets of impacts does little to help clarify which set of outcomes should take priority, and what level of health or peacebuilding impact constitutes success. This is especially challenging when success in one dimension comes at the expense of the other. How much of one outcome are programs willing to sacrifice for another outcome?

Furthermore, there are tensions concerning the time frame over which success is measured. Assessing the long-term impact of peacebuilding activities can be difficult over the short span of typical donor cycles and focus on short-term projects. The true impact of peacebuilding interventions is perhaps best judged over years and decades, if not generations. Nonetheless, to be relevant to donors, health-peacebuilding efforts must find ways to demonstrate impact within shorter time frames.

Because health peacebuilding will rarely if ever deliver political outcomes, such as negotiated settlements to conflicts, alternative objective measurements must be developed to assess the impact on conflict. Zwi et al. (2006) developed the Health and Peacebuilding Filter to help address this problem (Grove & Zwi, 2008). This filter identifies five core principles of health and peacebuilding (cultural sensitivity, conflict sensitivity, social justice, social cohesion, and good governance), each with sample indicators to consider in the design, monitoring, and evaluation of programs. While alternative impact assessment tools bring their own strengths and weaknesses (see Bush, 2009; Hoffman, 2004), the filter is particularly well tailored for structuring and capturing the impacts of health peacebuilding.

Funding and Evaluating Health-Peacebuilding Activities

Grove and Zwi (2008) note that even among advocates for peacebuilding through health interventions, those responsible for planning and delivering these activities often lack the necessary training, skills, and tools to operationalize such integrated programming. As a result, in practice many donors and agencies implement their peacebuilding programming separately from health programming. The Health-Peacebuilding Filter aims to help overcome this. Nonetheless, difficulties in attaining sufficient technical competence in the fields of both health and conflict resolution, alongside resistance to layering yet another lens into programming, continue to pose challenges for integrated programming.

Case Study 2: Peace Through Health Program in Bosnia-Herzegovina
Case taken from WHO/DFID, 1999.

Launched in 1997 in the aftermath of the Dayton Peace Accords, the WHO/DFID Peace Through Health program in Bosnia-Herzegovina established that health-peacebuilding programs can and should be rigorously evaluated. Operating on the level of health systems and public health issues, the program aimed "to integrate peace building awareness and capacity building for reconciliation into health care systems" (p. 51). This program was designed to impact the six domains of polarization, discrimination, manipulation of information, centralization of power and authority, isolation, and violence (WHO/DFID, 1999). Each of these was seen as a factor negatively affecting the formation of sustainable peace in the region.

Surveys of health professionals conducted as part of the program-impact evaluation suggested that exposure to inter-entity health activities was closely associated with increased comfort working with health professionals from the other side and more willingness or desire to collaborate with health workers from the other entity in the future. The assessment also identified over thirty-five achievements in the realms of political, structural, and social peacebuilding. These included negotiated freedom of movement and reciprocal treatment agreements for emergency medical services, inter-entity workshops for health professionals and students, regular communication between public health directors, and joint public health campaigns. Notably these successes occurred in the context of reluctant health ministers who did not hold reconciliation among their priorities, responsibilities, or interests.

The integrated Peace Through Health programming placed unique demands on field staff. Diversity of field staff was seen as an asset; the report suggested future programs consider enlisting a media professional, nursing specialist, legal/human rights specialist, and various technical health specialists. The program reported success with the combination of one medical professional and one nonmedical professional as co-coordinators of the program. The regular contributions of the DFID conflict resolution specialist were identified as crucial for the program. Additional external training on conflict resolution strategies, negotiation techniques, human rights principles, and working with the media were recommended for future field staff.

Despite being over a decade old, the WHO/DFID assessment remains one of the more comprehensive evaluations of any health-peacebuilding initiative. Yet there is a glaring need for additional evaluations using even more robust methodologies. Anecdotal comments by field teams and cross-sectional surveys alone are not sufficient to establish the types of cause-effect evidence that this health-peacebuilding field needs.

Key Institutions Working on Conflict Issues in This Sector

The central entities working on conflict issues within the health sector are local actors. Local governmental health officials, local health workers, and local communities engage on the front line of conflict and health. It often remains difficult to find case studies and evaluations of such programs in the international, English-language literature, making it a challenge for these experiences to reach a broader audience.

Numerous international health actors actively work on conflict issues. Just two sample organizations include Médecins sans Frontières and the International Committee of the Red Cross, both of whom deliver health services in conflict settings and have significant voices on policy levels. The Physicians for Human Rights movement is an example of a linking entity that engages health professionals for political advocacy on conflict-related topics.

Examples of the many academics and academic institutions contributing to this field include individuals based at McMaster University in Canada who have been at the forefront of the theory and practice of the Peace Through Health paradigm (see Arya and Santa Barbara, 2008; MacQueen, 2008). The University of Tromsø in Norway recently helped launch online training materials on medical peace work (Rowson and Melf, 2008). Researchers at the University of New South Wales in coordination with AusAid produced the Health Peacebuilding Filter tools (Zwi et al., 2006).

An equally broad range of donor governments and militaries are involved with this field. Donor countries such as Sweden, Norway, Canada, and the UK have been active for some years on integrating peacebuilding into the programs they fund. Cuba's longstanding international health engagement highlights the appeal health diplomacy holds for a wide range of actors.

CONCLUSION

As highlighted in the chapter, the domains of health and conflict are inextricably linked. Violence and war stand in opposition to health, while positive peace aligns with it. Health professionals who work in conflict regions have at a minimum a responsibility to ensure they do no harm, a duty that requires knowledge and skills borrowed from the field of peacebuilding. Increasingly practitioners seek additional criteria, through using conflict resolution skills to make health programs more effective, using health programs to build peace, and reframing conflict as a public health problem. Whether through health in the service of peacebuilding or peacebuilding in the service of health, the fields can and are recognizing innovative opportunities for synergy. Not all of these efforts will be wise, effective, or efficient; additional data on the impacts of these ventures will be crucial to guide the field going forward. Further attempts to integrate peacebuilding and health activities will open additional avenues to reduce suffering and improve the well-being of those who are most at risk—common goals shared by both fields.

QUESTIONS FOR FURTHER DISCUSSION

1. Given the limited resources available, is it ethical for health workers to also try to address conflict issues? Does this take away from their primary goal? How should the health field respond to critiques that conflicts are the domain of political actors, and nongovernmental actors are at best marginal contributors to peace?

2. Some criticize as overly simplistic the notion that because violence and armed conflict cause negative health impacts, health workers should seek to prevent them. Do you agree? In what circumstances might this argument not be sound?

3. Is it morally acceptable to instrumentalize health activities? Is it pragmatically wise to do so? How would you respond to concerns that this may undercut the trust and social legitimacy central to allowing health workers to be effective?

4. What is the proper role for the military in health activities in conflict zones?

5. Within medicine there is an ethical expectation that people will not extend outside of their realms of expertise and qualification. What level of expertise is required of health workers before they can ethically engage (or insert themselves *as interveners*) in conflicts?

6. Is it ethically appropriate to take the trust that people bestowed on health workers for their health intervention and use it to gain access for conflict resolution or peacebuilding activities? Does this misuse that trust? What happens if the peacebuilding intervention doesn't turn out well—how does that affect the health workers' relationship with the parties and any future health activities?

REFERENCES

ACQUIRE Project. April 2006. Traumatic gynecologic fistula as a result of sexual violence. *ACQUIRE Technical Update*. New York: Engender Health. Retrieved December 15, 2011, from http://pdf.usaid.gov/pdf_docs/PNADF980.pdf.

Anderson, E. W. 2006. Approaches to conflict resolution. In A. D. Redmond, P. F. Mahoney, J. M. Ryan, and C. Macnam, eds. *ABC of conflict and disaster* (pp. 31–33). Malden, MA: Blackwell Publishing Ltd.

Anderson, M. B. 1999. *Do no harm: How aid can support peace—Or war.* Boulder, CO: Lynne Rienner.

Arya, N., and J. Santa Barbara, eds. 2008. *Peace through health.* Sterling, VA: Kumarian Press.

Barsalou, J. 2001. *Special report 79: Training to help traumatized populations.* Washington, DC: US Institute for Peace. Retrieved December 20, 2011, from www.usip.org/publications/training-help-traumatized-populations.

Blumenthal, S., and S. Safdi. 2008, August. Peace through health: A mapping of cooperative programs in Palestine and Israel. A report of the Palestinian/Israeli health initiative. Center for the Study of the Presidency. Retrieved December 20, 2011, from http://pdf.usaid.gov/pdf_docs/PNADO476.pdf.

Bond Conflict Policy Group. 2010. Are we working "in, on, or around" conflict and insecurity? Retrieved December 23, 2011, from www.bond.org.uk/data/files/CPG_session_write_up.pdf.

Boyd, E. B. 2011, June 1. Women to women: In Afghanistan, Zoe Bedell '07 led female Marines in a new role. *Princeton Alumni Weekly.* Retrieved November 8, 2012, from http://paw.princeton.edu/issues/2011/06/01/pages/5436/index.xml.

Buhmann, C., J. Santa Barbara, N. Arya, and K. Melf. 2010. The roles of the health sector and health workers before, during, and after violent conflict. *Medicine, Conflict, and Survival* 26, no. 1: 4–23.

Bush, K. 2009. *Aid for peace: A handbook for applying peace and conflict impact assessment.* Londonderry, UK: International Conflict Research. Retrieved August 13, 2012, from www.incore.ulst.ac.uk/pdfs/Handbook-Aid_for_Peace-2009_Dec.pdf.

De Quadros, C.A., and D. Epstein. 2002, December. Health as a bridge for peace: PAHO's experience. *Lancet* 360: 25–26.

D'Errico, N., C. Wake, and R. Wake. 2010. Healing Africa? Reflections on the peacebuilding role of a health-based nongovernmental organization operating in eastern Democratic Republic of Congo. *Medicine, Conflict, and Survival* 26, no. 2: 145–159.

Diamond, L., and J. McDonald. 1993. *Multi-track diplomacy: A systems approach to peace.* Washington, DC: Institute for Multi-Track Diplomacy.

Faal, H., A. Sillah, and M. Bah. 2006. The Health for Peace initiative in West Africa. *Community Eye Health Journal* 19, no. 58: 24–26.

Feldbaum, H., K. Lee, and J. Michaud. 2010. Global health and foreign policy. *Epidemiologic Reviews* 32: 82–92.

Feldbaum, H., and J. Michaud. 2010. Health diplomacy and the enduring relevance of foreign policy interests. *PLoS Medicine* 7, no. 4: e1000226.

Fidler, D. P. 2005. Health as foreign policy: Between principle and power. *Whitehead Journal of Diplomacy and International Relations* 6, no. 2: 179–194.

Forsythe, D. P. 2007. The ICRC: A unique humanitarian protagonist. *International Review of the Red Cross* 89, no. 865: 63–96.

Galtung, J. 1990. Cultural violence. *Journal of Peace Research* 27, no. 3: 291–305.

Garfield, R. 2008. The epidemiology of war. In B. S. Levy and V. W. Sidel, eds. *War and public health* (pp. 23–36). New York: Oxford University Press.

Gordon, S. 2011. Health, stabilization, and securitization: Towards understanding the drivers of the military role in health interventions. *Medicine, Conflict, and Survival* 27, no. 1: 43–66.

Grove, N., and A. Zwi. 2008. Beyond the log frame: A new tool for examining health and peacebuilding initiatives. *Development in Practice* 18, no. 1: 66–81.

Hoffman, M. 2004. *Peace and Conflict Impact Assessment Methodology.* Berghoff Center for Constructive Conflict Management. Retrieved October 15, 2011, from www.berghof -handbook.net/documents/publications/hoffman_handbook.pdf.

International Committee of the Red Cross (ICRC). 1996. The fundamental principles of the Red Cross and Red Crescent. ICRC publication 1996, ref. 0513. Retrieved October 15, 2011, from www.icrc.org/eng/assets/files/other/icrc_002_0513.pdf.

James, S. (director), and A. Kotlowitz (producer). 2011. *The interrupters.* Kartemquin Films.

Kanter, E. 2008. The impact of war on mental health. In B. S. Levy and V. W. Sidel, eds. *War and public health* (pp. 51–68). New York: Oxford University Press.

Katz, R., S. Kornblet, A. Pace, E. Lief, and J. E. Fischer. 2011. Defining health diplomacy: Changing demands in the era of globalization. *Milbank Quarterly* 89, no. 3: 503–523.

Kaufmann, J. R., and H. Feldbaum. 2009. Diplomacy and the polio immunization boycott in northern Nigeria. *Health Affairs* 28, no. 4: 1091–1101.

Kickbusch, I., and P. Buss. 2011. Global health diplomacy and peace. *Infectious Disease Clinics of North America* 25: 601–610.

Labonté, R., and M. Gagnon. 2010. Framing health and foreign policy: Lessons for global health diplomacy. *Globalization and Health* 6, no. 14: 1–19.

Leaning, J. 2008. The brutality of war. In B. S. Levy and V. W. Sidel, eds. *War and public health* (pp. 6–9). New York: Oxford University Press.

Lederach, J. P. 1997. *Building peace: Sustainable reconciliation in divided societies.* Washington, DC: US Institute for Peace.

Levy, B. S., and V. W. Sidel. 2008. War and public health: An overview. In B. S. Levy and V. W. Sidel, eds. *War and public health* (pp. 3–20). New York: Oxford University Press.

MacQueen, G. 2008. Setting the role of the health sector in context: Multi-track peace-work. In N. Arya and J. Santa Barbara, eds. *Peace through health* (pp. 21–25).

MacQueen, G., and J. Santa Barbara. 2008. Mechanisms of peace through health. In N. Arya and J. Santa Barbara, eds. *Peace through health* (pp. 27–45).

MacQueen, G., R. McCutcheon, and J. Santa Barbara. 1997. The use of health initiatives as peace initiatives. *Peace and Change*, 22, no. 2: 175–197.

Manela, E. 2010. A pox on your narrative: Writing disease control into cold war history. *Diplomatic History*, 34, no. 2: 299–323.

McInnes, C., and K. Lee. 2006. Health, security and foreign policy. *Review of International Studies* 32: 5–23.

McInnes, C., and S. Rushton. 2010. Medical initiatives in conflict and peacebuilding. *Study commissioned by the Global Health and Foreign Policy Initiative at Johns Hopkins University*. Retrieved March 15, 2012, from http://cadair.aber.ac.uk/dspace/handle/2160/4644.

Pearrow, M., and L. Cosgrove. 2009. The aftermath of combat-related PTSD: Toward an understanding of transgenerational trauma. *Communication Disorders Quarterly*, 30, no. 2: 77–82.

Ramsbotham, O., T. Woodhouse, and H. Miall. 2005. *Contemporary Conflict Resolution* (2nd ed.). Malden, MA: Polity.

Rodriguez-Garcia, R., M. Schlesser, and R. Bernstein. 2001. How can health serve as a bridge for peace? *CERTI Crisis and Transition Tool Kit*. Washington, DC: George Washington University Center for International Health. Retrieved September 15, 2011, from www.certi.org/publications/policy/gwc-12a-brief.PDF.

Rowson, M., and K. Melf. eds. 2008. *The Medical peace work textbook*. University of Tromsø, Centre for International Health. Retrieved March 15, 2012, from www.medical peacework.org.

Rushton, S. 2005. Health and peacebuilding: Rescuscitating the failed state in Sierra Leone. *International Relations* 19, no. 4: 441–456.

Rushton, S., and C. McInnes. 2006. The UK, health and peace-building: the mysterious disappearance of health as a bridge for peace. *Medicine, Conflict and Survival* 22, no. 2: 94–109.

Santa Barbara, J., and N. Arya. 2008. Introduction. In N. Arya and J. Santa Barbara, eds. *Peace through health* (pp. 3–13). Sterling, VA: Kumarian Press.

Shah, S. 2011, July 11. CIA organised fake vaccination drive to get Osama bin Laden's family DNA. *Guardian*, p. 1.

Steel, Z., T. Chey, D. Silove, C. Marnane, R. Bryant, and M. van Ommeren. 2009. Association of torture and other potentially traumatic events with mental health outcomes among populations exposed to mass conflict and displacement. *Journal of the American Medical Association* 302, no. 5: 537–549.

Thompson, T. 2005, October 24. The cure for tyranny. *Boston Globe*, p. A15.

Ui, S., K. Leng, and A. Aoyama. 2007. Building peace through participatory health training: A case from Cambodia. *Global Public Health* 2, no. 3: 281–293.

Ursano, R., M. Goldenberg, L. Zhang, J. Carlton, C. Fullerton, H. Li, L. Johnson, and D. Benedek. 2010. Posttraumatic stress disorder and traumatic stress: From bench to bedside, from war to disaster. *Annals of the New York Academy of Sciences* 1208: 72–81.

Various Palestinian NGOs. 2005. An open letter to the Palestinian and international community regarding Palestinian–Israel cooperation in health. Retrieved October 15, 2011, from http://cosmos.ucc.ie/cs1064/jabowen/IPSC/articles/article0020634.txt.

Vass, A. 2001. Peace through health: This new movement needs evidence, not just ideology. *British Medical Journal* 323: 1020.

Woodside, D., J. Santa Barbara, and D. G. Benner. 1999. Psychological trauma and social healing in Croatia. *Medicine, Conflict, and Survival* 15, no. 4: 355–367.

World Health Organization (WHO). 1946. *Constitution of the World Health Organization.* Geneva, Switzerland: Author. Retrieved October 15, 2011, from http://apps.who .int/gb/bd/PDF/bd47/EN/constitution-en.pdf.

———. 1986. *The Ottawa Charter for health promotion.* Geneva: Author. Retrieved October 15, 2011, from www.who.int/hpr/NPH/docs/ottawa_charter_hp.pdf.

———. 2002. *Report on the Second World Health Organization Consultation on Health as a Bridge for Peace.* Geneva: Author. Retrieved October 15, 2011, from www.who.int/hac /techguidance/hbp/Versoix_consultation_report.pdf.

World Health Organization/Department for International Development (WHO/DFID). 1999. *WHO/DFID Peace Through Health Programme: A case study.* Copenhagen: Author. Retrieved October 15, 2011, from www.euro.who.int/__data/assets/pdf _file/0008/119375/E67081.pdf.

Zelizer, C. 2008, December. Trauma-sensitive peace-building: Lessons for theory and practice. *Africa Peace and Conflict Journal* 1, no. 1: 81–94.

Zwank, D. 2008. *On the road to empowerment? Heal Africa; research paper for Gueris mon people.* Maniema, DRC: Heal Africa. Retrieved October 12, 2011, from www.healafrica.org /pdf/road-to-empowerment.pdf.

Zwi, A. B., A. Bunde-Birouste, M. Eisenbruch, N. Grove, M. Humphrey, D. Silove, and E. Waller. 2004. *Considerations for policy: Peace conflict and development I: Investing in health and peace-building* and *Background paper I: Health and peace-building: Securing the future.* Sydney: School of Public Health and Community Medicine, University of New South Wales. Retrieved October 12, 2011, from www.sphcm.med.unsw.edu.au /SPHCMWeb.nsf/page/AUSCAN.

Zwi, A. B., A. Bunde-Birouste, N. J. Grove, E. Waller, and J. Ritchie. 2006. *The Health and Peacebuilding Filter* and *The Health and Peacebuilding Filter: Companion Manual.* Sydney: School of Public Health and Community Medicine, University of New South Wales. Retrieved October 12, 2011, from www.sphcm.med.unsw.edu.au/SPHCMWeb.nsf/page /AUSCAN.

NOTES

1. Though not the focus here, conflict resolution within health-care workplaces is itself a robust field with many integration opportunities for conflict specialists. Addressing workplace conflict may improve the effectiveness and efficiency of almost all health programming.

2. Some analyses include peace through health as a form of health diplomacy; see McInnes and Rushton (2010).

3. For further reading on health diplomacy, see Katz, Kornblet, Arnold, Lief, and Fischer (2011); Kickbusch and Buss (2011); Feldbaum, Lee, and Michaud (2010); Feldbaum and Michaud (2010); Labonté and Gagnon (2010); McInnes and Lee (2006).

4. PTSD is an anxiety disorder defined by symptoms of intrusive reexperiencing of the traumatic event, avoidance, and hyperarousal. Symptoms can be severe and disabling. See Ursano et al. (2010); Kanter (2008).

5. See Kaufmann and Feldbaum (2009) for a case study on diplomacy for polio eradication in northern Nigeria.

6. For further discussion, see Bond Conflict Policy Group (2010).

7. Rushton and MacInnes (2006) attribute the WHO's apparent shift of focus away from its Health as a Bridge for Peace program to personnel changes, lack of persuasive evidence, and changing organizational priorities.

8. For additional cases, see Rodriguez-Garcia, Schlesser, and Bernstein (2001); Rushton (2005); WHO case studies at www.who.int/hac/techguidance/hbp/Versoix_consultation _report.pdf.

9. For more on CeaseFire's work, see http://ceasefirechicago.org. See also the 2011 film *The Interrupters*.

10. For additional roles, see Buhmann, Santa Barbara, Arya, and Melf (2010).

11. For more on conflict stages, see Ramsbotham, Woodhouse, and Miall (2005, p. 12).

12. www.guardian.co.uk/world/2011/jul/11/cia-fake-vaccinations-osama-bin-ladens-dna.

13. Blumenthal and Safdi (2008); Faal, Sillah, and Bah (2006); Rushton (2005); Woodside, Santa Barbara, and Benner (1999).

chapter twelve

THE RULE OF LAW
AND PEACEBUILDING

Brian A. Kritz

The rule of law is key to coordinating peace operations, or peace-building activities in particular, in post-conflict regions. Its application describes a situation in which people respect the fundamental rights of others, offering greater stability to the society as a whole.

—HIDEAKI SHINODA (2001, P. 2)

THE RULE OF LAW (ROL) IS OFTEN CITED by governments, international organizations, the donor community, and civil society actors as a necessary component in a well-ordered and fully functioning society. While the relationship between the existence of ROL and peaceful society is well understood, the term itself lacks definitional specificity. The lack of consensus as to the exact meaning and proper indicators of ROL has engendered an atmosphere of confusion where it is unclear where ROL work begins and ends, and how it intersects with human rights, peacebuilding, and related fields. The goal of this chapter is to discuss the core issues related to the ROL sector, discuss relevant ROL theories, and explore the integration of peacebuilding into ROL. In furtherance of these goals, this chapter will explore the wide variety of ROL work being done in the field, the key institutions doing such work, and what skills future practitioners will need to succeed in the ROL field. This chapter will conclude with two brief ROL case studies, a profile of an exceptional ROL practitioner, and review of key questions that address cutting-edge concepts that are germane to the field.

A PROBLEM OF CREATION

In most legal regimes, there is a founding document that focuses the subsequent energies of practitioners and scholars. For example, in US jurisprudence, the founding document and the root source for guidance is the US Constitution. Similarly, genocide scholars or practitioners in the fight against human rights abuses rely upon the foundational framework of the Convention on the Prevention and Punishment of the Crime of Genocide (1948). Further examples include the Geneva Conventions (1949), which attempt to define the laws of war, the prohibition against torture codified in the UN Convention Against Torture (1984), and the rights of women detailed in the Convention on the Elimination of All Forms of Discrimination Against Women (1979). As recently as 2008, the codification of new guidance regarding the rights of the disabled was established in the Convention on the Rights of Persons with Disabilities. The field of ROL, however, does not enjoy such a founding document. Thus, there is no generally agreed-upon definition of the meaning of the term "ROL." In the absence of a foundational document to specify the established norms of ROL, international actors, members of civil society, and states have attempted, with considerable diligence, to capture the essence of the definition individually. Some of the more high-profile attempts are set forth below.

THE 2004 REPORT OF THE SECRETARY OF THE UNITED NATIONS

"For the United Nations, the rule of law refers to a principle of governance in which all persons, institutions and entities, public and private, including the State itself, are accountable to laws that are publicly promulgated, equally enforced and independently adjudicated, and which are consistent with international human rights norms and standards. It also requires measures to ensure adherence to the principles of supremacy of law, equality before the law, accountability to the law, fairness in the application of the law, separation of powers, participation in decision-making, legal certainty, avoidance of arbitrariness and procedural and legal transparency" (United Nations, 2004, para. 3).[1]

DECLARATION OF DEMOCRATIC VALUES AS AGREED TO BY HEADS OF GOVERNMENT OF THE SEVEN MAJOR INDUSTRIAL DEMOCRACIES IN 1984

"We believe in a rule of law which respects and protects without fear or favor the rights and liberties of every citizen and provides the setting in which the human spirit can develop in freedom and diversity" (Lancaster House, 1984, line 3).

THE WORLD JUSTICE PROJECT'S RULE OF LAW INDEX

The rule of law refers to a rules-based system in which the following four universal principles are upheld:

- The government and its officials and agents are accountable under the law.
- The laws are clear, publicized, stable, and fair, and protect fundamental rights, including the security of persons and property.
- The process by which the laws are enacted, administered, and enforced is accessible, fair, and efficient.
- Access to justice is provided by competent, independent and ethical adjudicators, attorneys or representatives, and judicial officers who are of sufficient number, have adequate resources, and reflect the makeup of the communities they serve. (Agrast, Botero, and Ponce, 2011, p. 2)

The Rise of Modern Rule of Law Practice

The notion of promotion and protection of ROL as an international issue has blossomed since the end of the Cold War. During the period, developing countries could rely upon the monetary support of the competing superpowers in an effort to secure their loyalty and support in the battle of ideologies and thus influence how they structured their legal systems. With the fall of the Soviet Union, such overwhelming support diminished, leaving developing countries to deal with the realities of modern governance without such vast support, and donor countries to discover a new way to continue to promote democracy abroad. One such method by which developing countries and donor countries continued their symbiotic relationship was through the auspices of ROL. The realization that conflict or postconflict countries "are frequently unable to respond to the basic protection needs of vulnerable communities and individuals, and crime is perpetrated with impunity" and that "the gaps in the rule of law sector are vast, and encompass a number of areas, from law enforcement, corrections and the judiciary, . . . as well as highly disputed issues such as compensation, land tenure, and many others," placed an emphasis on ROL as a vital issue of good governance, global security, diplomacy, and international development (UNDP, 2010, p.10). The hope is that the creation or reestablishment of stable national institutions will eventually provide security, foster development, and protect human rights worldwide (UNDP, 2010).

The Rule of Law as a Western Liberal Democratic Imposition

A misperception that confronts the ROL field practitioner in a transitioning or postconflict society is the accusation that the requirements of ROL require imposing Western values on the practices of the global South. This could not be further from the truth, as ROL, at its core, is simply an ideal of fairness present at most moments in human history. The imposition of allegedly Western values comes to the fore only when the necessary inclusion of democracy enters the ROL picture. This challenge will be discussed in the upcoming pages, but it is worth noting at this point.

A considerable amount of academic source material is available on the existence of ROL throughout the rich tapestry of human history.[2] The combined wisdom of such academic sources on the existence of ROL in non-Western societies, both historical and present-day, is well captured in the following selection from the Guide to Rule of Law Country Analysis: The Rule of Law Strategic Framework issued by the US Agency for International Development (USAID, 2010):

The rule of law is not Western, European or American. It is available to all societies. States differ in terms of laws and the treaties they have signed with respect to human rights. Legal cultures differ depending upon history, with many countries basing their legal system on the civil law tradition and others (including the U.S.) on the common law tradition, while many countries include elements of both traditions and may incorporate significant traditional, religious, or customary components. In many countries, religious law provides the foundation for family and other laws. Societies differ in terms of the values they ascribe to law versus other means of social organization, such as personal or family loyalty. Respect for specific laws and other norms varies depending upon cultures and circumstances. The principle of rule of law, however, transcends all these differences. (p. 6)

THREE THEORIES OF RULE OF LAW

As highlighted earlier, the lack of an international convention on the rule of law, as well as difficulty in defining the field, has posed a great challenge for the ROL practitioner. In the absence of such definitive sources of law, one can look to the ongoing debate among legal scholars as to the meaning of ROL. Professor William Whitford (2000), in his law review article "The Rule of Law," effectively lays out the legal philosophical debate regarding the scope of ROL, which will be set forth in short form below.

Formalism

The formalist theory of ROL mandates simply "the accountability of transparent government decisions . . . to predetermined standards applied by an independent body, probably a court, through a procedure that can be practically utilized by the aggrieved" (Whitford, 2000, p. 726). In other words, the formalist theory requires that the law be applied to everyone equally, that it is clearly set forth in advance and is available to the public, that it applies clear and fair procedure, and that it is adjudicated by a fair and impartial arbiter. Except in the requirement of procedural fairness, nowhere in the formalist conception of ROL is the specific substance of law considered; according to the formalist theory, ROL exists if the law is fair in process and procedure.

Example: In Sudan, Article 62 of the Evidence Law of 1994 provides the evidentiary requirements that at least four competent men must witness a rape to sustain such a criminal charge, as per the nation's interpretation of Islamic jurisprudence.[3] This national law is clearly set forth, available to the public, and sets a clear evidentiary standard for when a rape case can be properly proved and when it cannot. Assuming that the Sudanese judiciary, in toto, can act as impartial arbiter of such case and properly applies the evidentiary standard of Article 62, the formalist would find Article 62 to be consistent with ROL standards, despite the seemingly horrific and unjust imposition of such an evidentiary standard on the rights of victims of rape in Sudan.

Such an example, while arguably extreme, does inform the realities of ROL work, where punishments such as the death penalty for drug cases in Malaysia, public caning in Singapore for graffiti, and custodial sentences for defaming the royal family in Thailand are criticized as substantively unfair.[4] To these cries of substantive unfairness, the formalist would shrug and declare that if the hallmarks of procedural fairness are present, ROL is satisfied.

Substantivism

The substantivist theory of ROL jurisprudence rejects the seemingly cruel and heartless nature of the formalist. The substantivist philosophy contends that human beings represent certain ideals and that these ideals must be protected by, and incorporated into, the concept of ROL, lest we lose our humanity. To the substantivist, ROL cannot simply represent procedural fairness and equality; it must protect such rights deemed fundamental to our essence as human beings (Whitford, 2000). According to academic legal discourse, the substantivist's challenge is to decide which rights are to be protected by ROL as fundamental to all traditions, and which rights are considered secondary or not universal and therefore left out of the protective sphere of ROL prescription. The list of protections deemed fundamental to all societies, cultures, and legal traditions may be few and subject to great debate between states.

Example: One right that may be considered so fundamental as to gain universal acceptance to support the substantivist cause is the right to be free of genocide. Given that 140 states have acceded or ratified the Convention on the Prevention and Punishment of the Crime of Genocide, the prohibition of genocide has almost inarguably entered the realm of binding customary international law and may be the strongest example of a binding preemptory norm of international law (*jus cogens*). As such, the crime of genocide has been successfully prosecuted in the ad hoc tribunals for Rwanda and the former Yugoslavia, and has been codified in Article 6 of the Rome Statute of the International Criminal Court. Since an act of genocide receives practically universal condemnation and acceptance as an international and domestic crime, its place in the substantivist pantheon of universality seems secure. This is not to say that the exact definition of what constitutes genocide is free from debate, but the prohibition of genocide as a prohibited criminal act, whatever it may entail, may enjoy full substantivist acceptance.

The challenge for substantivist ROL theory is that the small groups of fundamental rights arguably protected by ROL tend to lean significantly toward the ideals of modern liberal democracy. While many of the major donors in the field certainly have the promotion of democracy high on their ROL agendas, the hallmarks of liberal democracy included in ROL programming can be deemed a meddlesome interference to state sovereignty, can be seen as an infringement upon traditional roles for women and children in society, and can offend national governments that do not wish for an expansion of democratic ideals, especially when promoted by international or foreign actors.

Example: One right that may not enjoy substantivist protection is the issue of child labor under the Convention on the Rights of the Child (United Nations OHCHR, 1989). Article 32 of this convention provides for the setting of a minimum age for employment and appropriate regulation of the hours of such work. In the US, such age, time, and place restrictions on underage labor have been in place for decades without significant domestic debate. Thus, it might be safe to assume that such protection is a universal idea that would fit within substantivist protection. However, this is simply not the case. In many developing countries, arduous manual labor conducted by children historically was, and is, the only solution to the specter of looming, or present, poverty. Specifically, the issues of the need for juvenile labor in mining facilities in the Democratic Republic of the Congo or in cocoa production in Côte d'Ivoire come to mind. In such countries, the argued societal need for child labor would negate the universality of the ban on arduous child labor. Thus, the role of children in different societies differs considerably, and it would be hard to argue that there exists a shared standard necessary for substantivist protection.

Functionalism

While the majority of the legal theoretical debate over the definition of ROL concerns the dual concepts of formalism and substantivism, there is a third school of thought. Functionalism expresses the presence of ROL as a converse expression of the presence of discretion in the legal system (Whitford, 2000). The lack of individual discretion by legal actors to deviate from standard outcomes on individual cases (in a system that enjoys the procedural fairness required in formalism) provides ROL because it allows for consistency. With the total lack of discretion on the part of legal actors to deviate from the norms set forth in law, full consistency of outcomes is present, and ROL is enjoyed. Conversely, in a system where an individual, whether a prosecutor, judge, or magistrate, has the professional discretion to deviate from the established norm, ROL suffers. Thus, as individual discretion rises, ROL goes down, and as discretion abates, ROL goes up. To the functionalist, an inherently fair system that enjoys the ROL is one that treats all like cases equally without the possibility of exemption based upon increased status or power. The critic of functionalism would claim that discretion, or the legal power to fix individual instances of unfairness within a legal regime, is vital to avoid fundamental miscarriages of justice, and a discretion-free system would lack the flexibility needed to provide justice.

Example: In 1998, the voters of California passed Megan's Law, requiring lifetime registration with local law enforcement by individuals convicted of enumerated sex offenses, including indecent exposure. Such registration requirements are applied retroactively, meaning that someone convicted of an enumerated sex crime prior to the 1998 establishment of Megan's Law is equally required to register. Thus, someone who pled guilty to indecent exposure for the arguably benign act of "mooning" or "streaking" in the 1970s in California is subject to the lifetime sexual offender registration requirements. In California, individual judges have little ability to use judicial discretion to eliminate the requirement of such registration for "streakers" or "mooners."[5] A functionalist might hail this significant lack of judicial discretion as an indication of the presence of ROL, in that all "mooners" or "streakers" in the state were, are, and will be treated equally under the law, while others might decry the lack of nuance and equity that treats such arguably benign offenders in a fashion more aptly applied to more serious sexual offenses.

THE LINK BETWEEN ROL AND PEACEBUILDING

In the introduction to the UNDP 2010 Annual Report on the Global Programme on Strengthening the Rule of Law in Conflict and Post-Conflict Situations, Jordan Ryan, assistant administrator and director of the Bureau for Crisis Prevention and Recovery, properly captured the known link between ROL and peacebuilding:

The poorest countries in the world are overwhelmingly those also most affected by conflict and vulnerable to natural disasters. Millions experience conflict and its effects—undermining basic security and access to justice. . . . The legacies of both conflict and disaster—including injustice, poverty and insecurity—are frequently among the root causes of renewed cycles of violence and instability. . . . During a crisis, national capacities must be empowered to tackle impunity and respond to immediate justice and security needs. In the aftermath of conflict, unobstructed access to functional justice and security institutions is crucial for rebuilding shattered societies and preventing relapse into violence. (UNDP, 2010, p. 4)

The structural link between the lack of ROL, poverty, and violent societal conflict is well established, outside of the above quote. When the needs of society are met by fair, impartial, and equitable legal systems, individuals and groups are less likely to resort to self-help and violence to achieve their personal and collective security and well-being (Kautz, 1999). When a legal system, whether formal or informal, can and does deliver timely, fair, and effective justice, such trust in the system gives individuals incentive to not engage in vigilantism or "street justice," or seek protection of organized criminal enterprises to meet those needs, furthering societal peace and stability. Thus, ROL work is inextricably linked to peacebuilding and should be considered a significant piece of the practitioner's toolbox. The upcoming pages will provide an exploration of the major areas of ROL in programming and practice, and will clarify the need for greater links between ROL work and the peacebuilding field.

TYPES OF ROL PROGRAMMING

Since the world of ROL is quite vast, a full discussion of all the different types of ROL programming is too difficult to capture in a single chapter. As a primer to the main types of ROL programming, however, one might look to the writings of Thomas Carothers, vice president for studies at the Carnegie Endowment for International Peace. In his book *Aiding Democracy Abroad,* Carothers (1999) sets forth five main targets of ROL programming: constitutions, judiciaries, legislatures, local governments, and civil–military relations. In a practical sense, the addition to the above of two targets, traditional and customary law, and land tenure, may be beneficial. Before this chapter discusses the above categories, a brief discussion of general lessons across the categories is warranted.

A number of cross-cutting challenges face a practitioner in any area of ROL programming. Some of the foremost include issues of institutional capacity, domestic/international control of ROL work, cultural competence, domestic will for change, and security for local partners.

Institutional Capacity

While not all ROL work is done in conflict or postconflict countries, a significant majority is. This being the case, the issue of institutional capacity is particularly problematic. Often, in a conflict or postconflict setting there exists a severe lack of well-trained and qualified lawyers, judges, security sector personnel, and other domestic ROL practitioners. Such individuals might have fled the country to avoid societal conflict, been forced into exile, or been killed en masse. It is often written that immediately after the 1994 genocide in Rwanda, a mere dozen lawyers were left alive in the entire country. As another example, "judges from many of the provinces of Afghanistan in 2003 had received less than a high school education" (Center for Law and Military Operations, 2009, p. 90). The issue of capacity and competence often arises in ROL work, especially during or in the immediate aftermath of conflict.

Cultural Competence

Early in the war against the Taliban, the US Air Force provided training to members of the service being deployed to Afghanistan. In the session, the trainees were shown a picture intended to show the average Afghan woman in traditional garb. Surprisingly, instead of a picture of an Afghan woman in a burka, they saw a slide of an Indian woman wearing a brightly colored sari and were told that this was a representative example of an Afghan woman. Such an error, while quickly corrected in subsequent training sessions, demonstrates the issue of cultural competence attendant to ROL practice. Vital to good ROL practice is a deep understanding of the local culture, its norms and traditions, and legal and nonlegal practices alike. The role of women and children, religion and faith, gender roles and sexual identity, and land and its importance in society are only a few of the many areas of importance that are vital to understanding one's role as an ROL practitioner in the country.

Domestic/International Power Struggle

ROL work is a major influence in the formation or re-creation of a legal/governance system in a postconflict country. Constitution writing, legal drafting, administrative organization, and other areas of ROL and governance work determine many important societal dynamics, such as political sway, influence and control, and the balance of power. The role of a nondomestic ROL practitioner, depending on the nature of the intervention, is often limited to peripheral status as an outside adviser unable to completely influence the form or substance of a newly written constitution, domestic code, or court system. Any domestic system will desire to keep these vitally important decisions of form and substance within the country and will be unwilling to cede such vital issues to foreign actors. Thus, the non-insider ROL practitioner should be aware of such concerns and restrictions, and be willing and able to work with them in mind.

Domestic Will and Buy-In

When a donor country is soliciting proposals for an ROL project in a country, members of their government will undoubtedly express willingness and desire to engage in the suggested ROL reform. Unfortunately, this may be simply an act of good business sense on the part of the host country. Such a project often entails significant capital influx and the granting of badly needed technological infrastructure, and provides a number of well-paying jobs for local elites. The question facing the ROL practitioner is whether the same host-country officials who welcome the foreign arrival in the country are truly dedicated to actual ROL reform or are simply giving lip service while taking advantage of the influx of ROL capital for their own gains.

Protecting the Security of Local Partners

With few exceptions, political and legal space for ROL advocates is normally not a concern in the US and other ROL donor countries. An ROL or human rights activist in such countries does not normally have to fear for his or her safety, or that of loved ones. Unfortunately, this sense of security does not translate to many of the countries that face ROL deficits. Intimidation, threats of violence, the threat of exile, and even extrajudicial killings of those working for greater adherence to the ROL are not uncommon in many countries. All domestic partners working alongside the international ROL practitioner must be properly protected. Many situations fall under the aegis of physical protection, for example, activists working on LGBT (lesbian, gay, bisexual, and transgender) rights in Uganda who have been intimidated, threatened, and even killed for engaging in their work. Additional security challenges include cyber security of the computer systems and data of ROL practitioners. As a recent example, the Egyptian offices of a number of NGOs working on ROL issues were raided by Egyptian government forces, and private documents and other sources of information were confiscated. These and other security challenges are part and parcel of ROL work and will undoubtedly become an issue while engaging in ROL programs in conflict and postconflict countries.

Targets of ROL Programming

As mentioned earlier, Thomas Carothers identifies five main targets of ROL work, discussed below. In addition, the issues of traditional and customary law, and the issue of land and land tenure, are added as key components of ROL work; a brief discussion of these seven areas are included below.

Constitutions

According to Carothers (1999), ROL work in the area of constitutional reform is fairly unfruitful. Significant ROL resources have been spent on all aspects of constitutional reform with little quantitative success, since most nations are not willing to cede the shaping of a constitution, a foundational legal document, to outsiders (even those with significant experience in constitution making). Certainly nondomestic ROL practitioners can lend a certain amount of technical support to constitutional drafting efforts, but the choices of final content and attendant form of the constitutional government will remain in the domain of domestic authorities. When engaging in constitutional reform work, outside parties need to know the history of the state in question and ensure that the advisory role is appropriate for the task at hand. After all, writing or rewriting a constitution is a seminal moment for any nation, and ownership of such an event will, and probably should, always remain local.

As an example of the potential perils of assisting in constitutional review, Carothers (1999) raises the case of Zambia circa 1991. Zambian President Frederick

Chiluba engaged in a campaign of constitutional review and established a powerful Constitutional Review Commission, with the significant monetary support and guidance of USAID and other international donors. The commission proposed an amended constitution that would secure an increased adherence to participation and other areas of ROL. With elections approaching in 1996, however, the president imposed a constitutional provision that disqualified his main political rival, Kenneth Kaunda, from running for president, and also withdrew the power of the commission and transferred it the National Assembly, which he controlled. USAID and the other international donors protested these changes, but President Chiluba prevailed, and "all the pressure, negotiations, and money the donors put in the constitutional review process came to little" (p. 163).

Judiciaries

One of the main working areas in ROL is support for and training of an independent judiciary willing and able to rule against the interests of benign or corrupt government entities and fight for equality before the law. Difficult but valuable endeavors for the ROL practitioner involve work in areas of judicial independence, due process, judicial capacity-building, judicial effectiveness, judicial consistency, and respect for human rights. As discussed earlier, often judicial capacity is very weak, particularly considering the challenges many conflict-affected countries face. The examples of post-1994 Rwanda and Afghanistan in 2003 were previously discussed, but the example of East Timor is equally important. "In East Timor, due to the legal vacuum created by the departing Indonesian Regime, almost all qualified personnel had left the country, including all experienced judges. . . . A decision was made to appoint East Timorese nationals who had law degrees but no prior professional experience as judges" (Center for Law and Military Operations, 2009, p. 89). Similar issues of judicial appointment occurred during the breakup of the former Republic of Yugoslavia and in Iraq after the fall of Saddam Hussein's government.

In addition to the issue of the partial or total destruction of a country's judicial and legal capacity, there remains a significant challenge to working with a competent and seemingly functional judiciary. Changing the law and attitudes about the law encompasses holistic societal change and cannot be done solely by working with the judiciary. Similarly, the judicial bench is not always an engine for change or reform in a country. Most judges, especially those most able to effect reform, are beneficiaries of the system as currently constituted and normally do not support judicial reforms that may minimize their power or influence. Often societal skepticism over the placement of even a modicum of trust in a previously untrustworthy judiciary similarly hinders such reform. The key factor in working with judiciaries is properly identifying judicial agents for change, and avoiding working with judicial officers who will preach reform on the surface but will work behind the scenes to maintain the status quo.

Legislative Assistance

As evidenced by the often gridlocked US political process, it is clear that US legislators wield considerable power against the executive and judicial branches of government.

This is not the case in many nations. Work on programs to strengthen the legislative branch abroad may yield positive results, but practitioners need to understand the political and legal history of the country in question to achieve this. In a state with a dominant executive branch, working to empower and strengthen the national legislature to effect change might be a waste of precious resources or, alternatively, place such legislators in danger of political retaliation. In addition, the relatively high turnover in legislators due to short terms in office often can negate any gains in legislative capacity, since individuals leave or are removed from public office shortly after being trained. Support for a strong legislative branch can certainly bolster the ROL, but it is essential to understand the country context before selecting the scope of work to be accomplished.

Local Government Assistance

Often ROL work in supporting the decentralization of power from a central authority to local government can be successful. Resulting programs often take the form of administrative, financial, and political support for local government bodies abroad. The issues correctly pointed out by Carothers are whether the central government will allow for the devolution of power from the center to the periphery, whether decentralization will fracture a spirit of national unity or central government capacity or authority needed in the country, and whether the strengthening of local systems will simply coronate a local elite and/or export the pathologies of the center to the periphery. Carothers (1999) offers as an example the case of Nepal in the 1990s, where "decentralizing a highly centralized political system immediately ran into powerful local patronage networks and often impossible to untangle controlling loyalties based on clan and ethnic group. Local governments began to receive regular grant funds from the central government, but in many areas of the country such funds did not work to change dysfunctional local political structures or habits but to reinforce them" (p. 195).

Civil–Military Relations

Assisting with the installation of democratic values in and civilian control over a foreign military is a challenging aspect of ROL practice. In many cases, militaries resist change and are unwilling to allow for increased civilian oversight of their activities. Also, as a matter of policy, some entities engaged in ROL work, such as USAID, are forbidden from working with foreign militaries (and military and national police), while other entities are significantly engaged in such ROL activities.

Traditional and Customary Law

International actors are increasingly engaging with traditional and customary legal systems as a more practical alternative to working solely with formal legal entities. Since worldwide a vast majority of complainants seek resolution of disputes through avenues other than the formal legal system, if one is even present and available, it behooves the ROL practitioner to engage with such customary legal systems. The question to ask before embarking on such programs is whether the customary practice adequately includes vulnerable populations, such as women, children, and indigenous and disabled persons, and whether the customary system violates basic tenets of international human rights and humanitarian law. Ensuring that interveners proceed with caution when engaging with customary or traditional practices that might violate the basic rights of the person is the true reason ROL work is done in the first place.

Land Reform and Land Tenure Issues

Conflict comes in many forms, of course, but a significant portion of conflict revolves around access to natural resources, specifically land and land tenure issues. Such a recognition that many conflicts are based not on group or ethnicity or historical hatred, but instead on land is dawning on ROL practitioners worldwide, and a considerable amount of future ROL programming will revolve around land reform and the resolution of land disputes. An understanding and appreciation of land and land issues will certainly enhance the ability of the ROL practitioner to effect positive change.

EFFECTIVE SKILLS REQUIRED IN ROL PRACTICE

The word "rule" in ROL is arguably misleading in that there are no mandatory rules or requirements for a society to enjoy ROL, and no binding international ROL treaty exists to set forth such black-letter law. Similarly, the word "law" in ROL may establish the unfortunate conception that ROL work is the province solely of the lawyer or the legally trained. Perhaps consideration should be given to changing the name of the field from ROL to something less technical, exclusive, and exclusionary, as ROL is simply the fight for increased fairness and equity in its most broad conception. This is not to say that a background in law is not an asset to the ROL practitioner, especially in the technical areas of legal code reform and prosecutorial, defense, and judicial capacity-building, but the field of ROL does, and will only, benefit from the continued inclusion of other disciplines, some of which include peacebuilding, conflict resolution, international development, psychology, anthropology, security sector reform, land tenure rights, riparian rights, and anticorruption.

Since the field of ROL is, or at least should be, welcoming of myriad disciplines, no one set of technical skills or a certain advanced academic degree is required of the ROL practitioner. However, a number of practical skills can assist the ROL practitioner, including an appreciation for cultural context and the ability to recognize true domestic buy-in, an essential component for any ROL work.

As to the former, donor agencies from developed nations have demonstrated an alarming tendency to attempt to re-create their home country's legal system while implementing ROL programming abroad. For example, the US Department of Justice and US Department of Defense have spent considerable time and effort in the past decade training prosecutors and judges in Afghanistan, often without devoting sufficient attention to ensuring cultural sensitivity programming. Initially, instead of fully understanding and appreciating the country's legal traditions and training to improve the system from within, and casting a blind, or even neocolonial, eye toward supporting and appreciating domestic legal traditions and practices. More recently, such assistance has become much more aware and supportive of Afghan legal traditions, working with such traditions to promote greater adherence to the ROL. These cautionary examples are not intended to pick on the initial efforts of such talented American prosecutors for feeling most comfortable teaching and training their foreign colleagues on US military law and American-style jurisprudence. It is always tempting to discuss or opine upon what one knows best.

Example: In its piece "Looking for Justice: Liberian Experiences with and Perceptions of Local Justice Options" (Isser, Lubkemann, and N'Tow, 2009), the US Institute of Peace (USIP) "provide[d] the Liberian government and other stakeholders in the country with more robust evidence than has hitherto been available on how both formal and customary justice systems are perceived and utilized by Liberians" (p. 3). USIP clearly and accurately established that a vast majority of Liberians prefer to seek to resolve problems in the venue of the informal and traditional system of dispute resolution, instead of resorting to the formal system based in the capital of Monrovia:

> According to the study conducted by the Centre for the Study of African Economics at Oxford University, of a total of 3,181 civil cases, only 3 percent were taken to a formal court; 38 to an informal forum; and 59 percent to no forum at all. Of 1,877 criminal cases, only 2 percent were taken to a formal court; 45 percent to an informal forum; and 53 percent to no forum at all. (p. 4)

In fact, most Liberians surveyed and interviewed felt that the formal system was under the control of the elite, acted on their behalf, and did not enjoy the hallmarks of equity and fairness required of ROL. To be sure, the informal traditional justice system in Liberia has considerable problems in regard to respect for human rights generally and the rights of women specifically, but this system, even with its flaws, is the venue of choice for the vast majority of Liberians. As succinctly put in USIP's report, instead of focusing ROL programming on simply reforming the formal court systems, "it would be wise to consider transitional policies aimed at providing the best possible justice under the circumstances, and at creating an environment of openness and trust between the customary and formal systems that seeks to bridge the gaps and move toward full realization of Liberia's goals for its justice system" (p. 6).

This demonstrates that the ROL practitioner should not be working to re-create America or a cookie-cutter Western liberal democracy. Understanding national legal history and tradition and clearly comprehending and pursuing national goals, as long as such national goals are consistent with basic standards of fairness, are the keys to success in improving adherence to the ROL and will increase the effectiveness of ROL practitioner efforts.

The second skill required of the successful ROL practitioner is the ability to understand, appreciate, and assess the vital requirement for domestic buy-in of any ROL work. When true domestic will to consider and implement ROL reforms is present, significant success can be had. Without such domestic will and buy-in,

ROL programming dollars will disappear like water through a sieve, without significant positive effect. Proper identification of moments and opportunities ripe for ROL reform and those less or not ripe for such endeavors will save the ROL practitioner considerable aggravation, heartache, and a considerable amount of precious funding. Proper planning through a complete assessment of domestic buy-in before beginning actual ROL programming will eliminate a good portion of the mistakes made in this regard and will lead to more efficient and cost-effective ROL programs.

ROL PROGRAMMING REFORM—THE INTEGRATION AGENDA

As mentioned above, increasing engagement with informal and traditional justice systems and casting a critical eye on whether true domestic desire for reform is present when considering program implementation are two areas of ROL that need significant attention in the coming years. Independent of those two items, another area in need of dire systematic change is the continued siloing and unnecessary duplication of ROL work.

As will be demonstrated in the proceeding section, myriad national and international actors are engaged in significant ROL training and programming. These actors rarely coordinate their work, however, or engage in significant communication about their respective ROL programming, leaving ROL efforts fragmented, siloed, and lacking significant coordination. Happily, the de-siloing of ROL work is occurring, albeit slowly. Two examples of cutting-edge collaborative efforts are below.

US GOVERNMENT INTERAGENCY ROL WORK IN SOUTHERN SUDAN

In a groundbreaking interagency effort, starting in 2010, the US State Department's Office of the Coordinator for Reconstruction and Stabilization and its Civilian Response Corps[6] sent about fifty democracy officers to southern Sudan. In cooperation and conjunction with USAID, these US government personnel conducted a full democracy assessment of South Sudan. Within the larger assessment, ROL experts from both agencies fanned out from the capital city of Juba and conducted a full assessment of legal capacity in the fledgling nation. This collaborative effort incorporated the knowledge of experts in human rights, judicial and court personnel capacity, police training, penology, and other ROL-related fields. The combined assessment report detailed the proper diplomatic and development role for the US to best support the new nation of South Sudan. This intensified diplomatic and development effort serves as a model for interagency collaboration to prevent conflict and promote regional stability through capacity-building and greater adherence to the ROL.

The ROL Collaborative at the University of South Carolina

An excellent example of breaking down the silos that exist in ROL education and programming is the Rule of Law Collaborative at the University of South Carolina (ROLC). The ROLC "draws on the expertise of more than 50 faculty associates from a broad range of disciplines who undertake research relating to rule of law, conflict resolution, and human rights promotion. ROLC organizes conferences and training workshops for U.S. Government agencies, human rights organizations, and foreign scholars and officials. ROLC also partners with other institutions, law schools, NGOs and the World Justice Project in striving to promote justice and human rights in fragile and post-conflict zones" (Rule of Law Collaborative, 2012). At the most recent ROLC training course, held in September 2011 at the Department of Justice, over seventy-five ROL practitioners from across the US government, including members of the Department of Defense, the State Department, the Department of Justice, USAID, and the Department of Commerce, received two days' worth of ROL training, designed to support and build an understanding of the ROL activities of each of the US government agencies and to support better collaboration and coordination of field activities between US government actors.

INDICATORS OF SUCCESS

In some areas of international work, success can be quantitatively measured. For example, in elections and political processes work, success, at least in the short term, can be measured by the peacefulness and credibility of a national election, and whether election or postelection violence ensues. In the area of ROL, success is difficult to monitor and evaluate, as changes in a legal system take years, if not decades, to take effect. Also, it is difficult to demonstrate that a particular ROL project is directly and fully responsible for a substantive change in ROL abroad, since ROL is a vast domain and not easily attributable to any one such ROL effort. A number of such efforts to quantify and qualify the ROL are under way, however, two of which are discussed below.

Rule of Law Index

The World Justice Project's Rule of Law Index monitors and evaluates progress or regress of the state of ROL worldwide on a country-by-country basis. The index "offers reliable, independent, and disaggregated information for policy makers, businesses, non-governmental organizations, and other constituencies to: Assess a nation's adherence to the rule of law in practice; Identify a nation's strengths and weaknesses in comparison to similarly situated countries; and Track changes over time" (Agrast,

Botero, and Ponce, 2011, p. 2). This "innovative quantitative assessment tool [is] designed to offer a comprehensive picture of the extent to which countries adhere to the rule of law, not in theory, but in practice" (p. 1). More specifically, the index provides detailed data on nine dimensions of ROL: limited government powers, absence of corruption, order and security, fundamental rights, open government, effective regulatory enforcement, access to civil justice, effective criminal justice, and informal justice (Agrast, Botero, and Ponce, 2011).

Freedom in the World Survey

Another example of an attempt to measure and assess ROL is Freedom House's Freedom in the World Survey.[7] Its annual Freedom in the World survey evaluates the state of global freedom as experienced by individuals. The survey measures freedom—the opportunity to act spontaneously in a variety of fields outside the control of the government and other centers of potential domination—according to two broad categories: political rights and civil liberties. The survey includes both analytical reports and numerical ratings for 194 countries and 14 select territories. Each country and territory report includes an overview section, which provides historical background and a brief description of the year's major developments, as well as a summary of the current state of political rights and civil liberties. In addition, each country and territory is assigned a numerical rating—on a scale of 1 to 7—for political rights and an analogous rating for civil liberties; a rating of 1 indicates the highest degree of freedom and 7 the lowest level of freedom. The survey uses these ratings to determine whether a country is classified as Free, Partly Free, or Not Free (Freedom House, 2010).

WHO IS CONDUCTING ROL WORK IN THE FIELD?

Within ROL, there are innumerable international, national, and private actors. On the international level, ROL work is conducted by the United Nations, the World Bank, the Organization for Security and Co-operation in Europe, the Organization of American States, the African Union, and dozens of other international bodies. As an example of such international ROL work, the

> United Nations rule of law initiatives are indispensable to international peace and security. In conflict and post-conflict settings the United Nations assists countries in establishing the rule of law by ensuring accountability and reinforcing norms, building confidence in justice and security institutions, and promoting gender equality. The Organization is increasingly focused on emerging threats to the rule of law, such as organized crime and illicit trafficking, and the root causes of conflict, including economic and social justice issues. (United Nations, 2011, p. 1)

The full panoply of bilateral donors is similarly vast. Among the many major national actors in ROL work are the US, Japan, Australia, the UK, Sweden, Norway, and Canada. An example of the vast nature of bilateral ROL work within the US government is that it is conducted simultaneously by actors that span the grid from the Department of Commerce, the Department of Defense, the Department of Justice, and the Department of State, to USAID, to the Environmental Protection Agency. As a representative example of the government's ROL work, this chapter will highlight that of USAID.

USAID

USAID currently maintains sixty-eight ROL, law enforcement, and anti-trafficking-in-persons programs around the world. Individual programs range in size from small grants and local organizations valued at a few thousand dollars, to multiyear, multi-million-dollar interventions designed to overhaul and reform entire portions of a country's justice system. The vast majority of USAID's ROL and associated programs are managed by the agency's in-country representatives, with Washington providing political, technical, and administrative support. Two examples of USAID's current applied ROL programs are described below: Afghanistan and Liberia.

Case Study: Afghanistan

USAID's ROL program in Afghanistan is the largest such USAID program, with a $15.8 million budget that focuses on a number of practice areas, including constitutional reform, justice and legal system strengthening, and human rights. The Rule of Law Stabilization Program works with both formal state institutions and informal community-based conflict resolution mechanisms. The program aims to build judiciary and legal education capacity, strengthen access to justice and the demand for ROL, increase the viability and human rights capacity of the informal conflict resolution system, and increase linkages between the formal and informal systems (USAID, 2011).

The challenges presented by such ROL work in Afghanistan are many, most significant being the lack of a historical culture of human rights and ROL in the country, in addition to weak legal infrastructure and an unstable security environment. Engaging with the informal conflict resolution system present in Afghanistan also may unfairly affect or exclude women, as their rights in the traditional system are decidedly unequal by favoring men. Also, the inability of US-supported ROL programming to engage with the Taliban or Taliban-related groups due to US federal law will hinder the ability to assist in total societal reconciliation. Time will tell whether such ROL programming, and that of the myriad other ROL entities working in Afghanistan, will make a positive impact on the state of ROL in-country.

Liberia

USAID's ROL program in Liberia is the agency's fifth-largest, with a $10.3 million budget. The program is designed to: (1) enhance access to justice by formalizing recourse to alternative dispute resolution mechanisms and increase societal availability of the formal legal system; (2) combat gender-based violence; (3) promote institutional capacity-building within legal institutions through the establishment of the Judicial Training Institute, improve the quality of legal education in partnership with the Louis Arthur Grimes Law School, support legal code reform, support the professional development of the Liberian National Bar Association, and provide scholarships to allow law students to work in ministries and the judiciary; and (4) enhance the legal institutions' capacity to combat corruption through training Ministry of Justice and Liberian Anti-Corruption Commission personnel and developing anticorruption policies for those agencies, and mentoring law enforcement personnel (USAID, 2009).

The challenges facing such an ROL program in Liberia are how to infuse international human rights standards into a traditional dispute resolution system that falls significantly short of such standards, ameliorating the disadvantaged position of women in Liberian society, overcoming the negative public perceptions of the formal justice system discussed earlier in this chapter, and solving the long-standing and well-entrenched specter of public corruption (Isser, Lubkemann, and N'Tow, 2009). Such challenges, while not necessarily on the level of the challenges of doing ROL work in Afghanistan, are many, and ROL work in Liberia seems likely to be needed for decades to come.

Nonstate Actors

Travel to any developing country with ROL challenges, and it will be immediately clear that a wide array of NGOs and other entities are conducting significant ROL work. Some of the larger private actors in the ROL field include Freedom House, the American Bar Association's Rule of Law Initiative, the International Center for Transitional Justice, the International Commission of Jurists, the Open Society Initiative, and Global Rights.

A DISTINGUISHED ROL PRACTITIONER

Otto Saki is an exceptional example of a practitioner who works across the discipline of ROL related to the pursuit of fairness and equity for civil society activists in Zimbabwe. A Zimbabwean lawyer and graduate of the University of Zimbabwe, and former acting director for Zimbabwe Lawyers for Human Rights, Saki has fought tirelessly on behalf of those threatened by Zimbabwean government repression, including embattled opposition candidate and current Prime Minister Morgan Tsvangirai. Saki received the International Reebok Human Rights Award in June 2006, recently served as a Human Rights Fellow at Columbia University Law School, and now serves as a senior democracy and governance adviser at USAID's mission in Zimbabwe. Only in his early thirties, Saki exemplifies the true spirit of the ROL practitioner, fighting across fields for those most in need of ROL protections.

ETHICAL CHALLENGES IN ROL

Whether one is working for the US government or another government entity, an international organization, an NGO, or an implementing partner of any of the above, the selection of local partnerships is a vital ethical question. If one chooses a local partner over another by providing funding and support to them, the favoritism could create a local power imbalance. Local or regional ROL groups that receive US government or international support often thrive, while other organizations, despite significant or greater merit, wither and die. The question to ask when selecting local ROL partners is whether the organization in question is an engine for justice, merely seeking precious funds to continue its existence, or an engine to maintain the status quo.

As mentioned earlier, another ethical challenge that often presents itself in ROL work is whether an ROL project or programming can engage with a customary legal practice that excludes or violates the rights of certain community constituents. An example of such an ethical dilemma is whether ROL practitioners can engage and work with the Sudanese legal system in regard to sexual assault cases, or whether the system, as currently constituted, violates women's rights and compels ROL practitioners to work *against* the system in order to change it. At present, a woman alleging sexual assault in Sudan needs multiple male witnesses to the sexual assault to sustain and prove her case, and the remedy for a rape allegation is that the perpetrator marries the victim to mitigate the harm done (Kritz and Wilson, 2011). Such an evidentiary standard and remedy certainly violates norms of international law; thus, the question remains whether ROL practitioners can work with Sudanese authorities to attempt to influence and change such law, or whether the law is so abhorrent that an ethical ROL practitioner cannot possibly work from within to attempt to ameliorate the law.

CONCLUSION

The field of ROL is a relatively new one, and thus, its four corners are still in development. Excitingly, for the future ROL practitioner such a state of flux will allow for the implementation of new ideas, new approaches, and innovation into the ROL agenda.

With the increased inclusion of the non-lawyer, the acceptance and appreciation of non-Western legal traditions, and the recognition of the need for true domestic buy-in to effect true reform, the next generation of ROL work is destined to better legally protect the fundamental rights of all humankind.

QUESTIONS FOR FURTHER DISCUSSION

1. Would the creation of a Convention on the Rule of Law be a positive step for the discipline? What would be the downside of creating an international treaty delineating the field?

2. In the hypothetical Convention on the Rule of Law, should the treaty espouse the formalist, substantivist, or functionalist school of thought?

3. Would the inclusion of the hallmarks of liberal democracy into the tenets of ROL transform ROL from a shared ideal of human history into a Western-dominated concept? Can democratic ideals and nondemocratic ideals coexist within the ROL?

4. In a conflict setting, can ROL work begin before the fighting has stopped, or before formal peace accords have been signed? If the answer is no, when should ROL work properly begin?

5. Is it feasible for US government and international donor agencies to work together on ROL programs? What are the upsides of such collaboration? What might be lost as a result of such coordination?

6. Will the greater inclusion of women in legal processes necessarily increase adherence to ROL?

7. Looking forward, how can the mainstreaming of peacebuilding positively affect global adherence to ROL?

REFERENCES

Agrast, M., J. Botero, and A. Ponce. 2011. WJP Rule of Law Index 2011. World Justice Project. Retrieved February 20, 2012, from http://worldjusticeproject.org/rule-of-law-index/index-2011.

Carothers, Thomas. 1999. *Aiding democracy abroad: The learning curve.* Washington, DC: Carnegie Endowment for International Peace.

Center for Law and Military Operations. 2009. Rule of Law Handbook. A practitioner's guide for judge advocates. US Army. Retrieved February 20, 2012, from www.loc.gov/rr/frd/Military_Law/pdf/rule-of-law_2009.pdf.

Freedom House. 2010. Freedom in the world. Reports. Retrieved February 20, 2012, from http://freedomhouse.org/reports.

Isser, D., S. Lubkemann, and S. N'Tow. 2009. Looking for justice. *Peaceworks* 63. Washington, DC: United States Institute of Peace.

Kautz, S. 1999. Liberty, justice, and the rule of law. *Yale Journal of Law and the Humanities* 11: 435–468.

Kritz, B., and J. Wilson. 2011. No transitional justice without transition: Darfur: A case study. *Journal of International Law and Practice* 19, no. 3: 475–500.

Lancaster House. 1984, June 8. Declaration on democratic values as agreed by heads of state or government. Ministry of Foreign Affairs. Retrieved February 20, 2012, from www.mofa.go.jp/policy/economy/summit/2000/past_summit/10/e10_b.html.

Rule of Law Collaborative. 2012, January 19. Rule of Law Collaborative. Retrieved February 20, 2012, from www.rolc.sc.edu.

Shinoda, Hideaki. 2001. Peace-building by the rule of law: An examination of intervention in the form of international tribunals. Retrieved February 5, 2012, from www.theglobalsite.ac.uk/press/108shinoda.pdf.

United Nations. 2004, August 23. United Nations and the rule of law: The rule of law and transitional justice in conflict and post-conflict societies. Retrieved February 20, 2012, from www.un.org/en/ruleoflaw.

United Nations Development Programme (UNDP). 2010. Annual report 2010 in brief. Retrieved February 20, 2012, from www.beta.undp.org/content/dam/undp/library/crisis %20prevention/UNDP_Rule_of_Law,_AR_in_brief_web.pdf.

United Nations Office of the United Nations High Commissioner for Human Rights (OHCHR). 1989, November 20. Convention on the Rights of the Child. Retrieved February 20, 2012, from www2.ohchr.org/english/law/crc.htm.

United Nations Security Council. 2011, October 12. The rule of law and transitional justice in conflict and post-conflict societies. Report of the Secretary-General, S/2011/634. Retrieved February 20, 2012, from www.un.org/en/ruleoflaw/index.shtml.

USAID. 2009, December. Support for rule of law and a culture of human rights in Liberia. Retrieved February 21, 2012, from http://liberia.usaid.gov/node/61.

———. 2010, January. Guide to rule of law country analysis: The rule of law strategic framework. Retrieved February 20, 2012, from http://transition.usaid.gov/our_work /democracy_and_governance/publications/pdfs/ROL_Strategic_Framework_Jan-2010 _FINAL.pdf.

———. 2011, June. Rule of Law Stabilization Program. Retrieved February 20, 2012, from http://afghanistan.usaid.gov/documents/document/Document/1743/Fact_Sheet _Rule_of_Law_Stabilization_June_2011.

Whitford, W. C. 2000. The rule of law. *Wisconsin Law Review* 3: 723–757.

Notes

1. As explained by the UN (2004), "The General Assembly has considered rule of law as an agenda item since 1992, with renewed interest since 2006 and has adopted resolutions at its last three sessions (A/RES/61/39, A/RES/62/70, A/RES/63/128). The Security Council has held a number of thematic debates on the rule of law (S/PRST/2003/15, S/PRST/2004/2, S/PRST/2004/32, S/PRST/2005/30, S/PRST/2006/28) and adopted resolutions emphasizing the importance of these issues in the context of women, peace and security (SCR 1325, SCR 1820), children in armed conflict (e.g., SCR 1612), the protection of civilians in armed conflict (e.g., SCR 1674). The Peacebuilding Commission has also regularly addressed rule of law issues with respect to countries on its agenda" (para. 4).

2. Four recommended discussions on historical ROL outside of modern liberal democracy are *Israel's Judicial System in the Preexilic Period* by R. R. Wilson, *Justice Without*

Frontiers: Furthering Human Rights (discussing, among other topics, ROL, historical Islam, and shar'ia law) by Justice C. G. Weeramantry, *On the Rule of Law—History, Politics, Theory* by Brian Tamanaha, and *The Rule of Law in the Arab World—Courts in Egypt and the Gulf* by Nathan J. Brown.

3. Qur'an 24:4 establishes that crimes of sexual immorality, *zina,* often interpreted as adultery, require four such male witnesses. Articles 145–160 of the Sudanese Criminal Code define rape as *zina* with consent. Thus, a victim complaining of rape must have four competent male witnesses of the alleged rape to sustain a rape charge.

4. It is not my intention to opine as to whether the hearings or trials in the above three examples are indeed fair in process and procedure. They are used as illustrative examples only.

5. The only remedies to the lifetime registration requirements are a certificate of rehabilitation from the court under significant strictures as per Penal Code Section 290.5(a)(3), or a governor's pardon, as per Penal Code Sections 290.4 (a)(1) and 290.5.

6. The office has since been renamed the Bureau of Conflict and Stabilization Operations. See www.state.gov/j/cso/index.htm.

7. Freedom House is an independent watchdog organization that supports the expansion of freedom around the world.

chapter thirteen

CONCLUSION

Craig Zelizer

Peacebuilding is about "how" things are done as much as about "what" is done.

—UNITED NATIONS SUPPORT OFFICE (2010, P. 14)

A S HIGHLIGHTED IN THE INTRODUCTION, the goal of this text is to explore the growing efforts to integrate peacebuilding across diverse sectoral areas. As discussed throughout the chapters, conflict-affected societies face an overwhelming number of challenges that range from poor economic performance, destroyed or underdeveloped infrastructure, and significant population displacement, to weak or nonexistent legal and political institutions, lack of health-care services, and ongoing violence. While stand-alone peacebuilding programming can have a significant positive impact, integrating peacebuilding concepts and practices into sectoral-based programming has significant potential to contribute to the creation of more peaceful and stable societies. It is important to emphasize, however, that integrated peacebuilding is not a magic bullet that will end conflict. There are many challenges to integrated approaches, as well as significant programmatic obstacles. Moreover, building peace is hard work, and many times, unfortunately, setbacks and failures take place at all levels.

The sectors covered in this book are a selection of key areas that have been negatively impacted by violent conflict and in which work has started (to varying degrees) to integrate peacebuilding approaches. For many years, the intersection of each sector and conflict was insufficiently explored in both theory and practice. It is only within the past fifteen years that scholars and practitioners have begun to link development and peacebuilding. Efforts by scholar/practitioners, including Mary Anderson (1999), Jonathan Goodhand (2001), Thania Paffenholz and Luc Reychler (2000; 2007), and organizations such as International Alert and CDA Collaborative Learning Projects, among others, have been critical in developing tools to improve policy and practice in diverse areas.[1] Furthermore, as the peacebuilding field has rapidly grown over the past two decades, there has been an increasing awareness that such an endeavor is invariably a long-term, cross-sectoral initiative. Increasing the chances of sustainable peace requires not only ending conflicts, but also creating economic growth and jobs, building sustainable and transparent legal systems, establishing a functioning media, and ensuring that basic needs for health and security are met (Woodrow and Chigas, 2009).

It is important to emphasize that integrated peacebuilding is not an entirely new phenomenon. For many years there have been fields such as health and peacebuilding, or a nascent peace journalism field. The difference now is that integrated approaches seek to mainstream peacebuilding across both the internal and external operations of organizations, and move beyond conflict sensitivity to implicitly or explicitly integrate peacebuilding goals into programs and policies.

Among the sectoral areas featured in this book, some have seen significant efforts to integrate peacebuilding, particularly development, humanitarian relief, and gender, while other sectors, such as business and rule of law, have been more limited. It would be impossible to cover all the sectors in which peacebuilding could be integrated, but other areas include education, agriculture, the arts, and infrastructure development.

This chapter summarizes the state of integrated approaches, explores the key themes raised across the chapters, and discusses the challenges of sustainability and impact, and lessons from integrated approaches.

THE STATE OF INTEGRATED APPROACHES

As described throughout the text, the integration of diverse sectoral concerns into international development programming (in the areas of gender, environment, health, youth, and peacebuilding) has become increasingly common. As Wisler and other authors highlight, a key focus of the book is that the overwhelming majority of development and sectoral aid work in the world occurs in fragile and conflict-affected environments. Attempts to foster sustainable development are frequently undermined by the threat or existence of violent conflict. Similarly, much of the peacebuilding work in the world occurs in societies experiencing severe development challenges.

Underdevelopment can take the form of fragile legal systems that can lead to corruption, impunity, or worse, as seen in Afghanistan. Health systems can fail to adequately provide for a population's needs, as in the Democratic Republic of the Congo. Media may be used to contribute to conflict and fuel violence, as occurred in Rwanda. Environmental degradation can exacerbate conflicts in weak areas, such as Darfur. In all of the cases above, a weak economy also hampers overall growth and development.[2]

Challenges and Opportunities in Integrated Approaches

The following section will explore a number of key issues regarding integrated peace-building approaches, including organizational issues, process, and challenges.

Organizational Issues in Mainstreaming.

A key issue organizations need to explore regarding integrated approaches is determining the appropriate structure for supporting these efforts. In a pioneering study in 2004, International Alert examined how a select group of development organizations sought to mainstream conflict sensitivity into their work (Lange, 2004). The study found several possible arrangements, including creating separate departments or units focused on conflict issues to infuse the issue across the organization, to embed staff in existing units, or to train all staff, and to try to adopt a peacebuilding perspective in all programming.

In considering how to integrate programming, organizations need to consider if specialized units for peacebuilding are best, or whether they need to infuse the issue across all programming activities. Ideally, the answer should be both. Given the high levels of conflict and violence in the world, and the need for specialized expertise and experience, there is a strong need for more dedicated peacebuilding approaches. But if peacebuilding is not integrated across sectors, then the chances of large-scale impact are lessened. There are challenges in both approaches. As Whitman and Thornton discuss, establishing a specialized gender unit or focal point may be a valuable step, but also risks marginalizing gender instead of facilitating deeper systematic change if not done properly.

As outlined in several chapters in the text, peacebuilding is a relatively small field compared to international development, and even smaller in comparison to the global security industry. For peacebuilding to maximize its impact in the world today there is also a need to greater integrate the tools and principles across sectors, despite many obstacles. In practice, many institutions have begun to undertake such efforts. Most bilateral donors have developed expertise and resources dedicated to conflict issues as well as integrated approaches. The goal of many of these units is not only to fund and support specific programs that directly address conflict, but also to help infuse peacebuilding across each institution's internal and external operations.

Peacebuilding ideally should be integrated into the external and internal operations of an organization. Internally, an organization can help advance the capacity of staff through training, coaching, and ensuring that conflict issues are factored into decision-making when hiring staff and contractors. Externally in program assessment, design, and implementation, explicit linkages to reducing conflict and building peace can be integrated into all aspects of the program life cycle.

Regardless of an organization's structure and choice of how it integrates such issues, creating system-wide change also requires support from top leadership. This should include a clear articulation of vision, goals, and metrics, and concrete allocation of staff and resources for integrating efforts (UNDP, 2006). Otherwise, there is a risk that such approaches will be diffuse, or that it will remain the effort of isolated individuals in the midst of a large bureaucracy competing against other issues (UNDP, 2006). Without larger institutional buy-in, such efforts are likely to be unsustainable and lead to frustration.

One of the key issues to emphasize is that peacebuilding is a more explicit process than conflict sensitivity or "do no harm" approaches. Although these are critical tools in conducting effective programming and are linked to implicit peacebuilding, truly affecting conflict systems requires more directly addressing conflict dynamics at both the local and policy levels (Woodrow and Chigas, 2009). As Woodrow and Chigas explain,

> Peacebuilding is a type of programming with particular aims. It includes a wide range of programming modes with a common aim: they all aim explicitly to address the key drivers of conflict and, ultimately, change the conflict dynamics, with particular emphasis on reducing or preventing violence as a means of addressing political, social and economic problems and injustices. (p. 12)

The Process of Integrating Peacebuilding

There are a number of key process lessons in integrating peacebuilding. First, there is a strong need to root programming attempts in a solid analysis of the context, from both a sectoral and a conflict perspective. Conducting programming without a solid understanding of the conditions on the ground runs the risk of making things worse. Furthermore, Wisler cautions against the danger of having a one-size-fits-all approach to programming and notes that analysis provides the means to gain an adequate understanding of the context.

A key issue raised by Jobbins is whether the conflict analysis should be a separate one focused on conflict/peace issues, or integrated into an existing sectoral-based analysis process. Conducting a stand-alone analysis requires a higher level of expertise, resources, and time and may not always be appropriate. However, integrating conflict concerns into an existing process can run the risk of marginalizing conflict concerns. Effectively integrating conflict is more than just a simple checklist of questions or boxes, and thus decisions about the analysis models, indicators, and process need to be considered carefully.[3]

It is also essential that an analysis is not seen as a simple static process. First it needs to be continually updated, and there is the sometimes difficult process of translating findings into effective programming and policy options (Saferworld and Conciliation Resources, 2012). As Saferworld and Conciliation Resources (2012) explain,

> There is a risk that so much effort is invested in the design, research and initial analysis phases, that little time and energy and few resources are left to translate the analysis into responses. However, as the primary purpose of conflict analysis is most commonly to inform programming and policy decisions, failings in this phase of the exercise undermine its whole value. (p. 30)

It is critical the process and product are tailored for the internal or external audiences that will use the data to make decisions (Saferworld, 2012). Woodrow and Chigas (2009) also raise a strong critique of organizations that think they are doing peacebuilding by conducting a conflict analysis but then fail to link this analysis to programming at the local operational and macro levels.

One of the issues related to integrated approaches is to what degree is programming conducted by or with locals, with international support, and technical assistance, versus implementing external solutions (Woodrow and Chigas, 2009; Paffenholz and Reychler, 2007). For example, Kritz emphasizes the importance of ensuring that rule of law programming in conflict-affected societies is based on local conditions; otherwise it can be perceived as Western imposition. As he describes, much of the initial rule of law work in Afghanistan was based largely on outside models that did not function well in the environment. Eventually greater emphasis was made to incorporate Afghan traditions.

It is essential to note that even the most conflict-affected societies have actors and often institutions actively engaged in peacebuilding activities (Anderson and Olson, 2003). Local peacebuilders often carry out work in the most dire circumstances at great risk to their own safety, and have the necessary commitment and contextual knowledge to foster change. The international community has an ethical and practical responsibility to make sure that programming is not imposed, but supports local peacebuilders, strengthens relevant institutions in society, and mitigates divisions where possible (Anderson and Olson, 2003). This is also critically important, as some international donors and implementing organizations may leave a conflict-affected environment due to changes in funding or priorities, and it is local people and institutions that will remain on the ground doing peacebuilding work.

Another issue that needs further exploration has to do with sequencing. There is the critical question of what needs to come first. Is providing basic security an imperative before undertaking health or legal reform? If security is present but there is no economic opportunity, will this lead to increased conflict and eventually insecurity? Does the sequencing depend more on the sources of funding, rather than the existing needs on the ground? And how can peacebuilding be effectively integrated across sectors, at various stages of conflict, and across diverse donors? And who has the power to make these decisions?

As many of the chapters discuss, integrated peacebuilding approaches remain a largely voluntary endeavor (see also Paffenholz and Reychler, 2007). As such, the issue of motivation comes to the fore. How can one motivate organizations to undertake the actions required to improve their operations, programming, and impact, when doing so is not required? For the foreseeable future, it is likely that peer networks and positive influence by counterparts who can demonstrate the positive results of integrated efforts will be one of the key areas to motivate change. In addition, donors can require organizations that want to obtain funding to implicitly or explicitly integrate peacebuilding concerns where appropriate.

At a minimum, one of the basic steps many organizations have taken (and should advance) is training staff on core peacebuilding and conflict resolution tools and principles. The issue raised in a number of chapters in the text discusses developing the capacity of private-sector actors, health professionals, the media, and others. As Charlton explains, health providers in conflict-affected environments need to negotiate a diverse set of challenging environments, ranging from working with armed actors to negotiating access. Providing health workers and others with adequate skills in these areas is a minimal step that organizations need to undertake. But this is not enough; staff need the analytical and practical tools to understand how their activities may impact a conflict context through analysis processes, and to understand how to link programs explicitly to peacebuilding goals and the challenges and opportunities in doing this.

CHALLENGES TO INTEGRATED APPROACHES

It is important not to oversell what integrated peacebuilding can accomplish, as there are significant challenges that are discussed in the chapters. Some actors, such as private-sector businesses or health providers, may be reluctant to take on roles that they view as outside their responsibility or sphere of influence. Jobbins emphasizes that as humanitarian organizations move into addressing conflict, there is a danger of diluting a focus on saving lives and/or raising unrealistic expectations about the ability of humanitarian actors to address core conflict issues. There is even the concern that such efforts could take away valuable resources that are needed for critical delivery of humanitarian assistance.

Furthermore, as MacDonald explains, private-sector actors define their primary role in society largely as conducting business. Profit-generating entities can act in socially beneficial ways by creating jobs, increasing revenue collected through taxes, and contributing to the overall welfare of a community. Many companies are reluctant to fully integrate environmental or consumer social responsibility into core operations out of concern that this could detract from their primary purpose. The idea of considering peacebuilding is an even more distant concern for many companies.[4]

Asking private-sector or other actors, such as health professionals, to move beyond their primary role has its own risks, such as opening up actors to new security risks, potential legal liability, and financial and personal costs. There is a need, as MacDonald discusses, to frame the benefits and costs of integrated peacebuilding in the relevant language of the audience. For example, some business actors may choose to integrate peacebuilding out of a higher ethical calling, but unless there is strong evidence that such actions can contribute to an improved bottom line or regulation requiring them to do so, widespread adoption in the business community is unlikely. As Paffenholz and Reychler (2007) explain, "Mainstreaming for the sake of it does not work—the involved stakeholders most validate the additional dimensions in their development work" (p. 125).

Another challenge is that some sectors, such as religion, may be undervalued by organizations in development and peacebuilding. Marshall and Huda explore that while religion is having a significant impact in the world and many faith-based actors are mainstreaming peacebuilding, the role of such actors in the larger development field is still contested. Many in development and international policy view religion or religious leaders as overly conservative or a potential obstacle to development. Thus, integrating religion and peacebuilding, while growing in acceptance, still faces significant resistance from the wider development community.

A core concept raised throughout the text is the danger of overintegration (UNDP, 2006). Given that organizations and staff are busy with the business of conducting programs, saving lives, writing reports, obtaining funding, and integrating a host of other concerns such as gender, environment, and HIV, the addition of peacebuilding poses additional challenges. To date there is no metaframework to support the integration of diverse sectors. Each issue that is being integrated, while important, raises a potential set of concerns that requires additional staff time and resources (Paffenholz and Reychler, 2007). It may be too much to ask a health program in an insecure region that is devoted to ending polio or reducing infant mortality to also seek to ensure that it is also gender-, conflict-, and HIV-sensitive. There are likely to be additional sectors integrated in the future, and each is of critical importance. How can the potentially competing issues of humanitarian relief and conflict be prioritized? In addition, there may be tensions over program or strategic goals, funding, or other key areas that can lead to complications.

Security/Risks

Many development and humanitarian organizations have long relied on the notion of impartiality to ensure that they have access to conflict areas to help save lives and reduce suffering. There is a potential danger, if an organization moves beyond delivering aid or development to seeking to influence, even if only to a small degree, that they could put their staff and operations at greater risk (Fast, 2010). Particularly in a post-9/11 world where insecurity for these humanitarian, development, and conflict actors is already at a greater risk, protecting the lives of staff, beneficiaries, and programming operations is a key concern. Attempts at explicitly integrating peacebuilding also need to balance security concerns of organizations and their staff working in difficult environments, though, as highlighted by Anderson (1999) and others, all organizations working in conflict environments are part of the conflict context and need to factor this into their operations.

An additional concern is the increasing securitization of aid. While international assistance has always had strong linkages to political goals, the relationship of aid to insecurity and direct military involvement is relatively new and raises concerns (CDA Collaborative Learning Projects, 2011). For example, Charlton cautions against the instrumentalization of health diplomacy as a tool of statecraft to win hearts and minds in conflict regions, particularly when undertaken by military actors. This is not to say it shouldn't be done, but in these cases, a careful discussion of the opportunities and potential ethical challenges is strongly needed, as blurring health and security lines put health workers and others at risk. As discussed in the security chapter, some of the new hybrid arrangements to integrate conflict into security practices, such as provincial reconstruction teams or human terrain teams, are highly controversial.

Ideally aid, peacebuilding, and development programming decisions should be based on the local needs of societies (CDA Collaborative Learning Projects, 2011). As emphasized in the chapter on the business of the field, however, decisions about how resources are allocated are often influenced by political considerations. While aid is given to help, there are also significant political factors, including the influence of diaspora communities, national security concerns, and private-sector interests. Jobbins emphasizes that an effective way for organizations to deal with this challenge is to be aware of the "political nature of assistance" and seek to integrate peacebuilding approaches into their programming and interactions with others.

There is a strong segment of the peacebuilding field that is based largely on pacifism and is critical of military operations. Some see any engagement with security actors as antithetical to their core, while others seek to infuse peacebuilding tools across sectors, including security actors. Regardless of one's perspective on the issue, it is likely that there will be increasing linkages between security and peacebuilding actors. This is also true of peacebuilding interventions, since much of the funding for the work comes from government sources.

Recently the Office of Conflict Management and Mitigation of USAID (2012b) issued a funding opportunity titled Programming Effectively Against Conflict and Extremism, which may award up to US $600 million to support programming on conflict issues over the next several years. Some of the core tasks include "conflict prevention, peacebuilding and development responses to violent extremism and insurgency" (p. 9). As outlined in the security chapter, many donors supporting peacebuilding and development are increasingly linking programming with security objectives, which raises questions about the primary goal of peacebuilding. While the goals may link to coherent programming at times, should a higher value be placed on hard security and stability or on fostering peacebuilding in a conflict-affected countries?

In the following section of the chapter, several key issues related to integrated approaches including sustainability and impact will be discussed.

Sustainability

John Paul Lederach (1997) has emphasized that building peace in societies that have suffered extensive conflict can be a long-term, multigenerational endeavor lasting twenty years or more. Considering the widespread havoc and damage long-term violent conflict inflicts on people, societies, and infrastructure, it is unrealistic to expect that a severe conflict that has disrupted many aspects of society can be addressed in a short period. One of the key questions related to peacebuilding is to what degree efforts are going to be sustainable in the long term.

As highlighted in the framing chapters, one of the challenges to sustainability is that international assistance is often provided on a project-to-project basis. To be eligible to receive support from the international community, activities in conflict-affected societies (whether carried out by locals or internationals) need to fit within the dominant paradigm of "fundable activity." Complex problems need to be projectified into discrete activities. This may mean that community-based efforts or other societal movements that do not fit the project may be overlooked or not receive support for critical efforts (see also Paffenholz et al., 2010).

In general, peacebuilding programs are funneled through an existing institution, such as a nonprofit, community-based organization or business. Institutions apply for and receive funds for projects designed to have a particular impact on a designated issue or area. For example, a project conducted by a nonprofit may bring together youth or educators to integrate peacebuilding dialogue into educational and community settings over a one- to two-year period. While such efforts often do have an impact and may lead to change, rarely are projects funded over an extended period of time.

While the issue of sustainability is frequently mentioned in the field, there hasn't been much progress in finding appropriate means to increase sustainability. The OECD/DAC (n.d.), for example, states that sustainability "is concerned with measuring whether the benefits of an activity are likely to continue after donor funding has been withdrawn." While donors now frequently require organizations seeking funding to include explicit discussion of how a project or the impact is sustainable in nature and greater emphasis is being placed on building the capacity of local organizations through funding, technical assistance, providing training in fund-raising and grants management, and encouraging potential local partners, it is not clear what impact this is having.

One of the goals for organizations conducting peacebuilding-related work is for them to become financially viable. As a recent USAID/DCHA (2012) Conflict Management and Mitigation Funding opportunity explained, "The proposed activity must promote, strengthen and be supported by sustainable local organizations that can champion sound concepts, innovative practices and changes beyond the life of the award" (p. 19). While many organizations have developed a sustainable long-term business model that enables them to conduct excellent work addressing the long-term challenges of society through a diverse range of donors and funds, in reality conflict-affected societies tend to remain largely or entirely dependent on international assistance and are largely unsustainable.

A fundamental mismatch remains in much of international peacebuilding work (and aid work in general). Projects (whether locally or externally driven) depend to a significant degree on resources provided by the international community. The average life cycle of a project may be one to three years. While some efforts may be supported for a longer period, there is a need to constantly find new sources of funding and develop new projects that fit the needs and interest of donors. As Dan Smith (2004) explains in the Ustein study of peacebuilding activities funded by four European governments,

> Peacebuilding must be responsive to context and able to adapt to new conditions and requirements as the context changes. It must also be sustainable: following bitter conflicts, sustainable peace is only available on the basis of sustained effort lasting a decade or more. This does not mean that all peacebuilding projects have to be sustained for so long, but that the overall strategy sees the process through. (p. 10)

For example, in a review of women's organizations in Bosnia-Herzegovina, Martha Walsh (USAID, 2000) notes how local organizations often changed their programming in response to changing priorities of the international community. As she explains about women's organizations moving from psychosocial to income-generating projects, "By 1997, the situation had changed. Funds for psychosocial programs began to dry up, and the emphasis switched to income generation. Most international and local observers agree that this transition was largely donor driven and corresponded with strategies to revitalize the economy and reduce overall dependence on international aid" (p. 6). While the desire to promote economic opportunities is critical, there is often a significant gap between donor priorities and local needs. Furthermore, this can mean critical areas that may need to be addressed can be overlooked when funding is short-term in nature.

When conflicts erupt or begin to subside, there is often a rush of international assistance, funding, and new organizations, but over time funding priorities change, new crises emerge, and organizations fail. There is a need to critically examine the notions of sustainability both at the project and organizational levels. This also raises the critical question of whether peacebuilding activities should be rooted largely in the nonprofit and civil society sector that to a large degree follows the structure Western donors seek. Or are other forms of organizations, such as community-based, faith-based, and business, effective (see Paffenholz et al., 2010)?

In terms of integrated approaches, it is also unclear how organizations can sustain their funding for such efforts. Should funding come from dedicated peacebuilding funding, as has started to happen with a number of donors, such as USAID, DFID, the UN, and private foundations? Or from sectoral-based resources? Or should special funding be available to support innovation in integrated approaches? In the fragile global economic climate, there is also likely to be increased competition for decreasing funding. Ideally donors would provide additional resources to organizations breaking new ground in this area.

Impact

In addition to the challenges in sustainability, a critical issue in integration and the peacebuilding field in general is determining the results of a particular programming effort. For many years the peacebuilding field has been weak in terms of evaluation.

As Wisler emphasizes, most of the evaluation work has been donor driven and is not adequately resourced. There is a need for improved evaluation processes, funding, and increased emphasis on ensuring that the results are geared not only toward donors and organizational learning, but also for local beneficiaries and partners on the ground.

In recent years, there have been some positive developments in this area. For instance, Search for Common Ground has done a great deal to advance the understanding and practice of evaluation in the field. The organization created a unit focused on building organizational capacity and also has shared many of its findings with the broader field.[5] The Alliance for Peacebuilding convened a yearlong process that brought together donors, peacebuilders, scholars, and more in the Peacebuilding Evaluation Project to reflect on the state of the field and recommend improvements. The project has led to several key publications and to a summit to share evaluations.

Part of the challenge of evaluation emphasized in the project is limited funding and lack of technical expertise (Chiu, 2011). But there is also the issue of competition for resources and that organizations are often reluctant to report on failed or negative outcomes. This is a significant issue, as organizations often need to reapply for funding from donors, and openly discussing failures could affect their chance of obtaining new support. As explained in the Peacebuilding Evaluation Project (Chiu, 2011), in the international aid system implementers rely on resources from external sources, and competition for these resources is often fierce.

One of the challenges in evaluation is that in conflict environments a host of organizations are conducting programming in diverse sectors. In general, most efforts are evaluated on a project basis, but it is not clear if such efforts are impacting peace writ large or at the macro level (Anderson and Olson, 2003). In a study of peacebuilding projects from four bilateral donors, Dan Smith (2004) critiqued the field for an overemphasis on project-level outcomes and lack of understanding about overall impact. As he explains,

> Output can be evaluated and often measured (numbers of mines removed and hectares returned to farm use, for example, or numbers of people engaged in dialogue activities and evidence of shifts in attitudes). Whether these project outputs have an impact that helps promote peace is less easy to establish; there are very many other factors at work, so their effects are hard to distinguish, and in any case, what seems a priori like a positive impact may generate a negative and violent backlash. (p. 14)

One of the methods Smith proposes to deal with this challenge is to encourage donors and implementers to work on more joint evaluations to look at the larger strategic impact. As outlined in the analysis chapter, such efforts are starting but are still in the early stages, and there are many obstacles.

A key challenge of success or measuring impact specific to mainstreaming has to do with determining the appropriate indicator of success. Whitman and Thornton question whether having more women participating in policy-making or peacebuilding is a measure of success, or if a conflict's end is the key benchmark. Furthermore, what is the appropriate time frame? Should impact or success be measured in the short-term, project-driven world of one- to three-year time frames, or in the long-term period that is required to help build a more sustainable peace? In integrated approaches there is the further challenge of measuring the impact of the particular sector and peacebuilding. As Charlton and Jobbins highlight, if there are multiple sectors and goals, which takes priority? Is health more important than reducing conflict or delivering aid? What are the indicators of success?

A key issue in peacebuilding as noted in a number of the chapters and emphasized by the work of CDA Collaborative Learning Projects (2011) is the need to go beyond local-level efforts to help change policies, institutions, and cultures. For example, in creating a more stable rule of law system in conflict-affected countries, Kritz emphasizes that this requires training of individuals, but also creating functioning institutions (formal and informal) in which the population of a society has sufficient trust. Thornton and Whitman discuss the critical importance of integrating peacebuilding and gender not only within specific programs, but in national and international policies as well. Thus, in considering impact, different levels need to be explored.

It is clear from the sectoral chapters that within each sector there are successful examples of integrated peacebuilding that have had an impact. For example, the work of the Community of Sant'Egidio in Mozambique played a significant role in the peace process and the work of women in Liberia who pushed the conflict actors to move toward a peace agreement. Sometimes success has been more on the policy level, such as the pushing through of UN Security Council Resolution 1325, which has been a tremendous advancement in encouraging positive action on women and peacebuilding around the globe. Success at the policy level helps to set a goal to encourage more transparent and accountable actions by actors in conflict-affected regions, but encouraging the broader community to achieve these goals can be a long and challenging process. At other times success may be at the micro or project level.

LESSONS FOR INTEGRATED APPROACHES

Key lessons for integrated approaches drawn from the chapters include the following:

1. *Analysis is key:* Any type of integrated peacebuilding needs to be rooted in a solid analytical framework in order to inform program design, implementation, and monitoring. Analysis needs to look at the key source, parties, and dynamics of conflict. In addition, it should link to programming design through developing an appropriate theory of change and have ongoing monitoring processes (Woodrow and Chigas, 2009).

2. *Local partnership and capacity are essential:* In almost all societies there are strong efforts by local actors to reduce conflict. Attempts at integrated peacebuilding, regardless of the sector, need to strengthen and work with local actors on the ground and not impose from the outside (CDA Collaborative, 2010; Paffenholz et al., 2010). Building on local expertise and ensuring local participation and accountability not only can assist in conducting more effective and sustainable programming, but are more likely to be ethically sound as well.

3. *Integration is more than just a checklist:* Integrating peacebuilding should be more than a simple checklist of things to be covered; it should be infused throughout an organization's internal and external operations. Institutions also need to decide on the extent to which they will implicitly work on conflict issues, while *explicitly* linking these issues to their organizational goals.

4. *Peacebuilding and conflict sensitivity are related but different:* Conflict sensitivity is an essential step to take for all organizations that work in conflict areas. Peacebuilding is more explicitly linked to transforming conflict, relationships, and systems in a conflict zone (Woodrow and Chigas, 2009).

5. *Selling integration:* While some sectors have taken significant steps to advance integrated peacebuilding, there is still significant resistance from some sectors. While not all organizations need be engaged in explicit peacebuilding—as conflict sensitivity may be sufficient in many cases—advocates of an integrated approach to peacebuilding need to frame the support of such efforts given the nature of their audience.

6. *Developing improved tools to deal with overintegration:* There is a danger that too many demands are placed on staff and organizations ill-equipped to handle additional sectoral mandates, which require a level of expertise and programming that is still being understood (Barbolet et al., 2005; Paffenholz and Reychler, 2007). While the sectoral mandates from health/HIV, peacebuilding, the environment, youth, and issues raised in earlier chapters are important, the need to balance competing demands must be weighed carefully. This begs the question of priorities, namely: Should one sectoral

mandate take precedence over another, and what methodology decides this? Given that organizations have limited funding, time, staff, and technical expertise, a robust understanding of mainstreaming across sectors is becoming increasingly important.

7. *Organizational structure and support are key:* To truly sustain and maximize impact, organizations need to develop systems that provide support throughout the organization. The top leadership must articulate clearly defined goals and then allocate the necessary resources, staff, and technical support in order to fulfill them. This once more raises the need to develop a clear understanding of the best way to infuse peacebuilding throughout the organization without creating mainstreaming overload (Lange, 2004).

8. *The value of integrated and stand-alone programming:* Dedicated peacebuilding work has a prominent role to play in addressing conflict dynamics. Integrated and stand-alone activities are both essential, and ideally should be complementary. The question remains: Is a stand-alone, integrated, or combined approach the most effective for maximizing the impact of aid? There are advantages and disadvantages to each approach, and the answer largely depends upon the context, mission, and capacity of an organization to meet the desired program goals (Lange, 2004).

9. *Understanding the business of the field is essential:* While many organizations and individuals are motivated by the desire to do good, given the scope of the industry, it is important to understand the motivations of donors and implementers.

10. *Building peace is a long-term process:* Often the project and donor-driven models of the field do not provide adequate space for the work needed to sustain long-term efforts. There is a need to explore new models of partnership and sustainability.

11. *Conflict resolution skills are critical:* In many sectors, practitioners often need to navigate between diverse constituencies and deal with challenging contexts. Conflict resolution skills such as dialogue, facilitation, mediation, process skills, cross-cultural interactions, and engaging with diverse stakeholders are important components of mainstreaming. For instance, actors in the private sector could benefit from increased training in conflict resolution to help them deal with the "messy" aspects of conflict. Practitioners also need specific knowledge of the sectoral issues such as environment, business, or humanitarian relief to be more effective and credible in their work.

12. *The danger in essentializing:* There is a need to be conscious of and to avoid essentializing or tokenism. For example, ensuring that a certain number of women are participating in a program does not mean that a program is integrating gender, just as bringing in a religious leader to share a faith-based perspective doesn't necessarily demonstrate an adequate integration of religion. The appropriate integration of conflict and sectors needs to be rooted in analysis and go beyond surface-level demonstration of mainstreaming.

13. *All sectors have the potential for positive or negative impact:* As emphasized throughout the chapters, actors in each sector have the potential to play a

negative or positive role in conflict. Marshall and Huda explore how faith-based actors may fuel conflicts in some contexts while acting as a pivotal force for peace in others. Similarly, Singh highlights how media have inflamed conflicts in many societies, while peace media can advance understanding and connections among conflicted parties.

14. *Internal and external pressure is needed to encourage integrated approaches:* Many organizations may conduct integrated approaches as a voluntary choice due to ethical concerns or evidence that doing so can improve operations. However, there is also a need to advocate for the adoption of mainstreaming through peer networks and other means, such as public advocacy (Paffenholz and Reychler, 2007).

15. *Change is needed at the program and policy level:* To create sustainable change, integrated peacebuilding efforts need to not only work at the programmatic level, but also seek to create change within national and international institutions. Initiating a project on business and peacebuilding in Colombia, for example, should push equally for integrated peacebuilding in private-sector operations across multiple companies in different regions, as International Alert has done through its innovative work.

CONCLUSION

As a relatively recent process, integrated peacebuilding has already made a significant impact over the past decade, as highlighted throughout the chapters. Integrating peacebuilding into development, health, media, and other sectors can greatly aid organizations in minimizing their negative impact in conflict areas, and ideally have a positive effect.

There is a need for much greater documentation of concrete efforts being conducted on the ground at the micro level. At the macro and strategic levels, there is a need to explore how organizations are advancing the concept of integrated peacebuilding and, more important, identifying the institutional opportunities and challenges across diverse sectoral areas. There is also a critical need to foster increased collaboration at all levels, among donors, implementing organizations, and international and local partners to be more effective in programming and impact. Given the many issues being integrated across programming, developing new tools or methods to reduce integrating fatigue is another critical area where innovation is needed. In the areas of sustainability and impact, more exploration is needed on innovations in documenting impact and long-term sustainability.

As emphasized repeatedly in the book, conflict is a complex social phenomenon and there are no easy fixes. Integrated peacebuilding will not magically solve issues that in some cases have dragged on for decades and caused untold suffering and damage. However, integrated approaches can provide a useful policy and programming lens to help organizations more carefully conduct their operations in conflict environments and maximize their positive impact.

References

Anderson, M. 1999. *Do no harm: How aid can support peace—Or war*. Boulder, CO: Lynne Rienner.

Anderson, M., and L. Olson. 2003. *Confronting war: Critical lessons for peace practitioners*. Cambridge, MA: Collaborative Development for Action. Retrieved February 1, 2011, from www.cdainc.com/cdawww/pdf/book/confrontingwar_Pdf1.pdf.

Barbolet, A., R. Goldwyn, and H. Groenewald. 2005. The utility and dilemmas of conflict sensitivity. In M. Fischer, H. Gießmann, and B. Schmelzle, eds. *Berghof handbook for conflict transformation*. Berghof Research Center for Constructive Conflict Management, Berlin Berghof Foundation. Retrieved January 5, 2012, from www.berghof-foundation.org/en.

Bush, K. 1998. A measure of peace: Peace and Conflict Impact Assessment (PCIA) of development projects in conflict zones. Working Paper #1, Peacebuilding and Reconstruction Program Initiative and the Evaluation Unit, International Development Research Centre. Retrieved December 5, 2011, from http://web.idrc.ca/uploads/user-S/10533919790A_Measure_of_Peace.pdf.

———. 2003. PCIA five years on: The commodification of an idea. Berghof Handbook for Conflict Transformation. Retrieved April 2, 2011, from www.berghof-handbook.net/documents/ . . . /dialogue1_bush.p.

CDA Collaborative Learning Projects. 2010. Reflecting on Peace Project. Consultation Report: Understanding Cumulative Impacts. Retrieved April 1, 2012, from www.cdainc.com/cdawww/news_announcement.php#key934.

———. 2011. The Listening Project issue paper: Perceptions of aid in places affected by conflict. Retrieved April 1, 2012, from www.cdainc.com/cdawww/pdf/issue/conflict_sensitivity_ip_Pdf.pdf.

Chiu, M. K. 2011. Starting on the same page: A lessons report from the Peacebuilding Evaluation Project. Alliance for Peacebuilding. www.allianceforpeacebuilding.org/?page=workpep.

Crost, B., and P. Johnston. 2010. Aid under fire: Development projects and civil conflict. Discussion Paper #18, Belfer Center for Science and International Affairs, Harvard University, Cambridge, MA. Retrieved March 1, 2012, from http://belfercenter.ksg.harvard.edu/files/Aid_Under_Fire.pdf.

Diamond, L., and J. McDonald. 1996. *Multi-track diplomacy: A systems approach to peace*. West Hartford, CT: Kumarian Press.

Fast, L. 2010. Mind the gap: Documenting and explaining violence against aid workers. *European Journal of International Affairs* 18, no. 1: 1–25.

Goodhand, J. 2001. Violent conflict, poverty, and chronic poverty. Working Paper #6, Chronic Poverty Research Centre and Intrac, Manchester, UK.

Lange, M. 2004. Building institutional capacity for conflict sensitive practice: The case of international NGOs. International Alert. Retrieved April 1, 2011, from www.usaid.gov/cgi-bin/goodbye?http://www.international-alert.org/pdf/pubdev/institutional_capacity_ngos.pdf.

Lederach, J. P. 1997. *Building peace sustainable reconciliation in divided societies*. Washington, DC: US IP Press.

Organisation for Economic Co-operation and Development (OECD). n.d. DAC criteria for evaluating development assistance. Retrieved March 1, 2012, from www.oecd.org /document/22/0,2340,en_2649_34435_2086550_1_1_1_1,00.html.

Paffenholz, T., and L. Reychler. 2000. *Peacebuilding a field guide*. Boulder, CO: Lynne Rienner.

———. *Aid for peace: A guide to planning and evaluation for conflict zones*. Baden-Baden, Germany: Nomos.

Paffenholz, T., C. Spurk, R. Belloni, S. Kurtenbach, and C. Orjuela. 2010. Enabling and disenabling factors for civil society peacebuilding. In T. Paffenholz, ed. *Civil society and peacebuilding: A critical assessment* (pp. 405–424). Boulder, CO: Lynne Rienner.

Saferworld and Conciliation Resources. 2012. From conflict analysis to peacebuilding impact: Lessons from the People's Peacemaking Perspectives Project. Retrieved June 10, 2012, from www.c-r.org/resources/PPP-lessons.

Smith, D. 2004. Towards a strategic framework for peacebuilding: Getting their act together. Overview report of the Joint Utstein Study of Peacebuilding. Royal Norwegian Ministry of Foreign Affairs. Retrieved December 5, 2011, from www.prio.no/Research -and-Publications/Project/?oid=92706.

Tiessen, R. 2007. *Everywhere/nowhere? Gender mainstreaming in development agencies*. Bloomfield, CT: Kumarian.

United Nations Development Program (UNDP). 2006. Evaluation of gender mainstreaming in UNDP. New York: UNDP Evaluation Office.

United Nations Peacebuilding Support Office. 2010. Peacebuilding orientation. www.un.org/en/peacebuilding/pbso/pbresources.shtml.

USAID. 2000. Aftermath: The role of women's organizations in postconflict Bosnia and Herzegovina. Center for Development Evaluation.

———. 2012a. Gender equality and female empowerment policy. Washington, DC: Author. Retrieved March 10, 2012, from www.usaid.gov/our_work/policy . . . /Gender EqualityPolicy.pdf.

———. 2012b. Request for proposals number SOL-OAA-12–00–000043: Programming Effectively Against Conflict and Extremism (PEACE). Retrieved June 10, 2012, from www.fbo.gov/index?s=opportunity&mode=form&id=bbbof5a43efa4543b66bad6b5 f8d3071&tab=core&_cview=1.

USAID/DCHA. 2012. Annual program statement FY 12 conflict mitigation and reconciliation programs and activities. Retrieved February 10, 2012, from www.usaid.gov/ba / . . . /usaid-dchacmm-fy12-reconciliation-aps.pdf.

Woodrow, P., and D. Chigas. 2009. A distinction with a difference: Conflict sensitivity and peacebuilding. Retrieved April 1, 2011, from www.cdainc.com/cdawww/news _announcement.php#key763.

World Bank. 2011. Select facts and figures on conflict and fragility. From http://web .worldbank.org/WBSITE/EXTERNAL/PROJECTS/STRATEGIES/EXTLICUS/0,,c ontentMDK:22934897~pagePK:64171531~piPK:64171507~theSitePK:511778,00.html.

NOTES

1. See www.cdainc.com and www.international-alert.org.

2. According to the World Development Report (World Bank, 2011), "Every year of organized violence is associated with lagging poverty reduction of nearly one percentage point" (p. 60).

3. This is also a core issue explored in the work by Bush (1998; 2003) on Peace and Conflict Impact Assessments.

4. Although it is worth noting, some companies have adopted such issues in all aspects of their operations, both out of an ethical desire to contribute to the world and with the understanding that it is good for business. For example, PeaceWorks is a small company that has moved beyond the triple bottom line of people, profit, and planet to add a fourth dimension of peace as an explicit goal in its operations.

5. For more information, see www.sfcg.org/programmes/ilt/dme_home.html.

APPENDIX A:
KEY RESOURCES FOR
INTEGRATED PEACEBUILDING

The following are selected recommendations of key institutions and resources to learn more about integrated peacebuilding. This is not meant to be an exhaustive list, only to help spark additional learning based on some of the sectors covered in each chapter.

KEY INSTITUTIONS

- **Alliance for Peacebuilding**
  www.allianceforpeacebuilding.org
  Leading network of peacebuilding organizations.
- **Amman Message**
  www.ammanmessage.com
  Statement by major leaders of Islam from around the world about relationship to peace.
- **Catholic Relief Services**
  www.catholicrelief.org
  Carries out diverse work on peacebuilding in multiple sectors.
- **CDA Collaborative Learning Projects**
  www.cdainc.com
  Carries out extensive work on "do no harm" and other aspects of peacebuilding.
- **Conflict Sensitivity Consortium**
  www.conflictsensitivity.org
  Group of organizations mapping relationships and developing tools to more effectively link development and conflict sensitivity and peacebuilding.

- **Department for International Development (DFID)**
  www.dfid.gov.uk
  The UK's main development agency.
- **Institute for Economics and Peace**
  http://economicsandpeace.org
  Publishes the annual global peace index and conducts active research on links between economics, business, and peacebuilding.
- **Institute for Inclusive Security**
  www.huntalternatives.org/pages/7_the_institute_for_inclusive_security.cfm
  Leading organization advancing the role of women in peacebuilding and security.
- **International Alert**
  www.international-alert.org
  Leading peacebuilding organization working in many sectors.
- **International Network to Promote the Rule of Law (INPROL)**
  www.usip.org/programs/initiatives/international-network-promote-rule-law-inprol
  Group of practitioners sharing experience and expertise sponsored by US Institute of Peace.
- **Internews**
  www.internews.org
  Works on media and peacebuilding in conflict and transitional societies.
- **Organisation for Economic Co-operation and Development (OECD) Development Co-operation Directorate**
  www.oecd.org/dac
  Brings together world's major bilateral donors in aid and peacebuilding.
- **Religions for Peace**
  www.wcrp.org
  Largest coalition of representatives from world's major religions.
- **Search for Common Ground**
  www.sfcg.org
  Leading peacebuilding organization working in over twenty-five countries.
- **Transcend**
  www.transcend.org
  Peace organization/network founded by Johan Galtung.
- **United Nations Development Programme (UNDP)**
  www.undp.org
  Lead development agency for the United Nations. Conducts extensive work in peacebuilding.
- **United States Agency for International Development (USAID)**
  www.usaid.gov
  Lead development agency for the United States.
- **United States Institute of Peace**
  www.usip.org
  Carries out research, training and policy-making related to peacebuilding and conflict prevention in many areas.

• **UN Women**
www.unwomen.org
Lead organization on gender issues in the UN.

KEY PUBLICATIONS

Anderlini, S. 2007. *Women building peace.* Boulder, CO: Lynne Rienner.

Anderson, M. B. 1999. *Do no harm: How aid can support peace–Or war.* Boulder, CO: Lynne Rienner.

Arya, N., and J. Santa Barbara, eds. 2008. *Peace through health.* Sterling, VA: Kumarian Press.

Boutros-Ghali, B. 1994, May 6. An agenda for development. United Nations Secretary-General's Report A/48/935. New York: United Nations. www.un.org/Docs/SG/agdev.html.

Bush, K. 1998. *A measure of peace: Peace and Conflict Impact Assessment (PCIA) of development projects in conflict zones.* Working Paper #1, Peacebuilding and Reconstruction Program Initiative and the Evaluation Unit, International Development Research Centre. web.idrc.ca/uploads/user-S/10533919790A_Measure_of_Peace.pdf.

Carothers, T. 1999. *Aiding democracy abroad: The learning curve.* Washington, DC: Carnegie Endowment for International Peace.

———. 2003. *Promoting the rule of law abroad: The problem of knowledge.* Rule of Law Series. Carnegie Endowment for International Peace. Democracy and Rule of Law Project No. 34.

Carstarphen, N., C. Zelizer, R. Harris, and D. J. Smith. 2010. Graduate education and professional practice in international peace and conflict. Special report 246, US Institute of Peace, Washington, DC.

Collier, P. 2007. *The bottom billion: Why the poorest countries are failing and what we can do about it.* London: Oxford University Press.

Collier, P., V. L. Elliott, H. Hegre, A. Hoeffler, M. Reynal-Querol, and N. Sambanis. 2003. *Breaking the conflict trap: Civil war and development policy.* Washington, DC: World Bank and Oxford University Press.

Conflict Sensitivity Consortium. 2004. *Conflict-sensitive approaches to development, humanitarian assistance and peacebuilding resource pack.* London. APFO, CECORE, CHA, FEWER, International Alert, and Saferworld. www.saferworld.org.uk/resources/view-resource/148.

DFID. 2010. Working effectively in conflict-affected and fragile situations. Briefing Paper B: Do No Harm. DFID Practice Papers. www.gsdrc.org/docs/open/CON77.pdf.

Do No Harm Project. 2004, November. The do no harm handbook (the framework for analyzing the impact of assistance on conflict). CDA Collaborative Learning Projects, Cambridge, MA.

Goodhand, J. 2001. Aid, conflict, and peacebuilding in Sri Lanka. Conflict and Security Development Group, King's College London. www.dfid.gov.uk/pubs/files/conflictassessmentsrilanka.pdf.

Lederach, J. P. 1997. *Building peace: Sustainable reconciliation in divided societies.* Washington, DC: US Institute of Peace Press.

Miall, H., O. Ramsbotham, and T. Woodhouse. 2005. *Contemporary conflict resolution* (2nd ed.). Cambridge: Polity.

O'Gorman, E. 2011. *Conflict and development: Development matters.* New York: Zed Books.

Organisation for Economic Co-operation and Development (OECD). 2007. *Principles for good international engagement in fragile states and situations.* Paris: Author.

———. 2009. Armed violence reduction: Enabling development. Policy paper. Paris: Author. www.oecd.org/dac/conflictandfragility/armedviolencereductionenablingdevelopment.htm.

Paffenholz, T. Y., and L. Reychler. 2000. *Peacebuilding: A field guide.* Boulder, CO: Lynne Rienner.

———. 2007. *Aid for peace. A guide to planning and evaluation for conflict zones.* Baden-Baden, Germany: Nomos.

Rogers, M., A. Chassy, and T. Bamat. 2010. Integrating peacebuilding into humanitarian and development programming. Catholic Relief Services. Baltimore, MD. www.crsprogramquality.org/publications/2010/10/5/integrating-peacebuilding-into-humanitarian-and-development.html.

Saferworld and Conciliation Resources. 2012. From conflict analysis to peacebuilding impact. Lessons from the People's Peacemaking Perspectives Project. www.c-r.org/resources/PPP-lessons.

Tiessen, R. 2007. *Everywhere/nowhere: Gender mainstreaming in development agencies.* Bloomfield, CT: Kumarian.

Tongeren, P., M. Brenk, M. Hellema, and J. Verhoeven, eds. 2005. *People building peace II: Successful stories of civil society.* Boulder, CO: Lynne Rienner.

United Nations Development Program (UNDP). 2003. Conflict-related development analysis. Bureau for Crisis Prevention and Recovery. New York: Author. www.undp.org/cpr/whats_new/CDA_combined.pdf.

United States Agency for International Development (USAID). 2004. Conducting a conflict assessment: A framework for strategy and program development. Office of Conflict Management and Mitigation. Washington, DC: Author. www.usaid.gov/our_work/cross-cutting_programs/conflict/publications/docs/CMM_ConflAssessFrmwrk_8–17–04.pdf.

Women Waging Peace and International Alert. Inclusive security, sustainable peace: A toolkit for advocacy and action. 2004. Washington, DC: Women Waging Peace (now the Institute for Inclusive Security) and International Alert. www.inclusivesecurity.org/explore-resources/toolkit-for-advocacy-and-action.

World Bank. 2011. *World development report: Conflict, security, and development.* Washington, DC: Author.

World Health Organization (WHO). 1999. *WHO/DFID Peace Through Health Programme: A case study.* Copenhagen: Author.

GLOSSARY

Bilateral donor Bilateral aid agencies are the official institutions through which more developed countries provide the bulk of their development assistance. It is aid from a donor to a recipient country. The bulk of bilateral aid is given by countries that are members of the Development Assistance Committee of the OECD.

Conflict analysis "Conflict Analysis is a means to understand better the complex dynamics of a conflict, set of conflicts or a situation of instability" (Saferworld and Conciliation Resources, 2012).

Conflict context The conflict context is the events, historical and present, and parties, with their backgrounds and points of view, in which the conflict is taking place. While achieving perfect understanding of a conflict context is often impossible, it is vital that a detailed understanding of the key issues and dynamics are developed.

Conflict prevention Seeks to stop or prevent conflict before it reaches a violent or highly escalated stage. This can take place at the latent or manifest stage of conflict. In general, conflict prevention activities can include mapping of the emergence of conflicts through new technology, media and analysis, creation of institutions and forums to bring together groups to constructively resolve issues, and rapid-response mechanisms to deal with violence before it spreads.

Conflict resolution There is considerable debate in the field over the term. For this book conflict resolution is defined as a set of conflict theories, skills (communication, listening), and specific processes of intervention, such as negotiation, mediation, dialogue, facilitation, and related applications that focus on ending conflict.

Conflict sensitivity A set of conflict analysis frameworks and tools to help organizations thoroughly examine their operations and projects to minimize their negative impact on a conflict context, maximize their positive impact, and help to understand how changes in the conflict context could affect operations and programs (Conflict Sensitivity, 2004).

Development Refers to the tangible political, economic, and social improvements that tend to manifest as aid to the poorer countries of the world. Often development is undermined in areas of intense conflict and does not fulfill its intended goal.

DFID The Department for International Development (DFID) is a UK governmental department committed to sustainable development and global poverty reduction. See www.dfid.gov.uk.

Do no harm Anderson (1999) coined the phrase almost as a Hippocratic Oath for development workers to, at a minimum, ensure that no harm is done before pursuing further development goals. Later known as the Do No Harm Project, named after its core principle, the project drew attention to the unintended consequences of humanitarian assistance, particularly during complex political emergencies. "Do no harm" and risk analysis have become foundational principles of humanitarian action and still provide a basis for most organizations in the responsible design of humanitarian response activities.

Greed versus grievance Collier and Hoeffler (2000) suggest a difference in conflict that arises from want of an unmet need (grievance) and pursuit of control over such resources (greed).

Humanitarian assistance "Aid and action designed to save lives, alleviate suffering and maintain and protect human dignity during and in the aftermath of emergencies" (Global Humanitarian Assistance, n.d.).

Integrated peacebuilding A set of processes and tools used by civil society and governmental actors to transform the relationships, culture, and institutions of society to prevent, end, and transform conflicts. An integrated approach requires that organizations apply these peacebuilding tools across their internal operations and external programs to ensure that, at a minimum, no harm is done, and ideally to achieve positive results in extremely difficult conflict environments.

Mainstreaming Mainstreaming cross-sectoral issues began in recognition that international development and relief efforts often overlooked critical issues in their programming. The mainstreaming movement, which strives to integrate sectoral issues into traditional development work, began with a push to include women and gender concerns in international development and now has expanded to include peacebuilding, youth, environment, health (HIV/AIDS), and other areas.

Nongovernmental organization A nongovernmental organization (NGO) is an organization that operates independently from the government. NGOs range from local to international in size and scope.

Organisation for Economic Co-operation and Development (OECD) OECD is an international economic organization that promotes world trade and economic progress. See www.oecd.org/home.

Overseas development assistance ODA is defined as "those flows to countries and territories on the DAC List of ODA Recipients and to multilateral development institutions," with the goal of helping to promote "the economic development and welfare of developing countries as its main objective." See Organisation for Economic Co-operation and Development (2008).

Peacebuilding Focuses on transforming relationships and structures in society to decrease the likelihood of future conflicts. For many years, peacebuilding was seen as a process that occurs after the end of conflict and violence. However, peacebuilding has become much broader and can take place at any stage of conflict.

Peacekeeping Preventing conflict and violence from spreading through the intervention of a third party, such as the military or police. Peacekeeping largely focuses on the immediate crisis and violence, although it can be an integral part of a long-term process. The goal of peacekeeping is to stop the violence or help enforce a calm environment to enable peacebuilding processes to take place.

Peacemaking An approach focused on resolving a specific conflict. Peacemaking takes place when parties gather and resolve specific issues through negotiations and/or other means, such as dialogue. These activities can include formal peace negotiations at the national level or efforts to bring together parties at the community level. A trusted third party, such as a mediator or convener, can help to facilitate the process.

Positive/negative peace Johan Galtung, often mentioned as the father of the peacebuilding resolution field, highlights a key distinction between actively pursuing peaceful reconciliation (positive peace) and attempting to prevent the outbreak of further violence (negative peace).

USAID The United States Agency for International Development (USAID) is the main US bilateral aid agency committed to international development and foreign aid. See www.usaid.gov.

INDEX